Witches and Witch-Hunts

THEMES IN HISTORY

Published

Wolfgang Behringer, *Witches and Witch-Hunts*
M. L. Bush, *Servitude in Modern Times*
Peter Coates, *Nature: Western Attitudes Since Ancient Times*
Mark Harrison, *Disease and the Modern World: 1500 to the Present Day*
Colin Heywood, *A History of Childhood: Children and Childhood in the West from Medieval to Modern Times*
J. K. J. Thomson, *Decline in History: The European Experience*
David Vincent, *The Rise of Mass Literacy: Reading and Writing in Modern Europe*

Witches and Witch-Hunts

A Global History

Wolfgang Behringer

polity

First published in 2004 by Polity Press Ltd

Polity Press
65 Bridge Street
Cambridge CB2 1UR, UK

Polity Press
350 Main Street
Malden, MA 02148, USA

ISBN 0 7456 2717 X
ISBN 0 7456 2718 8 (pb)

A catalogue record for this book is available from the British Library and has been applied for from the Library of Congress.

Typeset in 10½ on 12pt Times
by SNP Best-set Typesetter Ltd., Hong Kong
Printed and bound in Great Britain by MPG Books, Bodmin, Cornwall.

For further information on Polity, visit our website: www.polity.co.uk

Contents

List of Illustrations		vii
List of Tables		ix
Preface		x
Chronology		xi
List of Abbreviations		xix
1	**Introduction**	1
2	**The Belief in Witchcraft**	11
3	**The Persecution of Witches**	47
4	**The European Age of Witch-Hunting**	83
5	**Outlawing Witchcraft Persecution in Europe**	165
6	**Witch-Hunting in the Nineteenth and Twentieth Centuries**	196
7	**Old and 'New Witches'**	229
8	**Epilogue**	242
Notes		249
Bibliography		278
1	*Dictionaries, Handbooks, Source Editions*	278
2	*Demonologies and Literature before 1800*	279
3	*Witchcraft Monographs*	287

4   Essay Collections   295
5   Articles on Witchcraft   298
6   Occultism, Esotericism and 'New Witches'   305
7   General Standard Works   308

Index   316

Illustrations

Plates

1   *La lutte contre la Sorcellerie (Forces du Mal).* Postage
    stamp, Peoples' Republic of Benin, 1977   12
2   *Inca Official Killing a Family of Witches.* Drawing, in
    Guaman Poma de Ayala, *Nueva Cronica, c.*1612   20
3   *The Burning of Witches.* Drawing from the collection of
    Johann Jacob Wick. Zentralbibliothek Zürich, Wickiana
    collection Ms. F 19, f.147v   58
4   *Waldensian Witches.* Johannes Tinctoris, *Contra Sectam
    Vaudensium, c.*1460   70
5   *Weather Magic.* Frontispiece, Ulrich Molitor, *De Laniis et
    Phitonicis Mulieribus,* 1489   75
6   *The Witches' Dance,* 1568. Coloured painting from the
    collection of Johann Jacob Wick. Zentralbibliothek
    Zürich, Wickiana collection Ms. F 18, f.146v   84
7   *The Heresy of Witchcraft.* Title woodcut/frontispiece,
    Peter Binsfeld, *Tractat,* Munich, 1591   94
8   Heinrich Schultheis, Witch-commissioner of the
    Archbishop of Cologne. Copper engraving, frontispiece
    of his *Detailed Instruction,* Cologne, 1634   118
9   Mask, representing a Spirit, invoked in periodical
    witch-finding drives of the Songe. Photo: Lucy Mair,
    Witchcraft (1969), p. 62 © Axel Poignant Archive   203
10 South Africa's northern province as 'Witchcraft Zone':
    Public Perception Map from: *The Sowetan,* 9 July 1997
    Reproduced by permission of The Sowetan   215
11 Witches' dance, enacted by 'new witches'. Photo: Russels   234
12 Francisco Goya, *Reason's Sleep Generates Monsters.*
    Capriccio, 1797   246

Maps

1   Hotspots of witch-hunting in Europe, 1400–1800   105
2   The Holy Roman Empire in the sixteenth century   136
3   Countries with witch-hunts between 1950 and 2000   197

Tables

4.1 Major European demonologies and their context,
    1400–1700   102
4.2 The witch-bishops   109
4.3 The largest witch-hunts in Europe   130
4.4 Litigations over witch trials at the Imperial Chamber
    Court, 1500–1800   137
4.5 The severity of witch-hunting in Europe   150
6.1 Witchcraft eradication movements in colonial Africa   207
6.2 Countries with severe witch-hunts between 1950
    and 2000   227

Preface

I wish to express my sincere thanks to all those who commented on the manuscript of this book: Robin Briggs (All Souls, Oxford) as an official reviewer, James Sharpe (York) as a good neighbour, Johannes Harnischfeger (formerly Africa, now Kobe, Japan) as an anthropologist on four continents, Richard Golden (Austin, Texas), and my dear friend Erik Midelfort (Charlottesville, Virginia), who all decided to spend their precious time on parts of the manuscript. In particular I wish to express my thanks to my graduate students Paul Brand (York), who accepted the Herculean task of rectifying all mistakes, and Rob Boddice (York), who added some ideas. The anthropologists Iris Gareis (Frankfurt) and Ray Abrahams (Cambridge) provided important clues. Last but not least I wish to thank my Polity Press editors, Sally-Ann Spencer, Elizabeth Molinari, Helen Gray and Ali Wyke.

I dedicate this book to my colleagues in York, particularly those who supported our international 'Third York Cultural History Conference: Witchcraft in Context' in April 2002, including Nina Reinholdt and Andrew Cambers as conference assistants, then still graduate students and now young scholars; to John Bossy, my predecessor as Chair in Early Modern History in York; and to Richard van Dülmen (Saarbrücken), who encouraged me to write my first book on witchcraft. My greatest debt is to my wife Hizran, and to our children, Luis Alper and Aylin Carola. They were suffering from my extravagant habit of writing 'in the hours of night', although hopefully not 'seduced by illusions and phantasms of demons', as suggested by the *Canon Episcopi*.

Wolfgang Behringer
Osbaldwick, York, July 2003

Chronology

350–80	sorcery scares in the Roman Empire
358	Emperor Constantius II outlaws all forms of magic
380	Christianity state religion of the Roman Empire
385	Priscillian, the first convicted heretic, executed for magical crimes
426	St Augustine, *Civitas Dei*
c.500	catalogue of superstitious beliefs by Caesarius of Arles
534	*Codex Justinianus*
c.580	witch persecutions of Queen Fredegunde in Paris
c.820	sermons of Bishop Agobard of Lyon
906	Regino von Prüm, *Canon Episcopi*
c.1010	*Decretum* of the bishop Burchard von Worms
1071	witch killings in Russia; witches considered to be a threat to the state
1080	Pope Gregory VII instructs the Danish king not to hunt witches
1100	King Coloman of Hungary outlaws belief in witches (*strigae*)
1215	Fourth Lateran Council: ordeals dismissed; torture accepted
c.1270	Thomas Aquinas, *Summa Theologiae*
1271	famine, witch-hunts in Russia
1296	burning of two witches (*strigae*) in northern Italy
1305–78	popes reside in Avignon
1315–22	Great Famine
1324	burning of Alice Kyteler in Ireland
1324	Bernard Gui, *Practica Inquisitionis haereticae pravitatis*

1348–50	Black Death, followed by pogroms against Jews
1376	Nicolas Eymericus, *Directorium Inquisitorum*
1378–1415	Great Schism
1384/90	Inquisition trials concerning 'la Signora del Gioco' in Milan
1386	Christianization of Grand Duke Jagiello of Lithuania and Poland
1388	Inquisition trials against 'Waldensian witches' in Pinerolo, Piedmont
1398	University of Paris condemns sorcery
1399–1407	Vincent Ferrer's apocalyptic preachings in the western Alps
1400	the term *hexerey* first recorded in a Swiss trial
1407	a man burnt for witchcraft in Norse Greenland
1409	Papal decree mentions *novas sectas* in the duchy of Savoy
1418/22	Dominican Inquisition conducts two witch trials in Milan
1418–30	Bernardino da Siena's apocalyptic preaching campaigns
1424	burning of the witch Finicella in Rome
1427–36	first massive witch-hunts in Europe (Savoy, Dauphiné, Valais)
1428	witch burning at Todi
1429	Lucerne chronicler Fründ reports the new sect of the witches in the Valais
1431	Joan of Arc burnt for heresy and sorcery at Rouen
1431–49	Council of Basel: discussions about the new crime
1430–40	vernacular terms for the new crime (*hexen, bruyas, streghe*) emerge
1435	*Errores Gazariorum*: the first treatise about the new crime of witchcraft
1440	Pope Eugene IV decrees about *stregule* or *Waudenses* in Savoy
c.1450	flying witches in church paintings (Denmark, Slovenia)
1457	sceptical sermons of Nicolaus of Cusa
1459	persecution of Waldensian witches in Arras (Flandres)
1474	Heinrich Kramer/Institoris starts his career as papal inquisitor
1480–1520	endemic witch-hunts in Western Europe
1484	Innocence VIII papal bull *Summis desiderantes affectibus*
1485	unsuccessful witch-hunt in Innsbruck/Tyrol
1486	Heinrich Kramer, *Malleus Maleficarum* (the *Witches' Hammer*)
1489	Ulrich Molitor, *De Laniis et Phitonicis Mulieribus*
1493	first woodcuts of flying witches
1495–1525	witch-hunting by inquisitors in Italian Alpine valleys

1505–25	harsh criticism of witch-hunting in Renaissance Italy
1505	Samuel Cassinis, *De lamiis, quas strigas vocant*
1513	Niccolò Machiavelli, *The Prince*
1515	Andrea Alciati criticizes the 'new holocaust' in Alpine valleys
1517	Luther's ninety-five *Theses*; the religious Reformation starts
1519	the Aztec ruler Motecuhzoma II commissions a pogrom against sorcerers
1519	Agrippa von Nettesheim defends a suspected witch in Metz (Alsace)
1520–60	decline of witchcraft persecutions
1525	Peasants' War, Free Churches (Anabaptism) emerge
1525	Execution of a *striga* in Rome
1526	Spanish Inquisition objects to witch burnings
1531	Agrippa of Nettesheim speaks of 'bloodthirsty inquisitors'
1532	Niccolò Machiavelli, *The Prince* and *Discorsi* published
1532	the imperial law of Charles V ignores the crime of witchcraft
1538	Spanish Inquisition denies the authority of the *Witches' Hammer*
1539	burning of the Aztec kazike Chichimecatecuhtli in Texcoco/Mexico
1540	four men executed as witches in Luther's Wittenberg
1543	large-scale persecution in Denmark
1545	execution of witches in Calvin's Geneva
1551	witchcraft laws in Russia; fears of bewitchment at Czar Ivan IV's court
1560–1660	general climatic deterioration ('Little Ice Age')
1562	witch-hunting becomes common in parts of continental Europe
1562–5	controversy about the possibility of weather magic
1562–98	French Wars of Religion
1563	John Weyer, *De Praestigiis Daemonum*
1563	witchcraft laws in England and Scotland
1566–72	millenarian movements and witch-hunts in Peru
1568–1648	Eighty Years' War between the Netherlands and Spain
1570–3	continental hunger crisis; witch-hunts becoming endemic
1570–1630	endemic persecutions in western Switzerland and Savoy
1570–1630	endemic persecutions in northern Germany and Denmark
1572	witchcraft legislation in electoral Saxony
1572	Lambert Daneau, *Les Sorciers*
1572	Thomas Erastus, *Disputatio de lamiis seu strigibus*

1575	Nils Hemmingsen, *Admonitio de superstitionibus magicis vitandis*
1576–1612	age of Rudolf II, the melancholic emperor
1579/81	Union of Utrecht/Union of Atrecht/Arras: split of the Netherlands
1580–1620	massive witch-hunts in the Valais, Lorraine, Luxembourg and Trier
1580	Jean Bodin *De daemonomania magorum*
1584	witch-panics in Switzerland, Germany, France and England
1584	controversy about the swimming test
1584	Reginald Scot, *The Discoverie of Witchcraft*
1584	Johann Georg Goedelmann, *Tractatus de magis, veneficis et lamiis*
1586	Abraham Saur, *Theatrum de Veneficis*
1587	witchcraft crisis in France, the Parlement de Paris reacts
1587	*Historia von D. Johann Fausten*
1588–94	Paris occupied by League troops, climax of witch-hunts in France
1589	Peter Binsfeld, *De confessionibus maleficorum et sagarum*
1590	massive witch-hunts in Germany, France and Scotland
1592	Brussels encourages witch-hunts in the Spanish Netherlands
1592	Cornelius Loos, *De vera et ficta magia*
1595–1605	severe witch-hunts in Flanders
1595	Nicolas Rémy, *Daemonolatria*
1597	major persecution in Scotland, about 200 death sentences
1598	James VI of Scotland, *Daemonologie*
1598–1601	massive witch-hunts in the Spanish Netherlands
1599/1600	Martin Delrio, *Disquisitionum magicarum libri sex*
1600–4	fierce debates about witchcraft in Bavaria split the 'Jesuit party'
1600–32	witch-hunts in Burgundy
1602	Henri Boguet, *Discours de Sorciers*
1603	end of witch burnings in the Dutch Republic
1608	Francesco Maria Guazzo, *Compendium Maleficarum*
1609	witch-hunt in the French Basque territory
1610	expert opinion of Inquisitor Salazar on the Basque witches
1611–18	massive witch-hunt in the prince-abbey of Ellwangen
1611/12	programmatic legislation against witchcraft in Bavaria
1612	Pierre de Lancre, *Tableau de l'inconstance*
1616–18	witch-hunts in several German prince-bishoprics
1618–48	Thirty Years' War

1618–20	major persecution in Catalonia
1626	millennial frosts destroy crops at the end of May
1626–30	climax of witch-hunting in Central Europe
1626	Francesco Maria Guazzo, *Compendium Maleficarum*
1628	'year without a summer'
1628	major persecution in Scotland
1628	burning of Chancellor Dr Georg Haan in Bamberg
1628	Cornelius Pleier, *Malleus Judicum*
1631	Friedrich Spee, *Cautio Criminalis*
1633–4	witch panic in Lancashire
1635	Johann Matthäus Meyfahrt, *Christliche Erinnerung an gewaltige Regenten*
1635–45	witch panics among the Hurons in New France
1643	witch panic in the Languedoc
1644	witch panics in China
1644	witch panics in the Champagne, Bourbonnais, Burgundy and Gascony
1645–7	severe witch-hunts during the Civil War in England
1647	Matthew Hopkins, *The Discovery of Witches*
1648	John Stearne, *A confirmation and Discoverie of Witchcraft*
1651	Thomas Hobbes, *Leviathan*
1651–2	large-scale witch-hunt in Silesia
1652–60	the 'Big Witchkilling' (Groos Häxatöödi) in Graubünden
1658–61	witch-hunts in the Franche Comté
1659–60	witch-hunts in the Spanish Netherlands and parts of Germany
1661–2	major persecution in Scotland
1668–76	witch panic in Sweden
1669	last edition of the *Witches' Hammer*
1669	John Wagstaffe, *The Question of Witchcraft Debated*
1677–80	witch-hunt in the prince-bishopric of Salzburg
1679–81	witch panic in Moravia
1680	Pueblo Revolt
1682	Louis XIV limits witch trials in France
1684	Württemberg troops suppress a witch craze in the city of Calw
1685	last legal execution for witchcraft in England
1691–2	major persecutions in Slovenia
1692	witch panic in Salem, Massachusetts
1693	Balthasar Bekker, *De Betoverde Wereld*
1701	Christian Thomasius, *De crimine magiae*
1710–30	climax of witch-hunting in Hungary
1710	persecution in Slovenia
1712	trial of Jane Wenham in England

1714	royal decree stops witch trials in Prussia
1717	last legal execution for witchcraft in Italy
1727	last legal execution for witchcraft in Scotland
1736	repeal of witchcraft legislation in the United Kingdom
1743	late sorcery/witchcraft trials in France (Lyon, Dijon)
1746	last execution in Silesia
1749	a late execution in Würzburg triggers Catholic debates
1750	Scipio Maffei, *Arte Magica Destrutta*
1751	lynching of a witch in England
1755	wave of witch burnings in Hungary
1756	last execution in Bavaria
1766–70	'Bavarian War about Witches', an enlightened debate
1768	witch panic ('soulstealers') in China
1775	severe witch panic in Poland
1776	American Declaration of Independence
1777	a late witch execution in Kézmárk (Hungary)
1779	Ursula Padrutt dies in prison in Graubünden (Switzerland)
1780	burning of a male witch in Jamaica (British)
1782	the last legal execution for witchcraft in Europe: Anna Göldi in Glarus (Switzerland)
1783	August Ludwig Schlözer coins the term 'judicial murder' (*Justizmord*)
1783–1809	witch-hunts in Madagascar
1786	Gottfried Christian Voigt: 'nine million witches'
1789	French Revolution
1791	repeal of witchcraft legislation in France
1797	Francisco Goya's capriccio *Reason's Sleep Generates Monsters*
1800–5	Seneca chief Handsome Lake's anti-witchcraft movement in the USA
1816–28	witch-hunts in the Zulu empire
1828–61	witch-hunts in Madagascar
1835	Jacob Grimm interprets witches as 'wise women'
1843	Wilhelm Gottfried Soldan, *Geschichte der Hexenprozesse*
1854	traditional witch killings among the Pueblo Indians (USA)
1857	major persecution in India
1860	witch lynchings in Texas and Arkansas (USA)
1860–5	witch killings in New Zealand
1860–1900	illegal witch killings in Mexico and Russia
1862	Jules Michelet, *La Sorcière*
1863	lynching of a witch in England
1880–1900	witch panics among the Pueblo Indians (USA, New Mexico)

1880–1900	major witch-hunts in South Africa
1884	Navaho chief Manuelito orders the execution of forty witches (USA)
1900	Joseph Hansen, *Zauberwahn, Inquisition und Hexenprozeß im Mittelalter*
1900	US troops suppress witch-hunts among the Zuni in New Mexico
1900–65	anti-witchcraft movements in colonial Africa
1917	Russian Revolution
1935	Nazi ideologues reinterpret witches and witch persecutions
1937	Evans-Pritchard, *Witchcraft, Oracles and Magic among the Azande*
1944	Clyde Kluckhohn, *Navaho Witchcraft*
1946–60	decolonization in Africa and Asia
1948–80	hundreds of witches killed in western India
1950–60	witch killings in Chiapas, Mexico
1958	witch panic in the Belgian Congo
1960	witch panic in Tlaxcala, Mexico
*c.*1960	spreading of neo-pagan 'witch covens' in England and the USA
1962–88	witch-hunts in Tanzania, many thousands of victims
1965	Uganda legalizes witch trials
1966	witch-hunts in Uganda and Kenya
1968	women's liberation movement chooses WITCH as its symbol
1969	Lucy Mair, *Witchcraft*
1971	Keith Thomas, *Religion and the Decline of Magic*
*c.*1975	new legal witch trials in Cameroon
1975	witch panic in the People's Republic of Benin (former Dahomey)
1976	resurgence of witch burnings in the Republic of South Africa
1977	killing of a village sorcerer in France
1980–2	witch-hunts in Zambia
1982–4	witch panics in highland Bolivia and Peru
1985–99	endemic witch-hunts in South Africa's northern province
1987–8	witch panics in Indonesia and Papua New Guinea
1988	government committee on witch pogroms in Tanzania
1989	Carlo Ginzburg, *Storia Noturna. Una decifrazione del Saba*
1990–2000	hundreds of witches killed in South Africa's northern province
1992–4	witch-hunts in Kenya
1994–8	witch-hunts in Tanzania, thousands of victims

1996	government report on witchcraft in South Africa's northern province
1997	lynching of a suspected witch in Russia
1997	Peter Geschiere, *The Modernity of Witchcraft*
1997–8	witch-hunts in Ghana, establishment of 'witch sanctuaries'
2001	witch-hunt in Kenya
2002	witch craze in Mozambique, related to HIV infections

Abbreviations

AA	*American Anthropologist*
AESC	*Annales. Économies, Societés, Civilizations*
AHS	*African Historical Studies*
AHVN	*Annalen des Historischen Vereins für den Niederrhein*
AHWME	*The Athlone History of Witchcraft and Magic in Europe*, 6 vols, London 1999–2002
AJS	*American Journal of Sociology*
ARG	Archiv für Reformationsgeschichte/Archive for Reformation History
Ashforth (2000)	see bibliography – 3: Witchcraft Monographs
ASR	*African Studies Review*
Behringer (1997)	see bibliography – 3: Witchcraft Monographs
Behringer (2001)	see bibliography – 1: Source Editions
BM	*Berliner Monatsschrift*
Bond/Ciekawy (2001)	see bibliography – 4: Essay Collections
Briggs (1996)	see bibliography – 3: Witchcraft Monographs
Byloff (1934)	see bibliography – 3: Witchcraft Monographs
CA	*Current Anthropology*
Carolina	*Constitutio Criminalis Carolina*, law of Emperor Charles V of 1532
CEH	*Central European History*
CJH	*Criminal Justice History*
Clark (1997)	see bibliography – 3: Witchcraft Monographs
Cohn (1975)	see bibliography – 3: Witchcraft Monographs
Comaroff (1993)	see bibliography – 4: Essay Collections

CSEL	*Corpus Scriptorum Ecclesiasticorum Latinorum*, Vienna 1866ff.
CSSH	*Comparative Studies in Society and History*
Davies (1999)	see bibliography – 3: Witchcraft Monographs
Decker (2003)	see bibliography – 3: Witchcraft Monographs
Douglas (1970)	see bibliography – 4: Essay Collections
FAZ	*Frankfurter Allgemeine Zeitung*
FHS	*French Historical Studies*
Geschiere (1997)	see bibliography – 3: Witchcraft Monographs
GEW	Golden (ed.), *Encyclopedia of Witchcraft*
Ginzburg (1991)	see bibliography – 3: Witchcraft Monographs
Glaser (2001)	see bibliography – 7: General Standard Works
Gluckman (1956)	see bibliography – 7: General Standard Works
Goodare (2002)	see bibliography – 4: Essay Collections
GWU	*Geschichte in Wissenschaft und Unterricht*
Hansen (1900)	see bibliography – 3: Witchcraft Monographs
Hansen (1901)	see bibliography – 1: Source Editions
HNAI	*Handbook of North American Indians*, 20 vols, Washington 1978ff.
HZ	*Historische Zeitschrift*
IESS	*International Encyclopedia of the Social Sciences*, 18 vols, 1968–1979
IJAHS	*International Journal of African Historical Studies*
Iliffe (1995)	see bibliography – 7: General Standard Works
JAH	*Journal of African History*
JAS	*Journal of Asian Studies*
JIH	*Journal of Interdisciplinary History*
JMAS	*Journal of Modern African Studies*
JNES	*Journal of the Near Eastern Society*
JRAI	*Journal of the Royal Anthropological Institute of Great Britain and Ireland*
JWLG	*Jahrbuch für Westdeutsche Landesgeschichte*
Köbler (1995)	see bibliography – 1: Dictionaries
Kors/Peters	see bibliography – 1: Source Editions
Larner (1981)	see bibliography – 3: Witchcraft Monographs
Levack (1987)	see bibliography – 3: Witchcraft Monographs
Mair (1969)	see bibliography – 3: Witchcraft Monographs
Malleus (1486)	*Malleus Maleficarum*, 1st edn, see bibliography – 2: Demonologies
Malleus (2000)	*Malleus Maleficarum*, see bibliography – 2: Demonologies

Mansi	J. D. Mansi, *Sacrorum Conciliorum Collectio*, 31 vols, Florence 1757–98
Marwick (1982)	see bibliography – 4: Essay Collections
MGH	*Monumenta Germaniae Historica*
Midelfort (1972)	see bibliography – 3: Witchcraft Monographs
Monter (1969)	see bibliography – 1: Source Editions
Monter (1976)	see bibliography – 3: Witchcraft Monographs
Monter (2002)	see bibliography – 5: Articles (= *AHWME* 4 (2002) 1–52)
Niehaus (2001)	see bibliography – 3: Witchcraft Monographs
OER	*The Oxford Encyclopedia of the Reformation*, 4 vols, Oxford 1996
Ostorero (1999)	see bibliography – 1: Source Editions
Parrinder (1958)	see bibliography – 3: Witchcraft Monographs
PL	*Patrologia Latina*, ed. J. P. Migne, 221 vols, Paris 1878–90
Poole (2002)	see bibliography – 4: Essay Collections
PP	*Past & Present*
r.	ruled
Ralushai (1996)	see bibliography – 3: Witchcraft Monographs
Roper (1994)	see bibliography – 4: Essay Collections
RR	*The Russian Review*
Ryan (1999)	see bibliography – 3: Witchcraft Monographs
SCJ	*Sixteenth Century Journal*
Schmidt (2000)	see bibliography – 3: Witchcraft Monographs
s.d.	*sine dato*, date of print lacking
Sharpe (1997)	see bibliography – 3: Witchcraft Monographs
Sharpe (2001)	see bibliography – 1: Source Editions
Sharpe (2003)	see bibliography – 1: Source Editions
s.l.	*sine loco*, place of print lacking
Thomas (1971)	see bibliography – 3: Witchcraft Monographs
TLS	*Times Literary Supplement*
Wilde (2003)	see bibliography – 3: Witchcraft Monographs
Wilson (1973)	see bibliography – 7: General Standard Works
ZHF	*Zeitschrift für historische Forschung*
ZRGKA	*Zeitschrift der Savigny-Stiftung für Rechtsgeschichte, Kanonistische Abteilung*
ZSKG	*Zeitschrift für Schweizerische Kirchengeschichte*

1

Introduction

'So what do you think Madumo means when he says his life is cursed?'
I asked as I returned to the table with MaMfete's tea. 'Do you think
there really is something happening with his ancestors? Or could it be
that he has been bewitched?'

'You don't believe in witches, do you?' she asked, chuckling.

Adam Ashforth, *Madumo*, 2000

Let us start with a recent event, which to historians seems foreign and
familiar at the same time. In the last week of July 1990 a South
African village was shaken by several deaths. Six young men died in
car crashes, an elderly man committed suicide and a woman's corpse
was found outside her home with stab-wounds. At the funerals,
a leader of the African National Congress (ANC) Youth League
announced over a loudhailer:

> If five people die every week, more than twenty will die in a month. If
> things go on like this we'll all die. You yourself may be the next. The
> priests should pray to stop these deaths. But if these deaths are man-
> made the ministers should pray that the witches must stop . . . The
> witches think they are safe because I told my comrades to stop burning
> them.

Some mourners shouted: 'Away witches!' By December, thirty-four
people had been accused of being witches during the largest witch-
hunt in Green Valley's history. Youth League comrades were the most
prominent witch-hunters, but adults assisted them. ANC officials
tried to stop the Green Valley witch panic. Alarmed by the increasing number of witch-hunts during the previous decade, the ANC

Executive Council (after the end of prohibition of the party in February 1990) had strictly forbidden party members from acting against witches, because witch-burnings 'diverted the struggle from the real enemy'. Nevertheless, the supposed victims of witchcraft continued to seek the support of local ANC officials in having witches punished.[1]

Witch killings preceded the end of the apartheid regime, but did not stop after the first free elections in 1994, when Nelson Mandela (b. 1918, r. 1994–9) became president. An official 'Report of the Commission of Inquiry into Witchcraft Violence and Ritual Murders in the Northern Province of South Africa', chaired by Victor Ralushai, social anthropologist at the University of Venda, scrutinized 389 cases of witch killings between 1985 and 1995, and came to the conclusion that the existence of witchcraft had to be acknowledged.[2] People in many civilizations believe that certain individuals are able to cause harm by means of occult, mystical powers, although there are usually differences about the truth and likelihood of such attributions. In many cases witchcraft beliefs are under attack by a dominant ideology, a religion or, nowadays, Western rationalism. Witchcraft, however, has the potential to explain contingent events unequalled by rationalism, religion or political ideology, since it links human agency with supernatural powers. Basic human feelings, like envy or jealousy, anger or hate, derailed personal relationships or social tensions, can be linked to specific cases of misfortune. The basic hypothesis of witchcraft is that the origin of misfortune is social. In traditional societies, witchcraft is often a *synonym for evil*, characterized by the inversion of the central moral norms. It is the antisocial crime par excellence, the ultimate form of human depravity and malice, or the 'quintessence of immorality'.[3] Since deviance is at its core, fantasies of witchcraft are marked by similar attributes: deviant social and sexual behaviour, nudity and shamelessness, greed and intemperance, strange or ugly features, an affinity to darkness, to animals of the night, to unclean beings or objects, contact with spirits and demons, and secret nocturnal gatherings associated with horrible crimes, such as ritual infanticide or cannibalism. The belief in witches, as Norman Cohn (b. 1915) has pointed out, has much in common with conspiracy theories.[4]

Edgar Evan Evans-Pritchard's (1902–73) notion that 'witchcraft explains unfortunate events' is considered to be 'the main parameter in anthropological studies of witchcraft'.[5] However, witch-beliefs are not confined to functionally explainable features. There is a fascinating surplus of fantastical elements, fairy-like attributes, which cannot be explained by mere functionalism, such as the ability to fly through the air (magical flight), to shift shape (metamorphosis), to enter houses through closed doors, to become invisible or to be in two places at the same time (bilocation), skills in fortune-telling and divining the future or other secrets, the ability to speak with animals (master of the animals), and the presumed ability to influence the course of nature. With their supernatural abilities, witches resemble shamans, and in some cultures witches were indeed evil shamans, or shamans that turned evil. In a Christian perspective they resemble saints, who were able to harm their enemies.[6] However, fantasies of witchcraft, it seems, are not just strongly related to social or cultural features of society, but to individual and collective fears and hopes anchored in the human subconscious. In a Freudian sense they represent – like nightmares – a cultural *Id*, as opposed to the cultural super-egos of religion and rationalism.[7]

Witches in this book are primarily regarded as a subject of the disciplines of history and anthropology. Academic dissertations about witchcraft, however, have also been written in law, theology, psychology, sociology, medicine, language and folklore studies, and the disciplines dealing with ancient civilizations. Interdisciplinarity has added to our understanding, and earlier explanations for the witchcraft persecutions, like Christian demonology, the Roman inquisitorial procedure, legal torture, the misogynistic fantasies of clerics or fiscal aims of state authorities,[8] although still dominating the public perception, have lost their explanatory power. The surprising discovery that in early modern Europe witchcraft persecutions were initially demanded by the populace, and often carried out against the wish of the authorities, sheds new light upon these events. Although the emphasis on demand from below is not meant to justify the involvement of the Church, the judicial courts or the state, it has altered our interpretation and encourages comparisons. Surprisingly, historical European and present-day non-European witchcraft beliefs, and witch persecutions, have much in common. All the ambiguities of witchcraft can be found in Europe, too. White (beneficial) and black (harmful) magic, witches and witch-doctors, local terminologies of witchcraft, differing social systems, problems of translation, nuances of contextualization and overall discourses of knowledge and power, of morality and domination, of scarcity and misfortune, all seem familiar to historians.[9] The torturing and killing of witches is well known and widespread in many civilizations, and anthropologists are becoming increasingly aware of this.[10] Witches and witch-hunts are closer to being recognized as relevant for all mankind: they are – like magic and religion – a *universal phenomenon*.

On such a basis any narrow definition of witchcraft is no longer acceptable. The Christian definition of witchcraft as being based upon a pact with the devil is as limited in relevance as Evans-Pritchard's emphasis on witchcraft as a hereditary bodily quality.[11] As a consequence, we shall have to widen our scope. Some of the neatly drawn boundaries have to be blurred, as for instance the borderline between

European and non-European, between 'English' and 'continental', or between medieval and early modern witchcraft and witchcraft persecutions. There has never been a universally accepted definition of witchcraft. Within a given society the opinions about witchcraft and sorcery usually vary, as Claude Lévi-Strauss (b. 1908) demonstrated through the differing interpretations of the magical flight among Nambikwara Indians of Brazil.[12] In South Africa, or in Papua New Guinea, some people may believe firmly in the dangers of witchcraft, whereas their neighbours consider it to be unimportant. Even within shared beliefs the consequences can be radically different. In the 1940s, among the Maya of Central America, some villages lived in constant fear and discussed witchcraft on a daily basis, whereas others agreed only in principle and did not bother in practice.[13] Recent surveys emphasize the diversity of witch-beliefs, as far as issues like kinship, age groups or gender are concerned.[14] Since witchcraft symbolizes more fundamentally than other terms the fusion of human agency and evil, it seems unnecessary to add to the confusion by suggesting artificial new terms like 'wizardry'.[15] In this book *witchcraft* is used as a generic term for all kinds of evil magic and sorcery, as perceived by contemporaries.

In Europe, a number of clear-cut definitions have drastically challenged traditional notions of witchcraft. Each of these interpretations is rooted in a specific intellectual environment, and the starting point causes surprise even after centuries: Christian demonology equated black and white magic. Founded on the thought of the Church Father St Augustine (354–430), bishop of Hippo in Northern Africa, any kind of magic, and even superstitious customs like the wearing of amulets or watching the stars for astrological purposes, was thought to rely on a contract between a human being and a demon – the devil – either explicitly or implicitly, because the magician expected an effect from a ceremony or a thing which in itself could not work. In the wake of the Roman sorcery scares, and inspired by monotheism, any kind of magic seemed equal to witchcraft. Magicians and witches were seen as allies of the devil, they belonged to the *civitas diaboli*. As offenders of the law, biblical (Exodus 22:18) as well as Roman, they were to be killed.[16] For theologians of the early and High Middle Ages, such as Bishop Burchard of Worms (965–1025), author of an influential penitential, whose formulations would become part of canon law, witches were individuals who believed they possessed powers that in reality did not exist. In this period of mission devils were equated with pagan gods, which were not too powerful in comparison with Jesus Christ, and witches were merely considered to be deceived by devilish illusions. They were not to be killed, but corrected and educated.[17]

The rise of heretical movements changed this perspective. Some late medieval theologians, like the Dominican inquisitor Heinrich Kramer/Institoris (1430–1505), author of the *Malleus Maleficarum* (the *Witches' Hammer*), imagined witches to be members of a big conspiracy, directed against Christian society, which was allowed by God to cause immense physical and spiritual hardship. The witches' power, although supported by the devil with God's permission, was real. Witches therefore had to be physically eradicated, according to divine and to secular law, and hammered out by virtually any means, since exceptional crimes require exceptional measures.[18] Opponents of witch-hunting generally disapproved of the atrocities, and equated them with the persecution of Christians in Ancient Rome. But it took Johann Weyer (1515–88), a court physician of the dukes of Jülich-Kleve, to find a non-religious reason. The author of the most influential early modern book against witchcraft persecutions considered so-called witches to be melancholic females who needed leniency, love and medical care to cure their mental illness. These 'witches' were not strong, but weak, not evil, but sick, and they needed not punishment, but love. Their killing could not be justified under any circumstances, but was to be seen as a 'massacre of the innocents'.[19]

The European denial of witchcraft is firmly rooted in this pre-Cartesian opposition to atrocity, adopted by the representatives of European Spiritualism, rationalism and Enlightenment. Because they did not believe in the existence of witchcraft, for them witch killings were an ardent injustice committed by the authorities, 'judicial murder' (*justizmord*) as the enlightened historian August Ludwig Schlözer (1735–1809) called it on the occasion of the last legal execution of a witch in Europe.[20] Only a few decades later, however, when the execution of witches had already moved into the past, a completely new, post-rationalist interpretation turned up, inspired by Romanticism. Witches were reinterpreted as personifications of popular culture, or even of popular resistance, emphasizing the important role of women. Jacob Grimm (1785–1863), the godfather of language and folklore studies, redefined witches as *wise women*, bearers of ancient wisdom, unjustly persecuted by the Christian Church in order to destroy European national cultures.[21] During Romanticism, a Romantic paradigm was created, culminating in the fantasies of the French historian Jules Michelet (1798–1874), who reinterpreted the witches as heroines of folk medicine, victims of feudal suppression and predecessors of the French Revolution.[22]

Rationalism, however, remained the dominant ideology among academics during the period of Industrialization. Most historians were proponents of a rationalist approach, labelled as the *Soldan paradigm*,[23] a term referring to Wilhelm Gottlieb Soldan (1803–69), a Lutheran professor of history and Member of Parliament in Hessen, who published the first modern *History of the Witch Trials*, firmly based upon sources in a Rankean style.[24] Joseph Hansen (1862–1943), the most influential protagonist of the rationalist interpretation, considered witchcraft to be a *non-existent crime*,[25] and his interpretation has moulded historical research up to the present day. Nevertheless, it must have been evident to everyone reading the trial records that some of the accused had indeed experimented with magic, worked as healers, experienced visions and ecstasies, or even dared to invoke demons, very much like their educated male contemporaries, or witches outside Europe.

The European approach to witchcraft over the last two millennia has been characterized by what Eric J. Hobsbawm and Terence O. Ranger termed the 'invention of tradition'.[26] Augustine, Burchard, Kramer/Institoris, Weyer, Grimm, and Michelet, were founders of distinctive traditions, the latter two, for instance, of feminist and neo-pagan witchcraft, and even a new religion (see chapter 7). Witchcraft historiography was concerned with constructed realities long before the advent of deconstructivism or postmodern theory. Due to the rise of social theory the interpretation of witchcraft underwent a leap of abstraction around 1900, best illustrated by some contemporaries of Hansen, whose concepts have proved to be influential to the present day. Psychology since Sigmund Freud (1856–1939) views hidden desires of omnipotence and aggression, suppressed into the subconscious, as a driving force of witchcraft fantasies, and witches as objects of projection for anxieties and aggression.[27] The functionalist sociology of Émile Durkheim (1858–1917), and particularly his idea that societies define norms by deviance, has moulded social anthropology's doctrine that witchcraft should be considered to be a means of securing norms, and therefore identity.[28] Max Weber's (1864–1920) historical sociology linked the process of rationalization in Europe to complex changes in mental as well as economic structures, leading to a *disenchantment of the world*.[29] Anthropologists since Bronislaw Malinowski (1884–1942) have interpreted witch fears and anti-witchcraft movements as symptoms of a crisis in society.[30] European rationalism generally considered magic to be a product of the imagination, a consequence of deficient technology and lack of insight into the laws of nature in a primitive society.[31]

The widespread assumption that belief in witchcraft is characteristic of primitive, uneducated people, like peasants in the Middle Ages, or tribal societies,[32] proved untenable. In some urban centres of Western civilization, dissidents from the esoteric and feminist milieus have labelled themselves witches, or 'new witches'. But these neo-pagan movements are double-edged: even in Western Europe and North America, traditional anxieties about witchcraft persist, and individuals may still be suspected of being witches under certain circumstances (see chapter 6). The assumption of primitivism also fails to fit the experience of early modern Europe, where scores of educated people firmly believed in the existence of witches and urged their prosecution, for instance the famous French lawyer and economist Jean Bodin (1530–96), or James VI/I, king of Scotland (1566–1625, r. 1567–1625) and England (r. 1603–25). Neither Bodin nor King James were primitive, tribal or uneducated, and the same is true for present-day African intellectuals and politicians. There is also an obvious paradox, because for those believing in witchcraft its dangers are indeed real, since dreadful anxieties can cause psycho-somatic reactions, and thus real harm.[33] Such a conclusion makes it more difficult to explain away witchcraft as non-existent or irrelevant. One of the most recent observations of anthropological research is the *modernity of witchcraft*, which can no longer be considered as a marker of 'primitive cultures', or of a distant historic past, but of complex societies at the beginning of the twenty-first century.[34] It may well be that a majority of the world's population currently believes in witchcraft (see chapter 2). That is to say: witchcraft is a burning problem of *our time*.

Contemporary anti-witchcraft movements illustrate the meaning of traditional witchcraft as an explanation of evil. The prominence of witch-beliefs may depend upon the lack of alternative ways of explaining misfortune, like cosmic forces, gods, supernatural beings, ancestor spirits, or non-mystical reasons, as well as on a lack of concept of contingency.[35] Witchcraft can serve as a residual category with considerable explanatory power, if no other explanation seems to apply. At stake is the irresolvable and ever present question of reasons for subjectively undeserved suffering and hardship, hard luck, damage, loss of property, disease and death. This problem, like the question of *theodicy* (why does God permit or even cause evil?), is timeless, just like the struggle of mankind with the uncertainties of life, with the laws of nature and with the (im)possibility of tran-scending them. Like religion, the witchcraft paradigm is a universally existing pattern to explain the *condicio humana*. Maybe it is even possible to assume that at the core of religion is the fear of witch-craft. The beliefs in witchcraft, shamanism and religion have much in common anyway. Not by coincidence was Jesus seen as a magician by his contemporaries.[36]

The 'rational assumption' that atrocities like the witch-hunts would never again happen in Europe, as Sigmund Riezler had claimed at the end of the nineteenth century,[37] was wrecked by the First and Second World Wars, the war crimes and the holocaust. It was during this crisis of European rationalism that the new academic discipline of anthropology came forward with studies on witchcraft. The *social-scientific approach* dominated the academic perception of witchcraft throughout the twentieth century, with Malinowski and Evans-Pritchard as outstanding figures, surrounded by a corona of researchers who even reached a wider public, like Lucy Mair (1901–86) or Mary Douglas (b. 1921). Recent anthropologists like Niehaus or Geschiere have developed a stronger sense of the *his-toricity* of not only customs and mentalities, but also of institutions. With the rising importance of African states, and the integration of local economies into the world market, anthropologists are increasingly looking at the publications of historians, and starting to compare African and European developments.[38] The business of reviewing historical research of witchcraft on an international level, started by Erik Midelfort (b. 1942) in 1968,[39] has turned into a major challenge. More research has been done within the past ten years than in any previous decade, often within the context of workshops, for example, in Austria, Belgium, Denmark, Germany, Hungary, Luxembourg, the Netherlands, Norway, Scotland and Switzerland. Contributions of younger – and, to a greater degree than ever, female – scholars, have changed our perspectives. More studies are now characterized by interdisciplinary, comparative and experimental approaches. Whether there is already another *paradigm shift*, an entirely new approach in historical studies, is difficult to say. Anthropology, too, saw an upsurge of publications in the last ten years, while some scholars are claiming that new shores of interpretation have been reached already by interpreting witchcraft as a 'language' of the suppressed,[40] and we shall see where this will take us. The cultural turn, it seems, means different things to different disciplines.

This book is an attempt to treat the subject as an *anthropological phenomenon* with a historical dimension. I wish to sharpen the awareness of the fact that witchcraft and witch-hunts are not a closed chapter in the history of mankind, or a matter of folkloristic curiosity. Witchcraft is still considered to be dangerous by many people, perhaps the reader's next-door neighbour, or at least one of his or her friends or colleagues, if we can trust statistics (see chapter 2). And – quite unexpectedly – more people have been killed for suspected witchcraft in the second half of the twentieth century than in most other periods in the history of mankind, as far as we can judge from the existing sources (chapter 6). As a historian, I am emphasizing the *historical dimension*, and that of European history in particular, not least because African, Asian, Native American and Australian societies are struggling with the European-born idea that witchcraft does not exist at all. This is not meant to imply that European history is more important, nor to exoticize non-European histories. Rather the opposite is the case. European witchcraft is well-documented, and can therefore be compared with present-day witchcraft. The fifty years between 1580 and 1630 saw the fiercest witchcraft persecutions that we know of in the history of mankind. Its history may serve as a test case for theories of acculturation, of social change, or of the 'modernity' of witchcraft (chapter 4). The same years also saw the fiercest debates about the meaning of witchcraft. Present-day conflicts over witchcraft have their predecessors in early modern Europe (chapter 5).

The idea that witch-beliefs have been constructed by contemporaries, and are accordingly enmeshed in contemporary discourses, may appear postmodern, and has clearly inspired some historians.[41]

That reality can indeed be tricky was the subject of an early modern science, nowadays no longer accepted as such: the science of super-natural causation and effects, i.e. *demonology*. Its contribution to modern science is underestimated, although it has become a com-monplace that the natural magicians could be interpreted as precur-sors of modern scientists.[42] It might well be that we can learn from these medieval and early modern attempts to face 'the challenge of the unreal',[43] not because we believe in ghosts or spirits, but because we must acknowledge the serious attempt to classify inexplicable phenomena, and also because the demonologies enable us to analyse how divergent the perspectives on one particular subject could be in pre-modern times. I would not, however, subscribe to Stuart Clark's idea that those engaged in demonological debates were participating in the same discourse.[44] It is true that Puritan divines like William Perkins (1558–1602) were not far away from their Catholic counter-parts, who shared similar ideas on divine permission, satanic power and human agency.[45] However, those who wished to burn witches for God's honour did not share many assumptions with those who sug-gested an improvement in living conditions for impoverished old ladies. Such conclusions may come as a surprise to scholars who look for male misogyny in early modern texts on witchcraft, and under-line the importance of reading historical sources carefully. Authors like the Swiss physician Johann Jacob Wecker (1528–86) shared Weyer's opinion that suspected witches did not deserve prosecution, but went further in their suggestion that the remedy should be a more joyful life, dancing, music, sexual satisfaction and poor relief, or – translated into modern terminology – social reform and a more liberal cultural attitude, supportive to underprivileged and marginal-ized groups, and taking seriously their psychological demands.[46] To understand such differences requires the contextualization of the texts, and the exploration of social contexts. I am convinced that past and present realities are reconstructable to a certain degree, with the obvious limitations outlined by Weber.[47]

Finally, why is it that we are fascinated by the subject of witch-craft? It seems that there are many different reasons for different people, and more than just one even within the same person. It has become commonplace for the use of fairy tale to be regarded as healthy for children's development.[48] But even as adults we some-times like being enchanted and distracted by fantastic novels such as *The Mists of Avalon*,[49] to mention just one example, and we accept the suggested plot despite the obvious distortion of historical facts, and although we could easily obtain more accurate information about the underlying agenda.[50] Beyond sheer entertainment, it seems that the subject of witchcraft is a matter of *identity*. There are the ever-lasting attractions of sex and crime, the stereotypes of forbidden knowledge, hidden conspiracies, occult powers, secret circles, under-ground rituals, feminine power, misogynistic clerics, bloodthirsty persecutors or heroic fighters against suppression and persecution. For obvious reasons, the term 'witch-hunt' serves as a metaphor for certain types of oppression by forces we conceive as 'evil' nowadays, and the historiography of witchcraft seems to be sponsored by coded subjects: the suppression of human rights by specific institutions in specific political circumstances, the issue of religious fundamentalism, as emphasized by late nineteenth-century scholars in Europe and America alike, injustice in general, or the gender issue, so prominent in recent years. Students usually feel more attracted by witchcraft than by the drier subjects of their academic disciplines. And they are right in choosing the more exotic and entertaining subjects, which offer at least as many – and maybe more – insights as traditional and boring ones. For academics there is the fascination of witchcraft's cross-cultural prevalence, frequent cultural prominence and para-doxical attributes, with the potential for testing theories about structures, belief and social action. Furthermore, the subject is likely to generate more lively and controversial discussions in seminars, as well as in public, because there is *room for interpretation*. It is, however, helpful – perhaps even indispensable – to know the existing debates on the subject.

In order to provide firm ground for future discussions, the chap-ters beyond this introduction (chapter 1), deal with the belief in witchcraft, both in Europe and non-European societies (chapter 2); the persecution of witches in Antiquity and the Middle Ages (chapter 3); the European Age of Witch-Hunting (chapter 4); the process of outlawing witchcraft persecutions in early modern Europe (chapter 5); witch-hunting in the nineteenth and twentieth centuries (chapter 6); the relation between old and 'new witches' in our present time (chapter 7); followed by an attempt to make sense of all of this in a concluding chapter (chapter 8). All information provided is cited in the notes in abbreviated form. Full bibliographical details are to be found at the end of the book, where the bibliography lists: 1 a number of useful dictionaries, handbooks and source editions; 2 demonolo-gies and other texts published before 1800; 3 the most important monographs on witchcraft; 4 standard omnibus volumes, essay col-lections or readers on the subject; and – although I had intended to avoid it – 5 indispensable articles; 6 literature on modern occultism, esotericism and 'new witches'; and finally 7 a number of basic general works, necessary to understand the historical background and theo-retical classifications. Biographical data of scholars, artists and witches are attached to their first mention in the book. Dates are AD, unless indicated otherwise. The chronology at the beginning of this book provides a backbone to our story. And an index of the more important actors, places and subjects is meant to make the informa-tion accessible, serving as a guide to the realm of magic.

2

The Belief in Witchcraft

Lastly, to conclude this part: as we said in the beginning that the act of envy had somewhat of witchcraft, so there is no other cure but the cure of witchcraft.

Francis Bacon, 'Of Envy', 1625

The search for explanations of misfortunes and attempts to govern human affairs through occult forces are part of the human condition and know no time and place.

George Clement Bond/Diane M. Ciekawy,
Witchcraft Dialogues 2001

Witchcraft is a controversial subject and offers multiple opportunities for misunderstandings. During the first presidency of Mathieu Kérékou (1933–, r. 1972–91, 1996–), the government of Benin launched a campaign against 'witchcraft'. The president was asking for support for his policy of Africanization in the former French colony of Dahomey, and for the intended transformation into a Soviet-type 'People's Republic of Benin', based upon the philosophy of Marxism-Leninism. The campaign against witchcraft was meant to signify class war, since in traditional African societies wealth is considered to be suspicious: if everybody is working, how can some people get richer than others, except by mystical theft from relatives or neighbours? According to the concept of 'limited good',[1] the perception of a zero-sum economy is not unusual in traditional societies. It was present in pre-industrial Europe as well, where lack of milk or grain was attributed to magical theft. In Africa, the association of wealth and witchcraft is still widespread, and, although unexpected to European Marxists, the association with class war is not completely

Plate 1   *La lutte contre la Sorcellerie (Forces du Mal)*. Postage stamp, Peoples' Republic of Benin, 1977. ©

off the point. However, the government's intention was misinterpreted, and the campaign got completely out of hand. The populace began to chase old women, who were held responsible for a dramatically increased infant mortality. Child and infant mortality is generally high in Africa (Benin 25 per cent) compared to the developed world (USA 1.6 per cent, UK 1.3 per cent),[2] and a tetanus epidemic had added to the general misery in 1975. An expensive vaccination campaign was cancelled, and the government allowed the confessions of supposed witches to be broadcast on the radio. Some of the women reported that they had shifted shapes and become owls, and had bewitched children in order to transform their souls into animals, whom they devoured.[3] In 1977 the postal administration of Benin issued a stamp, advertising the government policy as a struggle against 'the forces of evil': *La lutte contre la sorcellerie (Forces du Mal)*. The stamp shows activists cutting down a huge tree, applauded by an enthusiastic crowd.[4]

This summary of a recent event in an underdeveloped country, with an illiteracy rate of more than 60 per cent, and a majority supporting traditional African religions (with only 18 per cent Catholics and 15 per cent Muslims) displays a number of motifs similar to beliefs held in the Ancient World, in medieval and early modern Europe, or in present-day Africa, south-east Asia, Australia or the Americas. A *basic set of beliefs* could be summarized as follows. There are evil forces around, and they try to cause harm. Some people, who are essentially anti-social, either incorporate such forces involuntarily, or form alliances with these forces intentionally in order to inflict harm by mystical means, mostly on their relatives or neighbours. They gain supernatural powers, such as shape-shifting, the transformation into animals, and the ability to fly through the air. They not only act as individuals, but rather, through their alignment to evil forces, they act in groups, being part of a conspiracy. In this capacity they manage to induce illness and death, to destroy livestock and crops. As the utmost symbol of their evilness, they kidnap babies in order to devour them or to use their body parts – for instance, baby fat in the fantasies of European demonologists (see plate 7) – for the preparation of powerful unguents. Some years ago, Geoffrey Parrinder, who compared witch-beliefs from different parts of Africa, pointed to these striking similarities between African and European perceptions of witchcraft.[5] But there are plenty of similar examples from all parts of the world, for instance from south-east Asia,[6] or the Americas. Laura de Mello e Souza has emphasized the similarity of notions of witchcraft among the descendants of European colonists, African slaves and native American Indians in Brazil. Concerning the witches' flight, only the destinations were different: European witches preferred to fly back to Portugal, Africans to West Africa and Indians to the Brazilian rainforest.[7]

Such similarities require explanation. Common origins could easily explain the similarities in the belief systems. However, they would have to reach back further than the prehistoric waves of immigration to the Americas, tens of thousands of years ago. This seems likely to some anthropologists,[8] although it is impossible to judge the age of shamanistic ideas, like magical flight, animal transformation or sympathetic magic. Prehistorians and archaeologists suggest magical-religious references, and even shamanistic motifs, in Palaeolithic artefacts, rock and cave paintings. Better evidence can be gained with the commencement of written sources. Magic formulae are certainly to be found among the most ancient written texts in the history of mankind.[9] But, however plausible, it is methodically impossible to prove a common pedigree of witch-beliefs. Malinowski claimed that magical belief and practice serve similar functions in all civilizations, and witchcraft beliefs from the Arctic to Australia have necessarily emerged with similar patterns.[10] This would imply that not only social or cultural factors, but also structures of the human psyche play a role. Psychologists have found magical assumptions and behaviour in childhood, even if not encouraged by the social environment. According to Freud, fantasies of omnipotence and compulsion neuroses are typical for early stages of infant development, and should be seen as part of the human subconscious. The popularity of magical or shamanistic motifs in folk tales mirrors children's demands rather than early stages of human development, as assumed by the Russian folklorist Vladimir Propp (1895–1970).[11]

Witch-beliefs are neither uniform nor distributed evenly. Studies on witchcraft in Africa have shown that witch-beliefs play a minor role in some societies, where misfortune is attributed to gods, ancestor spirits or states of pollution, whereas in other societies, even those under similar conditions of economy, kinship and social structure, beliefs in witchcraft seem like an obsession, and social relations as well as everyday events are described in a language of witchcraft. Early field studies like Evans-Pritchard's have presented examples of societies where belief in the activities of witches has structured social life to an enormous degree.[12] Max Marwick tried to provide a statistical foundation for such assumptions, and collected 200 cases of misfortune among the Cewa in Eastern Africa (Zambia), to compare the specific circumstances of these events and their subsequent interpretation. He found that all cases of misfortune (100 per cent!) were related to witchcraft when he asked in a general way, but only 54 per cent when specific cases were discussed. Only one quarter of those interviewed related misfortune to either natural causes or God; the residual cases were related to ancestor spirits or persons who were not considered as witches. In 74 per cent of the assumed witchcraft cases the witch or the sorcerer was identified by name (fifty-four males, forty-five females). In 78 per cent of these cases perpetrator and victim were matrilineal relatives, while in 21 per cent they were related through marriage or more distant relatives. Only in 1 per cent of all cases of suspected witchcraft did no kinship relation at all exist. It appears that categories of kinship and neighbourhood, social proximity in general, play a decisive role for witchcraft accusation not only among the Cewa, but in most societies.[13] Witchcraft, as Max Herman Gluckman (1911–75) summarized, 'is not just hatred, it is hatred working in some social relationships and not in others'.[14] As an extreme case, Susan Rasmussen has shown that among the nomadic Tuareg people in Niger witchcraft is often linked to threatening strangers, so-called 'external' outsiders.[15]

Intensive witch-beliefs are in no way confined to rural areas or the uneducated. In 1968 no less than 41 per cent of the students of the University of Ghana considered the existence of witches to be probable, whereas another 35 per cent were absolutely sure, adding up to 76 per cent of the educated future elite. Similar figures are known from high schools in Zambia in 1964, where 61.8 per cent strongly agreed with the statement 'witches make people ill', another 20.8 per cent agreed (together 82.6 per cent), 8.6 per cent remained uncertain and only 2.8 per cent denied the statement.[16] Such a widespread belief in witchcraft leads to a number of consequences. For instance, in 1992, the Ivory Coast football team defeated Ghana to win the African Nations Cup, hitherto dominated by North African teams. The champions were supported by witch-doctors, hired by the Ivorian sports minister, and this had sparked an ongoing debate about the use of witchcraft in African football. Some contributors to a recent web-chat on the BBC Sports Talk website have rightly pointed out that 'witchcraft' plays on the psyche of the opponents, just like other rituals, and is therefore generally used in sub-Saharan African football. But several Africans wrote with apparent irony that if witchcraft worked in itself, African teams should permanently win the World Cup.[17]

Only recently it has been demonstrated that the ongoing spread of AIDS – 15 per cent of pregnant women were infected in 1996, 25 per cent in 2000 (but close to 40 per cent in the province of KwaZulu Natal) – has led to a dramatic rise of witchcraft accusations in Zambia, since medical treatment is unavailable and death is traditionally attributed to witchcraft.[18] *Isidliso*, 'poison', an evil work of witches, is seen by many South Africans as the cause of the disease, not without reason, since the transmission of AIDS – by bodily fluids like blood, breast milk, semen or vaginal fluid, involving wounds, sexuality or nourishment – has much in common with the transmission of witchcraft. The disease becomes visible only after a delay, and the source of infection is not easily identifiable. Its symptoms, caused by the acquired immune deficiency, such as respiratory problems, coughing, wasting, tuberculosis, vomiting and diarrhoea, would earlier have been seen as signs of bewitchment. Even the language of medicine is compatible with traditional beliefs: viruses 'attacking' the immune system parallel the perception of witchcraft as an attack, and the agency remains hidden or occult. The victim of the virus, like the victim of the witch, is said to be in a constant struggle against invisible forces depleting his or her life. Witches are particularly keen on attacking the generative capacities of lineages, 'so an affliction that specialises in fertile victims passed through sexual contact is tailor-made for their craft'. Adam Ashforth amplifies these considerations with the insight that the deeper significance of AIDS is the *spiritual insecurity* created by the disease, which may surmount economic and social uncertainties in relevance.[19]

There is a mystical component, explaining the loss of weight as caused by supernatural creatures lodged in the gullet, resembling the shape of a crab, a frog or a lizard, devouring the victim from the inside out – literally eating his or her substance of life away. The poison of witchcraft is not to be understood in terms of toxicology. *Isidliso*, a Zulu word, is directed towards particular victims, 'not by chemistry, but by intention'. Another person could eat the poisoned food without being affected at all. It could even enter the victim's body while he or she sleeps. The witch places the *muti* in food consumed in dreams. The social ramifications of contracting either witchcraft or AIDS are severe: all kinds of social misfortune, such as divorce, unpopularity, family dissension, friendship and relationship breakdown, jobs disappearing and unemployment. The victim, or his or her family, must therefore engage a powerful healer to repel it. This does not mean that Western medicine is necessarily rejected, but a proper cure going to the roots of the disease requires African traditional and spiritual methods. Traditional healers and feasts for the ancestors are usually significantly more expensive than Western medicine, and will therefore put considerable financial pressure on the family's and their friends' income.

In urban areas, like Soweto, most people would not deny that witchcraft is a real disease, and few would reject Western medicine, but the witchcraft hypothesis requires answers to the questions identified by Evans-Pritchard: Why me? Why now? In the light of supposed *isidliso* witchcraft, social relations are scrutinized, recent quarrels within the family or with neighbours reconsidered, together with old conflicts being resurrected, and minutely re-examined in search of the cause of the crime. In a similar way to early modern European witchcraft cases, 'actions and gestures that once seemed innocent (like the loan of an article of clothing or the gift of food) can suddenly turn into ominous portents that were foolishly overlooked at the time'. Ashforth points out that the notion of AIDS as a social stigma was often reduced to sexual misdemeanour in public discussions, whereas the real meaning can hardly be understood without the dimension of witchcraft. No one would publicize being bewitched, because gaining intelligence of efforts to counteract this would enable the witch to take further action. Discretion is the norm, as long as the disease can be concealed, because witchcraft-related cases of disease or death will exacerbate tensions between a household and surrounding families. The notion of witchcraft means that the afflicted have reason to reconsider their social relations. Neighbours and friends become possible suspects, and targets of witchcraft themselves, since the afflicted will seek retaliation. The neighbours will also be wondering who amongst them might have been responsible for the disease, and many of them will have ready suspects. Community relations in general will be strained. The AIDS epidemic therefore 'becomes also an epidemic of witchcraft'.[20]

African authors have always stressed the fact that 'traditional concepts still form the essential background of many peoples'.[21] As a result of his recent representative survey, Ralushai suggests that only a small number of the citizens of South Africa do not believe strongly in witchcraft, namely whites and leaders of Christian churches of European origin, whose attitude is portrayed as a biased minority position.[22] Intensive witch-belief does not imply constant fear, but consciousness of latent danger, comparable to car accidents in big cities. Some scholars have assumed that the intensification of witch-belief could be related to colonial rule. But Isaac Schapera (b. 1905) demonstrated that in pre-colonial Botswana witchcraft was subject to the judgement of the chiefs, and torture and capital punishment had been instruments of traditional criminal justice.[23] Two collections of essays, edited by Marwick and Douglas in 1970, displayed the state of research on African witchcraft. The intensity of witch-beliefs and the increase in anti-witchcraft movements since decolonization are demonstrated by a number of publications on anti-witchcraft cults, and anti-witchcraft shrines,[24] and most impressively in a volume edited by Ray Abrahams on witchcraft in Tanzania.[25] Recent studies suggest an interrelation between the establishment of liberation movements and witch-beliefs, although sometimes in a concealed form. Documents like the Ralushai Report and other studies on South African witchcraft suggest that further studies will contribute decisively to our knowledge about witch-beliefs.[26]

In Australia and Oceania, at first sight witchcraft is a less significant subject. Melanesia was and is the hothouse of research, partly due to the fact that witch-beliefs were and are particularly strong, and partly as a legacy of Malinowski's seminal studies. Although this founding father of modern social anthropology is not quoted frequently by anthropologists of the present generation, his fieldwork on the Trobriand Islands during the First World War generated a number of surprising and systematic insights that implanted the importance of witchcraft research into the young discipline of social anthropology. In his *Argonauts of the Western Pacific*, Malinowski pointed to the belief in evil sorcerers (*bwagau*) and flying witches (*mulukwausi*), leaving no doubt that every important enterprise and all basic stations of life were necessarily accompanied by magic ceremonies.[27] Similar observations were soon made on the Pacific Islands.[28] Misfortune and death were almost always associated with witchcraft, as was soon ascertained for some other Oceanian and Australian societies, for instance by Reo Franklin Fortune (1903–79) for the island of Dobu,[29] and by Adolphus Peter Elkin (1891–1979) for the Australian Aborigines.[30] Shirley S. Lindenbaum and Mary Zelienitz have summarized research on Melanesian witchcraft more recently.[31]

Meanwhile, studies on South-East Asia have added considerably to our virtual atlas of witch-beliefs, allowing for comparison between more religions than in other parts of the world. The volume *Understanding Witchcraft and Sorcery in Southeast Asia* elucidates the omnipresence of witch-beliefs under completely different religious, economic and ethnic conditions. Christian-animistic belief systems from Papua New Guinea can be compared with the belief systems of Islamic countries like Indonesia and Malaysia, or Buddhist Thailand. Witchcraft could be ridiculed in one society, while being of overwhelming importance in a neighbouring ethnic group. Most of these studies still deal with traditional, rural or even tribal contexts, but they increasingly reflect the role of the modern state.[32] In Burma, where the saying is reported that 'out of seven houses, there must be one witch', the witchcraft paradigm as a theory of causation was equally important for the explanation of suffering among Hindus, Buddhists, animists and communists.[33] Nancy Levine has pointed out the similarity of witchcraft beliefs in Tibet and Nepal with those in Africa or Melanesia, and refers to the lack of research in Central Asian societies.[34] On Sri Lanka, appreciated for its beauty by Western tourists, the notion of sorcery or witchcraft is deeply connected to social practices and stages of life like birth, sickness, death or war, particularly among Singhalese Buddhists.[35]

Philip Kuhn's study about *The Chinese Sorcery Scare of 1768* demonstrates that fears of bewitchment were present in the classical Asian civilizations as well, and could occasionally cause outbreaks of persecution.[36] Recent research on the great peasant uprisings and the collapse of the Ming dynasty in the 1640s suggests that these were linked to witchcraft eradication movements.[37] In Communist China shamanism, spirit possession or belief in witchcraft and religion were labelled as 'feudal superstitious beliefs' (Criminal Law of the People's Republic of China, article 99), while sorcery and witchcraft were furthermore treated as fraud and politically dangerous (article 165), but it seems that all attempts at extinguishing these ancient beliefs were not entirely successful.[38] Intensive belief in witchcraft accounts for numerous killings in some Asian countries. Sohaila Kapur suggests in her *Witchcraft in Western India* that fears of bewitchment increased after 1948, and were clearly not just a rural but also an urban affair, at least in the region around Bombay.[39] Although strong witch-beliefs do not necessarily lead to witch killings, the evidence from different parts of Indonesia, the most populous Islamic country, is shocking.[40]

In America notions of witchcraft can be found among Native Americans (Indians), as well as among immigrants from Europe, Africa and Asia. For studies on American witchcraft, the cultural anthropology of Francis Boas (1858–1942) and his school has guided later research, as can still be learned from many contributions to the *Handbook of North American Indians* (Sturtevant (ed.), 1978). Clyde Kluckhohn (1905–60), a former student of Freud, pointed to the fact that for an understanding of the workings of Navaho society 'witchcraft is "important" in the same way that ceremonialism, social organization and other parts of Navaho culture which touch *every* Navaho are important'. In his careful judgement he comes to a conclusion that may bear significance for many non-European societies: witchcraft is not '*the* key' to an understanding, but it would be difficult or impossible to understand Navaho society without noting the decisive role of witch-beliefs.[41] Special cases are the ancient civilizations of Mexico and Peru, where the belief in witchcraft was closely related to the divine powers of the rulers, and to shamanism. In the Aztec empire it was widely believed that evil shamans bewitch humans as well as nature, use the evil eye and shape-shift into animals (*nahualli*), par-

ticularly into owls, for evil purposes, representing the dark, the creatures of the night or the dead.[42] Sixteenth-century reports provide
information about witch-beliefs for the pre-colonial period, for
instance in litigations about land ownership under Inca rule. Witchcraft was considered a severe crime with the populace concerned
about *maleficium* (harmful magic) and the ruling elite about treason,
as in other empires. Chroniclers like the Inca Garcilaso de la Vega,
as well as the Indian historian Guaman Poma de Ayala, report the
killing of witches. Public executions seem to have been the exception
in a permanent struggle against evil forces. In cases of 'very bad evildoers', however, not only the witch but all his or her family (except
for babies) were killed by Inca state officials (see plate 2), their
houses destroyed and the soil covered with lime.[43]

In Mexico *nagualism*, the belief in the animal souls of humans, has
survived the Christian mission, the colonial period and several revolutions.[44] The Catholic Church removed the evangelists' symbols
(bull, eagle, lion) from church façades to prevent veneration of these
supposed animal souls, who were considered to be more powerful
representations of the saints than their human shapes. Scores of
illegal witch killings are reported from nineteenth-century Mexico,[45]
and they continue to the present day. Beliefs in witchcraft are – like
in India or Africa – strong even in urban centres, and particularly
in Mexico City.[46] In a 'mean ranking' of forty-six forms of deviance
in a Zapotec village, witchcraft-related deviances occupy the rank
orders 4–7: behind murderers, abortionists (female) and robbers
come 'knows witchcraft' (male), 'spreads supernatural gossip'
(male/female), 'performs witchcraft' (male), and 'is a witch' (*brujo* =
male), whereas having the evil eye (male or female) ranks only 29,
and possessing a *nagual* (animal spirit, alter ego) only 43.[47] Although
Nathan Wachtel avoids the term 'witchcraft' in his ethnography of
village conflicts in Bolivia, the *kharisiri*, who are supposed to break
into people's houses at night to extract their fat or blood, until they
die, are witches, not vampires. Inquiries in the 1980s have shown that
a modernized version of this myth assumes that Americans are
extracting human fat in order to use it as a lubricant for industrial
machines, cars, airplanes and computers, procuring enormous profit
to the local traffickers, the *pishtako*.[48] Recently, American witchcraft
from Canada to Chile, including Inuit and black Caribs, has been
treated comparatively in Deward E. Walker's collection *Witchcraft
and Sorcery of the American Native Peoples*. The attribution of illness
and death to witchcraft was (and still is) widespread. Witch-beliefs
were particularly strong among Pueblo Indians, with an emphasis on
weather magic, echoing historic European examples. Given the tradition of this agriculturalist civilization, with similar structures of settlement reaching back many centuries, we can assume that their ideas
about witchcraft were equally persistent. But even among nomadic

Plate 2   *Inca Official Killing a Family of Witches*. Drawing, in
Guaman Poma de Ayala, *Nueva Cronica, c.*1612

tribes, like the Apache, witch trials can be traced back to the times of
their political and social independence.[49] Among the Netsilik Eskimo,
human wickedness seemed to be the source of all evil, and, if feelings
of envy or jealousy were involved, witchcraft was a likely explana-

tion for misfortune.[50] In West Greenland witches were thought capable of causing illness, death, sterility and poor hunting, i.e. capable of destroying the fundamental values of life for others. The control of witchcraft therefore counted among the most important tasks of shamans. Shamanistic seances would usually be held to explain why something had gone wrong, particularly in cases of bad weather, poor hunting, illness or death. In these cases the shaman served as a witch-finder.[51] In the Caribbean and in Brazil, despite all Christian missionary effort, a strong African influence is prevalent, fuelled by West African voodoo cults with their marked fears of bewitchment.[52]

Not even in Europe did violent actions against suspected witches stop completely after the legislation against witches had been abolished. Although the elites generally denied the existence of witches and the efficacy of sorcery from the age of the Enlightenment onwards, again and again elderly people, usually women, were bullied and sometimes killed (see chapter 6). Even nowadays traditional beliefs in witchcraft are widespread. Opinion polls in Western Germany (the former Federal Republic of Germany) brought to light the fact that the proportion of the population potentially fearing witchcraft varies between 10 and 30 per cent, depending on the mode of interviewing. In 1973 only 2 per cent of the population believed firmly in witches, but another 9 per cent considered witchcraft to be possible (11 per cent altogether). However, the results changed decisively when the term *hexen* (witches) was avoided, and witchcraft was discussed implicitly. To the suggestion that 'bad people' might cause disease by ill will, no less than 23 per cent of the population agreed (males 15 per cent, females 28 per cent).[53] These results proved to be relatively stable over a period of twenty years, with a slightly increasing tendency, although the majority still denied the existence of witchcraft. In 1986 about 13 per cent believed more or less in witchcraft, and 21 per cent agreed that bad people could cause diseases.[54] In 1989 the percentage of witch-believers rose to 16 per cent, but declined again to 14 per cent in 1991.[55] Those who believe in witches, it seems, represent a stable minority of about 10–15 per cent within one of the most developed industrial Western societies. Their social profile regarding age, sex, class, distribution between urban and rural areas, political preference, religion and education is not really surprising. To borrow a term from Max Weber, the *ideal type* of witch-believer actually seems to mirror the image of the stereotypical witch: she is female and aged, lives in rural areas, is characterized by low education and social position, and is politically conservative.

Unsurprisingly, there is a strong correlation between belief in witchcraft and religious belief. Pope John Paul II (Karol Woityla, 1920–, r. 1978–) has repeatedly confirmed that the Catholic Church continues to believe in the existence of a personal devil. Opinion polls among German priests showed in 1976 that 79 per cent of the Catholic clergy agreed, whereas only 40 per cent of the Protestant clergy shared this belief. Among regular churchgoers 24 per cent of both Catholics and Protestants believed in a personalized devil. However, only 3 per cent of the non-active church-members shared their belief. All in all 12 per cent of the population (males 9 per cent, females 14 per cent) subscribed to the existence of the devil, roughly as many as believed in the existence of witches.[56] Opinion polls by the Gallup Institute showed in 1988 that the proportion of people who believed in a personal devil was considerably higher in some Western societies. In Catholic Ireland, 57 per cent followed the teaching of the Pope. Most surprising, at least for Europeans, are the American results: no less than 66 per cent of US citizens believed in the devil,[57] surely a temptation for American politicians. Such degrees may only be surpassed in present-day Africa, where the concept of the prince of evil was only introduced more recently.[58] A personalized concept of evil seems to be implied by the custom of ritually stoning the devil during the annual Muslim pilgrimage to Mecca. As in other years, in 2003 more than a dozen people died on this pious occasion, and many were injured at Mena, according to the Saudi Arabian news agency SPA.[59]

Christians and Muslims would rather admit to belief in the power of a personal God, or even a demon, than belief in witchcraft. In contrast to the Bible, the Koran does not prescribe the killing of witches, although there is – in addition to chapters on jinns (c. 72) and soul-snatchers (c. 79) – an entire chapter referring in dark words to the evil in the creation, the magical rites of evil women, the evil of darkness and 'the evil of the envier when he envies' (c. 113). The underlying belief in witchcraft becomes evident when we look at rituals, benedictions and the use of sacramentals. Just to mention one object of cross-cultural importance: in Mediterranean countries virtually all children, and many adults, wear glass amulets on their body, around the neck, the arm or the waist, with further objects of that kind in their pockets, their homes and their cars. These eye-shaped beads are generally considered to guarantee protection against bad luck, and are often merely seen as part of common jewellery. However, these universally present objects are nothing but a protection against the *evil eye*, which can hardly be interpreted differently than as being an outstanding example of witchcraft,[60] as suggested already by Francis Bacon in his essay 'Of Envy'. The notion of the evil eye in the Middle East reaches back to Ancient Mesopotamia, and counts among the most persistent fears of mankind.[61] There are few studies yet on the fears of bewitchment in Muslim societies, but examples suggest that the concern about the evil eye, or deadly words, is of considerable importance, and indeed structures everyday behaviour and life among tribal people.[62] But even in urbanized countries like Morocco or Egypt the belief in magical powers of the eye and of words is present. But although counter-measures – like amulets, counter-magic, or ostracizing – are widespread, there are no recent reports about the killing of witches.[63]

The studies of Ernesto de Martino (1908–65) in southern Italy, Jeanne Favret-Saada in Normandy or Inge Schöck in south-western Germany have demonstrated that contemporary witch-beliefs work according to patterns of attribution well known to anthropologists and historians. The structure and persistence of witch-beliefs are regarded as a result of its anchoring in social life, its function for coping with situations of fear and danger, and of interpersonal conflict. Witch-beliefs structure the perception and simplify categorization of the environment, and serve as an organizing and relieving mechanism. Unexpected hardship or bad luck, sudden and incurable diseases, all can be accounted to the actions of *evil people*, to magical forces, sorcery or witchcraft, thus allowing for the reduction of contingency. The diagnosis of witchcraft opens up the possibility of combating the causes of hardship. Suspected witches often have a long history of suspicion in their village, where neighbours might collect evidence for years or even decades. Sometimes whole families are suspected, and sometimes for generations. Willem de Blécourt (b. 1951) has demonstrated with Dutch examples that the central role of witch-finders in contemporary European popular culture still resembles the examples known by historians from the archives, and by anthropologists from their field work in Third World countries. Witch-doctors are specialists in the fight against witches and are usually experienced in counter-magic, therefore running the risk of being suspected as witches themselves.[64]

The background to these findings is still Evans-Pritchard's study *Witchcraft, Oracles and Magic among the Azande*, conducted in British East Africa (today's Sudan), which demonstrated the normality and omnipresence of magic and witchcraft within a tribal society. Among the Azande certain forms of misfortune were related to the influence of witchcraft, illustrated by the classical example of a man stumbling over a root and breaking his leg. The argument that this could be considered to be a natural cause is refuted with the particular situation: the root is always there, but never before has anyone broken his or her leg.[65] This example illustrates a theory suggested some years earlier by Lucien Lévy-Bruhl (1857–1939), who had observed that 'to the native mind what has occurred cannot be accidental'. If three women were sitting on a river bank, and an alligator pulled one of them into the water, this could not be by chance because, although there are many predators, and many women, a specific crocodile had attacked a particular woman. In conclusion, 'someone must have incited this one to do it. Then, too, it knew exactly which woman to drag under the water . . . The only thing to

find out was *who* had done it'.[66] The lack of any concept of coincidence, chance or accident has attracted the attention of psychologists,
and Jean Piaget demonstrated that children under six also lack such
concepts,[67] a finding that has been backed by more recent psychological research. The concept of accident as an explanation of misfortune, it has been concluded, must be considered a social or cultural
construct.[68]

According to Evans-Pritchard, the accident raises unavoidably the
question: 'why me, and why now?', and serves as a reason to reconsider the victim's social relations, if necessary by consulting a diviner
or witch-doctor, who is expected to reveal the perpetrator by means
of oracular techniques. The social conflict is resolved as soon as the
victim manages to repair the disturbed social relation and thus to
remove the reason for further harmful magic. The idea of witchcraft
thus serves a clearly defined function, and plays a positive role by
keeping up moral and social balance in a given society. Witchcraft
among the Azande is imagined to be caused by an organ within the
human body, whose existence is inherited within the family. No individual, at least according to Evans-Pritchard, can be made responsible for the damage caused by witchcraft, because the witch-organ can
act independently of the witch's conscious will.[69] This construction
sounded exciting to historians, since the treatment of witchcraft runs
contrary to everything we know about the historical European experience, and also about anti-witchcraft movements in contemporary
Africa, where witches are publicly blamed, eventually tortured and
sometimes killed. Although the conclusion that no witches were
killed among the Azande may have been one of Evans-Pritchard's
famous constructions, his functionalist analysis of the social tensions
at the bottom of witchcraft and the reconstruction of the 'natives'
argumentation' nevertheless proved to be valuable for the understanding of witch-beliefs in other civilizations, from South-East Asia
to Europe.

Keith Thomas (b. 1930), Evans-Pritchard's younger colleague at
Oxford,[70] has not only demonstrated in his celebrated historical study
Religion and the Decline of Magic that early modern England was
permeated by specialists of magical services, but also that some
anthropological models also work in a completely different society.
Without mentioning Malinowski, Thomas tried to link the rise of
witchcraft persecutions in the sixteenth century to a major process in
European history: the Reformation, with its emphasis on the Gospel
(*sola scriptura*). Luther's teachings concerning justification by faith
alone (*sola fide*), and the Calvinist doctrine of predestination, deval-
ued and indeed forbade traditional and Catholic counter-magic. This,
in turn, led to rising fears of bewitchment, and therefore to increased
witchcraft accusations: 'Protestantism forced its adherents into the
intolerable position of asserting the reality of witchcraft, yet denying

the existence of an effective and legitimate form of protection or cure.'[71] Numerous regional studies have since demonstrated the importance of oracles and witch-finders for traditional European societies, and – following Evans-Pritchard's and Thomas' paradigm – looked for the social mechanisms behind witchcraft attributions and accusations.

The social historical theory culminated in the assumption that neighbourhood relations were disturbed to an unusual degree during the transition from feudalism to capitalism, when richer members of the communities withdrew their traditional support for poorer neighbours. Calvinist accumulation of capital, so to speak, stood against traditional Catholic alms-giving. Rising inequality caused envy, and the refusal to give bread and milk added feelings of hatred on the side of the needy, the elderly, poor women: the witches. Their reproaches and threats, with the possibility of some real attempts to use black magic, combined with feelings of guilt and bad conscience to encourage the wealthier to take action against the poorer villagers. And since the powerful controlled the legal institutions, they instrumentalized criminal justice against the witches. This 'charity-refused model' of accusation proved to be a powerful paradigm,[72] since it connected one of the most gruesome episodes of European history with one of the most celebrated changes in the social life of mankind.[73] Anthropologists, it seems, have more recently discovered the possible links between witchcraft and capitalism, or globalization, and became as fascinated with this idea as the historians a generation ago. However, the assumption that historical witch persecutions served the introduction of capitalism has proved untenable. Those attracted by this idea have failed to provide sufficient supporting evidence, and Thomas' student Alan Macfarlane (b. 1940), the most fervent supporter, subsequently discovered the roots of capitalism some centuries earlier, and recanted his previous theory.[74]

Envy, to be sure, is one of the most basic negative feelings on an anthropological Richter scale of emotions. Envy is not tied to any social or political structure in particular, but has been characterized as 'a pan-human phenomenon, abundantly present in every society, and present to a greater or lesser extent in every human being'.[75] According to George M. Foster (b. 1913), people in every society use symbolic and non-symbolic cultural forms to neutralize, or reduce, or otherwise control the dangers they see stemming from envy, and also the fear of envy, and – we should add – the fear of being labelled as envious, and this for good reasons: of about eighty cases of witchcraft collected by Henry A. Selby in a Zapotec village in Oaxaca during the course of six years in the late 1960s, all were linked to envy.[76] The most comprehensive response to Macfarlane's suggestions was given by Rainer Walz, who scrutinized hundreds of witchcraft accusations in the villages of the Calvinist lordship of Lippe. Unsurprisingly, he came to the conclusion that it was impossible to relate them to one single type of social conflict. Rather, they crystallized around all kinds of neuralgic points within the early modern village: disputes about love and affection as well as about property rights. Negative feelings like envy, hatred, jealousy or fear are decisive for witchcraft accusations, but due to its *multi-functionality* witchcraft could be related to any kind of crisis.[77] The examples of Thomas, Macfarlane and Walz demonstrate the seminal influence of anthropological research, and British functionalism in particular, on historiography. More recent anthropologists claim that the focus on accusation was no coincidence, because it 'automatically relates witchcraft to the reproduction of social order'.[78]

After a period of hectic searching for a key theory, it seems that scholarship on witchcraft has turned its back on 'ahistorical structural functionalism'.[79] Durkheimian functionalists may have provided the most elegant, but also the least accurate, interpretations, since they were neglecting both the importance of beliefs and the individuals' concerns, as well as their specific historical background. Anthropologists increasingly emphasize the historical dimensions of non-European societies, and develop an interest in institutions quite familiar to historians. State-building has been one of the subjects routinely scrutinized by historians because the institutionalization of conflicts within a legal framework, administered by trained jurists, and recorded by ever-growing bureaucracies, has moulded the treatment of witchcraft in Europe. It may well be that state-formation could be interpreted as part of the process of modernization. *Modernization theory* was invented after decolonization in order to design an alternative to communism for Third World countries in the mid-twentieth century, but from the beginning development was fashioned according to the European model, and this theory was therefore – or maybe foremost – applicable to European history. According to Neil Smelser, modernization is likely to cause 'social disturbances' during the process of acculturation: 'Three classic responses to these discontinuities are anxiety, hostility, and fantasy,' and these responses were linked to social and structural change. He even identified groups who were most likely to take action: 'There is plausible – though not entirely convincing – evidence that those drawn most readily into such movements are those suffering most severely the pains of displacement created by structural change.'[80]

Curiously enough, modernization theory could therefore serve a double purpose: it seemed to explain why European societies had been able to overcome witch-beliefs, because the factors favouring development – increasing division of labour, refinement of techniques, education and mobility, urbanization, rising social anonymity, institutionalization of conflicts and domination, economic growth, marginalization of subsistence farming, rationalization and secularization – were exactly the factors which rendered witches unimportant. On the other hand it was 'culture contact' (Malinowski) with developed, secularized European societies that increased the tensions within colonial or Third World societies and led to a sharp increase of fears of bewitching.[81] European diseases like smallpox often wiped out more than half of the population, and the traumatized survivors tried to determine what had happened, very much as in early modern Europe. The simultaneous appearance of disease and missionaries gave rise to witch-hunting in the early seventeenth century, when the Hurons in southern Ontario executed several French Jesuits, as well as their Native American followers in the 1630s and 1640s. As David Silverman has put it: 'Christian missionaries were less lethal than European diseases, but nearly as disruptive',[82] since they divided the local populations into accomodationists and nativists, who frequently fashioned their political conflicts in terms of witchcraft. Steady pressure from white expansion, land loss, alcohol abuse and economic dependency led to severe infighting. Among the Navaho of New Mexico there were two periods of increased fears of bewitchment and witch killings, the first period between 1875 and 1890, after their defeat by US troops and their captivity in a concentration camp at Fort Sumner. The people were 'pacified' and forced to settle within a narrowly limited area, a mental torture for hunters and warriors who were used to moving about freely over great spaces and not at all accustomed to permanent settlements. They were now also completely dependent on food supplies from their enemy. Traditional structures of authority collapsed, and witchcraft suspicions and accusations rose sharply, presumably alongside anxieties and aggressions. Kluckhohn argues that although the military defeat and captivity were a major trauma, still noticeable in interviews generations later, it was only during a period of adjustment in the overcrowded reservations that witchcraft gained unprecedented importance. A second period started around 1930, in a period of economic recession. Whereas the Navaho had remained unaffected during earlier crises, they were now integrated into the capitalist world economy and their products would no longer sell.[83]

Violent anti-witchcraft movements, it has since been argued, could be interpreted as a result of rapid cultural change, or social change, and the factors producing new tensions are of course numerous: disruption of traditional kinship relations; diminution in tribal chiefs' authority; difficulties in maintaining traditional patterns of reciprocity when changes occur in economic activity, particularly when money is introduced; the breakdown of agencies which formerly elicited social conformity and maintained social control; rising mobility causing new conflicts of values and giving rise to new jealousies or new envies.[84] It is an irritating form of Eurocentrism that exclusively European modernity is associated with rapid change, as it seems obvious that rapid social, economic and cultural change should be perceived as a more general phenomenon. It must have happened at all times, for instance due to changes in the natural environment, or due to cultural conflict. The Incas were confronted with a nativistic movement in the 1560s, the *Taqui Ongo* movement, which reacted primarily to the Christian threat and claimed that the indigenous deities, the Huacas, inflicted baptized Indians with sickness and death. Yet the Spanish invaders were also interpreted as witches, who had come to Peru in search of human fat, as reported by the chronicler Cristobal de Molina, an assumption with an obvious link to reality, since the Spanish invaders had involuntarily introduced a good number of epidemics, like smallpox and the plague, which took their toll. The Taqui Ongo prophets, claiming to be spiritually possessed by *Huaca* spirits, predicted the end of the world and its renewal in a new era.[85] The movement also threatened the indigenous rulers, and for Titu Cusi Yupanqui (1530–71), the rebel Inca of the Vilcabamba district, witches and false prophets were grouped together.[86] So it seems appropriate to assume that periods of intensive stress equally must have led to witchcraft accusations in earlier times, in the Americas as well as in Africa or in Asia. There was early criticism concerning generalizations,[87] especially from the 1990s, when it became clear that there was no mechanical link between social malaise and witch-hunting because, quite obviously, not all Third World societies reacted in the same way. Niehaus has therefore modified Marwick's assumption that witch crazes or witch-hunts could serve as an overall 'social strain-gauge',[88] and has pointed to the necessity of analysing the micropolitics of the witchcraft accusations, to reconsider them in terms of structures of domination and conceptions of power.[89] Adam Kuper concluded that witch-beliefs 'change and adapt, and respond to new anxieties and uncertainties'.[90]

As mentioned above, the Marxist government of Benin tried to utilize the traditional African perception that wealth, according to the concept of 'limited good',[91] can only be obtained by mystical theft, or witchcraft. There is plenty of evidence that not only hardship, but also rising inequality, can trigger suspicions of witchcraft, and it seems worth reconsidering similar phenomena in early modern Europe in this light, for instance the idea of the mystical theft of milk, attributed to peasant women whose cows were particularly productive, while those of the neighbours suffered from reduced output. A number of late fifteenth- and early sixteenth-century woodcuts portray the theft of milk by witchcraft. Unusual wealth is currently stimulating similar fantasies in Africa. In Nigeria, where a small group benefited from the oil boom, fantasies of ritual murder mushroomed in urban environments, eventually leading to violent action against some of the nouveaux riches, because the rich were suspected of killing children for the purpose of witchcraft.[92] Jean and John

Comaroff, with their postmodernist attitude to modernization, curiously end up suggesting that 'witchcraft is a finely calibrated gauge of the impact of global cultural and economic forces on local relations, on perceptions of money and markets, on the abstraction and alienation of "indigenous" values and meanings'.[93] This sounds like the kind of well-designed exaggeration to which historians would hardly subscribe. In the end, we may well have to return to the ingenious definition of Philip Mayer, who described the relationship between witches and their victims with the surprisingly efficient formula: 'Witches and their accusers are people who ought to like each other, but in reality refuse to do so.'[94]

Beyond all sociological explanations, ideas of witchcraft were related to the kind of religious speciality in non-European societies, which has been described with a Tungus word as *shamanism*. Due to the expansion of the Russian empire into areas of Siberia, where even nowadays shamanism is an important religious belief (Burjatia, Jakutia, Udmurtia), its exploration became the domain of Russian researchers. Their scholarship culminated in works like Sergej Michailowitsch Shirokogoroff's (1887–1939) *Psychomental Complex of the Tungus*, where the culture and function of these religious specialists, with their ability to make contact with the otherworld, to shape-shift, to fly magically, and to divine and cure, are portrayed in the context of an intact religious background.[95] In his summary *Le chamanisme et les techniques archaïques de l'extase*, Mircea Eliade (1907–86) came to the conclusion that shamanism was a powerful phenomenon throughout all of Asia, including China, Korea and Japan.[96] American cultural anthropologists, informed by Franz Boas' contacts with Russian and Scandinavian research, expanded the concept of shamanism to the circumpolar cultures and the Native Americans (Indians), and eventually to all continents. Anthropologists like Ake Hultcrantz or Louise Spindler made it quite clear that witchcraft and shamanism are to a certain degree interchangeable.[97] Shamanistic abilities not only resemble the properties of witchcraft, but shamans could turn evil and become witches themselves. The *Handbook of North American Indians* (Sturtevant (ed.), 1978) offers examples from various Native American and Inuit tribes or other peoples, where evil shamans were persecuted as witches and eventually killed through an alliance of chiefs and good shamans.

Like early modern Christian missionaries, twentieth-century anthropologists were surprised by similarities between, for instance, religious beliefs of American Indians or the Inuit (Eskimo) and the confessions of European witches, particularly regarding the central idea of the magical flight, but also of other-world contacts, spirit-helpers, the ability to talk with animals, shape-shifting and ecstasies.[98] When Carlo Ginzburg (b. 1939) first presented his famous *Benandanti* many scholars initially suspected that Ginzburg intended to prove the existence of a sect of witches. These charismatic individuals in sixteenth- and seventeenth-century Friuli, who experienced ecstasies and designated themselves healers and witch-finders, were believed to fight against witches in imaginary air battles, to defend the crop harvest and decide the fate of their communities.[99] Shamanistically gifted individuals have since been discovered in many corners of Europe. The *Krsniki* (Christians) were still considered to be opposed to the witches and were feared and sought for their divinatory powers until the 1950s, as Maja Boskovic-Stulli uncovered in her field studies on Dalmatian islands in the early 1960s.[100] Starting from the Hungarian *Táltos*, Gábor Klaniczay has collected similar ideas throughout Eastern Europe, from the Friuli over the Balkans down to the Black Sea, demonstrating that Ginzburg's seemingly erratic findings should be seen as part of a much wider puzzle.[101] From there a new access to the world of European fairy tales seems possible, where archaic folklore and literature meet. The nocturnal ride with Diana, the journey to Venus' mountain, the game of the good society (*ludus bonae societatis*), strange goddesses and contact with the deceased, together with the gaining of prophetic and healing powers, are all present in early modern sources, as in non-European cultures.[102]

In Europe the possibility of magical flights was strictly denied by the Christian Church. Laws in early medieval penal codes already forbade the belief in *strigae*, the term for owl-shaped flying creatures in Antiquity. In Greek and Roman times they were conceived as demonic creatures, capable of flying through the air, stealing children and devouring them.[103] Classical authors like Apuleius or Ovid clearly did not believe in their reality, but refer to a widespread belief.[104] During the Germanic invasions the notion was added that these creatures were in close contact with human allies. According to the Salic law (sixth century), it was one of the most severe insults to suggest that a man was carrying the kettle for *strias*. These Frankish *stri(g)as* convened at a fire to cook poisonous potions; they were human and their cannibalism was real: they were witches. The law imposes severe penalties, 'if a stria shall devour a man and it shall be proved against her'.[105] Legislation remained contradictory, however. The Frankish, the Lombard and the Alemannic laws all treat the subject with varying details. The Alemannic law, compiled around 600, forbade the burning of *strigae*. Likewise, the Lombard King Rothari (*c*.606–52) decreed in 643 that Christians must not believe that *women* devour a human being from inside (*ut mulier hominem vivum intrinsecus possit comedere*), and therefore supposed witches (*strigae*) must not be killed, particularly not convicted in court. The Anglo-Saxon missionary and bishop St Boniface (672–754) reported that the Saxons believed in witches and werewolves ('*strigas et fictos lupos crediderunt*'). A capitulary of Charlemagne (747–814) for the

Saxons in 787 imposed the death penalty on those who, like pagans, believed that a man or a woman could be a *striga*, one who devours humans, and burned them. Likewise, an Irish synod at around 800 condemned the belief in witches, and in particular those who slandered people for being *lamias* ('*que interpretatur striga*').[106]

These differences persisted well into the High Middle Ages, and we shall have to discuss whether the concept of *Carolingian scepticism* really makes sense.[107] Clearly, there was an increase in sceptical voices during the Carolingian period, even if we take into account an increase of surviving sources. The most important text on the subject is the *Canon Episcopi*, often erroneously attributed to the Church Council of Ankara,[108] but in fact collected, formulated and maybe even conceived by Abbot Regino of Prüm (*c*.840–915) in a penitentiary of the early tenth century. It is an admonishment for the bishops (*episcopi*) to proceed against sorcerers in their dioceses,[109] later to be adopted by the most important authorities of their times, first by Bishop Burchard of Worms, then around 1140 by Gratian of Bologna (*c*.1110–before 1179).[110] What made Regino's canon important was not only his rejection of the efficacy of sorcery, but his denial of certain witch-beliefs. After an introductory paragraph about the need to fight against sorcerers, male as well as female, suggesting lenient sentences, Regino inserts a long paragraph about certain women, who believe that they experienced nocturnal flights with the pagan goddess Diana. The great mass of believers in such fantastical tales were condemned for implicitly believing in a supernatural power rivalling God. The bishops should fight against these beliefs by means of their clergy, and make clear that these flights were not real, but were nothing more than a dream, a devilish illusion. The decree (canon) became part of the *Corpus Juris Canonici*, the Church law of Latin Christendom, and proved to be influential throughout the following centuries.

The *Canon Episcopi* not only remains the central text in European history regarding witchcraft, but also offers insights into the contemporary understanding of the subject. Regino wrote in Latin, although referring to popular beliefs, in a reference book for religious practice. The scores of copies offer different translations of central terms. The goddess the witches were suspected of flying with, Diana, was for instance described as *striga holda*,[111] combining the ancient Roman term for witch (*striga*) with a vernacular term, *holda*. *Hold*, which in present-day German still means lovely, kind or sweet, here possibly indicates a supernatural being similar to the Roman goddess Fortuna, perhaps a fairy queen. However, this label was so offensive to the contemporary clergy that other translations changed it into *striga unholda*, thus emphasizing its interpretation as a dangerous demonic being.[112] What kind of popular belief could be seen behind the label *striga* has not yet been explored thoroughly, and legislation remained contradictory. A decree of King Coloman of Hungary (*c.*1074–1116, r. 1095–1116) against the belief in the existence of *strigae* (*De strigis vero que non sunt, ne ulla questio fiat*) suggests that they were thought to be human beings with demonic affiliation: witches.[113] One of the oldest court account books from Tyrol contains a record about the burning of two such witches ('*pro exustione duarum strigarum*') in the lower parts of the court of Bozen/Bolzano in today's Italy in 1296.[114] The judge did not follow the recommendations of the *Canon Episcopi*, and regarded witches as real and dangerous. The transition from the ancient belief in *strigae* to the late medieval belief in witches was fluid. The witches discovered by the Inquisition in early fifteenth-century Savoy and Switzerland were called *stregule*. In Rhaeto-Romance Switzerland the witches are still called *striegen*, and the Italian term for witches is *streghe* up to the present day.[115]

The fragmentary nature of medieval sources makes it difficult to locate witch-beliefs exactly in time and space. Late Roman authors like Bishop Caesarius of Arles (*c.*470–503) provide catalogues of superstitions, widely used and copied by medieval authors, for instance to compile lists of sins in penitentiaries.[116] The penitentiaries contain accounts of false beliefs, such as the nocturnal flights mentioned in the *Canon Episcopi*. This key text itself influenced later notions. However, it remains unclear whether learned references or personal experiences were added to later texts, for instance the instruction by the Dominican inquisitor Bernardo Gui (1261–1331) in his handbook for inquisitors – in a chapter 'De sortilegiis et invocatoribus daemonum' – to ask the women whether they believed they flew with the *fairies* on certain nights.[117] There are many traces of popular beliefs in trial records of the Inquisition or of secular courts, including some erratic texts, such as two Inquisition trial records from Milan in 1384 and 1390, where women report in much detail nocturnal flights with a 'Good Lady', as their own real experiences.[118] Nicolaus of Cusa (1401–64), philosopher and bishop of Brixen, discovered beliefs in a *domina Richella* in remote Alpine valleys, and noted in his sermons of 1457 that this figure was called *Holda* in German.[119] Although there is room for argument, such images open the gates to Europe's *Dreamtime*, a sphere, according to the philosophy of the Australian Aborigines, where the boundaries between myths and reality, and past and present, are fluid.[120] Numerous motifs of fairy tales, as classified in Anti Aarne's (1867–1925) and Stith Thompson's (1885–1976) *Motif-Index of Folk Literature*,[121] appear in trial records, not as fiction, but as experienced 'facts'. Propp concluded that the roots of fairy tales are connected with layers of human consciousness, where linear perceptions of time and Euclidean space become meaningless.[122]

How far European perceptions of witchcraft were moulded by Christian theology becomes perfectly clear against the backdrop of

Roman Antiquity. Except for a few sceptical intellectuals during the late republic and the early imperial era, like Horace (65–8 BC) or Lucian of Samosata (120–80), the 'ancient Voltaire', who openly rejected and ridiculed vulgar superstitions, the possibility of magic was generally admitted, and its misuse (*maleficium*) penalized.[123] This is obvious from the earliest law codes (*c.*450 BC) to the late imperial legislation. Harmful sorcerers were to be burned alive according to a decree of Emperor Diocletian (*c.*245–313, r. 284–305), beneficial magic remaining unpunished. Contrary to the common differentiation between bad and good, or black and white magic, Christians questioned the efficacy of magic, but considered any kind of sorcery as diabolical. Starting with the era of the Emperor Constantius II (317–61, r. 337–61), *all* magicians were labelled 'enemies of mankind' (*humani generis inimici*), and the death penalty was imposed for black and white magic alike in a series of laws imposed in the years 357 (*Lex Nemo*; *Lex Multi*) and 358.[124] This paradigm shift had consequences. When the synod of Saragossa condemned the scholar Priscillian (*c.*340–85) as a heretic in 380, he was also subjected to an imperial investigation. Found guilty of magical practices, he and six followers were sentenced to death for *maleficium*. The first convicted heretic was thus actually punished for magic and, against the protest of several bishops, executed in 385.[125] The consequences can also be seen in the major Roman law codes, for instance the *Codex Theodosianus* of Theodosius I (347–95, r. 379–95), or the *Codex Justinianus* of Justinian I (482–565, r. 527–65). Due to the reception of Roman law in Europe, the imperial decrees created a lasting legacy. Their impact was increased by the semiotic theory of magic, as developed by Augustine.[126]

The consequences of this Christian demonology can be demonstrated with examples from various civilizations, and through the ages. To choose a more recent example, Deward E. Walker reports that in the religious universe of the Nez-Percé Indians there existed an opposition between witches and sorcerers on the one hand, and healers and shamans on the other. Both sides drew their powers from guardian spirits, but the former were considered as negative or evil, the latter as positive or good forces. The shaman with his or her divinatory power acted as a specialist for detecting and fighting witchcraft. The Nez-Percé remained untouched by Christian proselytizing until the end of the nineteenth century. Then they had to realize that the missionaries were confusing witchcraft and shamanism, by linking both to the devil, whereas Christian priests and medical doctors claimed to be associated with God.[127] The same kind of inversion must have worried the newly Christianized peoples in the Arctic circle, as well as in Africa, the Philippines or in early medieval Europe, for instance during the subjection of the Saxons under the rule of Charlemagne (747–814, r. 768–814). The problems surrounding conversion seem to have been similar,[128] and we must not forget when the Christian conversion of Europe was completed: Grand Duke Jagiello of Lithuania (*c*.1351–1434, r. 1377–1434) accepted baptism only on the occasion of his marriage to a Polish princess, in order to become King Władisław II Jagiello of Poland in 1386. But how many generations did it take for the common folk to learn the new beliefs?

Christian missions were often guided by the principle 'baptism or death', but with the newly converted the Church showed relative clemency towards errors in belief. Certainly there are examples when tolerance changed rapidly into massive persecutions, as for instance in the case of the converted Spanish Jews and Muslims, the *conversos* and *moriscos*, in the late fifteenth and early sixteenth centuries. The Spanish Inquisition, a symbol of intolerance until the present day, was founded at this time to combat heresy and false conversions. More characteristic, however, was the lenient treatment of converts, not only in the Americas or the Philippines, but also in early medieval Europe. The clergy treated those who believed in sorcery or witchcraft as individuals who erred in faith and had to repent. The penitentiaries are full of these kinds of rules. Jörg Haustein has pointed to the fact that the harsh implication of Mosaic law (Exodus 22:18: 'Thou shalt not suffer a witch to live') was reinterpreted by Carolingian theologians such as Hrabanus Maurus (*c*.784–856), archbishop of Mainz, who suggested mere exclusion from the community instead of physical extinction.[129]

The idea seems compelling, that 'the official church stance regarding magic shifted from a demonic association with paganism to a demonic association with heresy'.[130] This may work as an ideal-type model, but the reality was more complex. The law of Alfred the Great of Wessex (849–99, r. 871–99) clearly used the same reference (Exodus 22:18) as Hrabanus Maurus to impose the death penalty on women who received sorcerers or magicians. Witchcraft was considered to be a reality here. And it does not sound very much like Carolingian 'scepticism' when the French Carolingian king Charles II (823–77, r. 840–77) decreed in 873 that witches had caused illness and death in different parts of his realm, and should therefore – men and women alike – be put to death according to law and justice, together with their accomplices and supporters.[131] The position of the church seems to have remained at least ambivalent, as hagiography suggests. The great collection of the saints' lives, Jacob of Voragine's (1228–98) *Golden Legend*, compiled around 1260 but based on earlier narratives, was full of stories of conflicts between saints and demons and sorcerers, whose power obviously had to be real, in order to amplify the saints' achievements. Christian theology underwent a major shift of attitude only during the thirteenth century. In his *Summa contra Gentiles*, Thomas Aquinas (1225–74) not only confirmed Augustine's semiotic theory, according to which spells, amulets or magical rituals indicated a secret pact with demons, but gave the impression that sorcerers, through the support of the devil, could *physically* commit their crimes.[132]

Though mainly concerned with heresy, Bernardo Gui in his *Practica Inquisitionis*, in 1324, went into details of inquiring after magical techniques in a chapter on 'Sorcerers, Diviners and those who invoke demons'. These included cursing children, curing diseases, lifting infertility, gathering herbs with certain rituals, divining, conjuring with incantations and the use of wax or lead images (voodoo dolls). For Gui, sorcery by definition implied involvement of the devil, or perhaps even invocation of evil spirits, as in his questions about 'the fairy women whom they call the good folk, and who, they say, roam about at night'.[133] Sorcery was, however, still subject to secular law and secular courts, since the main indictment was *maleficium*. Subsequent inquisitors like Nicolas Eymeric (*c.*1320–99), inquisitor of Aragon, in his *Directorium Inquisitorum* of 1376 equated sorcerers with heretics because both were supposed to adore the devil.[134] Sorcery, or witchcraft, was thus redefined as a spiritual crime, subject primarily to ecclesiastical courts, and the Inquisition in particular. As we have seen, there were deep-rooted reasons for such a development: even the penitentials, where witchcraft had been treated as a fantasy, had claimed their spiritual relevance, and, as a legacy of the Augustinian semiotic theory, pagan priests and sorcerers had already been prepared for a career as devil-worshippers.

How far the diabolization of magic was accepted by the European peoples is difficult to assess, and remains an open question. On the one hand, it can be observed that in some ways the prominence of the devil increased in early modern trial records; on the other hand, most magicians persistently claimed in court that the efficacy of their rituals and spells was based upon 'natural' causes. This of course was anything but far-fetched, since *magia naturalis* was then a well-established learned discipline, with protagonists as prominent as Theophrastus Bombastus von Hohenheim 'Paracelsus' (1493–1541), Girolamo Cardano (1501–76), Gianbattista della Porta (1535–1615) or Isaac Newton (1643–1727). All were outstanding scholars of their period, who considered themselves to be natural magicians, dealing with the secrets of nature, and all are counted among the founding fathers of modern science.[135] Again, the relationship between high and common magic is anything but clear. Paracelsus, for example, claimed that he had learned many secrets of nature from hangmen, wise women and even witches. This, however, may have been just another populist move, since Paracelsus spent parts of his life as a freelancer, and despite the hostility of the authorities managed to gain widespread support and popularity. His ideas about sympathetic magic, his teaching of the *signatures* of plants and animals, whose form or colour revealed the hidden or occult relations between *microcosm and macrocosm*, were commonplace among the learned and the uneducated alike.[136] Moreover, in numerous trial records (although not the majority), suspected witches and witnesses report their magical activities as dependent upon 'white magic' and divination, with an impressively rich repertoire of spells and rituals, and without mentioning the devil at all. Whereas Keith Thomas claims that this kind of magic was characteristic of the British Isles, it was similarly frequent in all parts of Europe, among peasants as well as among nobles, and in the countryside as well as in towns. Harmful or black magic, on the other hand, was generally considered to be dangerous, and the sorcerers or witches themselves were usually regarded as responsible for the damage, not God or the devil as the theologians suggested. The use of magic was guided by the kind of instrumental approach analysed by Marcel Mauss (1872–1950).[137] Ernesto de Martino has rejected Durkheim's idea that the structure of magic was opposed to the rituals of the Church. As he explains in his famous field studies in southern Italy, both seem to serve quite similar purposes, crystallizing around decisive moments, steps and crises in life. In comparison to Church rituals, magic allows a more active role for the practitioner. Counter-magic, furthermore, offers active remedies against magical attacks, or witchcraft.[138]

These European findings remind us of reports from Africa or other parts of the world, where witches were thought to live in complex interrelation with supernatural powers on the one hand, and their relatives and neighbours on the other. Also, the figure of the *witch-finder*, or witch-doctor, whose magical abilities combine in the art of detecting witchcraft and witches by means of oracles and divination, seems to be a universal phenomenon. Recently, these kinds of diviners have been readmitted in courts in some West African countries to provide evidence for the indictment and conviction of witches. In Europe, due to the inimical attitude of both the Church and Roman law, and later enlightened rationalism, diviners have never been formally admitted to courts, although there are examples where their advice was sought. Most suspicions of witchcraft, however, were never brought to court, because those who considered themselves as being harmed by witchcraft avoided contact with the authorities for several reasons. There was a danger of getting involved more deeply in the case, and possibly even ending up as a suspect or being punished oneself. According to the *ius talionis*, accusers deserved punishment if they could not prove their accusations, and it was almost impossible to prove occult crimes, precisely because they were occult. The use of occult forces, of counter-magic or divination was considered to be a crime in itself by the authorities. The people therefore used diviners or oracles to detect witchcraft without going to court. In most cases they were more concerned with removing the spells than with punishing the witches. In order to restore health it was necessary to identify the witch. Only then could she be forced ritually, or be threatened personally, to remove the spell. In early trial records we can often find that the *maleficium* was successfully removed, and even the *Malleus Maleficarum* provides such examples.

Self-regulation of witchcraft cases without the interference of the authorities had a long-standing tradition in Europe. In court protocols of the sixteenth century the witnesses frequently say that certain individuals had been suspected for more than forty years, as had been her mother and grandmother. Families were labelled as being endowed with witchcraft for generations, without ever being formally indicted. The fact that there are no traces of indictments for slander in earlier court records demonstrates that coexistence with witches had been the rule, and prosecution the exception. As in contemporary Africa, in many European villages there were people who were known for their supernatural powers, good or evil. Their supposed power was checked by protective or counter-magic. One of the most important functions of the Catholic Church was its support in this never-ending struggle, giving protective powers such as sacramentals, like weather bells against hailstorms, blessed objects to counteract harmful magic, and benedictions and blessings of babies, the house, the stables, the cattle or the crops. In many cases, processions served no other purpose than securing protection against witchcraft, at least in the eyes of the rural population. Even the cross had an apotropaic meaning, and this explains the eagerness to eradicate the cross in the English Reformation.[139] Customs and rituals were penetrated by witch-belief, from the veneration of saints to the burning of bonfires, which often included the burning of an effigy on top. Many religious ceremonies were abandoned together with witch trials in the age of Enlightenment, just because these seemed to be two sides of the same coin.

The question why primarily women were associated with magic, as most historians assume,[140] or the *gender aspect* more generally, seems to allow only complex answers. One of the likely explanations for the prominence of female witches is the legacy of Christian theology, which has a long-standing tradition of claiming an increased female susceptibility to the temptations of the devil, starting with Eve. This was certainly the starting point of the misogynistic author of the *Malleus*, who devoted a number of pages to the reasons for female inclinations to witchcraft, and recommended the subject for preaching, because women had a particular desire for instruction. The first demonstration of the *malice* of females is the Bible; then he proceeds with instances of female credulity, and their physical qualities, in particular the changeability of their complexion, leading to a vacillating nature. He then refers to their slippery tongue, which makes them share their magic with friends, with whom they resort to *maleficium*, because they are too weak to take revenge otherwise. Worst of all, however, due to their changeability women are less inclined to believe in God. At this point, Kramer suggests his unique 'realist' etymology of *femina*, which consists of two components: *fe = fides*, and *minus*, literally translated, 'she, who believes less'. Lack of belief, in the eyes of the Dominican, is the basis for apostasy and witchcraft.[141]

Such an interpretation may appear basically crazy, and was even ridiculed by contemporaries, for instance nominalists, who would argue that a word (*nomen*) is just a signifier which has nothing to do with the signified, or humanists like Henricus Cornelius Agrippa von Nettesheim (1486–1535), who claimed that women are basically good, intelligent and beautiful.[142] Nevertheless the suggestions of the *Malleus* were shared by later demonologists, if they happened to touch upon the gender issue at all, even if this is not obvious at the first glance. Alexander Roberts, for instance, an obscure English Protestant clergyman, argued firstly that women 'are by nature credulous, wanting experience, and therefore more easily deceived'. After having referred to the fall of Eve and the physical quality of women's 'complexion', Roberts launches further assumptions:

> Fifthly, this sex when it conceiveth wrath or hatred against any, is unplacable, possessed with unplaciable desire of revenge, and transported with appetite to right (as they think) the wrongs offered unto them: and when their power herein answereth not their will, and are meditating with themselves, how to effect their mischievious proiects and designes, the divell taketh occasion, who knoweth in what manner to content exulcerated minds, windeth himself into their hearts, offereth to teach them the means by which they may bring to pass that rancour which was nourished in their breasts, and offereth his helpe and furthereance herein. Sixthly, they are of a slippery tongue, and full of words: and therefore if they know any such wicked practices, are not able to hold them, but communicate them with their husbands, children, consorts, and inward acquaintance . . . and so the poysone is dispersed.[143]

The *Malleus* is an outstanding example of Christian misogyny. Since the author was a Dominican friar, it has been argued that celibacy contributed to witch stereotypes by alienating the clergy from the female sex and increasing anxieties and aggressions. However plausible these assumptions may appear, there are major inconsistencies. First, women were generally considered as equal before God, and, in the Christian world view Mother Mary contributed decisively to salvation, as even the *Witches' Hammer* does not fail to admit. The Madonna was at the centre of a popular *protection cult* against the uncertainties of life, particularly disease and witchcraft, and her shrines in popular religion served – and still do serve – purposes similar to African fetishes or anti-witchcraft shrines.

Female saints offered protection against all kinds of hardship, and there are scores of examples of venerable queens, virgins, wives and mothers. Second, celibate members of Christian Orders served as devout defenders of women against the accusation of witchcraft (see chapter 5). And third, most importantly, and also most worryingly, the association of women and witchcraft has been in no way confined to Christianity. Within Islamic, Hindu or African civilizations, for instance, we can find similar stereotypes. The widespread division of labour, which conceives of witches as female, and witch-doctors male, can hardly be explained by Christian influence. In some European countries, like Iceland, Finland and Estonia, the idea of male witch-craft was dominant, and therefore most of the executed witches were male. As Kirsten Hastrup has demonstrated, only one of the total of twenty-two witches executed in Iceland was female.[144] In Normandy three-quarters of the 380 known witchcraft defendants were male.[145] Similar discrepancies may be taken from anthropological research. In Mexico the concept of witchcraft varies even within the same region. For the Tzotzil- and Nahuatl-speaking Mexicans witches are generally male, as during the Aztec empire, whereas the neighbouring Zapotecs mostly imagine witches and healers to be female.[146] All the witches killed among the Tzeltal-speaking Maya in the 1950s were male.[147] In a good number of African societies, for instance in parts of Zambia or South Africa, witches are expected to be male rather than female, an assumption closely related to the cultural affiliation of witchcraft and violence, and witchcraft and wealth.[148]

Despite such variations we have to acknowledge that in many societies witchcraft was conceived as a female art, or ability, or quality, and therefore those accused and eventually killed were predominantly women. Siegfried F. Nadel (1903–56) considered fears of bewitchment to be the result of gender conflicts, particularly if real women's capacities were contrasted to a subject legal position, but he could not see significant differences between matrilinear and patrilinear societies.[149] Attributions of witchcraft, although not simply the product of patriarchal society, were certainly shaped by it in the eyes of some scholars. Gluckman related to marriage customs the fact that among the Zulu, women were usually blamed for witchcraft. Misfortunes are attributed to women who have married into the group, daughters-in-law or sisters-in-law. Women are strangers, *internal outsiders* who can be held responsible for the ills of the group without destroying the loyalty of the group. In polygynic societies additional conflicts arise from women competing for limited power and property, with the obvious paradox that children, although desired, fuel the conflicts.[150] Andrew Apter argues that witchcraft accusations served as a weapon in a gender struggle during the Nigerian cocoa boom in 1950.[151] Esther Goody emphasized the fact that due to a lack of legal institutions, where aggressions could be acted out or articulated, women had to resort to witchcraft.[152] Similarly, Christina Larner (1934–83) pointed to the fact that men expressed aggressions according to their social positions by violent acts, women rather by words.[153] It was argued that the concentration of witchcraft accusations on elderly women was due to their bitterness, for which there were many reasons, and also their freedom from male control, or even economic independence.[154] Heide Wunder has emphasized the fact that widows were socially endangered when male protection was lacking. Accusations frequently arose within the social and cultural *domain of women*. According to a widespread division of labour in traditional societies, these were the areas of the extended household in general, including childbirth, education and nursing. Unusual diseases or sudden child death, for instance, in many societies a likely starting point for suspicions, were exclusively located within the female sphere, and so, therefore, were the popular remedies.[155] Robert Muchembled (b. 1944) and other historians suggest that the village discourse about witchcraft suspicions was predominantly female, and women were therefore responsible for the attributions of suspicions to a considerable degree.[156]

But there are more reasons for the association of women and witchcraft. Evans-Pritchard defined witchcraft, in contrast to sorcery, as a physical quality, which was not learnt but was seated within the body, being inherited from generation to generation. The Zande believed that there is an organ for witchcraft, seated within the abdomen, although some held the opinion that this was just a virtual organ, which could not be found physically through surgery. Standard subjects of anthropological research, such as female bodily qualities of menarche, menstruation,[157] pregnancy, breastfeeding or menopause, are yet to be explored in their relation to witchcraft. Borrowing from psychoanalysis, James Brain suggests that cultural prejudices towards women are related to early experiences, like birth trauma, 'womb envy' and weaning practices. Referring to Lévi-Strauss,[158] and to female capacities like menstruation, childbearing and lactation, he claims that in dichotomic classification systems of agrarian societies women are usually associated with changeability and disorder, *nature*, uncontrolled forces and danger, whereas men represent security, order and culture.[159] Monica Blöcker suggests that women in a pre-modern European cosmology were cognitively linked to nature and the elements, and earth and air in particular. Hailstorms were therefore part of the female domain.[160] This, however, is difficult to prove, although pregnancy and childbirth are undeniably connected to *fertility*, one of the most important preoccupations in agrarian societies, and particularly so in Africa with its hostile environment. The links between sex, or gender, and witchcraft, remain open to further discussion. Impressed by the fact that contemporaries have never interpreted witchcraft accusations as a result of gender conflicts, a majority of historians have adopted Larner's formula, that witchcraft was 'sex-related, not sex-specific'. However, it will be hard to sustain the feminist stereotype that 'the women who were accused were those who challenged the patriarchal view of the ideal women', and that they were accused 'by other women because women who conformed to the male image of them felt threatened by any identification with those who did not'.[161]

Lyndal Roper (b. 1956) has pointed to the fact that the *psychological dimensions* have hitherto not properly been taken into consideration, although early modern witch-trial records in particular would allow such analyses, since the suspects were asked to reconstruct, or in a way construct, their life stories, and to trace back the turning points of their biographical developments, not unlike in psychoanalysis.[162] The most surprising suggestion is that in order to understand European witch trials it will be necessary to ask why women confessed to being witches. Roper suggests that their narratives are 'littered with Oedipal themes', telling about the women's desires, their relations to father, mother, lovers and female competitors.[163] Even if the sexual implications of Freudian theory will not be universally appreciated, it is obvious that the women's psychology has generally been neglected by research, which makes it impossible to understand why some considered themselves to be witches, and – as in present-day Africa – confessed voluntarily. Among the unexplored themes are sexual fantasies, the perception of sexual difference, the concepts of individual self, the construction of guilt, the unconscious imagery of language and the conceptualization of the body, the female body in particular. Starting from the concepts of the psychoanalyst Melanie Klein (1882–1960), who interpreted the mother's body as a vessel containing evil and dangerous substances,[164] Roper emphasizes the importance of the bodily fluids (semen, milk, blood) and their exchange more generally. The observation that accusations of witchcraft were frequently generated by mothers whose children fell ill or died unexpectedly thus gains a deeper meaning.

Accusations were frequently directed against old, presumably post-menopausal women, whose envy targets those who are still able to share the pleasures of motherhood and exchange bodily fluids with males, experiencing the physical changes a woman's body undergoes when she bears children, gives birth and food. Motherhood is a symbol of fertility, whereas those accused represented exactly the opposite: 'their most common target was a post-menopausal, infertile woman, who was caring for the infant'.[165] The preponderance of lying-in-maids may be grossly exaggerated by Roper, but it is true that the majority of the accused were classified as being 'old'. And even if we have no data at all concerning the menopause, it may well be that these aged neighbours were identified with infertility. Witches – including those with a long-standing reputation – certainly were. The binary opposition of fertility (good) and barrenness (bad, or evil) seems to add to our understanding of accusations within the female sphere, particularly if we include the anxieties and ambivalent feelings mothers may have towards their children.[166] All this transcends the structures of (patriarchal, agricultural, or whatever) society, and constitutes a genuine concern of females, and of mothers in particular.

As mentioned above, Freud was interested in the phenomenon of witchcraft, magic and the relations between witch and devil, and witch and inquisitor. In his correspondence to Wilhelm Fliess he mentioned that he had read the *Malleus Maleficarum*.[167] Later Freud was concerned about the interpretation of occult phenomena, and finally he published an article about the story of the Bavarian painter Christoph Haitzman, who made a contract with the devil at the end of the seventeenth century. Freud interpreted witch-beliefs or encounters with the devil as forms of neuroses, related to events in early childhood.[168] Following this line of inquiry, Swiss ethno-psychoanalysts tried to explore the cannibalistic qualities of the witches within the society of the Agni people of the Ivory Coast. Frustrations, anxieties and aggressions are widespread in this society (and maybe in any society), but they are subconsciously projected onto appropriate scapegoats. Among the Agni these are usually aged females. Referring to Freud's 'oral phase', their greed appeared to be characterized by oral aggression. Old and frustrated persons are associated with greed and envy, and can therefore be imagined as devouring babies, or their souls. According to Parin, Morgenthaler and Parin-Mathèy, witches symbolize 'the man-eating phallic mother of the symbiotic phase' of early childhood, on to whom feelings of envy and greed are being transferred. They serve as scapegoats, since the mechanism of projection allows for the solution of psychic tensions.[169]

Another line of interpretation tried to locate gender in the relations between suspects and judges. As Lyndal Roper has suggested, many suspects had to endure prolonged imprisonment, intimate physical inspections, psychological stress and torture. During the reconstruction of their life stories, the suspects were guided by the leading questions of their interrogators. The confessions, in this interpretation, were constructed in a process of negotiation, as the suspect tried to provide a 'correct' version, for instance of her seduction by the devil, consistent with both her own experience and the demonological knowledge of the judges, in order to construct a narrative plausible to both herself and her tormentors. Her experience, of course, included both the correct data of her life, which had to be verifiable by the court, and her own fantasies about seduction, weddings, sexual pleasures, baptismals, dancing and feasting, flying through the air or harming her enemies.[170] Jonathan Durrant concludes that women naturally named more women than men as their accomplices, because they tended to nominate people with whom they were more socially intimate. 'These gender-aligned associations were not, however, the product of patriarchal ideology.'[171] Another reason for the high proportion of female witches was that accusations of males within the trials were suppressed by male judges, either because they did not meet their expectations, or for political and social reasons. For Africa, it could be added that not only the state courts, but also traditional courts and secret societies were male dominated. Several peoples employed associations of young men, frequently masked, 'to identify and execute witches, often with great cruelty'. Among the traditional masks in Yoruba secret societies there was explicitly a 'hanger of the witches'.[172] However tempting it may be to interpret witch-hunting as a result of 'male domination',[173] there are obvious difficulties. The leading expert on European demonological literature has claimed that the *Malleus* was a rare exception and the bulk of European demonology surprisingly ignored the gender issue.[174] And the most recent reviewer of early demonologies concludes that these authors were not interested in women at all, but merely instrumentalized the prevailing misogyny in order to fight against a rising tide of religious scepticism.[175]

A different strain of psychological research has dealt with superstitious beliefs. According to the *Studies in Prejudice*, an inclination to occult explanations, stereotyping and thinking in rigid categories was characteristic for the mental structures of the *authoritarian personality*. Conceived by a number of prominent German emigrés to America, known as the Frankfurt School, these empirical studies were meant to explore the psychology of Hitler's followers, but could equally serve to explain more generally the psychology of persecution, or of persecutors. Theodor W. Adorno (1903–69) supposed that a specific weakness of the self was one of the most important reasons for stereotyping.[176] The Freudian category of the defence mechanism, the projection of wishes, aggressions and anxieties in particular,[177] could also support *scapegoat theories*. American sociologists theorized about mechanisms of exclusion and the dynamics of stigmatizing, as developed by Erving Goffman (1922–82).[178] According to the *labelling approach*, social deviance was only one of many possible factors, with other deviations such as mental diseases or distinctive physical features, including warts or birthmarks, contributing to the identification of the witch.[179] The followers of the *Malleus Maleficarum* regarded the latter as *stigmata diaboli*, and tried to introduce the pricking test as means of obtaining circumstantial evidence in the courts. The coincidence of threats in disputes between neighbours, and subsequent diseases, was considered to be strong evidence for witchcraft (*semiplena probatio* – 'half of the evidence'), sufficient for applying torture in continental courts. Here Robert K. Merton's (1910–2003) theory of *self-fulfilling prophecy* is relevant.[180] Witch identifications are always reconstructions after the event (e.g. sickness), in which, according to Selby, four factors play a decisive role: dreams, suspicious encounters, motivational analysis and witch-doctors. Whether or not these criteria are applicable or convincing in a specific case is seen as a matter of discourse by interactionist sociologists, who define 'witch labelling [as] a sociological game'.[181]

In recent decades some anthropologists have accepted their African colleagues' point of view that witchcraft is real for those who believe in it. Case studies of death spells support the relevance of such a perspective.[182] Individuals whose right to life was formally denied by their communities as a consequence of their deviance died within a few days, without any physical violence involved. The reasons for their death seem easy to explain. In Australia, for instance, the victims die of dehydration, because they stop eating and drinking. Attempts by missionaries or anthropologists to save their lives have failed, because they could not be persuaded to resume the intake of food or to emigrate. The condemned reject such suggestions as hopeless, since they know that they are destined to die, and are unable to see the circularity of their argument. More recent findings about the psychosomatic causes of illness are calling the European idea of the non-existence of harmful magic into question. If sorcery and witchcraft are efficacious, due to a shared belief system of perpetrators and victims, it would be difficult to call them 'crimes without criminals'.[183]

The South African Witchcraft Suppression Act of 1895, amended in 1957 and again in 1970,[184] seemed completely off the point from an African perspective. Instead of persecuting the evildoers, it stopped the chiefs from handling cases of witchcraft properly, thus damaging their authority. Traditional healers, diviners or witch-doctors who could detect the witches were outlawed, and the witches protected instead. As a consequence, people took the law into their own hands, and started to kill, either secretly or in mob lynchings, those whom they suspected of having harmed their children or livestock. Numerous reports of such murders were published Zimbabwean newspapers. The alternative to handling cases of suspected witchcraft was to refer to a spirit-medium, who would try to negotiate between ancestral spirits and witch-spirits in order to restore the moral order, a solution ridiculed by European observers. But the opposition between witch and ancestor spirits stands at the heart of moral order, because the latter are benign, protect the lineage and promote health, fertility and continuity, whereas the witches are malevolent and create sickness, death and cessation.[185] Ralushai characterizes witchcraft as a marker of African identity: 'Belief in witchcraft and related practices form part of a basic cultural, traditional and customary principle of Africans in South Africa, and Africa as a whole. Belief in witchcraft itself is as old as mankind itself.' Rooted in counter-colonial discourse, the Ralushai Commission claims that 'no one can argue now that witchcraft is a myth which can only exist in the minds of the ignorant'. It comes to the conclusion that European law should be replaced by traditional 'African' methods of proving the guilt of suspected individuals, by admitting witch-doctors and spirit-mediums at court. In an attempt to curb extra-legal pogroms, the proposed Witchcraft Control Act of 1996, based upon the assumption that witchcraft exists, aims at its legal prosecution.[186]

Contrary to Evans-Pritchard's functionalist interpretation that witchcraft could be seen as a neutral means of keeping up moral and social balance within a given society, the majority of recent studies come to the conclusion that witchcraft is usually conceived as the epitome of anti-social behaviour. Ralushai provides the following definition:

> The word 'moloi' comes from the verb 'loya' which means to bewitch, and is attributed to those people who through sheer malignancy, either consciously or subconsciously, employ magical means to inflict all manner of evil on their fellow human beings. They destroy property, bring disease or misfortune, and cause death, often entirely without provocation, to satisfy their inherent craving for evil-doing.[187]

However appealing the Durkheimian approach may have been, witchcraft is an inappropriate subject, since it is by definition an inversion of positive values. It has often been argued that in Europe this is the result of a dualistic world view, imposed by Christian missionaries from late Antiquity. But similar examples stretch far beyond the Christian civilizations, reaching from the Arctic Inuit,[188] to peoples of the rainforest in Papua New Guinea, whatever their cultural background. Any symbolic system contains value judgements, and this is not in the first place a matter of language,[189] but of needs and everyday practice. Supernatural powers can be good, evil or ambivalent, not due to an arbitrary system of classification, but as a result of negative experience. Witchcraft symbolizes the negative pole, as far as human agency is concerned, and witches embody *negative charisma*.[190] Within traditional societies with personalized concepts of evil, suspected individuals are usually treated with caution, as a result of their supposed special abilities. However, as Gluckman put it, 'in a society which believes in witchcraft every misfortune potentially founds a case against another for harming you'.[191]

The variety of possible reactions comprises the option of bringing the suspected witches to account for their deeds. The *witchcraft paradigm*, a theory of causation attributing misfortune to human agency, enables action. The sanctions for witchcraft usually range from coerced withdrawal of the spell, intimidation or ostracizing, to more formal penalties, like coerced confession, pillory, fines or corporal punishment, to severe penalties, like enslavement, banishment or the death penalty, and this, across the cultures, through physical extinction. Fire is a widespread option, since it links in 'with crisis or great change, ritualises its value, und uses it to extinguish evil or to purify a state of defilement'.[192] This reminds us of the fact that the question of evil was above all actual hardship a classificatory problem: the good is always in danger of getting contaminated by evil, in dreams, thought and action, and burning some scapegoats could be taken as an expression of the everlasting problem of pollution, of purity and danger.[193] 'The problem with witches, like all forms of radical evil, is that you are either for or against them.' In a society where people believe in witches 'it's no use pretending they don't exist or seeking some ground of neutrality'.[194]

3

The Persecution of Witches

Thou shalt not suffer a witch to live.
God, Exodus 22:18

The persecution of witches is a consequence of witchcraft beliefs. However, beliefs as a necessary pre-condition do not automatically generate persecutions. As a consequence we must look at particular events and periods in order to find out which factors open the gates to prosecution, or persecution. This kind of research requires source material, and the sources in non-European civilizations are either shaky, or as yet unexplored. We can see from literate societies with codified law that certain forms of sorcery or witchcraft were severely punished, from the earliest law code of King Hammurapi (1792–1750 BC) in Ancient Mesopotamia. The Code of Hammurapi (§2) imposes a river ordeal (swimming test), if the charge could not be proved by means of witnesses. This offered an effective remedy against too frequent accusations: according to the principle of talion the accuser had to face the accused's punishment if the ordeal failed to prove the suspect's guilt. In cases of witchcraft this was the death penalty. We know similar laws from the Middle Assyrian Empire, and it is generally assumed that the death penalty was imposed on witches, male and female, throughout the Ancient Middle East.[1] The most comprehensive set of texts dealing with the struggle against witchcraft, about 100 incantations and prayers compiled during the rule of King Esarhaddon (680–669 BC), bears a title significant for the treatment of witches: *Maqlu*, which literally means 'burning'.[2]

The *divine law* of the Ancient Jews, possibly collected by Moses around 1250 BC, contains the rules that witches must be killed (Exodus

22:18), that equally those employing a spirit should be stoned to death (Leviticus 20:27), and that generally diviners and prophets were to be killed (Deuteronomy 13:5). However, we do not know whether or how these laws were enacted.[3] Our knowledge of non-literate societies depends on travellers' or ethnographers' reports. Herodotus (*c*.490–*c*.425 BC), for instance, reports the killing of sorcerers from the Scythians, a nomadic people from Central Asia, whose capital was then located north of the Black Sea, within the boundaries of present-day Ukraine. As in other societies, diviners or shamans were particularly suspect, and the penalty, if they turned evil, was burning. The procedure of proving guilt involved other diviners, who had to agree, and an accuser potentially faced prosecution himself in case of disagreement among these religious specialists.[4] The execution of witches was not unknown in the Ancient Greek city states, including Athens, as the prominence of witches in Greek literature may indicate, and surviving sources of some legal trials demonstrate.[5]

How decisively a change in the definition of witchcraft can alter the interpretation of witchcraft is shown by the case of Ancient Rome. Harmful magic was a punishable crime in Ancient Rome, and a case exemplifying the statute against magical theft of crops in the earliest Roman law code, the XII tables (*c*.450 BC), proves that the notion of 'limited good' was prevalent among the Italian peasantry.[6] The persecution of sorcerers assumed unprecedented dimensions in the late Roman Republic. In the context of an epidemic illness with high mortality, 170 women were executed as witches in 331 BC. It seems to have been an exceptional case though, since Livy (*c*.59 BC–AD 17) emphasizes that there had been no similar persecution in Rome before.[7] In the second century BC we hear of no less than three mass persecutions, in the years 184 BC, 180–179 BC and 153 BC, 'made possible by the effectively unlimited power of Roman magistrates', allowing for 'the fatal conjuncture [. . .] between popular "pollution" anxieties and state power'.[8] In the first case about 2,000 persons were executed for witchcraft, thanks to denunciation and routine employment of torture.[9] There is no way to prove or disprove these figures, but what is important here is the link between popular anxieties, torture and massive persecutions of magicians, which was to generate similar panics in the future. In correlation to an epidemic disease in the years 182–180 BC, another 3,000 persons were executed in Rome and further afield in Italy. Livy does not indicate how their crime was exactly defined. *Veneficium* usually referred to secret murder by means of magic, not just poison, but the sheer size of this persecution implies the notion of a threatening conspiracy. In a moral panic authorities and the population wanted to purge society of the evildoers, but even the Consul in charge eventually became worried that his 'investigation was assuming ever larger proportions by reason of the evidence received'.[10]

Due to the observation that different types of persecution affected local societies in different ways, and were conducted for different reasons, historians have distinguished between different *patterns of witch-hunting*, or types of trials, traditionally in vague terms like 'small' or 'big'. Midelfort was the first to suggest more clear-cut definitions, for analytical purposes focusing on 'large-scale witch-hunts' with 'more than 20 executions in one year'.[11] Soon after, Bill Monter (b. 1936) chose 'small panics' as a research category, with 'groups of four, five, six, perhaps ten people arrested, tortured, and often killed for witchcraft in one tiny jurisdiction over a span of eight to fourteen months'.[12] Larner introduced as a further category the 'national witch-hunt', based on the number of trials, not executions.[13] However, even during Larner's 'national hunts' the trials remained confined to certain regions (East Lothian, Fife, Aberdeenshire), whereas larger parts of Scotland (West and North Highlands, Hebrides and Orkneys) remained unaffected.[14] Based upon these definitions I suggested a more comprehensive classification, distinguishing between *witch trials* with up to three executions (Monter's), *panic trials* with 4–19 victims (Midelfort's), *large-scale witch-hunts* with 20–99 executions, *major persecutions* with 100–249 executions (as an equivalent to Larner's 'national hunts', which were never national) and, as a last category, *massive witch-hunts* with more than 250 victims within less than five years in one territory, or a cluster of neighbouring small counties or territories, as a marker of absolutely extraordinary events.[15] To be sure, this classification is anything but perfect, and misses some patterns of persecution altogether, as for instance outbreaks of *witch panics* with many suspects, but few executions (like in Salem); or major persecutions distributed over more than one territory; or chains of panic trials, or *permanent persecutions* adding up to large numbers of victims over a longer period (like in Lorraine). However, an imperfect classification seems to be more useful than terminological confusion.

By changing the scope we can see that the panics in Ancient Rome exceed by far any classification developed for the analysis of early modern witch-hunts. And it seems to make sense that Europe always perceived itself as the heir of the Roman civilization, particularly if we take into account that the persecutions in Republican Rome refer not to a vast empire, but exclusively to Italy. Since Livy's *History* is lost from 166 BC, we know of no details of the persecution of 153 BC, merely that it took place. Numerous incidents, like the sudden death of Germanicus (15 BC–AD 19), the governor of Syria and future emperor, show that the attribution of sorcery in the Roman Empire was similar to those in more recent cultures.[16] The known events explain the rising awareness of sorcery in Roman literature and law, starting with the *Lex Cornelia de sicariis et veneficiis*, promulgated by Lucius Cornelius Sulla (138–78 BC), one of the most important sources of European law on witchcraft in the late medieval and early modern period.[17] The equating of *veneficium, maleficium* and divination, mentioned above, paved the way to pogroms against these evildoers in the Roman Empire in the later fourth century.[18] Ammanius Marcellinus (330–c.95) reports of the sorcery scare during the reign of Emperor Constantius II, a period of famines and diseases: 'If anyone consulted a soothsayer [. . .], or if he used an old wives' charm to relieve pain [. . .], he was denounced through some agency which he could not guess, brought to trial, and punished with death.'[19] Extensive treason trials started in 359, conducted centrally in Scythopolis in Palestine against citizens of Alexandria (Egypt) and Antioch (Syria, today in Turkey) by 'an expert in the art of bloodshed'.[20] Apronian, a prefect of Rome who considered himself to be a victim of the black arts, 'made it his prime concern to arrest sorcerers' at the beginning of the 360s.[21] Around 370 persecutions resumed under Valentinian I (321–75, r. 364–75), who was driven by all kinds of anxieties, with scores of soothsayers, necromancers and magicians being condemned to death in the Roman Empire.[22] Valens (328–78, r. 364–78) conducted treason trials in the same years against diviners, sorcerers and magicians at Antioch, Ephesus and Constantinople, then capital of the Eastern Empire. Scores of men of all ranks, even a former ex-governor of a province, were tortured, decapitated or burned alive. As Marcellinus, a contemporary, recorded, the mass persecutions caused 'universal horror' in his home town.[23]

Some early modern examples from America, Asia and Africa may support the idea that not only the belief in witchcraft, but also the practice of witch-hunting was a universal phenomenon. We can only guess about the punishment of witches in the Ancient American civilizations, but can presumably draw conclusions from our earliest reports. With the crisis of his empire imminent, the Aztec emperor Motecuhzoma II (1466–1520, r. 1502–20) gave orders in 1519 to the governors of the provinces to summon all village magicians of Mexico to the capital Tenochtitlan. When they failed to read the signs, the ruler became dissatisfied and threatened them with torture. When the shamans managed to escape from prison – according to the chronicler they made themselves invisible, and flew away through the air to the boundaries of the world, as they used to do every night – Motecuhzoma gave order to the *cazikes* (chiefs) to kill the sorcerers' families. In this pogrom the women were hung, the children slain, and even the foundations of their houses were dug out. According to Bernardino de Sahagun (1499–1590), the ethnographer of the Aztec civilization, the purpose was to eradicate the witches.[24] In Peru large-scale persecutions were conducted in the sixteenth century by Inca officials, when the Inca rule in their remaining upland territories was challenged by local prophets.[25] Our knowledge of Ancient Asian civilizations is still shaky. But it seems to fit into a well-known pattern that the peasant rebellions in China in the 1640s, a period of famine and diseases similar to that of Europe, were linked to witchcraft eradication movements.[26]

African witch killings have been linked to the impact of colonialism, a view which is hardly sustainable since myths as well as early reports show that the killing of witches was common. The king of Ndongo, in present-day Angola, ordered the execution of eleven rainmakers who were held responsible for drought in 1563.[27] In Sierra Leone, witches were either killed or sold as slaves, a profitable form of 'social death'. Certainly there was slavery within Africa prior to the advent of Arabian or European traders, and enslavement was presumably a long-established custom. But as the demand for slaves increased, so too did the 'production' of witches within the Temne society.[28] Among the Kerebe in East Africa, a witch panic started at the end of King Mihigo II's reign (r. c.1780–1820). For about fifteen years the realm was ravaged by flooding, drought, unknown diseases, depopulation, rebellion and political instability. Two subsequent rulers died shortly afterwards, and two others were deposed because their attempt to restore control over the physical environment failed. Decades before cultural contact with Europeans, this society was in turmoil because its innovative ruler had introduced long-distance trade with Arabs from Zanzibar. Ivory trade had led to the introduction of new goods and crops, social inequality and new diseases.[29] It may well be that the crop failures and epidemics were due to climatic deterioration in the aftermath of the Tambora Freeze, which caused famine and disruption in agricultural societies from Europe to Japan.[30] Other African societies were also affected, for instance the Zulu empire under King Shaka (1789–1828, r. 1816–28), who summoned 'three or four hundred' witch suspects to his capital, and had them killed.[31] It is difficult to evaluate the contributory factors, such as state-formation, culture change or ecological disaster, but we know of severe droughts in 1800–3, 1812, and of course 1816–18. In these years, conflicts over land claims escalated, and Shaka's military revolution and warfare exacerbated the economic situation.[32] These massive witch-hunts gained their place in the collective memory and are still referred to in present-day South Africa.[33]

In the following pages of this and the next chapter we shall focus on persecutions in Europe and its colonies, and in chapter 6 on more recent persecutions in non-European societies. Hansen introduced the argument that in Europe witchcraft persecution, unlike trials for sorcery, has been *illegal* for most of its history, basically from the fall of the Roman Empire, when harsh imperial laws were replaced by the laws of the Germanic peoples, moulded by the Christian optimism of the first millennium.[34] However, it may well be necessary to review such ideas. Even if some laws, as indicated above, appear to be lenient, witchcraft was still liable to the death penalty according to biblical law. Harmful magic was considered to be devilish, and implied a demonic pact according to Augustine, and deserved the death penalty according to Roman law. Both legislations, divine and imperial, determined the development of European law to the end of the early modern period. And quite obviously the killing of witches was practised among the Germanic peoples. The laws of the Franks, the Ostrogoths, the Visigoths and so on rejected only the belief in *strigae*, but rarely questioned the danger of harmful magic. 'Carolingian scepticism' set aside, Charlemagne was quite clear about the treatment of harmful magic (*maleficium*): In his *Admonitio Generalis* the future emperor commented on a number of papal decrees, submitted by Pope Hadrian I (r. 772–95), and decreed in 789 that sorcerers and witches (*malefici, incantatores et incantatrices*) were not to be tolerated, explicitly referring to Mosaic law, and in later versions of this list weather-makers (*tempestarii*) were added.[35]

Witchcraft and sorcery were frequently placed together with murder, as for instance in Frankish and Anglo-Saxon law, which makes perfect sense if we consider present-day African ideas about witchcraft. According to the *Lex Salica*, those who could not pay for their magical crimes should be burned (*certe ignem tradatur*).[36] Numerous decrees of the later Carolingian period imply the death penalty for witchcraft. Such sorcerers were liable to suffer the extreme penalty under the rule of the Normans in England,[37] as well as in Sicily. The Venetian Republic issued draconian laws against *maleficium* in 1181, and many Italian towns did so in the thirteenth century. German law codes impose burning at the stake as the customary penalty for harmful magic. The *Schwabenspiegel* of around 1240, one of the most influential medieval compilations of imperial law, suggests that sorcery implies a pact with the devil, and apostasy.[38] This is only surprising at first glance, since the author, presumably a jurist close to the Franciscans at Augsburg, merely combined secular law with Christian theology. Demonic witchcraft was not a new invention, but required only basic knowledge of theology. Jean de Gerson (1363–1429) and the University of Paris came to exactly the same conclusion in their famous legal opinion of 1398.[39]

Since harmful magic remained punishable, why should we expect it not to be punished? We should rather assume that wherever certain forms of witch-beliefs were outlawed, witches were accused of *maleficium* instead, or, if this was impossible, of *veneficium* (poisoning). Trials were conducted orally in the Middle Ages, mostly without any written records, as in many non-European premodern societies. But if we collect events recorded in chronicles across Europe we can see that execution of witches was not unusual. We hear about death penalties against witches, diviners, sorcerers and weather magicians, imposed by secular or ecclesiastical institutions, based upon confessions, obtained by torture, or based upon ordeal, or mere assumption of guilt. Witches were executed after formal trials, or – in archaic northern societies – as private revenge. The sudden death of a king, as in Herodotus' case, was considered to be relevant to chroniclers, and here we learn about the treatment of witches. After the sickness of the Frankish King Louis (778–840, r. 814–40), his son Lothair I (795–855, r. 843–55) captured a nun called Gerberga at Chalon-sur-Saône. She was drowned as a witch (*malefica et venefica*).[40] After the sudden death of the Eastern Frankish Emperor Arnulf (*c.*850–99), a male sorcerer and a witch called Rudpurg were tortured and executed.[41] The sickness of Count William of Angoulême triggered suspicion against a woman in Aquitaine (France), who was subjected to an ordeal and, since this failed to prove her guilt, to torture. She and some accomplices were burned alive in 1028 – a panic trial. In Spain it was King Ramiro I of Aragon (r. 1035–67) who commissioned the burning of a number of sorcerers. When Count Dietrich of Flanders (Netherlands) fell ill, his supporters seized a woman (*quaedam incantatrix*) held responsible for the disease, and burned her alive at the stake in 1128.[42]

Further to such political trials, some traces of the persecution of ordinary sorcerers and/or witches have survived. In Anglo-Saxon England a widow was accused by a man called Aelsie of trying to murder him by driving nails into a puppet. The doll was indeed found in a house search. After the trial the woman was drowned at London Bridge around 970. Her son fled and was outlawed. Their property was confiscated by King Edgar (943–75, r. 959–75), and passed to the supposed victim.[43] The *Eyrbyggia Saga* describes how witches were stoned to death by Norwegian settlers in Iceland around 980.[44] The 'sorcerer' Kotkel from the Hebrides became suspect because of his effective incantations, and the damage caused by magical theft. After raising storms, and eventually resorting to murder by witchcraft, he was caught by chieftain Olaf Hoskuldsson (Olaf the Peacock, *c.*938–1006), and stoned to death, together with his wife Grima. The whole family was wiped out: Hallbjorn Kotkelsson was put to death by drowning, and was killed a second time after having reappeared as a revenant. Stigandi Kotkelsson, feared because of his evil eye, was soon after stoned to death by Olaf and his men.[45] In the Viking earldoms of the Orkneys, witches were killed on the basis of private revenge. Svein Asleifarson of Gairsey killed the pagan sorcerer Svein Breast-Rope, and around 1140 he locked up the sorceress Frakokk in her house, and burned her with her family.[46]

Witches were not only killed at the pagan peripheries, but also at the urbanized centres of Christian Europe. At Cologne a woman was killed for supposed love magic in 1075. In 1128 the citizens of Ghent (Netherlands) killed a witch (*incantatrix*). At Beauvais (France) a witch (*phitonissa*) was captured, tried by bishop and citizenry, and condemned to be burned at the stake in 1190. At Soest (Westphalia) a priest was burned alive as *maleficus et magus* around 1200 after a trial before the town court.[47] In England an alleged witch managed to survive the ordeal of hot iron in 1198.[48] One John of Kerneslaw in Northumberland slew a witch in 1279. The lynching was punished by confiscation of the murderer's chattels. That the woman's body was burned indicates that the assize court shared the assumption of her guilt.[49] In the same year peasants near Rufach (Alsace) tried to burn a suspected witch in a lynching, but the Dominican friars of Colmar interfered and saved the woman's life.[50] The outcome of serious trials against three women at Senlis in 1282 is unknown. Two witches (*strigae*) were burned after a secular trial in southern Tyrol in 1296. At Brussels a male sorcerer was tried and killed in 1304. At Paris several women were condemned to death by the Parlement in 1308, and another woman was executed in 1314. At Toulouse a male sorcerer was 'slowly roasted' to death in 1320. Lorraine saw legal burnings in 1327, 1358 and 1372, when three women and a man were sentenced in Metz. At Milan two female diviners and healers – Pierina de Bripio and Sibilla Fraguliati – were sentenced to death as relapsed heretics by an Inquisition court in 1390, because they persistently claimed to attend the meetings of the fairies. At Paris two 'sorceresses' (*quae cum invocatione diabolorum comiserant sortilegium*) were burned to death in 1390 and 1391, and a male sorcerer in 1399. Brandenburg saw burnings of women in 1400 and 1423, and a man was burned at Berlin in 1406. Many of these cases originated from the lower social groups, but there are also instances among the educated.[51]

Witchcraft, we can conclude from this random sample, was punished severely throughout the Middle Ages, presumably all over Europe, and in some towns or regions even more frequently than during the early modern period. The terminology (*striga, incantatrix, sortilega*) indicates clearly that these cases dealt with more than just harmful magic (*maleficium*). And there were more serious incidents: witch panics. These were treated at length by the chroniclers, like for instance the scandalous politically inspired persecution of witches (*maleficae et incantatrices*) commissioned by the queen Fredegunde (?–597) at Paris in 580, as reported by Gregory of Tours (538–94).[52] A Crown witness of 'Carolingian scepticism', Archbishop Agobard of Lyon (769–840), reports witch panics during the reign of Charlemagne. In his sermon on hailstorms he reports frequent lynchings of supposed weather magicians (*tempestarii*), as well as of sorcerers, who were made responsible for a terrible livestock mortality in 810. According to Agobard, the common people in their fury over crop failure had developed the extravagant idea that foreigners were secretly coming with airships to strip their fields of crops, and transmit it to *Magonia*. These anxieties resulted in severe aggression, and on one occasion around 816, Agobard could hardly prevent a crowd from killing three foreign men and a woman, perceived as Magonian people. As their supposed homeland's name suggests, the crop failure was associated with magic. The bishop emphasized that thunderstorms were caused exclusively by natural or divine agencies.[53] Although some details of these stories appear highly unusual, and may have been invented by Agobard, Carolingian laws render it highly likely that witch-hunts were not just a vulgar error, but were occasionally supported, or even launched by the authorities. In 1080 Harald of Denmark (r. 1076–80) was admonished not to hold old women and Christian priests responsible for storms and diseases, or to slaughter them in the cruellest manner. Like Agobard before him, Pope Gregory VII (r. 1073–85) declared in his letter to the Danish king that these catastrophes were caused by God alone, that they were God's punishment for human sins, and that the killing of the innocent would only increase His fury. No other source reports these witch-hunts, but there is no reason to cast doubts on this source, which implies frequent and severe witch-hunting.[54]

A complex situation can be observed on the occasion of the burning of three women near Freising, who were convicted of having harmed or poisoned the people (*veneficae*), and having spoiled or destroyed the crops (*perditrices frugum*), presumably by causing hailstorms. According to the chronicler, a Benedictine monk, it was only the fact that the nearby bishop's see was vacant in 1090 that enabled the rural rabble to carry out a persecution. The monk considered the whole procedure to be essentially illegal, and called the victimized women 'martyrs'. Their bodies were posthumously saved, and buried in sacred ground by the monks, within the walls of the monastery of Weihenstephan. The chronicler's report is detailed enough to reveal that the supposed act of lynching was a rather complicated procedure. After having been captured, the suspected witches first had to undergo an ordeal by water. Against the expectations of their persecutors, they passed and could therefore not be executed. Afterwards they were publicly tortured, in order to force them into confessions, again without success. Only then did the villagers turn to the nearby city of Freising, where two persons of high rank, presumably noblemen, summoned a public meeting. The women were transferred to the town, and tortured again. Although the suspects again refused to confess, they were carried to the banks of the river, and burned to death. However illegal the procedure may appear, the people did not simply kill the women straight away, but respected a set of procedural rules. And, even more importantly, a grassroots movement becomes visible, aiming at the eradication of a conspiracy of evil.[55] In 1115 a chronicle from Styria reports laconically that thirty women were burned in one day in the city of Graz (*concrematae sunt triginta mulieres in Greez una die*). Capital punishment for females was highly unusual throughout European history, and burning was restricted to a few secular crimes like arson, sodomy or counterfeiting. None of these were women's crimes, or likely to trigger a mass persecution. In heresy trials a more even gender distribution could be expected.[56]

In medieval Russia witch panics were related to weather-making and crop failure, very much like in the early modern period, when collective disaster was linked to fears of conspiracy. The *Primary Chronicle* reports the killing of a number of old people in Suzdal (north-east of Moscow) after a severe famine caused by drought in 1024. For the famine of 1070–1, a number of women were executed in Novgorod because they were held to be responsible for famine.[57] In 1153 the Arabic traveller Abu Hamid al-Gharnati (*c*.1080–*c*.1169) reported periodic witch-hunts from the Rus' capital Kiev (today Ukraine), suggesting that:

> every twenty years the old women of this country become guilty of witchcraft, which causes great concern among the people. Then they seize all those they find in this area and throw them, feet and fists tied, into a big river that passes through . . . Those who stay afloat are considered to be witches and are burned; those who, on the contrary, go under are declared innocent of all witchcraft and are set free again.[58]

Witches were executed at Novgorod in 1227, and after a severe famine in the years 1271–4 Bishop Serapion of Vladimir asked in a sermon: 'you believe in witchcraft and burn innocent people and bring down murder upon earth and the city . . . Out of what books or writings do you learn that famine on earth is brought about by witchcraft?' These people resorted customarily to the swimming test and burned those who did not pass the ordeal.[59]

Cohn suggests that 'the silence of the chronicles' of Western Europe implies for 'certain that there were very few trials for *maleficium*, whether as a secular or as a religious offence, between 1100 and 1300. It remains to find out why'.[60] It seems that recent research has found an answer. These centuries were generally benefiting from a favourable climate and abundant harvests. During the 'Medieval Warm Period' grapes were grown in England, northern Germany and southern Norway, and the Vikings settled in Iceland and 'Greenland'. Europe as a whole experienced an era of optimism, population growth, urbanization and expansion.[61] It seems that there was less misfortune in this period compared with the catastrophes of the fourteenth century, starting with the 'great famine' of 1315–22, and subsequent epidemics and mortality crises, as well as the related new anxieties.[62] The high medieval expansion came to its limits, and man-made factors (demographic growth, political and social organization, mode of agrarian production, storage facilities and infrastructure) coincided unfavourably with a climatic deterioration, which began to worsen the living conditions. Viticulture in the north came to an end, upland farming had to be abandoned, villages were deserted and the economy as well as the population numbers shrank, even before Europe plunged into the catastrophe of the Black Death.[63]

During the late Middle Ages, when papal inquisitors were persecuting heretics, Cathars, Waldensians or other religious minorities, magical crimes were repeatedly part of the accusations. As in the previous period, these accusations were usually made in political trials, for instance that of King Philip IV of France (1268–1314, r. 1285–1314) against the Order of the Knights Templar in 1307, which led to the burning of dozens of Templars for blasphemy, sorcery, homosexuality, heresy, apostasy and devil-worship. Similarly, Pope John XXII (Jacques Duèze, 1244–1324, r. 1316–24) was obsessed with fears of sorcery, and imagined himself to be the victim of a number of magical plots. One year after John's election, the bishop of Cahors, Hugues Géraud, confessed and was burned. Unsurprisingly, magical crimes figured highly in this Pope's decrees, for instance the famous bull *Super illius specula*.[64] Umberto Eco has convincingly contrasted his fearful credulity, and the authoritarian attitude of his inquisitor Bernard Gui (1261–1331), with the nominalist scepticism of the Franciscan philosopher William of Ockham, who had sought refuge at the court of Louis of Bavaria (1283–1347, r. 1314–47).[65] The accused in these trials for heretical sorcery were often clerics, who had access to books, and therefore to learned magic. However, there are other examples, like the famous case of Alice Kyteler (?–1324) of Kilkenny, who was accused of heresy, but also of *maleficium*, attending nocturnal gatherings of witches, sexual intercourse with the devil and devil-worship. Richard Ledrede, the bishop of Ossory, certainly knew how to conduct the trial, since he had learned his craft at the papal court of John XXII in Avignon. The accusations were launched by neighbours and her stepchildren, whose suspicions had been aroused by the deaths of three husbands, and her wealth acquired through these marriages. The burnings of Lady Kyteler and her servant Petronilla of Meath were the first executions of witches reported in Ireland.[66] Political trials lingered on throughout the late Middle Ages, in France as well as in Italy and in Russia. In England, kings such as Edward III (1312–77, r. 1327–77), Henry IV (1366–1413, r. 1399–1413), or Edward IV (1441–83, r. 1461–83) feared bewitchment and launched trials against wives, mistresses and clerics.[67] Most of these were trials for treason and sorcery. However, there are also more explicit cases of witchcraft, like that of Margery Gurdman (Jourdemain), the 'Witch of Eye', who was burned at Smithfield in 1440.[68]

The decisive step towards mass persecutions of witches was the construction of a *cumulative concept of witchcraft* during the late fourteenth and early fifteenth centuries, when the first large-scale witch-hunts and major persecutions were launched in some Alpine valleys. Alleged earlier mass persecutions in southern France, as well

Plate 3   *The Burning of Witches*. Drawing from the collection of
Johann Jacob Wick

as an early legal opinion by Bartolo de Sassoferrato, were spotted
as frauds in the 1970s by Cohn,[69] and independently by Richard
Kieckhefer (b. 1946).[70] These sources were forged by Étienne-Léon
Lamothe-Langon (1786–1852), an impoverished nobleman, who
made a living with spectacular publications on the Inquisition in
France. Since Hansen had accepted these sources and approved them

in his source edition,[71] scholars all over the world took their validity for granted. After eliminating the forgeries, it became clear that it was only around 1400 that different aspects of witchcraft and heresy were assembled to the specific European concept of witchcraft, which allowed witch-hunts of unprecedented severity. Harmful magic and the pact with the devil formed the core of the new cumulative crime, the first crime crucial for secular law, the latter for its qualification as a heresy. Around these crystallized a group of – even according to medieval perceptions – exotic accusations: apostasy, flying through the air, nocturnal gatherings at remote places, the witches' dance, sexual intercourse with demons and the adoration of the devil. In legal practice the idea of the nocturnal flights turned out to be the most dangerous part, since the suspects were asked to name their accomplices, whom they were expected to have met at the gatherings. If so, the use of torture could lead to chain-reactions, resulting in massive witch-hunts, reminiscent of similar events in the Roman Antiquity.

The structures and procedures that enabled, and maybe inspired, the European authorities to hunt witches in an organized manner had been developed during the persecution of heresy. This strain of our story begins with the emergence of the dualistic movement of the Cathars in the early twelfth century, and the movement of the Waldensians, spreading rapidly from about 1175. Inquisitors were appointed centrally by the Pope, and theologians of the newly founded mendicant Orders investigated the heretics officially (*ex officio*), that is, without necessarily having received previously specific accusations or complaints. During the Middle Ages this was quite an unusual procedure, since secular courts acted only if an accuser launched a specific accusation – at least in theory, because in cases of treason they always inquired actively, and this may be one of the reasons why many medieval witch trials from Russia to England were treason trials. The inquisitorial procedure was a legacy of Roman law, which had survived within the Roman Church, and was revived first for disciplinary measures within the higher clergy, and then applied in heresy trials.[72] At the 4th Lateran Council in 1215 the Roman Church accepted torture in trials run by the Inquisition, in order to obtain confessions from the suspects, and forbade archaic rituals like the ordeals of hot iron or cold water, the 'swimming test'. Ordeals became illegal subsequently, although we shall see that they were practised in lynchings throughout Northern and Eastern Europe, and were sometimes even commissioned by the lower courts.

Legal torture was initially conceived as an improvement to the legal procedure, because it aimed to achieve the material truth rationally, rather than by means of mystical intervention, as in ordeals. We have to keep in mind that the meaning of legal torture differed decisively from modern perceptions.[73] Although torture had been meant to replace ordeals, in practice judges sometimes used unlimited torture as if it were an ordeal, particularly in heresy trials. The interplay of physical coercion, systematizing all kinds of real or faked information, and mere fantasy or projection, led to the idea that the dissidents were members of a devilish sect, and worshippers of the devil. Such reproaches were not only made against heretics, but also against the Jews. Recent research has emphasized that anti-Semitic stereotypes influenced the emerging witch stereotype. Heretics were primarily conceived as enemies of the Christian Church, or of Christian society. Apostasy and magic were not yet thought of as joined together, and for the terrifying epidemics of the thirteenth century, and later on the Black Death, lepers were blamed. The idea that these outcasts might have poisoned the wells, however, was transferred to the Jews in fourteenth-century Savoy. The obscure powder that the Jews were said to have used for their harmful magic plays a central role in later witch trials, as well as the magic of the blood, ritual murder in order to prepare means of sorcery, the enmity against mother Mary, or secret nocturnal gatherings. Hebrew terms were used for the witches' dance, first by the persecuting authorities, who labelled it as *Synagoga Satanae*, alluding to the Apocalypse (Revelation 2:9). However, the term was soon popularized and widely used by common people in the western Alps, who called the witches' meetings 'synagogues', most likely with anti-Semitic connotations. Later another Jewish term, supposedly introduced by learned theologians, replaced the 'synagogues', and up to the present day we still talk about the *witches' sabbat*.[74]

The reasons why the earlier conspiracy theories of devil-worshipping heretics, or well-poisoning Jews, were transformed into the stereotype of a sect of witches in the decades around 1400 are still to be debated. Jean Delumeau has argued that European civilization was overwhelmed by collective fear during the fourteenth century. *La Peur en occident* was initiated by a number of terrifying changes, in particular the external threat posed by Islam, the increasing frequency of hunger crises, the return of the Black Death, and the split of the Roman Church in the Great Schism of 1378, which – at least in the eyes of some scholars – endangered the mental balance of Christian believers. The counter-popes condemned each other and their corresponding Church hierarchies, but still it seems doubtful that villagers were much concerned about the sacramental powers of their parish priest, which would have been theologically incorrect anyway. Frantisek Graus questioned whether the Black Death was the kind of *caesura* that other historians have claimed.[75] It will be difficult to prove that peasants in the high valleys of Savoy were concerned about the Mongolian conquest of Moscow, the fall of Constantinople and the rise of the Ottoman Empire. It seems much more likely that these peasants feared *streghe*, as the night-flying witches were called here since the Roman times, much more than anything else. In the Savoyan Alps the anxieties of the rural population began to infect the fantasies of their inquisitors, and it seems quite likely that social crises in the Alpine and Northern economies contributed to that change. The climatic deterioration, with some extremely unfavourable decades, left European society 'on the brink of the apocalypse'.[76] Climatic deterioration was first felt at the fringes of Europe, the far North. And it seems striking that the last news about the Greenland Vikings concerned a witch trial, resulting in the burning of a Greenlander named Kollgrim (?–1407), who had seduced a married woman from Iceland, Steinunn Hafransdotter, whose relatives claimed that her love had been caused by black arts. Kollgrim's trial was reported by Icelandic seafarers, who reached Bergen in 1410 – the last Greenland voyage recorded in Norwegian sources, and the last Norse record of the Viking settlements in Greenland altogether. The Black Death, famines and smallpox epidemics devastated the kingdoms of Norway, Denmark and Sweden, which had been forged into the Union of Kalmar during the reign of Queen Margarethe (?–1412). Greenland vanished behind walls of pack ice.[77] From Russia, the burning of twelve women is reported in the city of Pskov in 1411, but it is as yet unknown whether this was just a local event.[78]

Not only the far North was affected by climatic deterioration, but also a large region at the heart of Europe: the Alps. It seems that trials for sorcery became more frequent around 1400, particularly in Italy, France and Switzerland.[79] The very region where harmful magic and heresy were fused into a new cumulative crime of witchcraft was Savoy, under Amadeus VIII (1383–1451, r. 1391/1416–34). This duchy was an agglomeration of territories, stretching from the shores of the Mediterranean Sea around Nice well into present-day Switzerland, including the surroundings of Lake Geneva, and parts of the upper Rhone Valley, the Valais (Wallis) and the Pays de Vaud (Waadtland).[80] From his residence at Chambéry, the duke tried to build a 'modern' state, in order to integrate recent acquisitions like the Vaud (in 1359), the county of Nice (in 1388), the county of Geneva (in 1401), and the Piedmont (in 1418) by means of administrative and legal reforms, as well as Church reforms. This new state dominated the eastern Alps.[81] But state-formation had its costs: in 1417 the Savoyan chancellor Dr Jean Lageret received the death penalty, because Duke Amadeus felt bewitched. The persecution of Jews, Waldensians and witches gained momentum.[82] His ambitious law code of 1430, the *Statuta Sabaudiae*, emphasized the crime of sorcery, although still in a traditional language. Ten years later witchcraft surfaced in a much more prominent form. Pope Eugenius IV (c.1383–1447, r. 1431–47) mentions in a decree that Savoy bristles with '*stregule vel stregones seu Waudenses*' – female and male witches, or Waldensians.[83] It was in Savoy that the fusion of heresy, anti-Judaism and sorcery took place, and the new cumulative crime of witchcraft was born: European witchcraft.[84]

Duke Amadeus' further ambitions supported the spreading of the new crime. He became entangled more generally in the business of religious reform, and was elected Pope Felix V (r. 1439–49) by the conciliarist party at the Council of Basel. By the curial party he was considered to be illegitimate, a 'counter-pope', but during the schism it was uncertain who would win the power struggle. Pope Eugenius IV had good reasons for damaging his competitor Felix V's reputation by labelling his territorial power-base a hothouse of witchcraft. However, it was not an invention that Savoy had a particular problem, rather the curia Romana took advantage of a burning regional crisis. It was neither in Rome, nor Avignon, where Savoy's problem was defined further, but at the Council of Basel, where Amadeus triumphed. During the 1430s a number of treatises were written there by theologians in order to define the new crime, and all of them pointed to Savoy or its immediate surrounding area. The terminology of the treatise *Errores Gazariorum*[85] is similar to that found in the records of an Inquisition trial of 1388, conducted in the Piedmontese Alpine town of Pinerolo. Although persecuting Waldensians, a late medieval separatist church without magical ambitions,[86] the Inquisition recorded cases of sorcery, nocturnal gatherings of sorcerers and devil-worshippers. These meetings were called 'synagogues', reflecting the anti-Semitic sentiments in a region where fierce pogroms had taken place in the aftermath of the Black Death, a fourteenth-century holocaust.[87] The author of the treatise called these Waldensians, who performed black magic, *Gazari*, originally the Italian term applied to the separatist church of the Cathars. Their theology had been dualistic, with a good god being opposed by a bad god, the ruler of this world, and papal inquisitors had labelled them a demonic sect.[88]

The new demonic sect of the witches, the *secta gazariorum*, apparently was thought to have emerged around 1360/80, and this is about the period that later inquisitors, such as Bernard of Como,[89] or a Swiss secular judge quoted by Nider, dated the emergence of the *secta strigiarum*, the new sect of the witches.[90] Recent research has demonstrated that as early as 1317 a woman had been arrested because of alleged sorcery (*ex causa sortilegium seu de charaez*), and in 1346 legal torture had been used. The terminology in a case of 1368 seems to indicate a harsher attitude even then (*arte dyabolica sortilegii et charaez*), and in 1380 a sorceress, Willerma Meylissa, had been burned at Sion, preventing further executions only by exculpating her supposed accomplices. About the same time the first vernacular terms for witchcraft are recorded in Latin court records. In 1400 a woman called Agatha was indicted for knowing the art of sorcery, *vulgaliter dicitur strudiltum vel haxney*.[91] The French *charaez* and the Swiss *strudiltum* have disappeared from memory, but *haxney* turned into *hexerei* and became the term for witchcraft in most Germanophone areas, spreading from southern Switzerland.[92] Around 1400 we can find a number of trials in the Savoyan Piedmont, and the neighbouring French Dauphiné, where the charges of heresy, sorcery and the belief in *strigae* are linked, and the suspects were burned at the stake. Pope Alexander VI, elected at the Council of Pisa, mentions in a decree issued in 1409 for the Franciscan inquisitor Ponce Feugeyron, that 'innumerable Christians and perfidious Jews' had formed *novas sectas*, and the inquisitor should therefore have a close look at all kinds of sorcerers and diviners, specified as '*sortilegi, divini, demonum invocatores, carminatores, coniuratores, superstitiosi, augures, utentes artibus nefariis et prohibitis*'.[93] Obviously an established name for the new sect did not yet exist, therefore the Inquisition had to explain and define those whom they were supposed to persecute. The terminological uncertainty persisted for a number of years. In 1418 Pope Martin V (1368–1431, r. 1417–31) confirmed Feugeyron's position and his responsibility for Savoy,[94] as well as the decree against the new sects. And in 1434 Pope Eugenius IV confirmed the same bull for the same inquisitor.[95]

Feugeyron participated in the reshaping of the perception of heresy and witchcraft, and we know of at least one witch trial conducted by the friar himself, in 1434 in the Aosta Valley (today in Italy), then under Savoy rule. But he was not the only actor. Martine Ostorero suggested that the cumulative concept of witchcraft was transferred to Lausanne, when the former bishop of Aosta (in office 1433–40), Georges de Saluces, became bishop of Lausanne (in office 1440–61). The Dominicans of Lausanne were most active in spreading the new stereotype of the witches' sabbat in their inquisitions, and presumably their preaching. But the reference to Saluces is not compelling, since another inquisitor contributed decisively to the construction of the new crime: the Dominican friar Uldry de Torrenté (active *c.*1400–45). He supervised numerous witch trials throughout northern Savoy, in the dioceses of Lausanne, Geneva and Sion, and acted as an inquisitor in Switzerland, at Fribourg and Neuchâtel, mostly between 1428 and 1439, when he was prior at Lausanne.[96]

The significance of Torrenté's activities becomes obvious in the reports of an independent Swiss town chronicler. Hans Fründ (*c.*1400–68) wrote a detailed account of what is now believed to be the first large-scale witch-hunt of European history.[97] Fründ reports that a new heresy of witches and sorcerers, men as well as women (*ketzerye der hexssen und der zubrern, beide wiben und mannen, die da heissent sortilej ze Latein*), was detected in the Francophone parts of the Valais, but soon spread to the Germanophone valleys, all in the diocese of Sion, but under the rule of the dukes of Savoy. More than 200 witches, both men and women, were burned within only eighteen months, but the burnings were still carrying on (*und brennet man sy noch alle tag*), when Fründ wrote his report, presumably in autumn 1429. We have no reason to doubt his figures, since Fründ proves his reliability as a chronicler with much detailed information, presumably obtained from a Valaisian migrant to Lucerne. Fründ knew of further substantial burnings in the Francophone valleys of the Lower Valais, and around the San Bernardino, subject to Savoy, but refrained from quantifying these with similarly exact numbers. According to Fründ's report, first published by Hansen, the new witches had confessed to devil-worship, flying through the air, gathering in vine cellars, transforming themselves into wolves or becoming invisible. On certain nights they convened in their 'schools' (*schulen*) – obviously Fründ's equivalent for the term 'synagogues', suggested by the Dominicans – where they received instructions from the evil spirit, and cooked and ate children. The witches threatened and cursed their neighbours, killed children, made people sick, lame, blind or insane; they caused impotence in men and infertility in women, destroyed vine and grain, stole milk and damaged ploughs. The authorities succeeded in detecting a conspiracy, since these new witches suggested that the evil spirit had promised them the overthrowing of their lords, as soon as their 'society' had gained enough power.[98]

The new crime of witchcraft was born in these massive persecutions of 1428. Fründ mentions that the supposed witches were severely tortured, and some were even burned without confession, but does not clearly indicate whether the trials were conducted by inquisitors, secular judges, or both. Chantal Ammann-Doubliez managed to interpret these assertions by collecting source fragments from episcopal, monastic, state and city archives of the Valais. She identified twenty-seven executions between December 1427 and May 1436, indicating that Fründ wrote his report at the beginning of the persecution. The earliest executions indeed affected inhabitants of the Val d'Anniviers (Agnes Escor, burned in December 1427) and the Val d'Herens (Martin Bertod, burned in January 1428), as suggested by Fründ. Of the identified trials only sixteen were conducted during the period covered by Fründ's report. But eleven further executions, as well as three decrees from the years 1429–34, indicate that the persecutions lasted until at least 1436. In conclusion, we should expect many more than 200 victims, perhaps 300 or more in the Upper Valais alone, and perhaps similar numbers in the Savoyan Lower Valais and around Lake Geneva. The trials in the Germanophone Upper Valais and within the prince-bishopric of Sion were conducted by secular judges, local lords, like those of the Val d'Anniviers, Hildebrand and Peterman de Rarogne, relatives of the previous Prince-Bishop William V of Rarogne (r. 1402–17), or officials of Prince-Bishop André di Benzi de Gualdo of Sion (r. 1428–37). The trials in the Lower Valais, the Francophone areas under the rule of the dukes of Savoy, were conducted by Uldry de Torrenté, and possibly other Dominican inquisitors. If we follow Fründ's suggestion that the persecution started there, this would imply that the Dominican Inquisition was involved with the business of witch-hunting from the very beginning.[99]

Clearly the influence of the Dominicans can be seen from the fact that even in secular courts of the Valais the witches' sabbat was fashioned as an inversion of Christian ritual. The *Errores Gazariorum*, compiled by the Savoyan inquisitor in charge, most likely Uldry de Torrenté in 1436, with later additions by 1439, provides something of an official version.[100] These additions are particularly striking since they refer to a particular method of causing hail in a thunderstorm. A witch had confessed that she had caused the storm by carrying large blocks of ice up to the clouds, and dropping it from there onto the crops. Exactly this method of destroying crops had been confessed by Aymonet Maugetaz during her trial in 1438, a trial conducted by Uldry de Torrenté.[101] There is also a strong emphasis in Fründ's report on peasants' concerns, such as infertility, crop failure, children's diseases and mortality. These concerns point to the material background of an ecological catastrophe for the witch-hunts. The agriculture of the high Alpine villages of the diocese of Sion – nowadays, like Zermatt, famous as skiing paradises – was highly vulnerable. Historians of climate tell us that the 1420s were characterized by unstable climatic conditions, with a mix of extremely warm and cold years, severe storms, late frosts, floodings and droughts. The years of 1428 and 1429 were particularly cold and wet, the least favourable conditions for health and agriculture. And from 1431 a series of particularly cold years began, with late frosts and long winters, causing problems even in less hostile environments.[102] Only in 1430 are no climatic extreme events reported, and, although the sample of reconstructed witch trials is small, it may be no coincidence that for the entire decade 1427–36 it is only for this year that no execution is reported. The secular judges seem to have been particularly interested in weather-making, and – according to Fründ – some of the scapegoats indeed confessed that they had cursed and destroyed the crops, particularly those of vine and grain.[103] This kind of hardship, or the presence of the plague in 1420 and 1428/29, may have fostered social despair, but there were further sources of uncertainty: the consequence of the Great Schism, a kind of civil war (*Guerre de Rarogne*) in the second decade within the Valais. The fact that the present bishop was an outsider, implanted by the Council of Constance and interrupting the succession of the local Rarogne lords, supported the notion of political conspiracy. There was substantial migration within the valley, possibly related to changes in the environment. Immigrants from the Aosta Valley (today Italy), or from Germanophone Switzerland, proved to be particularly vulnerable during the witch-hunt.[104]

Most scholars agree that 'virtually all significant examples [of European witch-hunts] are located between the 1590s and the 1640s',[105] but this is evidently not the case, if we consider the large-scale witch-hunts around 1430. Fründ's report of the massive witch-hunts in the Valais is only the first of five contemporary accounts of these events. Interestingly enough, the four other reports focus on different areas within the same region: the Alpine valleys around Lake Geneva, nowadays in France, Italy and Switzerland. The second and most famous account of these persecutions came from a Dominican professor of theology, prior of the convent of Basel, a centre of the Observant reform movement, and also, during the council, a centre of European communications. Johann Nider (c.1380–1438) had gathered his information during the council from various parts of Switzerland, presumably from Torrenté, and possibly from Feugeyron, who had also attended the council, as well as from an unknown Dominican from Lyon, possibly Petrus Barra, who had carried out inquisitions in the diocese of Autun (archdiocese of Lyon).[106] Furthermore he relied on the accounts of a secular judge, Peter of Berne, who had conducted early trials in the Bernese Upper Simmental,[107] and whose stories of the arch-sorcerers Hoppo and Stadelin proved so convincing that a Jacobean playwright used them as helpers of the 'chief witch' Hecate centuries later.[108] Most of Peter's victims were male, and were not charged with heresy, but exclusively with popular magic, theologically recast by Nider as demonic. Witchcraft stories constitute the fifth book of Nider's treatise on spiritual errors, the *Formicarius* (*Ant-hill*), which was circulated widely in manuscript form and printed in 1475 as one of the earliest demonologies. Later, it was frequently bound together with the *Malleus Maleficarum*.[109]

Possibly the two most important accounts of these early persecutions were written directly by those responsible for them. Further to the *Errores Gazariorum* there was the treatise *Ut magorum et maleficiorum errores*, authored by the French lawyer Claude Tholosan, High Judge of the Dauphiné (in office 1426–49). He conducted no fewer than 258 witch trials, according to his financial records, and summarized his exceptional experience in 1436. The Dauphiné, close to the Pope's see at Avignon, had seen increasing activity by papal inquisitors from about 1335. From 1384, a formal crusade against the Waldensians had devastated whole valleys. After the physical extinction of the main heretics the number of trials lessened, but continued, and now went hand in hand with witch trials, integrating the peasants' concerns about black magic. Unlike Savoy, where trials of sorcery fuelled heresy trials and eventually grew into the large-scale witch-hunts of the late 1420s, the persecution in the Dauphiné never reached this massive level, but was characterized by a steady flow of individual or small panic trials.[110] One explanation for this contrast could be the different judicial system. In the Dauphiné, from 1349 subject to France, and the prince-successor (Dauphin) in particular, secular courts were responsible for witch trials, and the high judge, appointed by the Dauphin, referred mainly to secular law, to French jurists and to Roman law. Therefore Tholosan denied the witches' flight, and did not inquire into synagogues or sabbats, which he considered to be devilish illusions.[111]

Despite detailed research we do not yet know exactly how the massive witch-hunts of the 1420s came about. Andreas Blauert (b. 1956) suggested that, against the backdrop of all kinds of misfortune, the decisive spark may have come from inflammatory preaching campaigns that spread the notion of a conspiracy of heretical witches, offering the populace an opportunity for intervention.[112] In the French Alpine valleys Franciscan missions were implanted in order to combat Waldensianism. The Catalan Dominican St Vincent Ferrer (1350–1419) spread fears of a devilish conspiracy during his missionary trip through southern France, the Piedmont, Lombardy, Savoy, the Dauphiné and southern Switzerland during the years 1399 to 1409, and lashed out against all sinners who invoked God's wrath, including Jews, heretics and sorcerers. The observant Dominican Johann Mülberg (c.1355–1414) did the same at the Germanophone fringe of that area. When St Bernardino da Siena (1380–1444) excited Italy in the 1420s, witchcraft was already 'one of the enduring preoccupations of our friar's preaching career'.[113] The observant Franciscan had received his ideas about the witches' sabbat, sexual orgies, the preparing of unguents from baby fat, and shape-shifting from the Piedmont, doubtless from a local inquisitor.[114] The sermons of this moral entrepreneur bore fruit: several witches were burned at Rome during the reign of Pope Martin V, after Bernardino had asked for a general cleansing in June 1424, and four years later the same happened at Todi.[115] Bernardino's itinerary ought to be closely scrutinized, since witch trials started in some Italian Alpine valleys shortly after his appearance, for instance in the Milanese town of Bellinzona in the early 1430s. The future saint gained a reputation: during the next witch panic in the Val Leventina, when about thirty-five people were accused and eventually twenty burned to ashes in 1457, a chapel was built and devoted to Bernardino da Siena, who had a good chance of becoming the patron saint of witch-hunting.[116] All of these itinerant preachers belonged to the observant wing of their Orders, were driven by apocalyptic fears and were asking for direct action. We find some of the earliest witch trials in their aftermath, and one of the first authors to advertise the new demonology of witchcraft, Johannes Nider, had indeed accompanied one of these incendiary preachers, Mülberg, during his campaign.[117]

It is difficult to estimate the extent of the first wave of persecutions in European history. But taking into account that there were large-scale witch-hunts and even massive persecutions around 1430 in northern Italy (Savoy), eastern France (Dauphiné) and southern Switzerland (Valais), we can assume that they claimed more than several hundred lives. Martin Le Franc mentions in his account of the witch-hunts that more than 600 women had confessed to weather-making and sexual intercourse with the devil. There can be no doubt that all of these confessed witches were executed. We do not know whether the figure refers to the persecutions in Savoy alone, or is meant to include all victims of the entire wave of persecution in the region.[118] It would be interesting to explore the wider repercussions of these events. Fritz Byloff (1875–1940) pointed to the fact that the 1430s witnessed not only causes célèbres, like the trials of Joan of Arc (1410–31) or Agnes Bernauer (1411–35), but that in Tyrolean court account books for that decade there were also considerable expenses for burnings, for instance at Meran (today in Italy).[119] And it seems that a more general survey of this decade could be rewarding, since we hear of early burnings from other parts of Europe as well, such as the duchy of Milan, eastern Switzerland (Fribourg, Neuchâtel), Lorraine and Slovenia. If historians of climate are right in their description of the 1430s it is anything but a surprise that scapegoats were sought in so many places, and that the new concept of witch-craft spread rapidly.[120]

Three treatises provided almost simultaneously, and independently, exhaustive descriptions and interpretations of the new crime at the very moment when Pope Eugenius IV had accepted the Council of Basel, despite its conciliarist majority. Basel became the centre of Christendom for three years and, consequently, the Pope brought the issue of a new sect of devil-worshippers – the witches – to the attention of *all* inquisitors in 1437.[121] When the Pope tried to transfer the council to Ferrara in September, and the majority at Basel elected Amadeus VIII of Savoy as counter-Pope, this could only increase the attention to both the crime and its importance in Savoy. It is no coincidence that the counter-pope's secretary, Martin Le Franc (c.1410–61), was the next distinguished author to provide a detailed account of the new sect of witches. In his *Le Champion des Dames* he refers to Tholosan's persecutions in the Dauphiné, where '*vouldroies*' were meeting at their 'synagogues', in order to conceive their devilish 'sorceryies'.[122] Around 1440 the new sect had eventually received its name: they were labelled '*Vaudoises*' – 'Waldensians', or rather *Waldensian witches*, since they were clearly different from the real followers of the arch-heretic Valdès of Lyon. The original Waldensians had been accused of worshipping the devil, but were in fact a pious and peaceful evangelical sect, the only medieval heresy that has survived until the present day. Some branches of them joined the Reformation in 1532, while others remained independent.[123]

It is characteristic of the earliest witch-hunts – as well as for all papal decrees of the fifteenth century – that they targeted women and men equally. This could be due to the experience of the persecution of the Waldensians, which showed a balanced gender distribution, or to specific regional particularities. Even in the sixteenth and seventeenth centuries certain Alpine regions remained particularly concerned about male sorcery. However, the Church's paradigm shift regarding the reality of nocturnal flights during these first waves of persecutions had wider repercussions, as the popular fantasy – condemned in the *Canon Episcopi* – gained credibility. Like the followers of the pagan goddess Diana in that *Canon*, the participants in these journeys were primarily conceived as female in many regions. The Spanish theologian Alfonsus Tostatus (1400–55) legitimized the popular belief in the reality of these flights in his Bible commentary of 1446 (first printed in Venice 1507). In his register the subject – a discussion of the *Canon Episcopi* on the occasion of Christ's temptation by Satan in Matthew 4:5–11 – is indicated as *De maleficis mulieribus que vulgariter dicunter bruxas*, explicitly referring to the popular term *bruxa* for witch.[124] In its most aggressive form, Nicholas Jacquier (?–1472), a Dominican inquisitor and theologian at the Council of Basel, defended the new ideas about the witches' flight, gathered from inquisitorial practice and new 'experience' about the witches' sect, against the dogmas of the old *Canon Episcopi*.[125] Witchcraft theory gained momentum with the infamous persecution of the *vauderie* in the episcopal town of Arras (Flemish: Atrecht) at the end of the 1450s. These events provoked several reports about the new witches, drawing from the evidence of the confessions and the experience of the judges. Once again major authors tried to classify the new sect theologically. The Superior of the Lombard province of the Dominican Order, Girolamo Visconti (*c.*1415–78), agreed that *strie* should be judged as heretics, discussed the *Canon Episcopi* once more, and concluded that the witches' sabbat should be considered to be real.[126]

At this stage iconographic representations of the witches' flight began to play an important role. Although there is some uncertainty about two frescos in the cathedral of Schleswig – women riding on cats and sticks – which have been attributed to the thirteenth century, but are presumably forgeries, a wave of paintings on church walls was commissioned in the 1450s, or soon after, representing women riding through the air on sticks, plants, animals or devils. According to Jens Johansen, who analysed paintings in seventeen Danish churches, and compared them to similar paintings in other parts of Europe,[127] for instance in Slovenia,[128] these paintings must have been commissioned almost simultaneously. Perhaps they were part of an anti-witchcraft campaign, and were meant to illustrate *exempla* from early demonologies, building upon the mnemotechnique of the period, where complex theological matters were iconographically represented in comic-type illustrations, not unlike the *Bibliae Pauperum*.

Plate 4   *Devil Worship and Nocturnal Flight of Waldensian Witches.*
Johannes Tinctoris, *Contra Sectam Vaudensium*, *c*.1460

Possibly the painters were already using pattern books for these
paintings, and certainly they were drawing from popular fantasy. Soon
other media were employed to spread the new paradigm. Around
1460 pictorial representations of the witches' flight can be found in
books, first as miniature paintings in handwritten copies of the *Champion des Dames*, where the witches on broomsticks are still labelled
as *Vaudoises*, and then in Jean Tinctoris' *Contra Sectam Vaudensium*,
where the Waldensian witches are riding through the air on devilish
monsters. This was soon to become the exception. By the 1470s, when
the woodcut industry combined with book printing, with rising
numbers of printed illustrations to satisfy the customers' demands,

popular fantasy had triumphed over sophisticated theological concepts. Woodcuts of milk-stealing witches, or of the witches' shot, the widespread idea that witches harm their victims by the intrusion of objects,[129] were first inserted into prints of classical texts in Augsburg, then a centre of the printing industry. But from the 1490s illustrated demonological treatises inundated the market with images of witchcraft, and prepared the ground for more sophisticated iconographies around 1500 by the German painters (see chapter 7), who were already beginning a struggle against superstition. During the decades preceding the Reformation, the subject of witchcraft was tremendously popular.

The leading demonologist of this period was to be Heinrich Kramer. We know nothing of his childhood and youth. The surname Kramer, Latinized as 'Institoris', may relate to his ancestors' profession, literally meaning 'merchant'. He must have joined the Dominican Order at a young age, and was educated in the convent of his hometown Schlettstadt (today Sélestat), an imperial city south of Strasbourg. After receiving a doctoral degree in Rome, Kramer Latinized his surname in the humanist manner and published as 'Henricus Institoris'. If we believe autobiographical remarks, he participated in the trial against Friedrich Reiser (1401–58), a Waldensian and Taborite bishop, who was executed in Strasbourg. However, it was only on his appointment as inquisitor in 1474 that Kramer/Institoris became a persecution specialist. In 1475 *Frater Henricus de Sletstat* took an active part in the infamous ritual murder trial against the Jewish community of Trent (Trient, today Trento in Italy), then the capital of the prince-bishopric of Trent. Commissioned by Prince-Bishop Johannes IV Hinderbach (1418–86, r. 1465–86), Kramer collected evidence of previous trials for ritual murder in south-western Germany and the Alsace in order to support the bishop's persecution. Its legitimacy had been challenged by a representative of the Roman curia. Kramer, and the propaganda of the Dominicans, supported the prince-bishops in establishing a pilgrimage in honour of the supposedly martyred child, Simon Unferdorben. This enterprise soon proved profitable, and St Simon, the child, was venerated until the 1960s, when his shrines were eventually removed and the anti-Semitic cult terminated. Although ideas about Jewish conspiracies can be found in Kramer's later publications, this was not his main concern. Kramer persecuted *any* kind of deviation from what he himself considered to be the true religion. In addition to Jews, Waldensians, Hussites and Bohemian Brethren, he persecuted some women in the imperial city of Augsburg who desired the Eucharist too frequently. As a devout papalist, he tried to launch an attack on supporters of the conciliarist party. His lasting fame, however, results from his long-standing interest in witch-hunting, and in particular from his handbook of witch-hunting, the *Witches' Hammer*.[130]

The *Malleus Maleficarum* was the result of Kramer's experience as an 'Inquisitor Alemanniae Superioris' with witch trials in his designated areas of south-western Germany, western Austria, Switzerland, and his homeland, the Alsace. It is possible to find evidence of some of his trials in the region, particularly between 1482 and 1484. These activities were generally not well received by the local authorities, who disliked his interference in their administration of justice; and the populace, although sometimes initially welcoming him, soon tired of his persecutory zeal.[131] Annoyed by all the resistance, Kramer managed to obtain papal authorization for his inquisitorial rights regarding the persecution of witchcraft from Innocence VIII (1432–92, r. 1484–92). This was the decree *Summis desiderantes affectibus*,[132] which authorized formal Inquisitions against witches in all German Church provinces. Invested with such a carte blanche, Kramer tried to start a paradigmatic witch-hunt. Innsbruck, the capital of the duchy of Tyrol, was a significant place, since Archduke Sigmund of Tyrol was the most powerful Habsburg prince, ruling over a patchwork of territories stretching from northern Italy and south-western Germany into the Alsace (today eastern France), the inquisitor's homeland. Innsbruck was a gateway to the Holy Roman Empire.

Kramer's Inquisition in Innsbruck, starting in July 1485, employed a climate of intimidation, brutal force, unlimited use of torture, the denial of legal defence and distorted reports of his interrogations – scandalous conduct even according to late fifteenth-century legal standards. Therefore, not only the relatives of the accused, but the citizenship of the capital as a whole, along with the clergy, the Tyrolean nobility and, eventually, the responsible bishop, protested against the illegal procedures. Bishop Georg II Golser (*c.*1420–89), successor of the philosopher Nicolaus of Cusa at the see of Brixen, appointed a commission to scrutinize Kramer's Inquisition. Despite desperate resistance from the inquisitor's side, the bishop stopped the persecution immediately, nullified its results and – after having secured the archduke's support – liberated all suspected women. It is worth remembering that the secular as well as the ecclesiastical authorities of Tyrol deliberately decided to resist this papal inquisitor, and that they succeeded in their refusal to accept a witch persecution within their jurisdiction. Kramer was branded a fanatic, and Bishop Golser – who in his correspondence called Kramer/Institoris senile and crazy – went as far as to threaten him with force if he failed to leave his diocese voluntarily. The prince-bishops of Brixen never again allowed a witch persecution under their rule, and – even more importantly – the Tyrolean government had learnt a lasting lesson, and suppressed any attempts of lower courts to launch witch-hunts even in future generations. The Innsbruck Inquisition – in short – was an unprecedented defeat for the papal inquisitor.[133] The disaster at Innsbruck, and his apocalyptic fears, drove Kramer to develop his ideas further, and – starting from his reports to the bishop – he hastily systematized his notes into a major manuscript. The papal inquisitor was among the first of his profession to recognize the importance of the printing revolution, and with this manuscript he tried to turn his defeat into victory, by demonstrating the existence of witchcraft. Using his authority and experience, he urged the necessity of a campaign to eradicate witchcraft. The result was the *Malleus Maleficarum*, the *Witches' Hammer*.

There is a lot of confusion about the author, place of print and date of print of this crucial publication on witchcraft. Only recently could we demonstrate from a printer's account book that the *Malleus* was printed in autumn 1486 in the imperial city of Speyer. The printer was Peter Drach (*c*.1450–1504), who delivered the 'treatise against sorcerers' to his booksellers in December.[134] Since there was no title page at that stage, as with many early prints, the book's description in the account book varied. It was called 'treatise against sorceresses', or 'against sorcery', until Kramer eventually added a foreword, his *'apologia auctoris in malleum maleficarum'*, around Easter 1487. Even without a title page the book title was fixed then. Kramer promoted his publication in every possible way, notably by adding the papal bull of 1484, and a reference to approval by the University of Cologne, which was at least in part a forgery. He travelled to Brussels, to obtain a privilege from King Maximilian I (1459–1519), the future emperor. This document, if it existed at all, must have been so unfavourable that it was not inserted into the text. It is mentioned in the preface, thus conveying the impression that the *Malleus* was backed by the highest ecclesiastical, academic and secular authorities. Kramer's strategy was aimed at the princes, and their law courts. The educated theologians and lawyers must have noticed that authoritative authors, like St Augustine and St Thomas Aquinas, as well as the Roman law, are deliberately misquoted in the *Malleus*. Kramer was bold enough to emphasize the success of his inquisition at Innsbruck, and to thank the archduke for his support. He was right in his assumption that few would check his claims.[135]

The *Malleus Maleficarum* was welcomed by a curious audience as the first printed handbook of witch demonology and persecution. It was divided into three parts, the first treating theological, the second practical problems, and the third providing advice on legal procedures, constantly referring to the author's extensive experience with witch trials. Five points could be called original in the *Witches' Hammer*. First, it emphasized that witchcraft was a real – not just a spiritual – crime, and that witches therefore deserved capital punishment, and had to be prosecuted. Second, Kramer claimed that witchcraft was the worst of all crimes because it combined heresy, including apostasy and the adoration of the devil, with the most terrible secular crimes such as murder, theft and sodomy. Third, since it was not only the worst of all crimes, but also occult and difficult to trace, legal inhibitions had to be abandoned. Fourth, witches were primarily *women*. And, fifth, the crime needed to be prosecuted by secular courts – here again the inquisitor was drawing conclusions from his own experience, because he had seen how unpopular inquisitors were in Europe north of the Alps. Although Kramer was largely drawing from earlier theologians and from inquisitorial handbooks, such as Nicolas Eymeric's *Practica Inquisitionis* of 1376, the *Malleus* was a fresh product by an author of erudition and experience. With twelve Latin editions printed in Germany and France between 1486 and 1523, the *Witches' Hammer* could be called a success, although public interest was clearly strongest in the first ten years when the subject was still novel. Only two generations later two Venetian printers saw a new demand for the *Malleus* in 1574 and 1576, and in the 1580s three editions were printed in Frankfurt, with a fourth one in 1600. Surprisingly, France became the stronghold of *Malleus* reprints after the Reformation. The sales picked up in the 1580s, when two editions were printed at Lyon in 1584 and 1595, and after 1600 seven further editions were published at Lyon, the last one in 1669.[136]

Traditionally, the upsurge of witch trials in the early 1490s in Central Europe has been interpreted as a result of the publication of the *Witches' Hammer*, and there are incidents indicating that it did have a certain impact. In the monastery of Eberhardsklausen on the Mosel River, a chronicler reported that the region had been plagued by witches for some time, but due to the great uncertainty about the matter it had been impossible to prosecute them. Only after reading the *Witches' Hammer* did the authorities see how they could proceed against witches – and so they did. Here we do indeed have a kind of *conversion experience*, but this is a rare example, and it is not at all clear how the *Malleus* was generally interpreted. It is at least telling that an early opposition publication was printed even more frequently during the 1490s. Ulrich Molitor (1442–1507), a lawyer of the bishop of Constance, and courtier at Archduke Sigmund's court in Innsbruck, challenged even the central assumptions of the *Witches' Hammer*. Molitor fashioned his text as a conversation between a fanatic believer in witchcraft, Molitor himself as an opponent, and Archduke Sigmund as the wise arbiter, always coming to reasonable conclusions, and bluntly denying the possibility of the witches' flight, the witches' sabbat and shape-shifting.[137] This was nothing but the traditional attitude of the Catholic Church, and Molitor indeed promoted a conservative attitude towards sorcery. But this was the attitude that had hitherto prevented witch persecutions. And Molitor went one step further. The fact that he excluded theologians from his discourse meant that in his view Dominicans or inquisitors should have nothing at all to do with legal affairs. Molitor's dialogue instantly

Plate 5 *Weather Magic*. Frontispiece, Ulrich Molitor, *De Laniis et Phitonicis Mulieribus*, Cologne, 1489

became popular, with ten reprints in the 1490s, translations into the German vernacular and a number of exciting woodcuts.

Six woodcuts by an unknown artist, added to the 1493 edition of Molitor's treatise, triggered off a popular demand for the subject of witchcraft in European art. These illustrations represented the more fantastical components of the crime: the witches' shot, shape-shifting into the forms of animals, the witches' flight, the witches' congregation, intercourse with the devil and weather magic. Some of the most talented artists of the northern Renaissance, all of them young and open to new developments, started producing woodcuts and paintings of witches and witchcraft. Albrecht Dürer (1471–1528) may already have drawn the 'witch's flight' inserted into the famous Nuremberg *Liber Cronicarum* of 1493, and certainly he created a series of woodcuts on this theme in 1497. Many younger artists followed his example, such as Hans Baldung Grien (1485–1545), Niklaus Manuel Deutsch (*c*.1483–1530), Urs Graf (*c*.1485–1525) or Albrecht Altdorfer (1480–1538). According to Jane Davidson, witches became the most widespread subject of art during this generation,[138] and since woodcuts were printed for an anonymous market we must conclude that there was considerable demand for these representations. Quite in contrast to the woodcuts in Molitor's treatise, these avant-garde artists pleased their humanist audience with erudite allusions to classical texts, or with sheer pornography. Charles Zika argues that Baldung's and Dürer's nudes represent some kind of acceptance of demonological theory,[139] but it seems equally possible that just the opposite was the case. Willibald Pirckheimer (1470–1530), a famous humanist and town councillor at Nuremberg like Dürer, ridiculed the supposed power of witches and contemporary inquisitors alike in his publications.[140]

The extent of pre-Reformation witch persecutions has not yet been thoroughly researched. Kramer tells us in the *Malleus* that forty-eight women had been burned as witches in the diocese of Constance, and there is no reason to doubt this number, even more so as he indicates that he himself had searched this diocese more than any other. After his crushing failure in Innsbruck Kramer seems to have turned his attention towards the Alsace, particularly in the surroundings of his convent. The expulsion of the Jews from his home town of Schlettstadt might be placed in this context as well. In 1488 Kramer tried to incite witch-hunts in the neighbouring diocese of Trier, while in the same year thirty-five witches were burned in the nearby imperial city of Metz. In an expert opinion for the imperial city of Nuremberg, Kramer reported in October 1491 that 'more than 200 witches' had been burned so far due to his inquisitions.[141] Nevertheless, the further actions of the inquisitor remain shrouded in darkness, and recent research indicates that he may have been silenced by his own superior. Jacob Sprenger (1437–95), always thought of as co-author, sometimes even as the main author of the *Malleus Maleficarum*, turns out to have been Kramer's most bitter enemy. Quite in contrast to the Alsatian fanatic, a maverick who managed to get involved in trouble wherever he turned up, and who had developed into a wandering inquisitor and persecution specialist, Sprenger was an established exponent of the 'observant' reform wing of the Dominicans. He was first appointed prior of the large Cologne convent, then leader of the province 'Teutonia', and was also an influential theologian, promoting the veneration of the Virgin Mary and introducing rosary brotherhoods for lay people, which were organized by friars as well as by secular clergy. It seems likely that Sprenger was involuntarily included in the papal bull of 1484, as well as in the preface of the *Witches' Hammer* in 1487. Sprenger tried to suppress Kramer's activities in every possible way. He forbade the convents of his province to host his enemy, he forbade further preaching and he tried to interfere directly in the affairs of the Schlettstadt convent. There is not one fact or incident that associates Sprenger with witch persecutions, and he seems to have managed to expel the author of the *Malleus* from his province. Kramer had to spend his later years in Italy and Bohemia, where he died.[142]

It may well be that the rise of witch persecutions at the end of the fifteenth century was not at all related to the publication of the *Witches' Hammer*, but rather the other way round: the troublesome inquisitor tried to exploit popular fears for his purpose. The decades between 1470 and 1520 were years of severe mortality crises, and scapegoats were sought. In the early 1480s the plague had rampaged through large parts of upper Germany, Switzerland and eastern France, and even the *Malleus* linked witchcraft and the plague in one particular case, where a deceased witch had spread the disease from her grave. Imperial cities like Memmingen or Ravensburg lost considerable proportions of their population in these years, and fears of sudden illness and death were widespread, for good reasons. Not only witchcraft anxieties, but popular piety in general, soared, as we can see in the iconographical representations of the *Dance of Death*, or in the rise of millennial fears, with the idea that humanity was living in the last age – an age characterized by bitter hardships and terrifying signs of the end of the world. Like Third World prophets,[143] the author of the *Witches' Hammer* pointed to the Book of Revelation and argued that the emergence of the witches' sect should be seen as a sign of the imminence of the Antichrist.[144] Witch burnings, or small panic trials, took place not only in towns where Dominican inquisitors incited the populace, or where the town council had ordered a copy of the *Malleus*, but in many places in upper Italy, northern Spain, eastern France, Switzerland, western Germany and the whole of Burgundy down to the Netherlands, even prior to the publication of the *Malleus*, especially between the 1480s and about 1520. There are no reasonable estimates concerning the possible number of victims. At the end of the sixteenth century a Bavarian lawyer spoke of 3,000 victims, but without indicating how he had constructed this figure.[145]

Renaissance Italy was particularly involved in these early persecutions, with witch-hunts comparable in size to those of Switzerland and France. Valleys like the Valcamonica, well known for thousands of neolithic stone carvings, are remote places only from a modern point of view. Situated in the hinterland of Milan, the Valcamonica was actually close to one of the centres of Renaissance civilization, and one of the mightiest towns of Europe, being larger at that time than Paris, Rome or London, and a focus for all kinds of heresies. From the thirteenth century the Dominican convent of St Eustorgio in Milan became the headquarters of the Inquisition in the region. Kramer reports in the *Malleus* that the inquisitor of Como burned forty-one witches at Bormio, at the bottom of the Valtellina, in 1485. Surviving fragments of trial records prove that there were indeed a number of witch trials conducted by several inquisitors between 1483 and 1486 in the Valtellina, as well as in neighbouring valleys.[146] Reliable information exists for the Valcamonica, politically now part of the Venetian mainland territories. Trials had started in the 1480s. Bishop Paolo Zane of Brescia was already in power, and would later sponsor the burning of sixty witches in 1510, and of another sixty-four witches in 1518, when he appointed four inquisitors for different parts of his diocese.[147] But the diocese of Como remained a centre of the witch-hunts in Italy. The educated Dominican Bernardo Rategno (*c.*1450–1510), who claims to have burned great numbers of witches as an inquisitor of Como in the first decade of the sixteenth century, wrote down his experiences for posterity.[148] The Dominican Bartolomeo de Spina (*c.*1480–1546), who also provided examples from Inquisition tribunals at Ferrara, and in the Valtellina, suggested that the Inquisition of Como alone arrested an average of 1,000 people a year, and executed more than 100 of them annually.[149] Within ten years this could have added up to massive numbers of executions, and at least 300 executions are confirmed by a contemporary witness, a lawyer from Como, in 1514, when the trials had not yet ended.[150] During these massive persecutions, where inquisitors employed up to ten vicars in order to cope with the amount of work, the persecution peaked in Italy. The bishop of Trent conducted a persecution in his Alpine valleys, triggered by the narratives of a witch-doctor, Zuanne delle Piatte, who advertised his journeys to the other world, to the mountain of Venus, where he met Tannhäuser and the society of beautiful fairies, *ragazze bellissime*. There he received the power of healing, of divination and to recognize the witches. The witch-doctor and twenty suspected witches were burned at the stake at Cavalese between 1501 and 1505.[151] Prince Gianfranceso Pico della

Mirandola (c.1469–1533, r. 1499–1533) investigated sixty suspects in his principality, and executed ten of them.[152] Around 1520, persecutions were picking up at Bergamo, Piacenza, and even in the papal states, with executions in Bologna, the Apennine region and in Rome. In 1521 the Dominican inquisitor Silvester Prierias (1456–1523), then professor of theology at Rome – and, as *magister sacrii palatii*, an influential figure within the papal administration, as well as the first outstanding opponent of Luther[153] – corroborated the ideas of the *Malleus Maleficarum* with new examples,[154] as did Paolo Grillando, an educated lawyer employed by the papal states, in approximately 1525. No doubt northern Italy was suffering from large-scale persecutions between 1480 and 1525, when foreign troops invaded the peninsula and Rome was sacked. It is hardly surprising that these large-scale persecutions provoked resistance, as will be outlined in chapter 7.

In northern Italy the mass burnings did indeed stop, while in the Holy Roman Empire they ended even earlier. Papal inquisitors disappeared from northern Europe and the Reformation of Luther made the break definitive. Radical Reformers even denied the physical power of the devil, thus questioning the demonological concept of witchcraft altogether.[155] The focus of the debates shifted away from witchcraft in a decade of revolutionary uprisings and world-historical decisions. The flow of demonological literature stopped, and the *Malleus*, bestseller of the previous generation, disappeared from the book market. Popular demands for witch-hunting were subsequently crushed by the Austrian authorities. In Styria some peasants seized a number of witches and burned them at the stake in 1538, obviously because the courts did not accept accusations. Archduke Ferdinand I ordered the persecution of the lynchers.[156] Some contemporaries, like Johann Weyer, harboured the hope that the period of witch persecutions was definitively over.[157]

However, in retrospect it seems that wishful thinking was involved, since a closer look reveals that the generation between 1520 and 1550 experienced a considerable number of witch trials, and even some panic trials and small witch-hunts. Furthermore, as in present-day Africa,[158] witchcraft became a *media event*. Some of the burnings were communicated widely through the new mass media, the single-leaf broadsheet with woodcut. The earliest of these pamphlets reported the story of a woman in Schiltach near Basel, a supposed witch, accused of having caused a dangerous fire which burned down large parts of that small market town in 1533.[159] The case raised considerable attention, and Erasmus contributed a timid comment on the burning of this witch in his correspondence. In 1540, it was the powerhouse of the Reformation, Luther's Wittenberg, that suffered a sorcery scare in the context of a first regional wave of witch trials,[160] in response to cattle diseases and 'unnatural weather'. Four people were executed, three of them male, but their case was reported in a single-leaf woodcut by Luther's chief propagandist, Lukas Cranach (1472–1553), and his workshop. Although Luther was not involved,[161] this original sin of Lutheranism must have bewildered Protestants as much as similar occurrences in Geneva. Calvin's Godly city had formerly been part of the witch-ridden duchy of Savoy, and, after its secession in the 1530s, and a political revolution followed by a religious Reformation, it remained haunted by all kinds of strange fears, particularly the idea that the plague was being spread by a hidden conspiracy of poisoners. This was a Savoyan heritage too, and as in Savoy the supposed poisoners were gradually transformed into diabolical sorcerers, or witches. Shortly after Jean Calvin's (1509–64) arrival several men were burned, and the Reformer himself pleaded for an intensification of the persecution, calling for the 'extirpation' of the 'race' of the witches.[162] It should be noted again that the belief in poison-spreading witches is widespread. The ideas of the reformed pope of Geneva are akin to those of African herdsmen, such as the Dinka of southern Sudan, who think that witches smear the blood of the black cobra on the house-posts of victims.[163] Although some scholars try to enshrine the Calvinists as being 'gentle' in their treatment of witches,[164] clearly the opposite was the case. Geneva held an unusually large number of witch trials, with numerous executions. Likewise, there were witch burnings in the Protestant Swiss cantons of Zurich, Berne and Basel, as well as in Catholic Lucerne and the former imperial city of Constance on the Swiss border. Widespread attention was given to one broadsheet that is still frequently reprinted, of a witch burning in the tiny lordship of Regenstein in the Harz region, close to Germany's mystical mountain, the Blocksberg, where the witches held a dance on Walpurgis Night (the eve of 1 May).[165]

Even in the 1540s some countries still suffered from witch panics and major persecutions, and it seems that north-western Europe was particularly affected. Witch panics ravaged the Netherlands, with a number of witches being executed in major towns like Amsterdam, Utrecht and Roermond during the 1520s and 1530s. In the province of Limburg eleven witches were burned in 1539, then another five in 1551,[166] and there were also large-scale witch-hunts: Gelderland burned twenty witches in 1547, while in the county of Namur thirty-four were executed and thirty-three banished. In Lorraine eighteen witches were executed between 1545 and 1552. The most surprising case was Denmark under King Christian III (1503–59, r. 1534–59). The country had been through a tumultuous period of civil war, territorial expansion and rapid political and religious reforms, and here – for the first time in a Protestant territory – the panic turned into a large-scale persecution, with peasants hunting witches in the open

fields 'like wolves', according to the approving report of Peder Pal-
ladius (1503–60), a leading Churchman of his age, overseer of ecclesiastical affairs in Denmark, Norway, Iceland and the Faroes. In
Jutland alone fifty-two women were killed in 1543, but there were
also lynchings in other parts of Denmark and in Danish-controlled
southern Sweden. The government in Copenhagen tried to curb the
persecution by restrictive laws in 1547.[167] But persecutions were not
confined to Northern Europe. In the papal states some witches were
burned in the 1540s, and again in 1559, by the newly established
Roman Inquisition under the Dominican cardinal inquisitor Antonio
Michele Ghislieri, who was elected Pope Pius V (1504–72, r. 1566–72)
soon after.[168] In Tarragona the local inquisitor allowed the burning of
seven women in 1548. This so embarrassed the Supreme Council of
the Spanish Inquisition that he was subjected to punishment. The Tarragona case was the last witch burning ordered by the Inquisition of
Catalonia,[169] but trials before secular courts and lynchings persisted
well into the seventeenth century. Portugal saw its only panic trial in
1559, when the duke of Aveiro sentenced six women to the stake in
Lisbon.[170] In conclusion, the first generation after the Reformation
had its witch burnings, but the mainlands of France, Italy and
Germany remained largely unaffected. Altogether there were fewer
executions than during the generations before and afterwards.

Persecution for religious reasons, to be sure, was not absent; quite
the opposite was the case. New institutions for social discipline were
introduced, such as the Roman Inquisition. Ideological control was
by no means confined to the remaining Catholic areas of Europe,
where the developing state administrations supported the Church in
its efforts to tighten control over people's minds. Protestant territories developed new methods of disciplining, with reformed Church
courts or consistories minutely scrutinizing the believers' conduct.
The decade between the Peasants' War (1524/1525) and the Anabap-
tist kingdom of Münster (1533/34) saw a climax of religious persecution, with thousands of seditious peasants and Anabaptists, men and
women alike, suffering the most terrible death penalties. They were
burned or drowned because of their convictions, and the similarity of
their sentences to those of witches indicates that in the eyes of the
authorities the crimes were comparable. From 1520 to 1560 the campaign against heresy saw another climax, with roughly 1,500 legally
sanctioned executions for heresy.[171] Luther compared the *satanic
illusion* of the radical reformers to witchcraft, so that Menno
Simons (1496–1561) found it necessary to respond to the charges that
he and his followers were demon-possessed. Gary Waite has pointed
to the fact that Dutch courts, which treated witches and heretics
sometimes in the same week, regarded Anabaptists as forming a
conspiracy under the lordship of the devil, with nocturnal gatherings,
strange behaviour concerning babies, extravagant attitudes towards

marriage, sexuality and nudity, and of course their rejection of traditional Christian beliefs in saints, miracles and rituals. Clearly they had the idea that these heretics, and the Spiritualists – who rejected biblicism – were diabolically inspired. The president of the court of Friesland labelled them, unsurprisingly, as an 'evil race'.[172] Even centuries later, demonologists included religious revolutionaries like Thomas Müntzer (1489–1525) in their first chapter, usually dealing with the *discernment of spirits*, as in the demonology of the Swiss Calvinist Bartholomäus Anhorn.[173]

4

The European Age of Witch-Hunting

The causes of superstition are: . . . lastly, barbarous times, especially joined with calamities and disasters.

Francis Bacon, 'Of Superstition'

After 1560 the large witch trial became the new style of witch-hunting. The first major persecution in Europe is recorded in a printed pamphlet of 1563, the *True and Horrifying Deeds of 63 Witches*, who were caught, tried, convicted and burned in the tiny imperial lordship of Wiesensteig in south-western Germany, a territory of barely 5,000 inhabitants, some villages and two market towns, subject to the Lutheran Count Ulrich XVII von Helfenstein (1524–70, r. 1548–70).[1] This persecution of Wiesensteig was not 'an isolated event',[2] but quite the opposite: a visible sign of a *paradigm shift*. The *Episcopi* tradition was replaced by the *Malleus* point of view.[3] From the early 1560s witchcraft almost immediately gained new actuality from Lutheran Norway to Catholic Sicily. A witch-hunt started in the kingdom of France, in the northern Pyrenees, and the Parlement of Toulouse had to judge at least three dozen cases. Well-connected contemporaries like the Dutch-born Jesuit provincial for upper Germany and Austria, Petrus Canisius (1521–97), the main organizer of the Counter-Reformation in Germany, stated that witches were now burned almost everywhere, and never before had so many of them existed. Canisius fuelled the craze through sermons on witchcraft, as cathedral preacher in Augsburg, and through sensational exorcisms in noble families – to the dismay of his superior in Rome, Diego Laínez (1512–65), the second general of the Jesuit Order.

Plate 6   *The Witches' Dance*. Reprint from a trial in the Swiss
canton of Berne, 28 August 1568. Coloured painting from the
collection of Johann Jacob Wick

But why such a sudden change of mind, why such a large number
of *pogroms*? Researchers have traditionally pointed to a rising
acceptance of the *Witches' Hammer*, and the hardening of the confessional boundaries after the impact of Calvinism, the 'Second
Reformation' and, simultaneously, post-Tridentine Catholicism. Furthermore the process of state-formation or nation-building was
speeding up, allowing for a tighter grip on the religious or superstitious beliefs of the subjects, and state-formation and confessionalism
were intertwined in the process of *confessionalization*. In criminal
procedure, too, the introduction of inquisitorial law was emphasized
as one of the most important results of the reception of Roman law.
From then on, a public prosecutor would ex officio act on behalf of
the state, with torture as a legal instrument to obtain information or
confessions from the suspects. This was particularly dangerous in con-
junction with the idea of a witches' sabbat because suspects were
asked to name their accomplices.

If we take into account the divergent regional pre-conditions, all
these theories can hardly explain the synchronicity of the persecutory zeal. Even in countries where the Roman law was not applied,
traces of the new development can be found, as in Elizabethan
England, where a new Witchcraft Act was promulgated in 1563, the

first permanent legislation on the subject.[4] Although historians have not yet discovered related trials, it should be taken for granted that these laws were not enacted without reason. On the Channel Islands, the first death penalties do indeed correspond. Executions began by order of the royal court on Jersey in 1562, then on Guernsey in 1563.[5] The English witchcraft bill of 1563 fits neatly into the general picture of a rising vigilance concerning witchcraft. In Scotland legislation was introduced in the same year, caused by a considerable number of accusations.[6] The Conseil of Luxembourg promulgated an *ordonnance* (13 August 1563) in order to limit ongoing prosecutions in this part of the Spanish Netherlands. Church ordinances increasingly dealt with sorcery and witchcraft, as in the Lutheran duchy of Württemberg in 1567, in reaction to the ravaging persecutions from about 1562 onwards. But what exactly were these attempts to redefine the crime of witchcraft aiming at? Given the absence of sources regarding the British cases, combined with a lack of sources for the first full-scale persecution at Wiesensteig, the recent finding of the records of a trial for compensation before the Imperial Chamber Court (Reichskammergericht) may help to fill the gap. After an unsuccessful appeal to Emperor Maximilian II (1527–76, r. 1564–76) at the imperial diet in Augsburg 1566, the pub owner Anna Rentzin of Obereichheim, a village north of the imperial city of Kempten, with her husband and her two sons (citizens of the imperial city of Speyer), took Count Hans von Rechberg to court. The charge concerned his illegal witch trials, which had caused the death of Rentzin's seventy-year-old mother Anna Stirnerin (1493–1563), while her own health, reputation and property had been damaged when she herself faced trial in the years 1564 to 1566. The plaintiff was asking for considerable compensation for the pain and suffering caused – some 4,000 guilders, together with restoration of her previous rights. The Imperial Chamber Court, the highest court of the Holy Roman Empire, was famous for its fair but extremely slow trials, and the said litigation was not settled until 1603, after more than forty years, by which time both parties, their children and their lawyers had already died. Nevertheless, both parties were asked to tell their stories, and to retell them again and again, fortified by scores of witnesses, thus offering precious insights into the mechanism of an otherwise unknown witch panic in the tiny lordship of Illereichen, subject to the counts of Rechberg, just 50 kilometres from Wiesensteig.[7]

In short, we can see what the rural population was concerned about, and how the populace and the authorities reacted. Quite explicitly the peasants were upset about the damage to their fields and their cattle during the summer of 1562. An unwanted combination of rain, flooding and mortality of livestock led to the conviction that this accumulation of misfortune was *unnatural*. Therefore the peasants looked for culprits, and witchcraft seemed an adequate explanation to them. The lord and high judge of the territory did not at first act accordingly, which is not surprising, since witch trials were not yet common. Given his lack of experience, Count Hans von Rechberg was reluctant to step forward in such a dangerous matter. The peasants, however, gathered in the village to hold a protest demonstration, marching straight to the castle and strongly demanding action, playing upon the feudal promise of protection. Although we can assume that not all of the villagers were of one mind, and a small pressure group acted as the driving force, in the eyes of their lord they must have appeared an unstructured crowd. The villagers' actions were potentially frightening in a region where a largely un-intimidated population was always ready for action, and where many castles and monasteries had been destroyed during the great Peasants' War of 1525, just one generation before. Clearly theirs was again an initiative 'from below': no external driving forces are visible, and we do not hear of any clergy involved at all, although we may assume that the villagers heard their sermons in church.

Nevertheless, no one, neither suspects nor lawyers, nor witnesses, blamed the parish priest. Pressed by his peasants, the lord sought advice, and it is significant that he did not consult theologians or lawyers, nor did he seek the opinion of a law faculty, as he should have done according to the *Carolina*. Learned demonology, religious denomination and Roman law did not play much of a role in the first major witch-hunts. Instead, the lord consulted neighbouring lords and eventually hired an experienced witch-finder. As in so many sixteenth-century trials, the witch-finder was not just a cunning man, but an executioner, experienced in the trying and torturing of witches. These specialists used a range of magical techniques themselves, and theologically and legally bore much more of a resemblance to a learned magician than the suspected witches did. A number of experienced executioners had lived in the surrounding regions ever since the days of the papal inquisitor Kramer. At that time a first generation had learnt *the art of trying witches*, using certain Catholic sacramentals (holy water, holy salt and so on), taking guidance from the papal inquisitor, as well as employing other ingredients from the stock of popular customs, like the use of fire, shaving, pricking, ducking or telling the suspect's nature from the colour of her eyes. The executioners, in short, served as witch-doctors. 'Reading the signs' was as much a popular as a learned exercise, and the executioners were thus not far removed from Theophrastus Bombastus von Hohenheim, called Paracelsus (1493–1541), who claimed to have learnt techniques from them. Paracelsus had adopted a Neoplatonic superstructure of a sympathetic universe with its interdependence of macrocosm and microcosm in order to justify his medical theory of *signs* (*signaturenlehre*). But in practice there were puzzling similarities to the popular imagination, and Paracelsus certainly did not doubt the existence of witchcraft, although he avoided the suggestion of a demonic interpretation.[8]

The sources are not completely clear about the reasons or methods used that led to accusations of witchcraft being attributed to either Anna Stirnerin or Anna Rentzin, because this seemed unimportant in their litigation against the count of Rechberg. Both had been denounced by other women who had already been burned as witches. Landladies were often suspected of witchcraft, much more frequently than midwives. Pub owners were privileged outsiders within a peasant society, and the women dealt with food and were therefore a potential source of poisoning. They were relatively wealthy, well-connected beyond the village, and influential. Rather than anger at refused charity, envy, or a desire for revenge, the calculation that these influential families might be capable of stopping the persecution may have played a role for convicted witches. Whatever the intention, targeting the innkeepers made sense to them. It was the executioner who decided that Anna Stirnerin and Anna Rentzin were the ringleaders of the local witches, and it is striking to see the feudal lord and high judge of this territory completely dependent upon the actions of such an – according to the contemporary perception – infamous person. In fact, the count served as a witness during the interrogations, including the extensive procedures of torturing – torture so far beyond any existing law that the count's heirs finally lost their case. As the plaintiff rightly claimed, Anna Rentzin had been caught and tortured 'without the existence of any legitimate reason'. The *Carolina* did not acknowledge denunciations or rumours in themselves, nor did the imperial law allow for torture on such a ground. The repeated and unlimited torture Anna Rentzin and her mother were made to suffer was illegal.

Given the circumstances of the persecutions of the early 1560s, it will be difficult to prove that in these years, and in the afflicted tiny rural lordships like Wiesensteig and Illereichen, the transition from feudalism to capitalism, state-formation, the introduction of Roman law, the Reformation, religious strife, the acculturation of the peasantry, modernization or misogyny played any major role. Certainly there were social tensions in the villages, and presumably the usual amount of misogyny, but what the people were really concerned about, and the reason why they were looking for scapegoats, was the damage to their health and property – an 'unnatural' degree of hardship. Here the social historian has to ask whether this was merely a matter of interpretation, or perception, or whether evidence of rising hardship can be verified in the sources, not only locally, but in larger regions, even Europe-wide. One of the possible explanations for the rising attention to witchcraft is a phenomenon only recently acknowledged: the climatic deterioration labelled by glaciologists and geographers as the *Little Ice Age*.[9] Historians of climate are increasingly in agreement that a period of relative cooling occurred, roughly speaking, between the Medieval Warm Period, when the Vikings were able to settle in Greenland and Newfoundland, and the present period of warming in the Northern hemisphere, now labelled the Modern Warm Period. This cooling afflicted a society on the edge of subsistence. Climate-induced crop failures led to sharp price rises for wine and bread, because grapevines and wheat as plants of Mediterranean origin are affected by cold and damp. The weather therefore became a subject of concern, and one could argue that the scapegoat reactions changed accordingly.[10]

Throughout Europe, however, witchcraft was traditionally associated with weather-making – the creation of thunderstorms, rain, hail, snow or frost. Being described as infertile, the witches were thought to induce infertility in their enemies or their neighbours. The emergence of the new crime of witchcraft was related to climatic deterioration from the very beginning, if we remember that the high Alpine valleys of the western Alps, where the new crime was first discovered in the 1420s, are particularly vulnerable to cooling. The periods of frost and snowfall were extending, the glaciers growing, periods of vegetation shrank, grain harvests were endangered, and with them a peasant's 'daily bread'. Around 1400, grain-growing was abandoned in a number of Alpine valleys, and replaced by cattle farming, driving the cattle up to the mountain pastures in spring, then taking them back to the valleys in late summer. Historians of climate have been able to single out a number of particularly unfavourable decades in the course of the fifteenth century, for instance the 1430s or the 1480s. The core phase of the Little Ice Age, however, is thought to have started in the early 1560s, after several generations of more favourable climate.[11] The long, cold winter of 1560/61 was followed by frosts throughout the spring that damaged the grapevines, then an extremely dry, hot summer, with plenty of hailstorms, that damaged the grain harvest. The summer of 1562 was marked by heavy rains, and a number of extremely long, stormy periods in all seasons damaged the crops and caused floods, leading to cattle diseases. The winter of 1562/63 was another extreme winter, with massive snowfall, a freezing of the Alpine lakes, and plenty of heavy winter storms that sometimes lasted for several days. Spring, summer and autumn were unfavourable again, wet and cold, and the year of 1564 started with severe frost, like the subsequent winter of 1564/65, when the great lakes froze again. People died from hunger, and there are even reports of wolves entering some villages. It was these Little Ice Age events that were perceived as being 'unnatural', prompting people to suspect witchcraft.[12]

Weyer wrote in one of the later editions of his work: 'In this way it came to pass, not so very long ago, a poor old woman was driven by torture to confess – as she was just about to be offered to Vulcan's flames – that she had caused the incredible severity of the previous winter [1565], and the extreme cold, and the lasting ice.'[13] Being well aware of weather as a central issue, Weyer interfered with a debate about the causes of weather, prompted by a particularly severe hailstorm on 3 August 1562.[14] The preacher of the imperial city of Esslingen, Thomas Kirchmeyer (1500–63), called Naogeorgus, a former Dominican who had become a maverick Protestant superintendent, ascribed the thunderstorm to the weather magic of local witches, and demanded persecution according to the pattern of neighbouring Wiesensteig. However, these dangerous sermons were immediately opposed by two leaders of the Lutheran orthodoxy in the duchy of Württemberg, Matthäus Alber (1495–1570) and Wilhelm Bidembach (1538–72), both stationed in the capital Stuttgart. Due to the importance of the subject, their *Sermons on Hail and Witches* were printed within weeks, and were reprinted frequently during subsequent decades.[15] Alber and Bidembach criticized the excitement about witchcraft, with its general atmosphere of aggression, and completely denied the possibility of weather magic. They followed in the footsteps of the Württemberg reformer Johannes Brenz (1499–1570), who had argued that God alone was capable of influencing the course of nature and had emphasized the providential purposes and values of misfortune. Brenz's *Sermon on Hail and Thunderstorm* was flawed by the conclusion that witches should be persecuted despite their incapacity to harm, because of their evil intention.[16] This was pointed out by Weyer, who attacked the famous reformer of Württemberg publicly and vigorously for his lack of logic. If the witches were incapable of weather-making, their trials were not only inhumane but also illegal, since, according to law, death penalties could only be imposed in cases of maleficient magic, not for mere fantasies.[17]

Weyer succeeded in fundamentally altering the terms of the discourse on witchcraft by claiming that the suspected witches, if they admitted performing harmful magic, were not to be considered evil, but insane, and therefore not only physically but mentally incapable of bearing any legal responsibility for their supposed deeds.[18] In his ground-breaking *De Praestigiis Daemonum* (*On the Deceits of the Demons*), Weyer explained that witchcraft was an impossible crime, summarizing every argument he could gather from juridical, theological or medical authorities, as well as from the ancient philosophers, and finally from experience and experiment. Weyer concluded that the women accused of witchcraft were not guilty, that they must therefore not be burned to death, and, finally, that burning witches was an enormous crime in itself. Those who participated in such activities, lawyers and authorities included, were nothing but murderers. In his dedication to Emperor Maximilian II, famous for his disapproval of religious atrocities, Weyer called the witch burnings quite unmistakably a 'massacre of the innocents'.[19] Weyer's publication signified the paradigm shift on the side of the opponents of witch-craft persecution, and again was not 'an isolated event',[20] but a successful strategy of defence put forward exactly when a new strategy was required (see chapter 5).

Weyer's bold attack, however successful, could not stop the beginning of a new era of witch-hunts. Even in regions without major persecutions, recent research has uncovered a rising tide of magical crimes from serial sources such as decisions of law faculties, court records or expense registers. In Southern European Inquisition records, the various crimes of magic (harmful magic, love magic, divination and so on) replaced heresies in prominence. In Naples they dominate from about 1570, in Venice from 1585 and in Friuli from 1595.[21] In Siena they made up 34 per cent of the 1,725 cases between 1580 and 1640, and at the beginning of the eighteenth century the share went up to 42 per cent, whereas classical heresies had slumped to only 16 per cent. Altogether there were 761 cases of magic and related crimes (*magia, maleficio, stregoneria diabolica, negromanzia*) tried between 1580 and 1721, with a sharp rise at the end of the sixteenth century and a peak shortly after 1600, followed by only sixty-five cases being tried over a five-year period, then another peak at the beginning of the eighteenth century. Reducing the sample to witchcraft alone (*maleficium* and *stregoneria*), there are merely five cases after 1669, but the majority of the 166 cases cluster neatly between 1580 and 1630, just as in Central Europe. Only four cases referred to cumulative witchcraft (*stregoneria diabolica*), while the rest concerned *maleficium*.[22]

In Central Europe the hunger crisis of 1570 served as a milestone on the way to action. In several Swiss cantons, as well as in the Alsace, the Champagne or the prince-bishopric of Osnabrück, extensive – and previously unknown – systematic witch-hunts began. In the single district of Thann about 150 witches were burned between 1571 and 1630, while an overall estimate for the Alsace runs as high as 800,[23] distributed over a confusing mosaic of both Catholic and Protestant ecclesiastical and secular territories, and ten imperial cities, until 1680 mainly German-speaking. Again, some governments tried to place witch trials on a firm legal basis, for instance the Spanish Netherlands in 1570, and, in 1573, electoral Saxony, where the number of accusations had also sharply risen.[24]

New demonologies blossomed in all religious camps, partly in reaction to Weyer's attack, but partly resulting from the necessity to reshape the old teachings of the *Witches' Hammer* for Protestant purposes. This endeavour started from within the reformed camp. As the correspondence between the Swiss Reformers demonstrates, witch panics were widespread from Geneva to Zurich, and Zwingli's successor Heinrich Bullinger (1504–75) felt obliged to publish the first Reformed demonological advice.[25] Calvin's successor in Geneva,

Lambert Daneau (1530–96), followed one year later. His dialogue *Les Sorciers* reflected the resumption of massive witch-hunts in the duchy of Savoy – where eighty people were burned in a single town in one year – as well as those in Paris earlier in 1572, or in Protestant western Switzerland, and was immediately translated into English.[26] Also the famous French lawyer Jean Bodin, usually referred to as the author of a reasoned publication on political theory, drew on the persecutions of the 1570s. His *Démonomanie des Sorciers* was one of the most shocking publications of the period, even approving of the witch trials at Ribemont in 1576,[27] which had been condemned by the Parlement of Normandy for their unlawfulness.

Around 1580 reports about witch-hunting no longer referred to individual cases, or a single persecution, but rather offered a panorama of persecutions. For instance, a printed pamphlet, *Two Newspapers, what kind of witches were burned*, reported burnings across the whole of south-western Germany and the Alsace, in many different places, adding up to 114 executions. The witches had mainly confessed to having caused damage to cash crops like grain and grapevines by hail and thunderstorms, as well as the laming and killing of children. The devil had summoned a *landtag* (parliament) at a mountain castle near Colmar, and about 500 witches had travelled there, flying on cats or calves.[28] Johann Fischart, a lawyer at Strasbourg, who translated Bodin's *Démonomanie* into German the same year, added the idea that the witches regularly met at an even bigger meeting, a *reichstag* (imperial diet). In 1582 a similar news-sheet reported the devastating storms in August that had destroyed grain and grapevines, and the subsequent burnings: in the Landgraviate of Hessen, where ten women were burned; a small village in the Breisgau, where thirty-eight women were burned; the small town Türkheim in the Alsace, where forty-two women and a male ringleader were burned; and Montbeliard, where forty-four women and three men were convicted of weather-making and executed on 24 October. The sheer number of these burnings suggests a new quality of persecution.[29]

A number of European countries experienced the climax of their witch-hunting in the 1580s. In the papal lands around Avignon, subject to the Roman Inquisition, a persecution took place between 1582 and 1584, resulting in at least fifteen executions.[30] According to court records in England, such as the Essex assizes, the number of indictments peaked in the mid-1580s, during the reign of Elizabeth I. Between 1560 and 1680 an average of about 5 per cent of the criminal proceedings at the assizes concerned witchcraft, but in the decade of 1580–9 they constituted as much as 13 per cent in the county of Essex.[31] Not by coincidence, a Puritan divine resident in Essex contributed England's first demonology at this point.[32] In the kingdom of France the greatest number of legal burnings seems to have happened in 1587, during the reign of Henry III (1551–89, r. 1574–89), when the crisis of society approached its peak.[33] More death sentences for witchcraft were appealed to the Parlement in the 1580s than in any decade before or after. The procureur générale, Jacques de la Guelle, was puzzled by the persecutory zeal of the populace and the enormous pressure they tried to put on local judges: 'There is a madness in the province of Champagne, they think nearly everyone is a witch.' The Parlement agreed to only twenty-six out of the 109 proposed death penalties. However, a coup d'état of the Catholic party limited the capacity of the Parlement de Paris to interfere with the decisions of the lower courts.[34] It may appear that it ultimately made sense for the Catholic League to celebrate its triumph with some additional bonfires, which conceded relief to their supporters in the rural hinterlands, although this also curbed the hopes of their high-flying supporters. But even if it makes sense to correlate religious warfare with witch-hunting, and the attempt to rid a society of witches with religious zeal,[35] it would be a mistake to overemphasize the confessional aspect, because similar aspirations existed in all denominations.

Compared to population numbers, the Western European persecutions were virtually dwarfed by the developments in Switzerland. Whereas earlier publications played down the Swiss witch trials as 'clusters of small panics',[36] Peter Kamber has managed to prove from the sources that in the Calvinist Pays de Vaud, subject to the Reformed Swiss canton of Berne, no less than 970 individuals were burned for witchcraft between 1581 and 1620, scattered across ninety-one local jurisdictions. As in other parts of Europe, the Bernese trials had gained pace in the 1560s, and did not stop after 1620. It is quite likely that more than 1,200 people were sentenced to death in the Pays de Vaud in more than 2,000 trials, the Bernese government being responsible for one of the most extensive witch-hunts of Protestant Europe. The government explained in a decree that the peasantry was 'driven by poverty, despair ... envy, hatred, spirit of revenge'.[37] During the 1580s the number of witch trials rose even in remote parts of Christendom, such as the Baltics in the north-east, or Hungary at the border of the Ottoman Empire. The nature of these trials differed greatly among the countries involved: a Spanish Inquisition court, with judges trained in both ecclesiastical and secular law, and responsible to the Supreme Council in Madrid; an independent village court in Alpine Switzerland, where peasant jurymen decided; a town court in the Baltics, where civic bourgeois councillors acted on behalf of the urban government; a magnate's court in Hungary; French Parlements, which did their best to follow the rules of ancient Roman law; a Royal Commission in Scotland, consisting of local clergy and landholders, entangled in local politics; or an assize court in England, where educated lawyers, travelling through the six 'circuits' twice a year, decided independently from local pressure, only responsible to the central government.[38] However, all of these countries had to struggle with a rising tide of trials for magic, sorcery or witchcraft, independent of their political, legal, social or religious structure.

As far as Catholic countries were concerned, the prosecutions reached a hitherto unknown level in the late 1580s, with extensive burnings stretching from Catholic southern and western Germany over the duchies of Lorraine and Luxembourg, and from northern France into the Spanish Netherlands. A contemporary local chronicler gives a striking account of the witch-hunt during the reign of Archbishop Johann VII von Schönenberg (r. 1581–98) in his *Gesta Treverorum*:

> Hardly any of the archbishops had ever had to rule his diocese under conditions of such great hardship, such annoyance and such terrible poverty as Johann [. . .]. During the entire period of his government he suffered with his subjects from a lack of cereals, hardships of climate, and crop failure. Only two out of nineteen years proved to be fertile, and these were 1584 and 1590 [. . .]. Because of the common belief that these many years of infertility were caused by witches, driven by devilish hatred, the entire people rose for the purpose of their eradication.[39]

Clearly this account describes a persecution launched 'from below', and the unprecedented vigour of persecution requires explanation. Unsurprisingly, it was from the prince-bishopric of Trier that the first new Catholic demonology arose, the *Tractatus de Confessionibus Maleficorum et Sagarum*, published by one of the driving ideologues of the persecution, the suffragan bishop Peter Binsfeld (1545–98).[40] Two independent contemporary translations into the vernacular demonstrate the demand for such an explanation.[41] Binsfeld's was the first fully-fledged demonology since the days of the *Malleus* a hundred years earlier. The title woodcut, produced by an able carver, who preferred to remain anonymous, illustrates the vicious circle of the witches' crimes: malicious weather magic requires a pact with the demon, which enables them to fly to the sabbat, where they have sexual intercourse and worship their master, in order to receive their power for further horrible crimes. As in Africa, the preparation of the most powerful potions requires the most horrible ingredients: snakes, vermin and babies (plate 7).

As a Catholic, Binsfeld could refer to the *Witches' Hammer*, but nevertheless he managed to reshape the ideology of witch-hunting, leaving behind some of the monstrosities of his Dominican predecessor, such as the lustful fantasies about sexual relations between demons and women. Furthermore he dismissed some common superstitious practices, like the ordeal of the swimming test, or the referral to diviners, witch-doctors or executioners as specialists for

TRACTAT

Von Bekanntnuß der Zauberer vnd Hexen. Ob vnd wie viel denselben zu glauben.

Anfängklich durch den Hochwürdigen Herrn
Petrum Binsfeldium, Trierischen Suffraganten/ vnd
der H. Schrifft Doctorn/ kurtz vnd summarischer
Weiß in Latein beschrieben.

Jetzt aber der Warheit zu stewr in vnser Teutsche Sprach
vertiert/durch den Wolgelerten M. Bernhart Vogel/deß löblichen
Stattgerichts in München/Assessorn.

EXOD. XXII. CAP.
Die Zauberer solt du nicht leben lassen.

Gedruckt zu München bey Adam Berg.
ANNO DOMINI M. D. XCI.
Mit Röm:Bay:Mayt.Freyheit/ nit nachzudrucken.

Plate 7 *The Heresy of Witchcraft*. Title woodcut/frontispiece, Peter
Binsfeld, *Tractat*, Munich, 1591

recognizing witches by their eyes or other witches' marks, and certainly he outlawed the pricking test. In this sense Binsfeld curbed popular transgressions of both secular and ecclesiastical law, which were common from Russia to England (and are still in use in some African countries at the beginning of the twenty-first century). However, he replaced these transgressions with monstrosities of his own, denying the suspects their right of defence, and allowing for repeated and unlimited torture. Pushing aside more than 100 years of legal development, Binsfeld argued that witchcraft was an extraordinary crime, requiring extraordinary treatment. This meant in practice that the precautions of the imperial law should be ignored, and the ordinary legal process be replaced by an extraordinary one, the *processus extraordinarius*. This recommendation that judges break the law was to have far-reaching consequences over the next two generations, as had already been proved in the case of the prince-electorate. The author used the examples of a persecution he had led himself, drawing from the confessions in the trial records, that is, working from experience, a method usually ascribed to the new scientists following the advice of Galileo and Bacon. As a consequence the treatise doubled in size within a few years, becoming a 'work in progress'.[42]

The atmosphere in the bishop's capital was gloomy in the 1580s, when a long-standing struggle for power was decided in favour of the prince-bishop, and the town had to abandon all hope of gaining the status of an imperial city. The town council's authority was shattered, a princely governor was introduced, and the newly established Jesuit College started to reshape the city's life by means of virtual terror. As professors at the university, and as preachers, Jesuits embarked on Binsfeld's ardent campaign against witchcraft, building upon the widespread concern in the countryside, and exploiting common fears in a period of hardship, not unlike comrades in late twentieth-century sub-Saharan Africa. Students from the Jesuit school and from the university roamed through the streets, spreading rumours of witchcraft, and attacking individual citizens in a charivari-type manner. From September 1585 the Jesuits kept in custody young boys who served as spirit-mediums, claiming that they had attended the witches' sabbat as drummers and were able to recognize witches, thus generating suspicions against citizens of the capital. The Jesuit Fathers used this unique source of information for their local politics, steering accusations as they felt appropriate. Despite attempts by neighbouring Jesuit rectors, for instance in Mainz, to expose these incredible machinations and bring them to the attention of the Jesuit General Claudius Aquaviva, the rector of the Trier College, the English immigrant John Gibbons SJ (1546–89) protected his source of power, backed by his close ally Binsfeld. That the Jesuits were able to steer these persecutions, as Rita Voltmer (b. 1961) suggests, does not mean that they were responsible in the last instance, since the economic and social situation – combined with pressure from the populace, who organized village committees – drove the authorities to action, and, if they failed to comply, lynchings were likely. The witch-hunt of Trier, some formally independent monasteries like the imperial Abbey of St Maximin included, probably accounted for more than 1,000 victims, the largest ever witch-hunt at this time, and provided a shining example to all those Catholic authorities who needed encouragement to begin their own witch-hunts.[43]

Authorities referred to the example of Trier during the next decade, firstly because of the sheer numbers of witches burned, but secondly because this example had demonstrated that not even the noble and rich could feel safe any longer, and justice was enacted more radically than ever before. Starting with Binsfeld, authors repeatedly referred to the case of Dr Dietrich Flade (1534–89), an educated lawyer and wealthy citizen, who had been denounced in the course of the persecution by convicted witches. Previously, a persecution had stopped as soon as high-ranking or rich and politically influential individuals were accused. In Trier the judges had scrutinized the testimonies with particular care, and encouraged other suspects to denounce Flade. The women convicted of witchcraft may have had any number of reasons to do so, because Flade had served as councillor to the prince-bishop, as a law professor and chancellor of the university from 1585, and furthermore held the position of chief-prosecutor in the capital of Trier. In 1587 one of the boys kept by the Jesuits accused Flade not only of participating in the witches' activities, but of serving as a president at the witches' sabbat, and of being responsible for the sickness of the prince-elector. When these rumours spread, and Flade tried to leave the town, the government classified his attempt to flee as circumstantial evidence. Flade was severely tortured until he confessed, and was burned as a witch on 18 September 1589. Historians do not agree whether he was an opponent of the witch persecutions, but it seems clear that his strategy of defence borrowed from Weyer's arguments. Recent researchers have argued that Flade was presented as a defender of the witches by his prosecutors to add further support to his death penalty. His trial records, partly in the municipal library of Trier, and partly in the collections of Cornell University (Ithaca/New York), do not confirm any opposition from Flade's side. Nevertheless, this was a sensational case, and Binsfeld participated in its proceedings, as well as in the trial against Cornelius Loos (1546–95), a priest of Dutch origin who had sharply criticized these witchcraft trials.[44] His case is particularly intriguing, since this educated humanist had been commissioned by Binsfeld to write a refutation of Weyer, presumably because Bodin as a suspected heretic could no longer be considered an authority by Catholic hardliners. By reading *De Praestigiis Daemonum*, however,

Loos became convinced that Weyer was correct, and that witch-hunting was a serious error. Clandestinely, he wrote an inflammatory pamphlet, *About Real and Fictive Magic* (1592), arguing that witch-craft did not exist in reality and was a fictitious crime, but it was real magic to turn the blood of innocent victims into money, another allu-sion to the trial of Flade, whose property had been confiscated by the bishop.[45]

The Trier persecutions were of decisive importance because the previous pattern of witch-hunting broke down. Hitherto most con-victed witches had been female, with a majority of them also being relatively old and poor, thus matching the traditional witch stereo-type. However, Flade, the wealthiest citizen, not only educated and noble but also a princely councillor, came from the other end of the social spectrum. In addition, this persecution swallowed up half a dozen former lord mayors, councillors and even some members of the higher clergy, as well as scores of parish priests. Even members of the aristocracy could no longer feel safe, such as Count Arnold von Manderscheid (?–1614), a canon of the cathedral chapter. These victims were male, rich and powerful. In the popular imagination, perhaps fed by Jesuit sermons, there were good reasons why the wealthy merchants cooperated with the witches, or were part of their conspiracy: if witches were destroying crops by frosts, or hailstorms, the wealthy usurers would earn even more money for their stockpiled grains. The rich were imagined as driving to the witches' sabbat in golden coaches. As in present-day Africa, the witch-hunt at Trier, where the populace managed to target the rich, revealed a remark-able association of wealth with witchcraft. For contemporaries, the Trier persecution demonstrated that witch trials, unlike any other trials, were as dangerous for the elite as for the populace. Some might have found this truth menacing, but for others it may have been more favourable, since accusations of witchcraft could be turned into a powerful weapon, an instrument for social revenge. In the imperial Abbey of St Maximin, one-third of the roughly 400 people executed for witchcraft were male, most of whom held leading positions in their villages. Therefore it made sense that Binsfeld gave up the female stereotype and spoke of confessions of 'male and female witches' (*de confessionibus maleficorum et sagarum*). The carver of the title woodcut preferred to represent the witch as female. But unlike earlier artists he no longer fashioned the witch as poor and marginal, but dressed as a lady, wealthy and powerful. This new type of persecution aimed at the core of contemporary society.

Until the mid-1580s witch trials were still a novelty in many places, but the frequency of reports from certain corners of the continent, like Savoy, Switzerland, Normandy, the Alsace, or Trier, increased. A major persecution started in 1584 in the prince-bishopric of Osna-brück. From 1586 persecutions gained momentum across the politically scattered landscape of the German parts of the Holy Roman Empire, which alerted the book market. In 1586 the Frankfurt publisher Nikolaus Basse (?–1599) reacted to a public demand for information, and commissioned a comprehensive reader about witchcraft and demonology for the book fair, compiled by the prolific writer and Lutheran lawyer Abraham Sawr (1545–93). His *Theatrum de Veneficis* (*Theatre of the Witches*), playing upon the title of the *Theatrum Diabolorum* published in Frankfurt some years earlier, was a summary of Protestant literature on the devil[46] that presented a selection of earlier important demonologies and pamphlets on the subject. It started with Abbot Johannes Trithemius' famous answers to the questions of Emperor Maximilian I,[47] and included Molitor, but focused on Protestant opinion leaders like Daneau and Bullinger, contrasting their traditional viewpoints with some radical followers of Weyer, such as Johann Jacob Wecker (1528–86), Johann Ewich (1525–88) and Herman Witekind (1524–1603), who denied the existence of witchcraft. It could rightly be interpreted as a symbol that another Frankfurt publisher in 1587 printed a piece which was to inspire world literature, the *History of Dr. Johann Faust*, the story of a bold magician who made a devil's pact in order to understand the universe.[48] Given the fact that there were indeed a number of natural philosophers who had used the art of magic in an attempt, we now recognize, to gather experience and knowledge by means of experiments, but perhaps also by invoking spirits, this was an explosive subject. The list of natural magicians comprises celebrities like Agrippa von Nettesheim (1486–1535),[49] Girolamo Cardano (1501–76) from Milan,[50] Giambattista della Porta (1538–1615) from Naples[51] and John Dee (1527–1608), the favourite of Queen Elizabeth I of England.[52] No wonder the Faust story was immediately adapted by the English dramatist Christopher Marlowe (1564–93), whose *Tragical History of Doctor Faustus* was first published in 1592, and fascinated the public for decades.[53]

It would take too long to give a list of all the tiny territories and free cities within the German parts of the Holy Roman Empire that started witch trials in the late 1580s, that were afflicted by small panics, or fell into major persecutions. Such a list would be incomplete, anyway, because there was no central authority providing a comprehensive body of sources for the region. Nevertheless, after one generation of research we are pretty sure that we know at least the more important events, having analysed the court council records of larger territories like the duchies of Bavaria and Württemberg, and of prince-bishoprics like Augsburg or Passau. Furthermore, the extensive criminal records of more important imperial cities like Augsburg, Nuremberg, Ulm, Memmingen or Rothenburg have been studied, and the surviving criminal records of prince-bishoprics like Eichstätt, Bamberg, Würzburg, Trier and Mainz have been reconstructed. In addition, the records of a good number of law faculties, which served as supra-regional high courts according to the Carolina, have been analysed, including for instance Tübingen, Helmstedt, Leipzig, Rostock and Greifswald. At least at some points contemporary publications shed light on the growing wave of persecution. The *Expanded News about Witches*, printed anonymously and concealing the place of publication, reported in the summer of 1590 on dozens of smaller territories engaged in witch-hunting, providing a panorama of weather anomalies, crop failures, and diseases of people and cattle, which were attributed to the devastating activities of the witches.[54] Concern about unusual weather, it is sometimes argued, was a peculiarity of Central Europe. But this could well be mistaken, because major persecutions started in the Spanish Netherlands, where the Conseil of Luxembourg tried to stop the worst excesses by means of a decree on 6 April 1591. However, a decree of King Philip II encouraged witch-hunting anew in September 1592, with no trace of doubt about the witches' abilities to harm and raise storms. Similarly the Scottish trials reacted to weather magic, for one of the suspected ringleaders of the witches claimed to have created the storms that had hampered King James VI's return from Denmark after his marriage to Princess Anne (1574–1619) in August 1589.[55] Presumably without knowledge of the Central European events, one of those responsible for the Scottish witch-hunts reported in the *News from Scotland*.[56]

It may be surprising that the Catholics were slower to embark on the business of witch-hunting after the Reformation. But as soon as they did so, they could build upon the tradition of the persecution of heresy, and could refer to the *Witches' Hammer* without any necessity for whitewash. Already in 1590 Ludovicus a Paramo, who had served as an inquisitor in Sicily, was boasting of the burning of 30,000 witches (*triginta lamiarum milla fuerint concremata*) during the last 150 years (but without indicating where these figures were derived from).[57] Although we shall see that witch-hunting was never obligatory for Catholic authorities, and a number of Catholic countries produced fewer victims than their Protestant neighbours, the most terrible persecutions were conducted by Catholic princes and the leading politicians of the Counter-Reformation. While a comprehensive and comparative study on the duchy of Lorraine is yet to be written, we can already say that during the government of Duke Charles III (1543–1608, r. 1552–1608) by far the largest witch-hunt in Francophone Europe took place. In his *Daemonolatria*, the procureur générale Nicolas Rémy (c.1528–1612) boasted in 1595 of 900 witch burnings over his previous fifteen years of office,[58] which might be an exaggeration. But he carried on to burn witches after this for another ten years, only to be succeeded by his son Claude Rémy (in office 1606–31), who continued the burnings during the reign of Duke Henry II (1564–1624, r. 1608–24). Robin Briggs, the expert on the Lorraine witch trials, has estimated a total of 3,000 trials with 2,000 victims during the whole period in the duchy of Lorraine – a country with roughly 400,000 inhabitants – and the attached prince-bishoprics of Metz, Toul and Verdun, as well as the tiny duchy of Bar.[59] The Lorraine witch-hunts rank among the largest persecutions in European history. Monter casts doubt on Rémy's claim, arguing that he only mentions 125 confessions by name in his book. However, a witch-hunting specialist like Binsfeld names only the case of Flade: following this line of argument, we should imagine that only one person was ever burned in Trier. Monter suggests that about 900 victims can be verified in the sources, and a total of about 1,500 might be likely.[60] Given the neighbourhood of Trier, Luxembourg and the Spanish Netherlands, as well as the religious zeal of the house of Lorraine, it seems more likely that the permanent prosecutions in Lorraine added up to at least 2,000 victims.

In any case, Lorraine served as a mediator between France and the Holy Roman Empire, the dukes being, at least in theory, vassals of the emperor until 1648. It will therefore be necessary to have a closer look at the micro-relations between the leading force of the French Counter-Reformation and Bavaria, the leading force of the Counter-Reformation in the Holy Roman Empire, with its Wittelsbach dukes presiding over another Catholic League, and maintaining close dynastic relations to Lorraine.[61] It would be misleading, however, to consider the duchy of Lorraine as a territory within the imperial universe. Although there was a Germanophone minority in the Baillages d'Allemagne, the majority was French, and so were the clergy, the magistrates, the judges and the legal system. The office of procureur générale was alien to the German legal system. No other dynasty was more heavily involved in French politics than the house of Lorraine. The Guise branch triggered off the French Wars of Religion with the massacre of Vassy in 1562, sponsored the infamous massacre of St Batholomew's Night in 1572, founded the Ligue de Défense de la Sainte Église Catholique, and invaded Paris in May 1588 in order to chase off King Henry IV. In his book on the Godly warriors of sixteenth-century France, Denis Crouzet diagnosed an apocalyptic mood in all levels of society.[62] Processions of 'white penitents' confirmed popular ideas of a witches' conspiracy in the Ardennes and Champagne, and triggered massive (illegal) witch-hunts or lynchings. Religious warfare was responsible for the most terrible cruelties of this period, and witch-hunting was part of the programme, perhaps used to secure popular support.[63]

During recent decades it has become obvious that massive witch-hunts must also have taken place in the Grand Duchy of Luxembourg. Legislation from 1563, 1570 and 1573, and more frequently from 1591 onwards, displays the usual Central and Western European pattern. Recently, it has even been claimed that the persecutions in the Spanish Netherlands during the reign of Philip II (1527–98, r. 1556–98) almost reached the size of those in neighbouring Lorraine, eventually amounting to about 3,000 trials, and apparently around 2,000 victims. As in Trier and Lorraine, it turned out that with so many victims the female stereotype was unsustainable. In all three cases about 20–30 per cent of the executed were male.[64] These massive persecutions inspired another demonology, building upon the expertise of Kramer, Binsfeld and Rémy, but designed more elegantly, and authored by one of the most prolific scholars of the period, the Jesuit Martin Antoine Delrio (1551–1608). Born in Antwerp, the son of a high Spanish-Dutch official, Delrio studied law in Paris, Douai (Spanish Netherlands) and Salamanca (Spain), where he received his doctoral degree in 1574. Delrio gained administrative and political experience through his appointment as procureur générale of Brabant in 1577, thus becoming a colleague of Rémy. Soon after, Delrio was made vice-chancellor and Philip of Spain's chief fiscal officer for the province of Brabant in the years 1578 to 1580.[65] At this stage, for unknown reasons, Delrio abandoned his political career, joined the Jesuit Order, studied theology in Valladolid, Louvain and Mainz, and gained a reputation as a scholar. He was soon to be recognized for his erudition by one of the brightest spirits of the period, the humanist and proponent of neo-Stoicism Justus Lipsius (1547–1606), who praised Delrio as 'the wonder of our time' in a poem. Delrio served from 1591 as teacher in Liège and Louvain, and from 1600 in Graz (Austria) and Salamanca (Spain). His *Six Books of Discussions on Magic* were published in twenty-five editions between 1600 and 1755, and practically replaced the *Witches' Hammer*. It served as a handbook for judges, providing numerous examples from contemporary legal practice, most of them collected during the persecutions in the Spanish Netherlands,[66] with some updates in later editions up to Delrio's death. Delrio's demonology outgrew all earlier products as a kind of demonology of all demonologies, and was also quoted approvingly by Protestants. Even opponents of witch-hunting, such as Robert Filmer (1588–1653), referred to Delrio in order to demonstrate that the demonological assumptions of Puritan divines like William Perkins rested on exactly the same ideas as those of the Jesuit.[67]

As a general rule it can be said that in the background of most demonologies we can find a particular witch-hunt, and it is methodologically necessary to relate the texts to these specific contexts, in order to understand the intention, the argumentation, and the examples chosen and newly provided. Many of the demonologies not mentioned in table 4.1 were linked to smaller panic trials, or waves of persecution, that consisted of small trials, very much like the scores of pamphlets produced between 1560 and 1700. Sharpe has counted no less than 100 for England alone.[68] During his time in Louvain and

Table 4.1 Major European demonologies and their context, 1400–1700

Date	Title	Author	Persecution
1435	*Errores Gazariorum*	Anonymous inquisitor	1428–35 Savoy
1436	*Ut Magorum Errores*	Claude Tholosan	1428–35 Dauphiné
1437	*Formicarius*	Johannes Nider	1390–1435 Switzerland
1486	*Malleus Maleficarum*	Heinrich Kramer	1481–85 Upper Germany
1490	*Lamiarum Opuscula*	Girolamo Visconti	1480–90 Upper Italy
1505	*De la Strie*	Samuel Cassinensis	1480–1505 Milan
1506	*Apologia Dodi*	Vincente Dodo	1480–1505 Milan
1508	*De Strigibus*	Bernard of Como	1480–1505 Como
1520	*De Lamiis*	Gianfrancesco Ponzinibio	1510–20 Milan
1523	*De Strigibus et Lamiis*	Bartolomeo de Spina	1510–20 Milan
1563	*De Praestigiis Daemonum*	Johann Weyer	1562–3 Netherlands
1571	*Von Hexen*	Heinrich Bullinger	1568–71 Switzerland
1572	*Les Sorciers*	Lambert Daneau	1568–72 Savoy
1575	*Admonitio*	Nils Hemmingsen	1570–5 Denmark
1580	*Démonomanie*	Jean Bodin	1570–80 France
1584	*Discovery of Witchcraft*	Reginald Scot	1581–4 Kent
1589	*De Confessionibus*	Peter Binsfeld	1581–9 Kurtrier
1595	*Daemonolatria*	Nicolas Rémy	1580–95 Lorraine
1597	*Daemonologie*	James VI	1590–7 Scotland
1600	*Disquisitiones Magicae*	Martin Delrio	1592–1600 Netherlands
1602	*Discours des Sorciers*	Henry Boguet	1600–2 Franche Comté
1612	*Tableau de l'Inconstance*	Pierre de l'Ancre	1609–11 Labourd
1627	*Malleus Judicum*	Cornelius Pleyer	1626–7 Franconia
1631	*Cautio Criminalis*	Friedrich Spee	1626–30 Kurköln
1634	*Ausführliche Instruction*	Heinrich Schultheis	1626–30 Kurköln
1647	*Discovery of Witches*	Matthew Hopkins	1645–8 England
1648	*Confirmation*	John Stearne	1645–8 England
1689	*Invisible World*	Cotton Mather	1690–2 New England

Liège, Delrio took a particular interest in the trial of Jean de Vaulx (?–1597), a monk of the Benedictine prince-abbey of Stavelot, then under the rule of Ernst of Bavaria (1554–1612), the powerful arch-bishop and prince-elector of Cologne (from 1583), pluralist prince-bishop of Freising, Hildesheim, Münster, and of Liège (from 1581), to whom Delrio dedicated his demonology. The inquiry had started in 1592 after a series of mysterious deaths among the Benedictines, including that of the prior Antonius von Salm (1512–92). The remain-ing monks had suffered from exhaustion, all of which was attributed to either poisoning or witchcraft. The noble monastery was close to collapse, with a number of monks having fled already, and the remain-ing eight brethren sick or mentally disturbed. When the panic began to spread to the town, the new prior Gilles de Harzé incarcerated de Vaulx for supposed witchcraft. Stavelot represents the rare case of a male convent afflicted by a witch craze. Jean de Vaulx turned out to be of fragile temperament, confusing the emotions of the inquisitors by erupting with attacks of contrition, bursting repeatedly into heavy sobbing and crying, which made the clerics doubt whether such a compliant culprit could be executed at all – quite in contrast to Attorney General Jean Molempeter, who simply wished to burn him. The Belgian Benedictine did not only confess what his judges expected, but managed to feed their fantasies with ever more expan-sive amplifications. Delrio's famous description of the witches' sabbat, the most comprehensive account in demonological literature so far, as Julio Caro Baroja had recognized, depended exclusively on the fantasies of de Vaulx, who claimed to have been introduced to the witches' sect as a youth by Dr Flade of Trier, who had presided over the sabbats. Flade, the ringleader of the Trier witches, subse-quently forced de Vaulx to join the Benedictines in Stavelot.[69]

What may sound to us like a bad joke proved to be explosive stuff. Jean de Vaulx, a member of the regional lower nobility, did not just invent powerful stories, but also incriminated more than 200 mem-bers of the regional elite as participants in the witches' sabbat. At dinner they were seated according to their rank in the witches' society, which clearly mirrored their social position.[70] The noble monk was mainly acquainted with the rich and powerful, as he had shown in his imagined participation in the Trier events. Under these cir-cumstances, it turned out that the clerics as well as Delrio's friend Dheure were reluctant to start a major persecution. They were clearly aware of the psychological problems of de Vaulx, but also of the legal, social and political consequences of such an Inquisition. Eventually the Benedictine was degraded, convicted and decapitated, but the subsequent Inquisition into the supposed witches' conspiracy remained hesitant, and thus disappointed those who had expected a more fundamental sweep. Ernst of Bavaria, the prince-abbot, a remnant of pre-Tridentine Catholicism and personally not really interested in religious affairs, forbade further defamations for witch-craft in 1598.[71] Delrio was hardly satisfied with such an outcome, but in his demonology criticized only the lenient form of death penalty, honourable decapitation instead of burning.[72] Like Kramer or Binsfeld, he passed in silence over disappointing results. Witch trials were only worth describing if they were successful, and the examples given were intended to encourage future persecutions, not to promote the discussion of problems and failures. Delrio's recommendations were well in line with those of Binsfeld, whom he seems to have known in person, and whom he quotes repeatedly. The former attor-ney general of the Spanish Netherlands developed the theory of the *processus extraordinarius*, and became the most important proponent of a hard-line position in witch trials in Europe, a major player on the stage of international demonology, and quoted for the next 150 years all over Europe, by Catholics as well as Protestants, for instance in Johann Heinrich Zedler's enlightened *Universal-Lexicon*, as late as 1749.[73]

To assume that Delrio's books on demonology caused the wave of persecutions immediately after 1600, trials that reached from Belgium to Burgundy, would be an exaggeration. Rather it could be said that Delrio had summarized demonological knowledge at just the moment when another period of misery terrified the peoples of Central Europe. If we compare the waves of persecution with the movement of grain prices, and the recent findings of climate history, a striking pattern emerges. Although it will never be possible to link every witch trial to economic or social causes, the large-scale perse-cutions were clearly linked to years of extreme hardship, and in par-ticular the type of misery related to extreme climatic events, the *Little Ice Age type of events*.[74] The Little Ice Age was not a period of con-stant deterioration, but rather a period characterized by an increased frequency of extreme events. The years around 1600, for instance, were extremely cold, with prolonged winters, plenty of snow, an unusual number of nights of frost and an accordingly short vegeta-tion period. These particular events were not just a local, a regional or a European event, but an example of global cooling as a result of volcanic dust in the atmosphere.[75] The winter of 1600/01 saw a tem-perature of 5.5 degrees Celsius below the average in Central Europe, far from the statistical standard deviation. Such conditions caused extreme stress to food stocks, and led to substantial price rises. The year of 1601 was extremely cold throughout, resulting in crop failure, sour wine and hunger in many regions. The next year, in contrast, suf-fered from an unusual abundance of precipitation, storms, flooding and also late frosts, and was altogether equally unfavourable for agri-culture, and for subsistence farming in particular.[76]

Like other waves of persecution, the wave around 1600 was marked by new demonologies and an increasing number of pam-

1) South Scotland
2) East England
3) Denmark
4) Holstein
5) Mecklenburg
6) Pommern-Wolgast
7) Pommern-Stettin
8) Spanish Netherlands
9) Kurköln
10) Luxemburg
11) Kurmainz
12) Nassau
13) Würzburg
14) Bamberg
15) Lorraine
16) Alsace
17) Ellwangen
18) Franche Comté
19) Vaud
20) Vorderösterreich
21) Valais
22) Dauphiné
23) Savoy
24) Milan
25) Hungary

Raimund Zimmermann 2003

Map 1   Hotspots of witch-hunting in Europe, 1400–1800

phlets, not to mention the reprints of earlier demonologies, collections of sermons and related material. After Delrio's massive compendium, however, the new publications added hardly any new ideas
or concepts – the subject was exhausted. However, scores of new
examples were added from hitherto neglected territories, which were
now drawn to the European public's attention. Henry Boguet
(1550–1619), a Burgundian lawyer, Grand Judge of the lands of the
Abbey of St Claude from 1587, reported on his persecutions in the
Franche-Comté. Like Rémy, Boguet boasts of his successes.[77] Monter
considers this to be a shameless exaggeration, because few trials and
executions are mentioned in Boguet's book.[78] Recent research has
demonstrated, however, that there were substantial persecutions in
Burgundy, Boguet's demonology having been published at the beginning rather than at the end of it. The trials reached a first peak
between 1600 and 1614, and a second, particularly fierce witch-hunt

was launched simultaneously with the climax of persecutions in the German prince-bishoprics between 1627 and 1632. Brigitte Rochelandet has collected information on about 800 trials, just over half of which ended in executions, with the death penalties confirmed by the Parlement. The Franche-Comté experienced a third and final wave of persecutions between 1658 and 1661, with hundreds of trials again, and dozens of executions. Like Luxembourg and the area of today's Belgium, the Franche-Comté was under Spanish rule, but the population as well as the legal system, and the lawyers, were French, with the Parlement at Dole as its high court.[79]

By the time of Boguet's demonology, the French Parlements had already grown sceptical about the crime of witchcraft. Nevertheless, his demonology was a bestseller in France, with three different editions (Lyon 1602, 1603, 1610), which were reprinted six times (Paris and Rouen 1603, Lyon 1605, 1607, 1608, 1611). Monter assumes that Boguet feared that his publication might damage his aspirations to a see in the Parlement at Dole, and therefore stopped further reprints.[80] However, it was far beyond the capacity of a provincial judge to prevent printers in France, Switzerland or the Holy Roman Empire from reprinting his booklet, and it seems more likely that Delrio's rising star and more recent and thrilling publication simply replaced him. Francesco Maria Guazzo (?–c.1640) for instance, an Ambrosian monk from Milan, published a *Compendium Maleficarum*, attractively illustrated with woodcuts which have been recycled down to the present day. In contrast to Binsfeld, Rémy and Boguet, he was not directly involved in any persecutions, as far as we know. But, like Delrio, he had a more than impersonal interest in the subject. When he was called to Düsseldorf in order to exorcize the mad Duke Johann Wilhelm of Jülich and Kleve and Berg (1562–1609), Guazzo first diagnosed possession, but after five months of unsuccessful attempts at spiritual healing in the summer of 1604, the diagnosis changed to bewitchment as the cause of the poor duke's mental illness.[81] What makes this encounter so particularly striking is that the exorcist had been sent by Duke Charles III of Lorraine on behalf of his daughter Antoinette (1569–1610), Duke Johann Wilhelm's wife.[82] Guazzo had exorcized some members of the house of Lorraine before, namely the bewitched Cardinal Charles of Lorraine (1567–1607), and Eric de Lorraine, the bishop of Verdun,[83] and took most of his examples from Lorraine's leading lawyer and demonologist, Rémy. It is striking to see all these Lorraine examples turn up again in an Italian demonology with exact names and dates, mostly from the late 1580s and early 1590s. Guazzo also included examples from Binsfeld and Delrio, but few from Italy, mostly from the beginning of the sixteenth century.[84]

Another French lawyer, Pierre de Lancre (1553–1631), a member of the Parlement de Bordeaux, surprised the French public with a massive account of his Inquisition in the French Basque territories. His *Tableau de l'Inconstance des mauvais Anges et Démons*, published in Paris in 1612,[85] was a first attempt at redesigning the subject, followed by a lengthier publication ten years later.[86] De Lancre had been commissioned to investigate a witch panic in this southernmost corner of France in 1609 by King Henry IV, only to become deeply entangled in the business of witch-hunting himself. This is all the more surprising since the Spanish Inquisition had inquired into a similar witch panic in the Spanish Basque territories.[87] As Gustav Henningsen (b. 1934) has noted, the inquisitor in charge, Don Alonso de Salazar Frias, performed such a thorough analysis that it reads like a piece of sociological research, only to come to the conclusion that all the accusations were mere inventions, and that the imprisoned suspects must be released at once (see chapter 5). De Lancre, bursting with classical humanist and theological erudition, concealed the outcome of the Spanish Inquisition, and built upon demonologists like Delrio, concluding that the demons recently driven out of Japan and 'India' (the Americas) had returned to the Labourd, where more witches could be found than in all the rest of Europe. De Lancre does not simply refer to the Labourd as another example of an afflicted territory, as Binsfeld had done with Trier or Boguet with Burgundy, but he attempted to discuss the specific conditions, very much like the missionaries Diego de Landa (1524–79), bishop of Yucatan,[88] and José de Acosta (1540–1600), rector of the Jesuit College in Lima,[89] who had served as ethnographers of their respective American territories, and whom de Lancre quoted. Labourd's soil was barren and the men, therefore, were driven to deep-sea fishing off the coasts of Canada. The women were alone for half of the year, and frequently their marriages collapsed.

Numerous details add up to a lively picture of the Basque culture around 1600, and for de Lancre many of its qualities, like their love of smoking tobacco and dancing, and their manner of dress and hairstyle, made them suspect. Although some details would not fit into the picture, like the Basques' bravery, their sense of honour and their abhorrence of theft, his general conclusion is unfavourable. Their dancing, with their bodies agitated and distorted, resembled a witches' sabbat, where the same tambourines were employed, presumably by the same musicians. Basque women, given the beauty of their hair and the fascinating gleam in their eyes, seemed particularly susceptible to witchcraft. According to de Lancre, 'among this whole population there are few families who are not touched by witchcraft in some way'. The expert drew his examples mainly from his own trials, and those of three other French lawyers and demonologists, Bodin, Rémy and Boguet, adding only a few stories from Delrio, but dismissing completely the accounts of other theologians. As de Lancre admits, the lawyers quoted considered witchcraft to be an

extraordinary crime (*crimen exceptum*), unlike the French Parlements. According to Monter, de Lancre saw about eighty people
executed within three years, until the Parlement de Bordeaux
stopped the trials. This was a major persecution, but no massive
witch-hunt like in the Valais or Lorraine.[90]

At the beginning of the seventeenth century witch burnings
became so frequent in Central Europe that it is impossible to local-
ize exactly the starting point of individual waves of persecution. It is
amazing to see the most prominent princes of the Holy Roman
Empire, the three ecclesiastical prince-electors, ranking high among
the witch-hunters. The archbishop of Mainz was by far the most
powerful ecclesiastical prince north of the Alps, with an archdiocese
stretching from close to Hamburg almost down to Milan, comprising
the bishoprics of Hildesheim, Paderborn, Strasbourg, Worms, Augsburg, Eichstätt, Konstanz and Chur in Switzerland. This bishop of
Mainz was of prime political importance, because his was the first
vote among the seven prince-electors. He crowned the elected king,
or the emperor, and had the right to serve as imperial chancellor, the
most prominent office in the empire, with influence over the imperial administrations in Prague or Vienna. Furthermore, the archbishop
ruled over a territory of his own, the prince-electorate of Mainz (Kurfürstentum Mainz, or Kurmainz), geographically scattered across the
middle of the empire, with a large portion in the Rhineland, another
portion stretching east of Frankfurt in upper Franconia, and a third
patch in Thuringia around the university town Erfurt, where Luther
had received his university education. There were further tiny particles of land elsewhere. Altogether this territory added up to about
8,300 square kilometres, with close to 400,000 inhabitants, and generated around one million gulden of income annually. The prince-
bishops were usually members of the lower regional nobility, and
were elected by the cathedral chapter. The witch craze in Mainz
started under Johann Adam von Bicken (1564–1604, r. 1601–4), a
man of fragile health, whose short reign saw about 650 burnings.
Under his successor Johann Schweikhard von Cronberg (1553–1626,
r. 1604–26), a powerful imperial politician, the persecution slowed
down, but, even so, 361 people were executed as witches. Witch-
hunting speeded up again and climaxed under Archbishop Georg
Friedrich von Greiffenklau (1573–1629, r. 1626–9), when 768 witches
were killed within just four years. All in all about 1,800 people
were legally killed as witches under the rule of these three
prince-bishops.[91]

Nineteenth-century scholars were eager to attribute these persecutions to Counter-Reformation zeal, and Catholicism in general.
Recent research, however, has demonstrated that the attribution of
responsibility is more complicated. The prince-electorate of Mainz
was one of those fragmented territories where state-formation had

Table 4.2 The witch-bishops

Victims	State	Ruling bishop	Persecution
2,000	Electorate Cologne	Ferdinand von Bayern	1624–34
900	Bishopric Würzburg	Philipp Adolf von Ehrenberg	1626–30
768	Electorate Mainz	Georg Friedrich von Greiffenklau	1626–9
650	Electorate Mainz	Johann Adam von Bicken	1602–4
600	Bishopric Bamberg	Johann Georg II Fuchs von Dornheim	1626–30
550	Ellwangen/Eichstätt	Johann Christoph von Westerstetten	1611–30
361	Electorate Mainz	Johann Schweikhard von Cronberg	1616–18
350	Electorate Trier	Johann VII von Schönenberg	1581–99
300	Bishopric Würzburg	Julius Echter von Mespelbrunn	1616–18

failed. There are some obvious reasons for structural weakness: first, there was no continuity in office, since ecclesiastical lands were not hereditary. Second, the bishops had considerable difficulties in introducing reforms, one of their prime tasks as proponents of the Counter-Reformation. However, the cathedral chapters that had elected them were irremovable and frequently pursued their own politics, dominated by interests of the regional nobility rather than a universal Church. Third, in Mainz, as in the prince-electorates of Cologne and Trier, the regional nobility, the towns and even the peasants retained considerable rights of self-government, and they did not suffer from a lack of self-confidence. Taxation was difficult, and legal administration was not directed by the central government, but fragmented among competing jurisdictions. Fourth, and most embarrassingly, there was a conflict between the call for religious reform and the reality. Prince-bishops were temporal as well as spiritual lords, and in theory the process of confessionalization should have been particularly easy. In actual fact, some prince-bishoprics were Catholic only in name, whereas the greater part of the nobility, and a number of towns, like Erfurt, or portions of the citizenry remained Protestant, so that one of the most prominent laws of the Empire, the famous *cuius regio eius religio* (subjects are to follow the belief of their ruler), introduced by the Religious Peace of Augsburg in 1555, could never be put into practice. Until the end of the six-teenth century even members of the cathedral chapters remained Protestant, and some bishops had to accept Protestant councillors because they were unable to find able Catholics among their subjects, and would not risk employing foreigners. As late as 1582, one of the most eminent ecclesiastical princes, Gebhard II Truchsess von Wald-burg (1547–1601, r. 1577–83), archbishop of Cologne, converted to Protestantism, a traumatic experience for the Catholic party. The nobility was split into a lower branch, subject to the princes, and a higher branch, subject only to the emperor, virtually independent, and organized in cantons. Both branches were closely interlinked by marriage and represented a powerful social stratum, particularly in Franconia, Swabia and the Rhineland. Many imperial knights, and many of the lower nobility too, were Protestants, and when the bishops tried to embark on the business of Counter-Reformation they faced considerable resistance.

It was symbolic of their weakness that Balthasar von Dernbach (1548–1606, r. 1570–6 and 1602–6), the prince-abbot of Fulda, an ecclesiastical territory almost as large as the neighbouring prince-bishoprics of Bamberg and Würzburg, failed to reform his territory. To the great displeasure of his subjects, including members of the nobility who constituted the cathedral chapter, this abbot was among the first generation of ecclesiastical princes who tried to introduce the rules of the Council of Trent. Like other reforming princes, he tried to use the reforms for the purpose of disciplining his subjects, as well as for state-formation. According to the Peace of Augsburg, dissenting burghers, clerics and nobles could be driven into exile, and local society could be reshaped by discipline and education, with the Jesuits serving as intellectual cadres supporting monarchical rule. The struggle against concubinage usually served as a means of disciplin-ing the clergy, and the members of the cathedral chapter in particu-lar. The public whipping of concubines, one of the zealous abbot's 'reforms', was however considered to be insulting to the noble canons, as well as to the citizens of Fulda, who had accepted these unofficial 'marriages' of their daughters, which conveniently united various strata of the society. The opposition to the Counter-Reforming abbot was therefore considerable, and it was not merely a Protestant affair, but was also supported by leading Catholic fami-lies, who were slow to accept the new religious zeal. Supported by the bishops of Würzburg, the opposition managed to force the abbot into resignation. However, the abbot managed to regain his territory due to a decision of the Imperial Court Council (Reichshofrat). Back in office, he launched one of the fiercest witch-hunts in the Holy Roman Empire, claiming 276 victims within three years, in a territory with less than 90,000 inhabitants. Only after the abbot's death could the persecution be stopped. Under the new abbot the infamous judge Balthasar Nuss (1545–1618) was imprisoned and – after years of power struggle behind the scenes – eventually executed for his atrocities.[92]

For our purposes, it is rewarding to explore the microstructures of these ecclesiastical territories. The persecution of Fulda has links to three other later large-scale persecutions, that in the lands of the Teutonic knights in Mergentheim 1602–6, and the two in the prince-bishopric of Bamberg in 1616–19 and 1626–30. Among those who had triumphed over the resignation of Prince-Abbot Dernbach in 1576 had been an influential citizen, Hans Haan. After the zealous abbot's return, however, Haan's wife Anna was among the first to be accused of witchcraft. The family's appeal to the Imperial Chamber Court was one of the reasons why Judge Nuss was put on trial, and eventually executed for his severe abuses. Not even during the confessional age were witchcraft persecutions meant to serve as an instrument of political or religious power struggles, or of revenge, and a contemporary report labelled the Fulda persecution as 'unlawful, cruel and tyrannical'.[93] But this was not the end of the story. Recent research has suggested that the chancellor of Bamberg, Dr Georg Haan (1568–1628), was Anna Haan's son. Formerly a councillor in the interim administration of Fulda, he was accepted as a councillor in Bamberg afterwards. Under Johann Philipp von Gebsattel (1555–1609, r. 1599–1609), a pre-Tridentine bishop, who indulged in the Renaissance joys of loving music and women, with at least one concubine and half a dozen children, Haan became vice-chancellor. After Gebsattel's death, Councillor Haan, as the designated successor of Chancellor Dr Karl Vasoldt (?–1611), was charged with the care of the bishop's daughters, whose rights were threatened by the bishop's four sons. But now the Catholic League installed an ardent Reform bishop, Johann Gottfried von Aschhausen (1575–1622, r. 1610–22), already bishop of Würzburg. The new suffragan bishop Friedrich Förner (1568–1630), a theologian akin to the demonologist Binsfeld, began to form new alliances, and immediately lashed out against the witches. A first witch-hunt started in 1612, and Haan must have felt uneasy about that change for more than one reason. He himself was probably the son of a suspected witch, and his wife's mother had been burned as a witch in the territory of the Teutonic knights, at Mergentheim.

Factionalism entered politics as proponents of the Counter-Reformation established their power. Förner found support in the former chancellor's son, Councillor Dr Ernst Vasoldt, who was eager to serve as a witch-commissioner. The conflict came to a peak in 1618. Haan had already indicated that he disliked the new zeal for persecution, and when the Thirty Years' War began to cause financial problems he took the chance to cut back the budget of the persecutors, thus putting an end to the persecution. The hardliners had lost a battle in the struggle for power. This changed again with the election of Bishop Johann Georg II Fuchs von Dornheim (1586–1633, r. 1622–33), another candidate of the Catholic League, whose election had been organized by suffragan Förner. While Haan remained in office, the hardliners began to prepare the ground for takeover more carefully. In 1625 Förner delivered a series of thirty-five sermons on magic and witchcraft, dedicated to the prince-bishop of Eichstätt, Johann Christoph von Westerstetten (1565–1637).[94]

Westerstetten represented the new fundamentalist type of Counter-Reforming ecclesiastical prince, and was known for his persistent witch-hunting. At first he had initiated a permanent persecution in the territory of the prince-abbey of Ellwangen (r. 1603–12), leading to no fewer than seventy-five days of execution (at which groups of four to twelve were burned).[95] Then he added another sixty group burnings in the prince-bishopric of Eichstätt (r. 1612–36). Even if Jonathan Durrant's revisionist figures are accurate, and Westerstetten's reign in the prince-bishopric resulted in 'only' 240 executions in Eichstätt,[96] he would still be responsible for about 550 burnings, once we include the Ellwangen persecutions. In both cases the witch-hunts lasted exactly as long as Westerstetten was in power.[97] Guided by Förner, the most prominent victim of the Bamberg witch-hunts was the leading politician of the territory, the educated and experienced Chancellor Dr Georg Haan, who had served the bishops of Bamberg and the Catholic League for many years. Eventually the whole Haan family was burned at the stake: the chancellor's wife Catharina Haan (1581–1628), their daughter Maria Ursula Haan (1610–28) and their son Dr Georg Adam Haan, who had received his doctorate in law some years earlier and was one of the most promising young jurists of the territory. And the eradication included related families, like the son's wife Ursula Haan, née Neudecker (1602–28), and her father Georg Neudecker (1580–1628), the wealthiest citizen of the prince-bishopric with an estimated property of 100,000 gulden, as well as Neudecker's wife Anna, who died after repeated torture in 1629. It even included their daughters Anna Barbara Neudeckerin, who had tried to flee with her servants but was executed in 1630, and Magdalena Neudeckerin (1585–1630), who was also linked to the circle around Chancellor Haan.[98]

Even in comparison with earlier large-scale witch-hunts there was a new rationale in these persecutions. The grassroots persecutions in Lorraine and Trier worked away for years, or decades, and therefore accumulated large numbers of victims. The new type of persecution, however, was started deliberately, gained momentum within weeks, and led to the burning of hundreds of witches within a few months.

Although even these persecutions were not always started from above, the authorities grasped their chance to gain support from the populace in order to centralize the legal administration. The persecutions were coordinated and performed by a new type of judge, a direct representative of the prince, later to be called a witch-commissioner (*hexenkommissar*). Although this term was not used at the time, the prototype may be seen in the Fulda judge Balthasar Nuss. Whereas the persecutions in Mainz in 1602 were driven by village committees,[99] following the example of Trier from the 1580s, the prince-abbot's friend in Fulda was responsible for the whole territory. He used the chance to bypass the district courts (*zentgerichte*), and even the central government, like an inquisitor, or a French procureur générale – Rémy's role was of course known by his publication. This effective model of persecution was adopted by Prince-Abbot Westerstetten, who appointed two lawyers as commisioners in Ellwangen immediately after he saw the chance to launch a persecution in May 1611. The commissioners developed a standard procedure by minimizing outside interference and by combining torture and denunciations most effectively. Thus they became independent of traditional circumstantial evidence, and created the proverbial witch-hunt, based upon a minimum of evidence and guaranteeing a maximum number of convictions, along with the opportunity to steer the persecution.[100] From Ellwangen this type of witch-hunt was exported to Eichstätt in 1613, and the other Franconian bishoprics (Bamberg, Würzburg) in 1616. In the 1620s there were political struggles in many territories over the question of whether witch-commissioners should be appointed or not. Both sides were clearly aware of the implications. Bavarian politicians managed to dismiss the new model, and to avoid large-scale persecutions. The prince-elector of Cologne, on the other hand, decided to deploy witch-commissioners and managed to claim the largest number of victims ever in the German lands.

Like other waves of persecution, the wave around 1600 was triggered by extreme climatic events, crop failures, famine and diseases, and the same was true for the persecutions around 1611 and between 1616 and 1618.[101] The worst was still to come. The crisis started with an extreme climatic event. The diary of a citizen of Stuttgart reports that on 24 May 1626 a hailstorm dropped about a metre of hailstones. Two days later a bitterly cold northerly wind set in, carrying on for several days throughout Central Europe. Overnight all rivers were frozen, and grapevines, rye and barley destroyed. The trees lost their leaves, which had become black overnight. These polar nights in late spring frightened the people, who interpreted them as signs, as usual during this period of uncertainty, and suspicions were aroused. The chronicler Johann Langhans, lord mayor of the market town of Zeil in Franconia, wrote:

Anno 1626, the 27th of May, the grapevines all over Franconia, in both the Bishoprics Bamberg and Würzburg, were destroyed by frost, as well as the dear corn, which had faded already. In the Deichlein, and in the Aue, in Altach [placenames], as well as everywhere around Zeil, everything was destroyed by the frost, which has never happened in people's memory, and caused substantial price rises [. . .]. Whereupon an intensive pleading and begging started among the common rabble, why the authorities went on tolerating that the sorcerers and witches are damaging even the crops. Therefore his princely highness was alerted to punish such an evil, and therefore the witch persecutions started this year.[102]

The devastating frosts of May 1626 with subsequent crop failure, cattle diseases, price rises and epidemics moulded the persecutions of the subsequent years. As late as 1630 the suspects still had to confess that they had been responsible for these events. According to the confessions, the Franconian witches had discovered how to make the frost. They prepared an unguent from children's fat, flew through the air on the night of 27 May 1626 and dropped the poison on the crops, until everything was frozen.[103]

Very much as in the 1580s, when a series of unfavourable years had caused misery, as the contemporary Trier chronicler had indicated, the populace again demanded witch persecutions in the mid-1620s. Since the climate stayed unfavourable or 'unnatural' – climate historians call 1628 'the year without a summer'[104] – the demand for persecutions persisted. The late 1620s count among the harshest years of the Little Ice Age, and it is no coincidence that they saw the climax of witch-hunting in Europe. The weak prince-bishops complied with popular demands to persecute witches, or took their chance. In 1629 an anonymously published pamphlet reported with a good deal of insider knowledge about the *Six Hundred Witches, Sorcerers, and Black Magicians, who have been burnt by the bishop of Bamberg*, clearly making the link between the extreme climatic events, crop failure and witch-hunting.[105] This report emphasized the male minions of the devil, because the Bamberg witch-hunts were so severe that many lord mayors, councillors, canons and even members of the princely government fell victim to the persecution, all of them wealthy and male, and of a variety of ages. As in the earlier large-scale persecutions of Trier, Ellwangen or Eichstätt, all former stereotypes broke down, and *kinship* became the most important indicator for suspicion. But it would be an exaggeration to suggest that 'witchcraft can be characterized as the dark side of kinship', as suggested by anthropologists.[106] In his secret letter to his daughter Veronica, the lord mayor of Bamberg, Johannes Junius (1573–1628), explained why he had confessed, and was to be executed as a ringleader of the witches. He had been denounced by so many convicted witches that there was no escape, and torture was used so excessively that he had eventually agreed to confess to whatever the judges expected. So he admitted the devil's compact, sex with a *succubus* (devil in the shape of a woman), dancing at the witches' sabbat and adoration of the devil. The witch-commissioners discussed every single street of Bamberg, and Junius had to name fellow-witches, most credibly of course his relatives and friends. Junius and all the members of his family were killed, save Maria Anna Junius, who survived as a Dominican nun, and reported the persecutions in her chronicle, with laconic shortness. Junius' heart-breaking letter reveals the mechanism of large-scale witch persecutions, based upon torture and denunciations. These persecutions were completely different from sorcery trials, or small panic trials, where suspicion was often linked to magical practice.

Bamberg already represented the 'ideal type' of a massive witch-hunt, but was outnumbered in terms of victims by those in the electorate of Mainz (Kurmainz), as mentioned on page 108. And both were surpassed by the prince-bishopric of Würzburg, where about 900 people were burned at the stake during the same five years (1626–31), including some noblemen and a good number of clergy.[107] This came after an earlier persecution of around 1616–18 in the same territory under the famous reforming bishop Julius Echter von Mespelbrunn (1545–1617, r. 1573–1617), the German counterpart of Carlo Borromeo of Milan, when about 300 witches were burned at the end of his long reign. The burnings under Philipp Adolf von Ehrenberg (r. 1623–31) gained a proverbial reputation. 'It will work out like in Würzburg',[108] argued a town councillor about 500 kilometres further north-west, when persecutions started in the electorate of Cologne (Kurköln), and this prophecy was anything but exaggerated. In the duchy of Westphalia, subject to Ferdinand, prince-elector and arch-bishop of Cologne (1577–1650, r. 1612–50), about 2,000 people were burned for witchcraft between 1626 and 1634. Ferdinand was responsible for the most terrible witch-hunt in the German parts of the Holy Roman Empire. Gerhard Schormann argued that this was due to a 'centrally implemented programme of eradication', a *war against the witches*, prepared by earlier legislation against witchcraft of 1607, when Ferdinand had served as coadjutor for his uncle Ernst von Bayern (1554–1612, r. 1583–1612), his predecessor as archbishop and elector of Cologne.[109]

Labelling the prince-elector as a congenial predecessor of the Nazis and their 'War against the Jews'[110] would explain these developments most elegantly, and it seems to fit neatly that Ferdinand had already been educated in Trier during the great witch-hunt of the 1590s. However, evidence for such parallels is surprisingly weak. Ferdinand had already been appointed coadjutor of Cologne in 1594, and during the first twenty years of his rule nothing happened as far as witchcraft persecutions were concerned. Clearly Ferdinand was more interested in religion than his uncle, Ernst von Bayern, bishop of Freising, Hildesheim, Liège, Münster and Cologne. One of the most powerful Catholic rulers in Europe, Prince-Bishop Ernst had replaced his heretical predecessor in the Cologne War as the candidate of the Counter-Reformation party, but was indeed more interested in the worldly pleasures of an aristocratic life: hunting, music, dancing and feasting in the company of women. As mentioned on page 103, Prince-Bishop Ernst had even terminated the witch trials in Stavelot. But obviously he was not the one who prevented his zealous nephew and successor Ferdinand from starting witch trials. Even after 1612 the new ruler saw no reason for launching Inquisitions, not in Cologne or Westphalia, nor in Hildesheim, Liège, Münster or Paderborn, his other sees. Therefore Thomas Becker has rightly challenged Schormann's interpretation. By scrutinizing serial sources – the protocols of the court council in Bonn – he managed to prove that the persecutions had indeed not started 'from above', as suggested by Schormann, and were not at all centrally planned and implemented. At the root of the problem, we can again find the agrarian crisis of the mid-1620s, devastating crop failures and unusual diseases, with an urgent demand 'from below' putting pressure on the numerous noblemen who were in charge of the criminal courts. Even if the central government had intended to launch a witch-hunt, it would have been incapable of doing so, because most of the criminal courts had been pawned to the nobility, and due to a deficient degree of state-formation there was not even an obligatory system of reporting to the court council, as existed in contemporary secular territories, such as Württemberg, the Palatinate or Bavaria, where the court council (Hofrat) tightly controlled the district courts (Landgerichte). In most of the ecclesiastical territories the central authorities were only coincidentally informed of cases, when the owners of the courts were seeking advice, or subjects tried to appeal to the higher court. From such patchy references we are able to reconstruct when and where the persecution started in the electorate of Cologne (not to be confused with the imperial city of Cologne).[111]

Only after the persecution had gained momentum did Prince-Elector Ferdinand try to step to the forefront of the movement. He appointed witch-commissioners in order to gain control, and possibly to win back a number of the pawned criminal courts. However, these appointed commissioners soon got out of control, and started implementing their own policies, terrorizing whole regions and trying to gain money and reputation. They used their arbitrary power extensively and in an anarchical manner, very much like the English witchfinder general Matthew Hopkins during the Civil War. And the Thirty Years' War in Central Europe had indeed created a similarly anarchical environment, with the grip of legal administration loosened to a certain degree. Due to the sheer size of the Cologne witch-hunts, but also due to the fact that the imperial city of Cologne was a university town with a number of independent monasteries and printers, these persecutions resulted in a number of publications both for and against witch-hunting. The most powerful attack on the illegal procedures under the prince-elector's government was published anonymously by the Jesuit Friedrich Spee (1591–1635) in 1631, and we shall refer to his *Cautio Criminalis* later (p. 179). Here it is important to recognize that Spee, then a member of the Jesuit College at Paderborn, had intimate knowledge of the developments in the prince-electorate. And although he formally disguised all names, contemporaries could easily decode the text, and understand the allusions to particular actors and events.[112] The government as well as the commissioners understood the purpose, and tried everything to catch the author, who was, however, protected by his superiors. The most powerful defence of the persecutions was published soon after by one of the princely witch-commissioners, the lawyer Heinrich von Schultheis (c.1580–1646). In his *Detailed Instruction, How to Proceed in Inquisition Cases against the Horrible Crime of Sorcery*, he referred of course to Binsfeld and Delrio as the main authorities, and classed the author of the *Cautio Criminalis* as a patron of the witches, one of those suspects who should – according to Delrio – be treated as harshly as the witches themselves, being even more dangerous than the witches. In his dialogues Schultheis had one of the speakers threaten the author of the *Cautio*, as well as Adam Tanner (see chapter 5), with torture by one of the commissioners.[113]

The prince-electorates of Mainz, Cologne and Trier, the prince-bishoprics of Bamberg, Würzburg, Eichstätt, Fulda, Minden, Osnabrück, Augsburg, Strasbourg, Breslau and Ellwangen, the prince-abbacies of Fulda and Ellwangen, and the lands of the Teutonic Order were ecclesiastical principalities particularly susceptible to witch persecutions. Since this type of territory was a peculiarity of the Holy Roman Empire, their susceptibility contributed considerably to the number of burnings in Central Europe.[114] However, there were plenty of ecclesiastical territories that were less afflicted, and some not at all. It seems worth emphasizing that the majority of the imperial abbacies avoided persecutions. None of the extensive monastic lands, usually associated with the culture of the Baroque, such as the imperial prince-abbacies of Berchtesgaden, Buchau, Corvey, Ettal, Irsee, Kempten, Kornelimünster, Marchthal, Ochsenhausen, Ottobeuren, Prüm, Salem, Schussenried, St Blasien, Ursberg Weingarten, Weissenburg or Zwiefalten, can be connected with any witch-hunt, and our perception has been deceived by a few outrageous cases, like Fulda and Ellwangen, St Maximin or Stavelot. If we look at the prince-bishoprics, we might be tempted to arrive at the

Plate 8   Heinrich Schultheis, Witch-commissioner of the Archbishop of Cologne. Copper engraving, frontispiece of his *Detailed Instruction*, Cologne, 1634

reverse conclusion, because so many of them were engaged in witch-hunting. But even here we find a good number of examples to the contrary: there were only a few trials in the prince-bishoprics of Speyer and Worms, Passau and Regensburg, Brixen and Trent, which were tiny anyway, but equally few in Münster, the largest ecclesiastical territory of the empire, which bordered on the prince-bishopric of Cologne and was indeed ruled by the same prince-bishops, Ernst and Ferdinand of Bavaria. Even in areas where severe witch-hunts took place, they were usually confined to the period between 1580 and 1640. We have already mentioned factors that may have contributed to their susceptibility: structural weakness, the failure of state-formation, the demand for persecutions from below and the hardship caused by climatic deterioration. We can add lack of medical care or social security, and presumably spiritual insecurity due to the competing confessions, as well as the tensions between official and popular religion. Certainly the transport infrastructure was deficient, which was in turn connected to economic misery and underdeveloped institutions. Most of these factors were also true for all monastic territories, so what made the difference?

One of the reasons may have been that the political aspirations of prince-abbots were usually smaller than those of the prince-bishops. Only a few of them, like Fulda or Ellwangen, embarked on the business of state-formation, or *confessionalization*, and attempted a power struggle with their estates, or their subjects, or dared to force them violently into a uniform belief. Quite the opposite, as Marc Forster has demonstrated for some smaller prince-bishoprics, which, like Speyer or Constance, resembled the monasteries in their leniency, and did not aspire to state-formation, did not try to force their subjects into confessionalized Catholicism and did not systematically persecute witches or heretics. There may have been spiritual insecurity as well, but certainly less ideological stress.[115] Furthermore, it seems that the prince-abbots, for reasons of Christian charity or as a strategy for survival in an area where the threats of Protestantism and secularization were imminent from the 1520s, had developed a particular kind of social provision, which helped to alleviate social crises and to provide their subjects, if necessary, with capital for investments. The welfare system of the monasteries assumed a proverbial character among the peasantry during the early modern period in southern Germany (*unter dem Krummstab ist gut leben*). Third, although for various reasons this is not yet well explored, it seems that at least some prince-abbots harboured their own interpretations of the regulations of the Council of Trent. All prince-abbots of Kempten, for instance, had their concubines and children, as the chroniclers in the neighbouring Protestant imperial city of Kempten meticulously and maliciously recorded. The abbots of the wealthy abbacies were usually not religious zealots, and their attitude towards sin, as well as their attitude towards women, may have been more relaxed than those of some Counter-Reformation bishops.

Here we are touching upon another difficult subject, at least for historians: the *psychology of the persecutors*. In many cases we can see that those bishops engaged in witch-hunting shared quite specific personalities. They were the first generation of bishops educated in the spirit of the Counter-Reformation, with a character of fanatical

severity, against themselves as well as others, and this may have contributed to their inclination to radical solutions. The basis of such a
mental hardening was certainly a darkened world view, occasionally
propelled by a chiliastic mood. The perception that they were living
in an exceptional historical situation allowed for exceptional solutions, including the use of violence. One cultural historian has
described the Reforming bishop of Würzburg, Julius Echter von
Mespelbrunn, a key figure of the German Counter-Reformation, in
terms reminiscent of psychoanalysis: 'The whole generation . . . was
dominated by a spirit of extreme austerity, which was directed in part
against religious enemies, in part against opponents in their own
camp, but foremost against their own "I", and everything that could
be perceived as sinful within themselves.'[116] Friedrich Spee interpreted the witch-hunts as 'the disastrous consequence of Germany's
religious zeal'.[117] It seems to fit neatly with this interpretation that the
most terrible witch-hunters of the Holy Roman Empire, at least of
its Germanophone parts, were prince-bishops, or *witch-bishops*
according to a contemporary term coined for Johann Georg II Fuchs
von Dornheim. This witch-hunting bishop of Bamberg was indeed,
like his colleague in Würzburg, a nephew of Julius Echter, who had
sponsored their education and prepared their careers. But witch-
hunting was a matter of education rather than a family affair. We can
see that many of the zealots had been educated in the same institutions, and by the same academic teachers, for instance at the universities of Dillingen (prince-bishopric of Augsburg) and Ingolstadt
(Bavaria), Freiburg (Swabian Austria) or Dole (Burgundy). The
subject of witch-bishops (and their advisers, councillors and confessors) as members of the same age group, in the sense of Karl
Mannheim, moulded by similar key experiences, moods or mentalities,[118] is yet to be explored. Religious fundamentalism was supported
by the contemporary confessional strife, and it is not by coincidence
that the most terrible witch-hunters in Germany were all members
of the Catholic League. Their inclination towards violent solutions,
with the theory of an extraordinary trial (*processus extraordinarius*)
for an exceptional crime (*crimen exceptum*) in the case of witch trials,
climaxed in advance of the Edict of Restitution of 1629, the attempt
by the Catholic party to regain all the territories lost to the Protestants since the Peace of Augsburg in 1555. However, this was not the
official policy of the Catholic Church, and – as Robert Bireley demonstrated – Pope Urban VIII (1568–1644, r. 1623–44) looked with con-
tempt upon the religious zealots in Germany.[119]

In comparison to the conduct of the ecclesiastical principalities, the
development in Bavaria deserves particular attention. The duchy had
gained a position of supremacy among the Catholic estates of the
Holy Roman Empire. The Counter-Reformation ideology served
Duke Albrecht V (r. 1550–79) well in his struggle against a Protes-

tant Fronde in the 1560s. Having defeated the Lutheran nobility and driven out the Protestant citizens, he introduced the regulations of the Council of Trent, imposed religious uniformity and gave the country's university to the Jesuits. Ingolstadt became a breeding ground for Counter-Reformation politicians, and many of the later witch-hunters – almost all of the 'witch-bishops' – were educated there. The business of Catholic renewal had, at least in part, been started for political reasons, but it seems that the duke, as well as his successor Wilhelm V (1550–1622, r. 1579–97), became ideologically involved as well, and underwent conversion experiences. After a severe health and identity crisis in the early 1570s, Wilhelm, later labelled 'the pious', led the life of a ruling saint, visible in symbolic actions like pilgrimages, Corpus Christi Processions and the ritual foot-washing of twelve selected poor by the duke on Maundy Thursday, an act of self-humiliation and a symbol of Christian service. This commitment, however, also implied a new militancy, inspiring not just a renewed persecution of Anabaptists, but also political action against non-Catholic princes, for instance during the Cologne War, when the Bavarian dukes levied troops and kicked out of his office the prince-elector, who had joined Protestantism and thus endangered Catholic supremacy in the Holy Roman Empire. The Cologne War had the side-effect that the prince-electorate was secured for the second-born Bavarian princes (*sekundogenitur*), jointly with a cluster of ecclesiastical principalities, like Münster, Paderborn, Hildesheim and Liège, or the prince-abbacies of Stavelot and Malmedy, all of which were grouped under the label 'Bavarian Bishops' Empire'. Bavaria thus managed to assume the leading role within the Catholic party in the Holy Roman Empire, institutionalized in the Catholic League, which was founded by Duke Maximilian I of Bavaria (1573–1651, r. 1598–1651).

The Catholic League served as stage for the 'witch-bishops', many of whom were actually sponsored by the Bavarian dukes. Their affiliation with witch-hunting apparently deepens when we look at their dynastic policy. Duke Wilhelm was married to Princess Renata of Lorraine (1544–1602) in 1568, and their son Maximilian confirmed the dynastic coalition between Bavaria and Lorraine through his marriage to Princess Elisabeth of Lorraine-Vaudémont (1574–1635), daughter of Charles III of Lorraine, a would-be leader of the French Catholic League. The princesses imported Lorraine servants, courtiers and clerics, who could be sure to meet like-minded theologians in Munich. Duke Maximilian had been educated by the Spanish Jesuit Gregory of Valencia (1551–1603), a leading moral theologian and a firm supporter of witch persecutions,[120] and during his studies at the University of Ingolstadt, Gregory introduced his pupil to the pious enterprise of persecution, spending considerable time at contemporary witch trials. The correspondence between the prince and his father, Duke Wilhelm, contains detailed reports from the torture chambers. It is hardly surprising that Bavaria became part of the first wave of persecutions, which spread eastwards from eastern France in the late 1580s, since Jesuit theologians, like Petrus Canisius (1521–97), Gregory of Valencia (1551–1603) and Jacob Gretser (1562–1625) enthusiastically supported the persecutions. Their attitude seemed so coherent that there was the perception of a uniform Jesuit party, with the dukes of Bavaria firmly under their influence, and that of their Jesuit confessors in particular.[121]

Perhaps unexpectedly, the first wave of persecutions remained confined to just a handful of Bavaria's 100 district courts, and was stopped after a couple of months. The experiment of a large-scale witch-hunt was never repeated, and Bavaria became a stronghold for the opponents of witch-hunting within the Catholic camp. It was Bavarian *politicians* – we remember the derogative usage of the term by Delrio – who stopped the persecutions, dismissed the idea that witchcraft was an extraordinary crime (*crimen exceptum*), and secured the maintenance of a regular legal procedure (*processus ordinarius*) according to the regulations of the imperial law code (see chapter 5). The Bavarian example, as well as the examples of Spain, Portugal and Ireland, demonstrate that witch-hunting was not automatically a Catholic affair, even if some major witch-hunts took place in Catholic lands like Lorraine, the Spanish Netherlands and – not yet mentioned – Austrian territories in Swabia and the Alsace, where another 1,000 witches must have been burned between 1570 and 1630.[122] The latter seems quite striking, as Austria had exerted strict control over the lower courts since the days of the *Witches' Hammer*. The Tyrolean government in Innsbruck never allowed a witch-hunt, and repeatedly punished local magistrates who dared to lash out on their own against suspected magicians.[123] The administration of justice was similar to Bavaria, where the central government decided whether witch trials took place or not. No district court was allowed to use torture without explicit written order from the court council, and the proceedings had to be recorded in written protocols, which were controlled by the government in a steady flow of communication. The western lands of the Habsburgs (*Vorderösterreich*), however, were not directly subject to Innsbruck, but to the regional government in Ensisheim/Alsace, or were virtually independently controlled by district governors in Hagenau, Ortenau and Breisgau. Many courts were pawned to the nobility, to prelates or towns. Although under Habsburg suzerainty, the border region between France and the empire was politically among the most fragmented regions of Europe.[124]

If we compare these observations to *Calvinist Europe* in its widest sense, that is, where either Calvinism, Zwinglianism or Anglicanism had assumed cultural hegemony, we can discover some similarities. On the one hand there are larger countries, wealthy and powerful with established institutions, like England, the Netherlands or the Palatinate, with few trials. Here we can find no large-scale persecutions, with the exception of brief periods of anarchy, such as during the English Civil War. On the other hand there are marginal or fragmented territories, with weak institutions and difficulties in guaranteeing survival in years of hardship. The Calvinist Pays de Vaud in Switzerland, subject to the Calvinist city-state of Berne, saw endemic persecutions between 1580 and 1620, very much like Catholic Lorraine, or Trier. In the Francophone canton of Neuchâtel at least 250 witches were burned between 1580 and 1660. State-formation had failed in a good number of middle-sized Calvinist earldoms, as in Catholic ecclesiastical territories. Schormann has pointed to the various territories of the counts of Nassau, the relatives of Maurice of Nassau-Orange (1567–1625), where 400 witches were burned. In a similar position were the related counts of Isenburg-Büdingen, with another 400 victims,[125] the counts of Schaumburg and of Lippe, with about 300 witch burnings each, and the landgraviate of Hessen-Kassel, a larger territory with more elaborate structures, which had become Calvinist in 1604, but was politically as fragmented as the neighbouring earldoms, which saw a surprising 250 victims.[126] The exception was Scotland, an already consolidated nation-state, although with some characteristic limitations, which suffered from major witch persecutions. As in England and Central Europe, there had been increasing awareness of witchcraft since the early 1560s, and Scotland was shaken by five waves of frenzied witch persecution, or *national witch-hunts* in the terms of Larner[127] – in the 1580s, twice in the 1590s, again in the late 1620s, and once more in the 1660s.

Among the unique pre-conditions of the Scottish witch-hunt are the circumstances of the ruler's life. James VI had decided to marry in 1589, but his meeting with Anne of Denmark was severely disturbed by a number of storms that prevented the princess from sailing to Scotland, and blew her fleet to Norway instead. Their difficulties in travelling to the coronation in Edinburgh were attributed to witchcraft, and a number of witches were burned in the Danish capital of Copenhagen at about the time of the queen's entry into Edinburgh in May 1590. Meanwhile, some Scottish suspects had also confessed to having made the storms. The king himself became involved in the trials, and listened to the interrogations of the peasant women by members of the privy council. In January 1591, Agnes Sampson, the supposed ringleader of the witches, was burned at Edinburgh's Castle Hill. King James VI would later refer to his experiences in his *Daemonologie*.[128] The king's fears of conspiracy may have been reinforced by a real rebellion, championed by his cousin, Francis Stewart

Hepburn, Earl of Bothwell (?–1612), who had to be defeated by means of a military campaign, and who was subsequently accused of being part of the witches' conspiracy, dying in exile.

However, the persecution was not simply the king's private pleasure. The late 1580s were decisive years in the Scottish Reformation, and some more radical Church leaders, who had been forced into exile, returned in 1587 and managed to introduce a regime of tight social discipline. Agnes Sampson was arrested at Haddington, parish of the radical Presbyterian James Carmichael, who explained the meaning of the Scottish persecutions in his pamphlet *News from Scotland*. Carmichael reports how Sampson confessed before king and privy council her attendance at the witches' dance at Halloween, where they adored the devil, and pledged to harm the king. According to her deposition, she had been present during the king's encounter with his bride in Oslo, and again in Copenhagen; she had raised the storms in September 1589, and had tried to poison the monarch.[129] But again, this was not the whole story. As in Central Europe, the populace was extremely interested in witch-hunting. Scotland, and the Highlands in particular, was suffering from extreme climatic events, and the storms that had hampered the king's journeys were representative of the severe hardship suffered by the population. In the late 1580s and the mid-1590s there was a series of extremely unfavourable years. Natural disasters and harvest failures caused widespread poverty, famine, social instability and anxiety. The two waves of persecution in 1590–2 and 1594–7 can easily be connected with these events.[130] Based upon Larner, historians arrived at an estimate of about 1,350 executed witches in Scotland, a country of roughly 900,000 inhabitants in something like 2,300 trials between 1560 and 1700.[131] Larner, however, was more careful, adding that 'in the Highlands, especially those parts outside the Kirk sessions system and within the dominion of the clans there was no witch-hunting, or none that reached the records'. In other words: nobody knows what happened up there.[132]

If we have a look at *Lutheran Europe*, we can discover similarities. Again we find problematic states with rudimentary institutions and many victims. The duchy of Mecklenburg, a territory of roughly 200,000 inhabitants, was divided in the dynastic lines of Mecklenburg-Schwerin, and Mecklenburg-Güstrow, but shared institutions. Economically, Mecklenburg was part of Eastern Europe, with few towns, and large lordships (*gutsherrschaften*), who had pressed the peasantry into a 'second serfdom' since the late Middle Ages. The jurisdiction was fragmented, while the criminal courts were owned by feudal lords (*gutsherren*). Many of their archives are lost, but from legal opinions by universities like Rostock we get an impression of how intensive the prosecution must have been: close to 4,000 witch trials were held between 1560 and 1700. There was an increase in the 1570s, and massive peaks between 1600 and 1630, and again in the 1660s, eventually adding up to at least 2,000 victims, as Katrin Moeller (b. 1967) discovered. The conditions were not too different in the neighbouring duchy of Pomerania, another frequently divided territory, with shared institutions such as the University of Greifswald. The division of 1569 split the country into Pommern-Wolgast (today in Germany) and Pommern-Stettin (today in Poland), and some smaller particles. In Pommern-Wolgast alone there were at least 1,000 trials, and maybe twice as many, with at least 600 victims. No estimates for Pommern-Stettin exist yet, but the conditions were similar. In 1648 the western part of Pomerania became Swedish, while the eastern part was annexed to Brandenburg, but despite all legends about Swedish or Prussian leniency in witch trials nothing changed in either part of Pomerania, as the legal opinions indicate, although Queen Christina of Sweden (1626–89, r. 1632/1644–54) tried to stop the trials by decree in 1649.[133] Equally confusing is the story of the twin-duchies of Schleswig and Holstein, with a number of divisions but again with shared institutions, mostly under Danish rule, Schleswig being under Danish law, while Holstein was a fief of the emperor and subject to imperial law. Despite these political and legal differences, there were no differences in persecution. Both duchies suffered equally from witch trials, altogether at least 846 between 1530 and 1750, with again roughly 600 victims.[134] For the fragmented states in Thuringia, the dozens of Saxon lines and other princes, not to speak of imperial cities, the estimates come to between 1,000–1,500 trials, with at least 500 victims, but distributed over dozens of independent territories.[135] There were more than 100 burnings alone under the dukes of Saxe-Coburg, famous for their dynastic connections all over Europe. Curiously enough, the Protestant clergy tried to stimulate more severe persecutions, pointing to the Franconian prince-bishops as an example, whereas the lawyers referred to Catholic Bavaria in their attempt to restrain the clerical zeal.

There are only vague suggestions about the extent of the persecutions for some major Lutheran territories, such as the electorate of Brandenburg, whose ruler adopted Calvinism privately in 1613, but left the Lutheran orthodoxy intact. A first panic trial is reported from 1530, and persecutions seem to have peaked in the second half of the sixteenth century. The territory's university at Frankfurt/Oder issued about 269 legal opinions in cases of witchcraft.[136] The death toll was surprisingly low in electoral Saxony, despite its harsh legislation, and in the duchy of Saxony, probably due to a tight supervision of the lower courts by the central government, similar to that of the Lutheran duchy of Württemberg in the south. Although Saxony and Württemberg were much more densely populated, the number of victims seems to have remained under 300 in both of these states.[137] If it is correct that 350 witches were killed in Lutheran Norway, and another twenty-two in Iceland, this could mean that the persecution was far more intensive there, but certainly not as intensive as along the southern coast of the Baltic Sea (Holstein, Mecklenburg, Pomerania). The persecution seems to have been less severe in Sweden, Finland and Estonia, but considerable in Denmark. There it had started in the 1540s, and flared up again in the 1570s, leading to the first Danish demonology by Nils Hemmingsen (1513–1600), a Protestant theologian who may have inspired the demonological writings of King James VI of Scotland, whom he met in person during the king's wedding trip to Copenhagen.[138] Although King Frederick II (1534–88, r. 1559–88) tried to limit witch trials by a decree in 1576, making the checking of judgments by the high court compulsory, there are no indications that this law had much effect. The witch-hunt flared up again in 1590, simultaneously with the Scottish witch-hunts, partly in order to explain the mishaps of the royal voyages. After 1600 the trials remained endemic, very much as in the Danish duchy of Schleswig, apparently adding up to about 1,000 victims.[139] The tiny Lutheran territory of Montbeliard, then subject to Württemberg, but Francophone (now in France) and with a considerably more severe persecution, managed to burn 150 witches between 1580 and 1660.

One of the conclusions of recent research is that strong governments in developed secular states tended to establish a legal system that would not allow for irregular witch-hunts. The government of the *Electoral Palatinate* at Heidelberg held a strong grip on the lower courts, which were threatened with immediate punishment for any irregularities. Since the privy councillors in Heidelberg did not believe in witchcraft, much like the members of the law faculty and the medical faculty at the University of Heidelberg, they would not permit witch trials. In 1572 the provincial government at Amberg reported a witch trial in one of the district courts of the Upper Palatinate. The privy council in Heidelberg strictly forbade the use of torture, and ordered the release of the prisoners if there was not sufficient circumstantial evidence – which there rarely was in witchcraft accusations. Although the Palatinate was the most prominent Calvinist territory in the empire, and Prince-Elector Friedrich V (1596–1632, r. 1610–19) stepped to the forefront of international Calvinism with his election as king of Bohemia in 1618, which triggered the Thirty Years' War, it is an interesting question whether the peculiar attitude towards witchcraft had anything to do with Calvinism at all. The electoral Palatinate had not turned to Calvinism until 1563, and even after that there were interim periods when the subjects had to return to Lutheranism, or even to Catholicism.[140] Furthermore, the Calvinist clergy, with Thomas Erastus (1524–83) an eminent member, did not agree with the government's attitude, and – pointing firmly to Geneva – asked for systematic persecutions instead.[141]

What we can learn from the example of the Palatinate is that a number of convenient stereotypes really do not work. Certainly its subjects suffered from the usual crises, and as vine-growers they were particularly vulnerable to climatic hardship. Also, the arguments of political fragmentation and of proximity do not work. The Electorate, politically almost as fragmented as Electoral Mainz, was surrounded by hotspots of witch-hunting. The government's determined attitude, however, made no concessions to either populace or clergy, and managed to avoid the execution of witches. In comparison, countries like France or England suffered severe witch-hunts. The Home Circuit alone, one of England's six assize circuits, covering the counties of Essex, Hertfordshire, Kent, Surrey and Sussex, tried 785 cases of magical crimes between 1559 and 1709, identified 474 alleged witches (89.7 per cent women), of whom 209 were found guilty and 104 eventually hanged.[142] The Channel Islands of Jersey and Guernsey, possessions of the English Crown, with a population of barely 15,000, saw 167 witch trials and at least 90 executions between 1562 and 1661, one of the most severe persecutions in Europe.[143] None of these atrocities happened in the Electoral Palatinate, a territory of the Holy Roman Empire, with about 300,000 inhabitants, comparable to Lowland Scotland although more densely populated.

Sometimes regulations had to be introduced or enforced after the beginning of a witch-hunt in one corner of a country in order to stop it, and to prevent similar occurrences in the future. It was *reason of state* that made the councillors stop the persecutions in larger, well-developed states. A small count could perform a trial in his court, but where would it lead if a territory with more than 100 district courts started persecuting systematically? An interesting case is Bohemia, afflicted by the growing incapacity of its king, the Habsburg Emperor Rudolf II (1552–1612, r. 1576–1612). The emperor became melancholic, or maybe even mad, and did not wish to see his councillors for weeks. As Midelfort has demonstrated, mad princes were not uncommon during the decades around 1600, and some princes may have developed the feeling that the whole world was turning mad altogether, being literally surrounded by melancholic relatives.[144] However sick the emperor might have been – and his illegitimate son Don Giulio Cesare de Austria, who killed his mistress, dismembered her and threw the body parts out of the windows of Krumlow Castle, was certainly insane – it did not affect government in a well-constructed state. Although the Jesuits and Capuchins, whom Rudolf hated deeply, suggested witchcraft, or at least possession, the imperial councillors were not concerned. Diseases in the centre of power did not trigger witch-hunts. Witchcraft was not a major subject in either Bohemia or Austria, where the governments always had a firm grip on the lower criminal courts. The Habsburg capitals Prague and

Vienna, centres of the Counter-Reformation, even served as a refuge for witch suspects from the Catholic prince-bishoprics, very much like Holland or some imperial cities, such as Frankfurt or Speyer, the see of the Imperial Chamber Court. From these safe havens the refugees organized resistance against the hellish persecutions in their homelands.

Witch-hunting was considered unnecessary, useless or disgusting in the major capitals of Europe – political capitals like Paris, London, Madrid, Naples or Stockholm, as well as powerful city republics like Antwerp, Amsterdam or Nuremberg, and even vibrant commercial centres like Leipzig, Lyon or Siena. Although there were sorcery trials in all European towns, sometimes even executions for witchcraft, as in Amsterdam where four women were burned in 1533, these capitals did not experience major persecutions. It is hardly possible to imagine a witch-hunt in a politically independent and economically successful urban centre like Venice. Peasants hoping for pogroms had no chance where a self-confident aristocracy or a successful merchant class, rich and powerful, dismissed stories of witchcraft as fairy tales, regardless of their denomination. Rome, the centre of Catholicism, saw no witch craze either, and the Roman Inquisition reliably suffocated any ambitions of the rural subjects. Governments in major cities tended to dismiss witchcraft accusations with urbane arrogance, and this attitude may have contributed to the paradigm shift visible among the lawyers of the Parlement de Paris in the 1580s (see chapter 5). Real power, at least in Europe, dwarfed imagined powers, which were considered to be unimportant, or non-existent. Some authors started ridiculing magic and witchcraft altogether, and asked maliciously why generals never tried to save money by employing cheap witches instead of paying for expensive armies.[145]

It is instructive to study a conflict between the Tyrolean government and the valley of *Prättigau*, whose villages had repeatedly tried to incite the authorities to lead witch-hunts. The court council in Innsbruck relentlessly suppressed the aspirations of these peasants in their remote Alpine valley. Between 1649 and 1652 the valley managed to free itself from the Habsburg government, and joined the Swiss canton of Graubünden, or Grison. The villages were now allowed to govern themselves. They seized jurisdiction, organized in three autonomous criminal courts in the Prättigau, with judges elected by the villagers. This kind of democracy proved to be highly explosive. A massive witch-hunt started, a period known as 'The Big Witch Killing' (*Groos Häxatöödi*) in the local dialect. During these witch-hunts between 1652 and 1660 neither Roman law nor theological considerations played any role. The peasants were pressing the judges to 'eradicate the evil', with fifty-eight death sentences in 1655 alone.[146] Within a few years more than 100 witches were killed in the Prättigau, which had become Swiss by then – more than were exe-

cuted in centuries in the neighbouring, much more densely populated, Habsburg territory of Vorarlberg.[147] The peasants' model was
the earldom of Vaduz, where Count Ferdinand Carl Franz von
Hohenems conducted a massive persecution between 1648–51, and
between 1677–80, burning about 300 subjects. This was about 10
per cent of a population of roughly 3,000 inhabitants. However, in
contrast to the peasants' judges in the Prättigau, the count was still
subject to Emperor Leopold I (1640–1705, r. 1658–1705), who commissioned Prince-Abbot Rupert Bodman of Kempten to hold an
inquiry, eventually stripping the count of his rights. The count died in
the prison of Kempten after years of confinement. His lands were
given to the princes of Liechtenstein, who managed to retain their
possession up to the present day as an independent European
country.[148]

For a number of years historians have argued that Europe suffered
a general crisis in the decades around 1600,[149] with an increasing
number of severe food shortages and hunger crises. Accordingly, this
led to a rising number of marginalized people, who left their home
towns in order to earn their living elsewhere, without ever arriving
anywhere, thus contributing to rising numbers of migrant travellers,
or *masterless men*.[150] Henry Kamen has pointed to the fact that some
contemporaries characterized their time as an 'Iron Century',[151] and
Hartmut Lehmann has repeatedly emphasized the rise of apocalyptic feelings and millenarian expectations.[152] Theodore K. Rabb interpreted the turbulent years around 1600 under the heading of a
'Struggle for Stability'. This classical diagnosis did not get to the
bottom of the story, that is, the agrarian crises which put such enormous stress on the European societies, and those of continental
Europe in particular, but it saw ingeniously that a common factor of
all the political and social crises of the later sixteenth century was
their effect on society as a whole, although different sectors or groups
were affected in different ways, and eventually found expression in
religion and the arts.[153]

Hugh Redwald Trevor-Roper (1914–2003) analysed the different
moods at four Habsburg courts, pointing to the peculiar atmosphere
at the courts of Archduke Albrecht VII (1559–1621, r. 1599–1621) and
Isabella of Spain (1566–1633, r. 1621–33) in Brussels.[154] Emperor
Rudolf II and Queen Elizabeth I were both immensely interested in
the arts, and in the occult sciences, both employing one of the foremost magicians of the period, John Dee (1527–1608), who was in
search of hidden messages from the supernatural, the secrets of the
future, and the secrets of nature.[155] The imperial court at Prague was
generously investing in artistic productions, and the grotesque paintings of the Italian artist Giuseppe Arcimboldo (1527–93) add particularly to our sense of the tortured picture of the period. In varied
forms, he portrayed aspects of infertility and personifications of

Table 4.3 The largest witch-hunts in Europe

Victims	Former state	Confession	Dates	Today in
2,000	Duchy of Lorraine	Catholic	1580–1620	France
2,000	Spanish Netherlands	Catholic	1580–1620	Belgium
2,000	Electoral Cologne	Catholic	1626–35	Germany
2,000	Mecklenburg	Lutheran	1570–1630	Germany
2,000?	Duchy of Milan	*	1480–1520	Italy
1,800	Electoral Mainz	Catholic	1590–1630	Germany
1,350	Scotland	Calvinist	1560–1670	UK
1,200	Bishopric Würzburg	Catholic	1616–30	Germany
1,200	Vaud	Calvinist	1580–1620	Switzerland
1,000	Denmark	Lutheran	1540–1680	Denmark
907	Vorderösterreich	Catholic	1560–1650	France/ Germany
900	Bishopric Bamberg	Catholic	1616–30	Germany
800	Kingdom of Hungary	Catholic	1710–50	Hungary
600	Pommern-Wolgast	Lutheran	1600–60	Germany
600	Pommern-Stettin	Lutheran	1600–60	Poland
600	Schleswig-Holstein	Lutheran	1600–60	Denmark/ Germany
500	Duchy of Savoy	*	1428–36	Italy
500	Valais	*	1428–36	Switzerland
500	Dauphiné	*	1420–50	France
450	Franche-Comté	Catholic	1600–61	France
450	Ellwangen	Catholic	1588–1627	Germany
400	Earldom of Nassau	Calvinist	1590–1660	Germany
400	Earldom of Büdingen	Calvinist	1590–1660	Germany
387	Mergentheim	Catholic	1590–1665	Germany
358	Luxembourg	Catholic	1580–1630	Luxembourg
350	Electoral Trier	Catholic	1581–95	Germany
300	Earldom of Vaduz	Catholic	1648–80	Liechtenstein

* Pre-Reformation persecution

barrenness, and, in contrast, a picture of the emperor's head was made up of all kinds of fruits and flowers, like the ancient god Vertumnus, symbolizing fertility and abundance.[156] Once Pieter Brueghel (1525–69) had invented the genre of the winter landscape in the 1560s, displaying even traditional subjects like the adoration of the magi in thick snowfall, the production of winter landscapes expanded into a major industry. These turbulent years eventually resulted in a number of terrible European wars, like the Thirty Years' War (1618–48), rebellions and revolutions, as in England and some other countries, with even non-European civilizations being affected, such as China, where under Emperor Chuang-Lieh Ti (r. 1628–44) peasant uprisings and civil war eventually led to the disintegration of the empire and the collapse of the Ming dynasty. The widespread turmoil in Europe, with civil wars in France, the Netherlands, Germany and England, and rebellions in Catalonia and Naples, has led historians to invent the concept of a 'general crisis of the 17th century',[157] although the crisis had in fact begun in the 1560s, when frequent subsistence crises began to shatter the foundations of society.[158]

The early 1640s, when large parts of Western and Central Europe were in turmoil, ravaged by rebellions, civil war and international conflict, were particularly fertile times for witch panics. The general feeling of uncertainty was presumably supported by another cluster of unfavourable years, and crop failure combined with man-made disruptions of commerce and trade. Not only England, but also France suffered from severe witch panics. The Ursuline convent of Louviers saw another outbreak of demonic possession in 1643, and widespread popular witch-hunts affected the Champagne, the Bourbonnais, Burgundy, parts of Languedoc and Gascony, as well as the Bordelais, the Pyrenees and the Toulousain in the years 1644 and 1645.[159] The archbishop of Reims complained in July 1644 that witches were 'maltreated, driven out, or physically attacked; they are burned, while it has become customary to take the suspects and throw them into the water, then if they float it is enough to make them witches. This is such a great abuse that up to thirty or forty are found in a single parish'. The same year the Capuchin Jacques d'Autun described how 'most of the towns and villages of Burgundy were in a state of consternation because of the rumour which spread that the witches were the cause of the changes in the weather, that it was they who through their spells had destroyed the grains by hail and the grapes by frost'. Witch-finders, like a young shepherd known as the 'little prophet', went around, and the lower courts 'whose officials were at risk of their lives if they tried to examine these extravagances' felt intimidated by the popular demand for witch-hunting.[160]

How closely witch scares were connected to extraordinary situations can be seen from the persecutions of the self-appointed *witch-*

finder general, Matthew Hopkins (?–1648), who managed to use the turmoil of the English Civil War to launch the greatest ever witch persecution in the kingdom of England, in a situation where apocalyptic and millennial fears and hopes were mushrooming.[161] This gentleman from Manningtree in Essex, son of a Calvinist minister, felt disturbed by the prevalence of witches in his region in the winter of 1644/45,[162] and his concerns were obviously shared by others. An inquiry into witchcraft led to a trial against thirty-six women in Chelmsford, about half of whom were executed in July 1645. Meanwhile, the suspicions had spread to East Anglia, first to Suffolk, the county that saw the highest number of executions, following which prosecutions were started in 'Northamptonshire, Huntingdonshire, Bedfordshire, Norfolke, Cambridgeshire, and the Isle of Ely in the County of Cambridge, besides other places'.[163] In Bury St Edmunds alone sixty-eight witches were condemned in the summer of 1645, if we may believe John Stearne, Hopkins' fellow witch-finder.[164] The witch-finders often used the 'swimming' of the witches, an archaic water ordeal, used in ancient Babylonia, but outlawed by the Roman Church in 1215. The swimming of witches was revived in the course of the sixteenth century, from Russia to England, but was always opposed by the clergy and educated lawyers, with only a few exceptions.[165] The *ducking*, as the ordeal was mockingly called in England, became widespread during the years of civil war anarchy. Stearne emphasized that he had used 'the bath' only 'at such time of the yeare as when none tooke any harme by it, neither did I ever doe it but upon their owne request'.[166] He claimed that public criticism of the 'extremities' in their trials was unjustified: 'Only at first, before he [Hopkins] or I ever went, many Towns used extremity of themselves, which after was laid on us.'[167]

The imperfect nature of the surviving records makes any reconstruction difficult, but estimates suggest that at least 250 individuals were tried, and a minimum of 100, but perhaps considerably higher numbers, were executed for witchcraft during these persecutions. Stearne clearly admits to the execution of 'about two hundred in number' from May 1645 onwards, and there seems little reason to doubt his claim, because we could assume that he tried to minimize the numbers in his apology. As Jim Sharpe emphasizes, the Hopkins persecutions pose a major challenge to current interpretations of English witchcraft, not just because of the large numbers of the persecuted, but also because the records demonstrate that fantasies of demonic witchcraft were anything but absent from England. Clearly, for the witch-finders the witches' 'League and Covenant with the devil' was central to the crime, including sexual intercourse, and the *stigma diaboli*, the devil's mark. The familiar spirits in animal shape, or *imps*, a speciality of English witchcraft, were also a token of their alignment to the devil. According to their confessions, the witches did not restrict their activities to simple maleficient magic, but gave details of their pact and of their witches' assemblies, which took place 'in our owne Kingdome' as 'in all countries', as Stearne emphasized, and where they worshipped the devil, as Elizabeth Clarke from Manningtree confessed, obviously the first suspect interrogated by John Stearne and Matthew Hopkins.[168] Furthermore, the treatment the suspects received from their persecutors included general mal-treatment, sleep deprivation and the use of leading questions, an aspect emphasized by Francis Hutchinson, who claimed to have spoken to surviving witnesses.[169] The breakdown of central govern-ment, the erosion of traditional authority, and the atmosphere of political strife and religious zeal obviously made it easier to stage witch trials, and this interpretation is confirmed by a number of unconnected incidents, from Kent to Newcastle-upon-Tyne, where a Scottish witch-pricker was invited to help the authorities hunt witches. Sharpe concludes that the events in East Anglia 'show clearly that England had as great a potential for mounting large-scale witch crazes as any other European nation'.[170]

There were earlier occasions which had the potential for a large-scale persecution in England, for instance the Lancashire trials of 1633/34, where at least nineteen witches were executed, while another sixty were under suspicion, and some jailed, with several people dying in prison.[171] The confessions show the fully developed fantasy of a witches' sabbat, revealing ideas about a permanent meeting point 'at Harestones in the forest of Pendle', where the witches flew for feast-ing and dancing, shape-shifting and having sexual intercourse, where they adored the devil and practised harmful magic ('killing and hurting of man and beasts', weather-making). This dangerous perse-cution was ultimately stopped by the privy council, aided by a medical team headed by William Harvey (1578–1657).[172] The Lancashire trials demonstrate a remarkable divide between Puritan zealots and Angli-can moderates, reminding us of the fact that all major English demonologies were published by Puritan divines (George Gifford, Henry Holland, William Perkins, James Mason, Alexander Roberts, Thomas Cooper and Richard Bernard), whereas those advocating moderate scepticism after the Restoration, like Joseph Glanvill (1636–80) and Meric Casaubon (1599–1671), were Anglican minis-ters, inclined to restore unity and order, and more concerned about atheism than witchcraft. In 1634 it seems that even the privy council was split into moderate and radical factions.[173] It also seems psycho-logically likely that those who aspired to a Godly republic would be more easily tempted to adopt the role of moral entrepreneurship, whether they were Presbyterian divines like James Carmichael, or Catholic zealots like Peter Canisius. For both, the devil's pact was an inversion of the covenant with God, and, again for both, witch-hunting served as an instrument to raise attention to their cause.

It is striking, however, that unlike earlier witch-hunts, which had been announced to a wider public by means of broadsheets and pamphlets, as indeed an earlier Lancashire witch panic had been,[174] the later outbreak led to the publication of a comedy, touching upon all the exotic features of witchcraft: the witches' flight, shape-shifting into the form of animals, familiars, love magic, harmful magic causing impotence and so on.[175] The performance at the Globe Theatre in August 1634 was attended by 'fine folke gentlemen and gentlewomen'. It was the fourth play about witchcraft within one generation,[176] and the excitement lay clearly in the fact that some of the Lancashire witches were still in prison. However, the comedy did not promote the cause of the witch-hunters. It 'consisteth from the beginning to the ende of odd passages and fopperies to provoke laughter, and is mixed with diverse songs and dances'. And although the performance was a bit dull, 'it passeth for a merrie and excellent new play', as the contemporary reviewer Nathaniel Tomkyns wrote.[177] Likewise, on the continent witchcraft became a subject of plays and novels, and experienced authors like Martin Opitz (1579–1639) or Johann Christoph Grimmelshausen (c.1622–76) treated it in a way that was not dissimilar to Shakespeare. Their witches are archaic figures reminiscent of classical Greek drama, or they are but a folkloristic motif open to the ridicule of the educated.[178]

As Rabb has recognized, it was the general mood that changed in the second third of the seventeenth century, due to a general struggle for more stability in a world shaken by persecution, wars and revolutions. The civil wars ended, the monarchies were restored and international conflicts were stopped by treaties like the Peace of Westphalia in 1648, or the Peace of the Pyrenees in 1659, which solved the age-old conflict between the Habsburgs and the French monarchy. A general disillusionment deflated the fanatical religiosity, which had fuelled religious and civil wars, as well as international conflicts, and – last but not least – witch persecutions. Furthermore, the European economy seemed to stabilize to a certain degree, partly due to the enormous loss of population, and partly due to improvements of agriculture in Western Europe. Dangerous diseases like leprosy and the bubonic plague disappeared from the European stage, although we still do not know exactly why. It could have been an increase in hygiene or an improvement in nutrition, or, as a contingent development, due to changes in ecology. One of the suggested explanations is that the vector of the disease, the rat flea, did not like a new rat population that had managed to replace the previous one. Furthermore, there were changes in the cultural system. An intellectual elite, tired of warfare and intolerance, managed to separate religion and science, and started to offer secular explanations in physics, medicine or meteorology. The educated in general, it seems, embarked on the enterprise of secularization, equating religion with superstition, leaving behind them a curious alliance of theologians and the general populace.

The struggle for stability had been successful to some degree, and the uncertainties of life became fewer and less important. In Western Europe the witch-hunts faded out, or were forcibly stopped, as the power of the central governments increased. The result is traditionally labelled as *absolutism*, although states could be strong without an absolute monarch, as the examples of England or the Netherlands show. France of course was the model case, where centralization had succeeded in suffocating not only popular unrest, but also popular witch-hunting. The Parlements had usually managed to control their districts tightly, and the Parlement de Paris accepted few death penalties after 1625. Louis XIV (1638–1715, r. 1643/51–1715) brought the executions to an end by royal decree in 1682: all further cases had to be reported to the king, and the execution of witches could be carried out only with his signature. Earlier historians saw something heroic in the decree, but now we know that France was by and large mirroring common European developments, not as an avant-garde, but somewhere in the middle ground. All over Western Europe the witch-hunts and executions of witches petered out in the 1680s, in England as well as in Denmark, Norway and Iceland, in the formerly panic-stricken duchies of Holstein and Mecklenburg, the whole of northern Germany, the Swedish realm in the Baltics, the Spanish Netherlands and Lorraine, the Rhineland and the Saar region, where particularly fierce hunts had been common only decades before. All the national, regional or parochial historians tell us their heroic tales, with local heroes, professors, theologians, law faculties or princes successfully fighting the sea of superstition. However, the executions stopped even in places where we cannot find a single hero. A new generation of rulers and politicians, educated at the same universities – whether Catholic or Protestant – and usually raised in the spirit of rationalism, such as the new generation of prince-bishops in Mainz, Cologne and Trier, began to suppress any attempt at witch-hunting, if necessary by sending in troops – an instrument of power not available to their predecessors before 1630.

Most territories of Central Europe were ruled more efficiently, but even where state-formation had failed the rulers could rely on the support of the imperial circles, which now coordinated regional concerns of the Holy Roman Empire. The Imperial Chamber Court, the highest independent court of appeals in the empire – first located in Speyer, then moved to Wetzlar after the demolition of Speyer by troops of Louis XIV – had no responsibilities in criminal justice, but people could appeal to it in cases of faulty legal procedures in their territories, if their rulers had not managed to gain a *privilegium de non appellando*. We have only recently discovered that, despite all limitations, this court of appeals was more successful in influencing

Map 2 Heartland of the witch craze: The Holy Roman
Empire in the sixteenth century

Table 4.4 Litigations over witch trials at the Imperial Chamber Court, 1500–1800

Generation	Litigations by victims	Total number of litigations over witch trials
1500–29	1	3
1530–59	10	17
1560–89	19	39
1590–1619	50	97
1620–49	29	46
1650–79	17	30
1680–1709	3	6
1710–39	2	6
1740–69	0	1
1770–1800	0	2
Totals	131	247

the politics of persecution than formerly assumed. Even at the climax of the persecution, in the late 1620s, it issued harsh decrees against the Franconian witch-hunts, and – although not immediately – the judgments did influence both public opinion and the conduct of lawyers in the territories. The number of litigations over witch trials in no way mirrors the amount of witch trials in the empire. However, it is a surprisingly accurate representation of the general course of the persecutions: a substantial rise from the 1560s, the climax between 1590 and 1630, a gradual decline until the 1680s and only a few trials afterwards.[179]

Witchcraft persecutions from the second half of the seventeenth century onwards have to be seen against the backdrop of these more general developments, which will be explored in chapter 5. There were still further waves of persecution, although on a much lower level than in the previous decades. We can find major waves for instance in the 1660s, in the 1670s[180] and again in the 1690s, when the massive cooling of the *Maunder Minimum* (1675–1715) made the climate particularly unfavourable again,[181] and some countries at the periphery, such as Scandinavia, Eastern Europe or the English colonies in North America, started witch-hunts for the first time in their history. The European elites had departed from their former frenzies, and were generally looking for rational or natural explanations, increasingly excluding the supernatural forces, demons, angels, or God, from their considerations. Furthermore, new modes of education contributed to these developments, because ever more doctors and lawyers were required for the administration of ever-growing bureaucracies. The process of state-formation, or the formation of national states in Western Europe, had induced professionalization of many offices, and the growing self-confidence of these new elites contributed to their departure from superstition. Developments in technology, with the invention of the telescope or the microscope, had contributed to an increasing interest in the natural sciences. With the new philosophy of this rational elite, belief in witches was marginalized, and witch persecutions were increasingly seen to be irrational by those who no longer felt endangered by magic. Since witch-beliefs became ridiculous to them, the demand for witch trials became an unwelcome irritation, and the execution of witches, if it still happened, was consequently seen to be an outrage. Increasingly, therefore, witch trials were driven first to the more remote areas of the realms of Western Europe, and eventually to the European peripheries, where academic institutions, strong state administrations and wealth were absent, and traditional lifestyles still prevailed.[182]

There were still sufficiently backward areas within Europe to keep the irritation alive for a while. The Swedish empire, including Swedish Finland and the Baltic fringes, only started to be concerned about witchcraft in the second half of the seventeenth century. It has been argued that returning soldiers from the Thirty Years' War imported the notion of cumulative witchcraft to Sweden.[183] However, if this had been the case, it should be possible to prove in detail that returned soldiers brought about the witch-hunt of Dalarna, which started in 1668 with the accusations of a fifteen-year-old boy, eventually involving more and more children, who gave elaborate reports of full-blown witches' sabbats at the *blakulla*, an immense green meadow with a pleasant dining hall. There the feasting, dancing and sexual activities with devils took place, and every witch was baptized and inscribed in the devil's black book.[184] The teenagers and children generated large numbers of denunciations of parents, neighbours and other children, and kept the courts busy as long as they were willing to take these stories seriously. The witch craze swept through northern Sweden and spilled over to Swedish Finland. These events took place during the minority rule of Charles XI (1655–97, r. 1660/72–97), a prince of the Protestant branch of the Wittelsbach dynasty (Pfalz-Zweibrücken), still a child himself when the trials began. More than 200 people were killed during the persecutions between 1668 and 1676, and, as in so many other cases, the demand for witch-hunting seems to have come from below. Several royal commissions dealt quite ponderously with the subject, certainly in comparison with the Spanish inquisitor Salazar for instance, and the government wavered. The court council finally stopped the trials after a witch craze began to seize the capital of Stockholm in 1675. There had been critical voices in the commissions, but these were a minority, whereas the majority was ready to follow the pressure from the local populations. Finally the king, now himself in charge of the government, stopped the hunt by decree,[185] and soon after he intervened in the Swedish Baltic, and actually stopped the trials in Finland, Estonia and Livonia, which had also peaked in the 1670s.[186] The Swedish witch-hunts aroused a lot of attention, mirroring the fact that Sweden was a strong political player in Northern Europe in the seventeenth century, engaged in a number of successful wars. Whereas the continuous executions of witches in Denmark, Mecklenburg and Pomerania went almost unnoticed, the Dalarna trials were commented upon by all demonologists of the period, and by a wider public. A report of the Dalarna parish priest Elaus Skragge was translated into Dutch, English and German, and widely reprinted, in England by Joseph Glanvill,[187] in Scotland by George Sinclair[188] and in America by Cotton Mather.[189] Balthasar Bekker (1634–98) integrated a second English version into his *Betoverde Weereld*, which was in turn translated into all the major European languages.[190]

Although the notion became suppressed by the contemporary elites as well as by historiography, late witch trials were not confined to the peripheries, but continued to surface in Central Europe well into the century of the Enlightenment. When occasional witch burnings continued after 1700 in southern Germany, Austria and even northern Italy, Protestant Europe consoled itself that all of these countries were Catholic, and therefore backward by definition. However, these religious stereotypes, or certainties, were fragile, since Protestant Swiss cantons were also part of this development, and the last legal killings of witches took place in Calvinist Swiss cantons like the Grison and Glarus. If we have a look at these late trials, an interesting observation can be made: the classical witch stereotype of the old lonesome hag had largely collapsed. During one of the most notorious late persecutions, the so-called 'Sorcerer-Jack Trial' (*Zauberer-Jackl-Prozess*) in the prince-bishopric of Salzburg between 1678 and 1680, about 80 per cent of the victims were young men – some of them still boys, most of them teenagers, and just a few above twenty – all supposed to be followers of Jacob, or 'Jackl' Koller (1655–?), the vagabond son of a suspected witch. Koller, Sorcerer-Jack, was never caught by the authorities, becoming an almost legendary figure during his own lifetime, and he still appears in regional narratives. But more than 140 of his supposed minions, most of them beggars, were tried and executed in the district courts of the bishopric. The hunts for witch-beggars spread to neighbouring territories, such as the prince-bishoprics of Freising, and Passau, the prince-electorate of Bavaria, and the arch-duchies of Tyrol and Austria, within a radius of more than 100 miles from Salzburg.[191]

What made these young people, mostly male, but including a minority of girls, so extremely dangerous? These travelling children were a symptom of crisis: some had lost their parents in epidemics, others had abandoned their families and joined one of the existing gangs. It is striking to hear of these gangs of children roaming around the countryside, sleeping in stables or haystacks, under market stalls or behind bath sheds in the towns, avoiding contact with adults as much as possible, and creating a subculture of their own. What comes to mind are the street children in Third World towns, who make their living from petty crime, begging and occasional work, and also – not to forget – their persecution by local 'law and order' factions, who often hire killers to get rid of beggars who disturb business. In early modern Europe, there were different strategies for dealing with begging children. The secular states usually opted for internment, putting them into orphanages, or, if old enough, into workhouses. In contrast, the ecclesiastical territories tended to support them by means of alms, which the children clearly found preferable. Since they were entitled to receive charity for only a limited number of days, they had to move from bishopric to bishopric, developing a kind of round trip through southern Germany, from Salzburg to Passau, from there to Regensburg and Freising, then on to Dillingen, capital of the prince-bishopric of Augsburg, and so on, with the monasteries as bases in between, as we can see from the narratives. These children and teenagers seem to have been fascinated by magic, and a number of their fantasies cannot be traced back to learned demonologies, for instance the creation of mice and rabbits. Whenever the authorities chose to round up one of these gangs, they could hear numerous stories of that kind. As long as they were willing to persecute witch-craft, they could easily do so on such grounds.

But how could witches turn into young men? What could be the reason for such a striking development, which looks like an inversion of the witch stereotype? First of all, male witches were never com-pletely absent in the Alpine regions, where their proportion was always higher than the European average.[192] There were also other regions with considerable numbers of male witches, Northern Europe for instance, Iceland, Finland and Hungary, all regions with long-standing shamanistic traditions, used to the idea that men had something to do with magic.[193] Furthermore, all opponents of witch-hunting, from Agrippa and Alciati to Weyer, Scot, Spee or Thomasius, had always emphasized the protection of women, who were imagined to be innocent victims, maybe for tactical reasons. Their strategy of containment proved to be pretty successful, since the image of the dangerous witch was gradually replaced in the public mind. The jurists' insistence on proper circumstantial evidence in the ordinary trial (*processus ordinarius*) against suspected criminals deci-sively limited the trials. With the crime still existing in the law codes, some groups of potential victims remained, and it is not by coincidence that exactly the same groups can still cause substantial problems for courts in our own time, as the accused or as witnesses: mentally disturbed or handicapped people, melancholics who are determined to commit suicide and children who enjoy living out their fantasies, or are mentally ill – or, as it happened to be defined in a religious age, possessed.

Possession counts among the conditions foreign to the modern reader or observer in Western cultures, and is one which came to be defined as a kind of mental illness. However, in many civilizations, and to a certain degree also in Christendom, 'possession' happens only when an evil spirit, a devil, invades an individual and takes control of his or her body. In such cases, traditional Christian Churches, for instance the Roman Catholic, the Greek and Russian Orthodox, or Ethiopian Churches, would call for a specialist in devilish invasions in order to fight back the forces of evil within the body, and regain control. Indeed, exorcists played a great role in late medieval and early modern Europe. Christendom recognizes not only evil spirits, or demons, but also good spirits, or angels, and like the demons they kept a science of their own busy, angelology, the counterpart of demonology. One of the key events in Christian history is of course Pentecost, when the Holy Spirit invaded the apostles. *Inspiration*, therefore, although not usually associated with possession, also has positive connotations in our culture. In many non-European civilizations, inspiration forms a crucial part of religious experience. In shamanistic cultures, for instance, inspiration is seen as the most important sign of individual election of the religious specialist, the shaman, and a rich variety of techniques, including meditation, dancing, drugs, asceticism or pain are used to induce inspirations.[194] In Afro-Caribbean religions a spirit-medium makes contact with the spirits during a possession. African as well as Amerindian cultures, as in historical Europe, can interpret involuntary possession as being induced by witchcraft.

Among the standard procedures for exorcism is the question of whether the devil has decided to possess somebody, or was asked, or maybe even forced to do so, by a human being, a sorcerer or witch. Possession cases could therefore easily spark off witch trials, as can be seen from an exorcism conducted at Vienna in 1583 by Georg Scherer SJ, who later published an account of his procedures.[195] Some of the most scandalous trials started from possession cases, for instance the trial against Louis Gaufridy (1572–1611) from Marseille, who had served as a confessor in a monastery of Ursuline nuns at Aix. The Parlement of Aix-en-Provence accepted the depositions of Madeleine de la Palud (1593–1670), and some more juvenile nuns, that the attractive priest had bewitched them. Gaufridy was imprisoned, and tortured, until he confessed the devil's pact, and finally was executed as a witch, although he recanted his confession. Equally exciting was the case of Urbain Grandier (?–1634) of Loudun, another Ursuline convent, with a roughly similar problem, but with repercussions all the way up to Cardinal Richelieu, who became interested in the case. Cases like the Loudun witch trial, with all the religious, and supposedly sexual, fantasies involved, attract novelists and film directors to the present day.[196] Nunneries, priests' seminaries, boarding schools and hospitals were breeding grounds for all kinds of group dynamics, and, in a religious age, mass possessions could spread like epidemics.

The most vulnerable group among those who acted as witnesses in witch trials, or were forced to do so, were children. When the first publication on the subject of children in witch trials was put on the book market at the very climax of the European witch-hunts,[197] more than one generation of experience in the subject had already passed. Weyer did not mention child-witches, and the publications of the 1570s did not mention them either. It seems that Binsfeld was the first author to do so, and he had every reason, since the Jesuits kept boys in the College of Trier who had confessed to witchcraft and were willing to denounce others as participants in the witches' sabbat. We do not know all the detailed circumstances of these confessions, because the Jesuits later had every reason to suppress the scandal, and all our information is derived from surviving correspondence between Jesuit Colleges, unearthed by the great Jesuit historian Bernhard Duhr (1852–1930).[198] The Dominican inquisitor Kramer had claimed already in his *Witches' Hammer* that witches' daughters were likely to become witches themselves, not by inheritance, but because the mothers devoted them to their master, the devil. However, it was only after the massive witch-hunts of the late sixteenth century that great numbers of children started to generate witch stories, obviously reflecting the stories they had heard in church, at home, in school or – most likely – in their peer groups. During the persecutions of the 1580s, for the first time children served as key witnesses in witch-hunts, with their stories being taken seriously, and at least some of them seem to have enjoyed their new importance, the attention adults were paying them and the opportunity to exercise power. From then on, we can find children acting in witch trials, and in a number of well-documented cases we can see that some of them acted voluntarily, without being encouraged to do so. We can equally see how difficult it was for the authorities to dismiss their narratives as nonsense.[199] During the great witch-hunts in the 1620s, children again played a prominent role, as has rightly been emphasized.[200]

When the great witch-hunts had stopped, it proved difficult to stop the children, who went on with their fantasies, which might have been realities for them. In some cases they articulated their accusations so stubbornly, and in public, that the authorities felt it necessary to take action. As nowadays in cases of child abuse, the courts had the utmost difficulty in dealing legally with these children's allegations.[201] According to the imperial law it was unnecessary to pursue self-accusations of teenagers up to the age of fourteen, but what about the allegations against their seducers? Mothers or aunts, whom they accused of having introduced them to the devil, with whom they had sex on several occasions at the witches' sabbat, but first at home or in the neighbour's flat? Some of these narratives are similar to those found in present-day cases of child abuse. Recently, some scholars have tried to suggest that these witch-children had indeed experienced sexual abuse. We cannot exclude the possibility, but in some cases there are reports of midwives in the trial records. The courts commissioned them to test the virginity of young girls, in order to dismiss their fantasies of sexual intercourse with devils, and maybe also to find out whether cases of incestuous child abuse were lurking in the background of their demonical fantasies. Among all these mid-wives' expert opinions I have seen, I have found no case so far where intercourse had indeed taken place. The children's fantasies posed a major problem, and it was as difficult for early modern courts as it is nowadays to understand that some children, for whatever reasons, liked to cause damage to their relatives or neighbours. When the traditional witch trials had faded away, the witch trials against children remained, and a rising percentage of all trials were caused by children. Maybe this contributed to the Enlightenment's fascination with pedagogy, since superstition was always closely associated with lack of education, and clearly the child-witches demonstrated that children needed adequate guidance.

The discussion of legal witchcraft persecutions within the influence of European civilization requires some comments on *the colonies*, because the persecutions occurred during the period of European expansion, or colonialism. Here we arrive at intriguing results, contrary to previous assumptions about the rule of law, or the role of the Spanish Inquisition, or the meaning of Christian denominations. The largest realm of the early modern world was the Spanish empire, fiercely Catholic and centrally governed. Clearly, the Spanish Inquisition was most successful in suppressing witch-hunts, not only in early modern Europe, but even more so in the colonies. The records survive in surprising completeness, and, while a certain number of trials involved crimes of magic, very few executions for witchcraft, magic or sorcery are reported from the vice-kingdoms of Peru in South America, or from Mexico in Central America. No death penalties are reported from the Spanish Philippines in south-east Asia, from the Spanish territories in northern Africa, or from the Mediterranean islands. In colonial Mexico, twenty burnings are recorded, but none by the other Latin American tribunals. Even the number of trials remained marginal, with 119 cases in Lima (Peru), 144 cases in

Mexico City, and 188 in Cartagena de Indias (today in Colombia). The tribunal in Cartagena almost convicted a woman for witchcraft in 1633, but the Supreme Council in Madrid forbade it. A witch panic among the black populace between 1621 and 1641 was suppressed by the authorities. A similar picture arises from the archives of the Portuguese empire. From the Inquisition tribunal in Brazil only thirty-three witch suspects were transported to Lisbon for their conviction. What is particularly remarkable here is that the colonies in Latin America – unlike New England – included the entire population (white colonists, Native Americans and black slaves), and Mexico and Peru as ancient civilizations were much more densely populated than the French, Dutch or English colonies in North America.

In colonial New France (Canada) only one person was executed for witchcraft, and none in the Dutch colonies. Accusations were hardly ever launched against the indigenous peoples. Although shamans or witch-doctors were generally branded devil-worshippers, they rarely seem to have worried the religious or secular authorities, with the single exception of Cacice Chichimecatecuhtli of Texcoco, who was burned for witchcraft in 1540. Only members of their own civilization seemed to matter, and the *enemy within*, or the internal outsider, appears to have been perceived as much more dangerous than real outsiders. This may shed some light on the fact that European countries under Ottoman rule, the later states of Bulgaria, Romania, Greece, Serbia and Albania, were not allowed to hunt witches by their Muslim superiors, and why other European countries governed by foreign rulers, like Ireland, had equally few witch trials. The native population was treated as a primitive people, who were basically left to themselves as long as there were no riots. In such cases, however, for instance in colonial Colombia, the authorities stepped in and crushed the local movements, whether they were rebellions or pogroms against suspected witches.

There is one remarkable exception to this rule that indicates how things in Spanish America might have developed without the tight rule of the Spanish Inquisition, and also how indigenous witchcraft and European fears could interact. The colonization of the Upper Rio Grande Valley was a private endeavour of Juan de Oñate, who – licensed by the king – entered the valley in 1598 with about 400 soldiers, colonists, friars and servants in order to conquer the territories of the Pueblo Indians, an agrarian, but complex, civilization. The Spanish nobleman's harsh measures provoked resistance, but the yoke of Spanish colonial rule lasted for generations. Taxes were extracted with great violence, and the Franciscans established a particularly oppressive Christian mission. As their endeavour proved unsuccessful, they blamed witchcraft for the failure, and in 1650 troops raided the Pueblo religious chambers and confiscated masks, fetishes and other ritual devices for burning.[202] In 1675 the tensions came to a head after the deaths of several friars and citizens were attributed to witchcraft by the Spanish. Governor Juan Francisco Trevino now arrested the Indian leaders. Three of them were hanged, while forty-three others were publicly whipped and condemned to slavery. Five years later one of those flogged for witchcraft became the leader of an Indian uprising. During the Pueblo Revolt twenty-one missionaries and some 400 colonists were killed. The Spanish abandoned their capital of Santa Fe and fled. Anthropologists have characterized the revolt as a *nativistic movement*. The interesting point here is that the friars, as well as the Spanish governor, considered the Indian leaders to be witches and feared their spiritual power. On the other hand the Pueblo shamans did use sorcery, and certainly invoked their guardian spirits, in order to fight the foreign invaders who were trying to destroy their religion and culture.[203]

It may come as a surprise that the severest persecutions of all early modern European colonies happened in the English colonies of North America. The settlers carried witch-beliefs in their baggage when they emigrated to the colonies, as did all European emigrants. However, the English colonies had much less metropolitan supervision than their Spanish counterparts, and magical crimes were a matter for secular courts. According to Westerkamp there were altogether 344 accusations of witchcraft (78 per cent women) between 1620 and 1725, of which 103 came to trial (86 per cent women).[204] Before 1700 about forty people were executed for witchcraft, from a population of barely 100,000 people. Most of the accusations belonged to only three major witch panics. The first of these occurred in Bermuda, which suffered an outbreak in 1651. Even more severe was a panic in Hartford, Connecticut, between 1662 and 1665, when thirteen people were accused of witchcraft and four eventually found guilty and executed. At the centre of the third panic, in Massachusetts, where the death penalty for witches had been decreed in 1641, was Salem Village. In the years 1692 and 1693 no less than 185 people were involved, with twenty-seven convicted and nineteen eventually executed for witchcraft. According to our definition this is to be classified as a 'small panic trial', as far as the number of death penalties is concerned. The number of convictions, however, indicates that this was a considerable persecution, and the number of suspects shows that there was the potential for a large-scale persecution.[205] Such a persecution may have developed 100 years earlier, but at the end of the seventeenth century these colonial persecutions fit well into the European pattern, where witch trials were most frequently triggered by diabolical possession, with children as accusers, and families at the core of the suspicions.

The Salem witch-hunt is one of the best researched events in the history of witchcraft, and even the sources have been published.[206] Among the publications there are books as famous as Kai Erikson's

Wayward Puritans,[207] exemplifying the sociological theory of deviance in the environment of an insular Puritan community; Paul Boyer's and Stephen Nissenbaum's attempt to explore the social-psychological dimensions of possessed young girls;[208] and Carol F. Karlsen's attempt to detect a male conspiracy against powerful elderly women, by scrutinizing their social position in the colonial society.[209] The Salem hunt was remarkable in several respects: the interaction between English settlers and Native American magicians, the role of children in the craze, and the fact that a prominent member of the Puritan clergy, Reverend Cotton Mather, was a driving force in the persecution. He even provided a kind of apology for his deeds, like some European witch-hunters before him. In his *Wonders of the Invisible World* he mourns: 'I believe there never was a poor plantation more pursued by the wrath of the devil than our poor New-England.'[210] This renowned member of the Royal Academy had been interested in demonic possession well before the outbreak of the Salem witch craze, and had reprinted a report on the Swedish Dalarna witch craze in his first North American demonology.[211] The literature on Salem has become a major industry in itself over the past decades, and more books have been published on the subject than people were executed. Skilful marketing has secured Salem a disproportionate share of publicity, for instance on the World Wide Web, where the keyword 'witch village' guides the researcher exclusively to Massachusetts, whereas there is no chance to get any information about the refugees from actual persecutions in the Republic of South Africa, who are interned in 'protected' settlements, witch villages or 'sanctuaries'(see chapter 6). Virginia had a witch trial as late as 1701, and even in the 1730s occasional 'duckings' were performed in Connecticut. The interesting observation here is that the more serious incidents all happened among the devil-fearing Puritans of the north, whereas 'the more easy going Anglicans' in the slave-holding southern colonies were less concerned about witchcraft, and killed very few witches.[212]

Researchers have often been positive about the treatment of supposed witches in the European colonies, but we cannot be sure that we fully know what actually happened. As in the peripheries of the Russian empire, it is quite unlikely that the peripheries of the English, Spanish, French and other empires have provided adequate documentation. A blind spot seems to be the treatment of slaves. The Africans kidnapped from West Africa certainly brought their ideas about witchcraft to the Americas, and there were intensive fears of bewitchment among them. The colonial authorities, however, seem to have feared the mystical powers of the healers or shamans as well, and it will be necessary to have a closer look at all the cases of 'rebels' executed for acting as ringleaders, like an 'Obeahman' condemned to death after the Antigua rebellion of 1736. The 'Obeahman', responsible for the cult of Obeah,

> transmitted the whole technique by which men lived and died, coerced nature, protected and destroyed property, cursed and bewitched their fellows and masters, and prospered in love or deviltry. The worship of Obi involved secret meetings at night in the forest, licentious dancing, blood sacrifices of chickens, goats, and at infrequent intervals . . . the sacrifice of 'a goat without horns', a human being or child.

In 1760 a law was passed in Jamaica (Act of 18 December 1760), threatening 'any negro or other slave' with 'death or transportation', if they 'pretend to any supernatural power and be detected of making use of any blood, feathers, parrots, beaks, dogs teeth, alligators teeth, broken bottles, grave dirt, rum, egg shells or any other materials relative to the practice of Obeah or Witchcraft'. A Jamaican planter claimed to have lost 100 slaves between 1760 and 1775 from Obeah practice, which obviously implies that he believed in its efficacy. An old slave woman, who was considered to be a source of evil, was sold to the Spaniards. In 1780 an Obeahman and bandit named Plato, who had threatened people with witchcraft, was captured and burned at the stake 'in the county of Westmoreland', Jamaica. In a 'Memorial' the council of Barbados claimed in October 1788 that negroes became sick and often died when they discovered that they had been cursed or bewitched. In 1816 an old Obeahman was caught in action, with 'a bag containing a great variety of strange materials for incantations; such as thunder stone, cats ears, the feet of various animals, human hair, fish bones, the teeth of alligators, etc.'. After the sorcerer's imprisonment in Montego Bay, 'depositions were poured in from all quarters'. The culprit was 'convicted of Obeah', and sentenced to deportation, since 'the good old practice of burning has fallen into disrepute'. As the contemporary chronicler reports, this sentence was executed 'to the great satisfaction of all colours – white, black and yellow'. Although these reports are quite impressionistic they seem to imply that a chapter of colonial witchcraft has not yet been written.[213]

If we try to provide a survey of the historical witch-hunts we can see immediately that the picture is much less favourable for Europe than for its colonies. Although in some cases the research is not yet far advanced, we are nevertheless able to determine the intensity of witch-hunting for the European continent. One of the surprising results is that the persecutions were much more intensive in the centre of the continent than at the peripheries, and some years ago scholars felt attracted to centre-periphery models, then in vogue in the social sciences. Even then it was difficult to define the concept of 'centre', and it never really became clear whether it was supposed to mean an economic and political centre, as in *dependence theory*, or just referred to geography.[214] Anyway, at first glance the concept seemed promising, since the countries at the Western fringes had clearly never suffered severely from witch-hunts, as the examples of Spain, Portugal, England, Ireland or the Netherlands demonstrate. On the Iberian peninsula we can be absolutely clear about this, since the administration of both Inquisitions, the Spanish and the Portuguese, kept reliable records. Recent Inquisition research has explored these sources in detail. In Portugal, the Inquisition in Evora, for instance, dealt with 11,743 cases of spiritual crimes over a period of 300 years. Only 2.5 per cent of these, or 291 cases, concerned magical crimes, including superstitious behaviour, divination, sorcery and witchcraft. The inquisitors imposed the death penalty just twice, in 1626 and 1744.[215] During the entire period the Inquisitions in Coímbra and Lisbon, responsible also for the Portuguese territories in Africa, the Atlantic isles, and Brazil, voted for capital punishment for witchcraft in only three other cases (1694 and 1735). In the whole of the Portuguese empire, at the end of the sixteenth century still more important than the Dutch and English empires, there were only six other executions of witches before secular criminal courts (in 1559).[216]

In Spain more than 100 witches were executed in secular trials between 1580 and 1620,[217] virtually unhampered by the Inquisition. Only after a major witch panic had started in 1618 did the viceroy alert the Inquisition of Aragon to take action against a witch-finder, who was soon condemned to the galleys. Likewise, witch-finders had to be checked by the Inquisition of Aragon.[218] Henry Kamen suggests that future research will reveal more local witch-hunts, since local and baronial jurisdictions rejected any interference, and their archives are yet to be scrutinized. In the tiny district of Vic forty-five witches were sentenced to death between 1618 and 1622, a large-scale witch-hunt, and dozens of witches were hanged in towns of Catalonia, because the local authorities responded to the demands of their citizens, who asked for action whenever the crops were destroyed.[219] Nevertheless, the relative leniency of the Spanish authorities repeatedly led to lynchings, as for instance on the Canary Islands.[220] In Catholic countries like Portugal or Ireland the persecution of witches was significantly less severe than in Protestant countries like England or the Dutch Republic.[221] Traditional stereotypes about economic development and witchcraft, or denomination and witchcraft, must therefore be revised.

Local historians usually acknowledge that there was a witch burning in their village, but emphasize that it happened 'just once', or that the witch-hunter was a foreigner, or invent other excuses. Dutch historians, for instance, explain witch burnings in the Netherlands by claiming they happened under foreign rule, and were not really Dutch. Any burnings under Dutch rule, they claim, were an *exception* to the rule that the Dutch did not burn witches.[222] For the English, the large-scale persecution of the 1640s was an exception, for Swedes the persecution of the 1670s, and for historians of Bamberg the super-hunt in their bishopric around 1630, because it happened 'just once' in a thousand years. But such exceptions were not limited to the Netherlands, England, Sweden and Bamberg. As a general rule we can conclude that the burning of witches was an exception – everywhere. Or at least almost everywhere, since there are a handful of regions with low-scale prosecutions over a longer period, eventually adding up to large numbers of suspects executed (for example, Vaud, Lorraine and Mecklenburg). But normally people are not interested in burning their neighbours, and governments do not wish to wipe out their tax-payers. Nevertheless, the sheer number of exceptions adds up to an overall picture of persecution.

Due to the achievements of recent scholarship it is possible to assemble a more concise overall picture of the severity of witch-hunting in Europe. The figures presented – and in part discussed below – display the present state of research, and contain some interpretations as well, in an attempt to avoid exaggerations or underestimations. They are intended to serve as an invitation to provide more accurate results, and any rectification is welcome. In my eyes a deficient survey makes more sense than none because it can serve as a basis for further discussion, and may indeed provoke future research that leads to improved figures in a process of iteration. To comfort the present-day reader, the numbers presented in table 4.5 are arranged according to present-day boundaries, and compared to estimated population numbers around 1600.[223] This may not do justice to the historical realities in all cases (and may possibly embarrass most of my colleagues), but makes it easier to understand the historical geography of witch-hunting. Statistics work miracles of their own. Although table 4.5 is a crude calculation, and the data fragile to a certain degree, we are able to arrive at a pretty clear-cut and reliable picture: there were at least 50,000 legal executions for witchcraft in Europe, but despite gaps in the sources and a lack of research in some areas we no longer expect that the numbers could increase by more than 20 per cent. Half of the victims were killed within the boundaries of present-day Germany. However, compared to population numbers, there were more intensive persecutions. The tiny Liechtenstein saw by far the most intensive persecutions of all European countries (ratio 10), and we shall see how this observation links in with this princedom's history. Switzerland constitutes the worst case among the larger units (ratio 250–500). Belgium, Luxembourg, Denmark and Poland suffered from persecutions to a degree

Table 4.5   The severity of witch-hunting in Europe

Country	Executions	Inhabitants	Ratio per capita
Turkey	0	unknown	
Ireland	4	1,000,000	250,000
Portugal	10	1,000,000	100,000
Iceland	22	50,000	2,273
Croatia	30	unknown	
Lithuania	50?	unknown	
Estonia	65	unknown	
Finland	115	350,000	3,043
Latvia	150	unknown	
Netherlands	200	1,500,000	7,500
Russia	300	unknown	
Sweden	300	800,000	2,667
Spain	300	8,100,000	27,000
Liechtenstein	300	3,000	10
Norway	350	400,000	1,143
Slovenia	400	unknown	
Slovakia	400	1,000,000	2,500
Austria	500	2,000,000	4,000
Czech Republic	600	1,000,000	1,667
Hungary	800	3,000,000	3,750
Denmark	1,000	570,000	570
Britain	1,500	7,000,000	4,667
Italy	2,500	13,000,000	5,200
Belgium/Luxembourg	2,500	1,300,000	520
Switzerland	4,000	1,000,000	250
Poland	4,000	3,400,000	850
France	5,000	20,000,000	4,000
Germany	25,000	16,000,000	640

comparable to Germany (ratio 500–1,000). A third group is constituted by the Scandinavian countries (Norway, Iceland, Sweden) and
the Czech Republic, Slovakia and Slovenia (ratio 1,000–3,000).
Britain, Austria, France, Italy, Finland and Hungary experienced persecutions of lower, but still considerable, intensity (ratio 3,000–6,000).
And there was a remarkable, though lower, number of executions in
the Netherlands (ratio 6,000–10,000). The final group is probably the
most surprising one: Catholic countries like Spain (ratio 27,000),
Portugal and Ireland, Orthodox countries, and countries under
Ottoman rule, where the danger of witch-hunts was practically
absent. Out of an estimated 80 million inhabitants, one in 1,600 was

executed for witchcraft: this is the average European ratio in our example.

'Germany, mother of so many witches!' was Friedrich Spee's cry in 1631,[224] at the climax of the Central European persecutions, and his desperate diagnosis is confirmed by retrospective statistics. But we have to keep in mind that Germany as a national state did not exist before 1871, and Spee used the Latin term *Germania*, referring to the Germanophone areas. Most of these areas were part of the Holy Roman Empire, but many were not: German-speaking parts of Switzerland, Denmark (duchy of Schleswig), Poland (Prussia and Silesia) and a number of towns in Estonia, Livonia, Hungary and Romania (Transylvania). The emperor was not 'German', but – as a remnant of the Middle Ages – was meant to be the successor of the ancient Roman rulers, and a protector of the Holy (Roman) Church. In 1519 the candidates for succession in the Holy Roman Empire were Francis I of France, Henry VIII of England and Charles I of Spain. The fragile structure of the Holy Roman Empire served in practice as an umbrella for many hundreds of virtually independent territories. It consisted of 7 prince-electorates, 43 secular principalities, 32 ecclesiastical principalities, 140 independent earldoms or lordships, about 70 imperial abbacies, 4 cantons of the Teutonic Order, about 75 imperial cities, and scores of independent imperial knights – in Swabia about 670, in Franconia 700 and in Rhineland about 360. Due to constant fluctuation it is impossible to provide a definite number of all these territories, with their independent jurisdictions, but there must have been more than 2,000 independent territories within the boundaries of this empire.[225] The constitutional pluralism allowed for the coexistence of a multitude of lifestyles, the Reformation with a plurality of denominations, and the invention of the printing press, as well as of the periodical press.[226] This pluralism, however, enabled imperial lords, knights or abbots to commit the most incredible crimes. Only a few of them were ever punished, such as the witch-hunting count of Hohenems and Vaduz, who was stripped of his feudal rights and kept in prison for the rest of his life. His territory was awarded to the princes of Liechtenstein.[227]

Our retrospective statistics for the European witch-hunts require extensive comment, but here it is possible to refer to the literature only where the figures are discussed for each country. Here is an example of the kind of scrutiny to be found in the better cases. In his thorough study of the court protocols and expense registers of Norway, Hans Eyvind Naess has found 863 witch trials, leading to 280 capital punishments. Due to some gaps in the sources, and the steady flow of trials, Naess decided to extrapolate the number of death penalties to an estimated maximum of 350.[228] Rune Hagen has added to these findings that in the northernmost parts of present-day Norway, the Finnmark, the intensity of witch-hunting was considerably higher. In this region, with just a few small fishing villages, he found no less than 167 trials with at least ninety executions between 1600 and 1660. Related to the low population numbers, the 'witchcraft hysteria in the far north' amounts to one of the fiercest persecutions in Europe. It is possibly not by chance that major persecutions were conducted by District Governor John Cunningham (1575–1651), who had been recommended by King James of Scotland/England to King Christian IV of Denmark and Norway, and Cunningham's successor Jon Olafsson (1593–1679).[229]

In contrast to comprehensive studies that provide firm ground for estimates, there is uncertainty about the number of both trials and executions in Eastern European countries. In Russia the sentences of local courts were never recorded, and therefore it is impossible to establish secure numbers. Records of the central authorities refer exclusively to political trials from the reign of Ivan IV 'the Terrible' (1530–84, r. 1547–84) onwards, including the early Romanovs. Despite inquisitorial procedure and excessive use of torture, the number of death sentences was small, and the suspects – approximately 140 – in the known treason trials are around 60 per cent male. But clearly this is the tip of the iceberg. William Ryan was the first to admit that the punishment of serfs would never appear in court, while few cases would ever reach the level of higher courts, where records exist. Recent historians point to the 'Time of Troubles' (1598–1613), a period of unrest, devastating famine, mass popular uprising, civil war and anarchy, and indicate that not just Tsars Boris Godunov (r. 1598–1605) and Dmitri (r. 1605–6) were living in fear of bewitchment, while considered to be sorcerers themselves, but that also the rural population was in turmoil, excited by revivalist preachers and prophets, and exhausted by famine, terror and warfare.[230] As in Western Europe, the witch craze seems to have peaked in the later sixteenth and early seventeenth centuries. However, further research may well demonstrate that among the rural population female victims prevailed in the Muscovite period, as under Kiev Rus, or in nineteenth-century mob lynchings. The period of Mongol domination in Russia is *terra incognita* altogether.

Equally difficult to assess is the source basis in Ukraine, in Belarus, and in Lithuania, formerly mostly under Lithuanian, Polish or Russian rule. Only by coincidence, for instance, was the burning of six witches reported, which was conducted in 1667 in the town of Gadich by a *hetman* (military leader) of the Zaporozhie Cossacks. Some researchers claim that the execution of witches was much less frequent than in Central Europe, but clearly they do not include all the medieval witch-hunts reported in the chronicles or by travellers in their considerations, and the documentary evidence is patchy,[231] except for the more urbanized Baltic areas.[232] Examples such as the lynching of a nobleman in Wolhynia, who was put to the stake by an agitated rabble, led by the parish priest, because he was thought to be responsible for an epidemic, are only recorded because his wife sued the murderers. Janusz Tazbir claimed that half of all victims in Poland and the Ukraine were burned by mobs.[233]Although he forgot to provide supporting evidence, it seems likely that acts of self-defence against supposed sorcerers and witches occurred frequently. Studies of the history of crime and punishment in the Balkans, for Serbia, Bosnia, Bulgaria, Romania, Macedonia, Greece and Albania, are lacking, but, since these countries came under Ottoman rule, death penalties for witchcraft may have been rare and in any case illegal. In tripartite Croatia, some lynchings but no legal trials are recorded from areas under Ottoman rule, few from under Venetian rule and some small panics from Hungarian Croatia. However, trial records from the 1360s in Zagreb, and an execution in Sibenik in 1443, demonstrate the potential for panics. In the eighteenth century, trials conducted by Muslim Bosnians did not differ much from those of their Catholic or Orthodox Christian neighbours.[234] A similar picture seems to emerge from Serbia and Bosnia, Montenegro and Albania, where the populace occasionally resorted to ordeals by water or fire, and stoned women to death, according to the pre-Ottoman legislation of Tsar Stephan Dusan (r. 1331–5), who had pre-sumably corroborated customary law. This practice prevailed far into the nineteenth century and seems to have become less frequent only after a Serbian law code forbade 'searching for the witches, and killing women' in 1810, and the Austrian occupation of Bosnia in 1878.[235]

In the case of Poland the exaggerated number of 10,000 victims, suggested by a Polish historian,[236] has been narrowed down to less than 1,000, but this might be an exaggeration at the other extreme. It seems that there were few executions further to the east, just as in Lithuania, but these were thinly populated areas. The number of exe-cutions in Wielkopolska, 'Greater Poland', around Poznań, was modest as well, and maybe for 'Little Poland' too, but reliable research is lacking.[237] However, the persecution in Pomerania-Stettin claimed up to 600 victims, and Karen Lambrecht collected 593 instances of death penalties for the politically fragmented region of Silesia, the first execution reported from 1461, the last from 1746. Since most suspects in trials with known outcomes were executed, Lambrecht assumes that this applies to a large proportion of the further 264 suspects as well, which would bring the numbers up to 800, and – given a considerable loss of sources – presumably even higher. The frequency of witch trials increased from the 1570s onwards, climaxing only between 1650 and 1670, with two witch panics (Lanken/Lekanów, Jägerndorf/ Karniów), three major perse-cutions (Grünberg/Zielona Góra, Kolzig/Kolsko, Ratibor/Racibórz), but only one large-scale witch-hunt in the principality of Neisse

(Nysa). This territory was subject to the bishop of Breslau (Wrocław), Carl Ferdinand of Poland (1613–55, r. 1613–55), a son of the Polish king. Under his reign the first major persecution occurred in 1649–51, with twenty-seven documented executions, although the actual figure was probably higher, followed by a large-scale hunt in 1651/2, when 250 witches were burned.[238]

After the first mass execution – the burning of eleven witches – in October 1639 the bishop commissioned the construction of a *witch oven* to burn the witches more cheaply and safely, and more rationally – quite macabre in retrospect, since Neisse is not far from Auschwitz. It seems, however, that there were earlier permanent constructions for executions by burning, for instance in the prince-bishoprics of Würzburg and Bamberg from 1627. And the Counter-Reformation bishops presumably learned the technique from Spain, where the Inquisition had constructed burning sites, called *quemadura*, from 1481 onwards.[239] Another peculiarity of the Silesian sample is the importance of deceased witches, who were believed to smack their lips noisily in their graves and eat away the substance of life. The idea that they assumed the quality of vampires – such as in Hungary or Transylvania – was widespread, as was the belief that they caused the plague by *magia posthuma*. As a consequence, supposed witches or revenants were dug out of their graves and their remains burned, with cases evenly distributed from 1337 to 1732. Furthermore, a number of witch trials were conducted against grave-diggers from 1542 to 1681, who were also supposed to spread the plague by extracting poison from those who died of the bubonic plague, then secretly applying it to door-handles.

The numbers for Italy are particularly provisional, since it seems currently impossible to assess the severity of the fifteenth- and sixteenth-century persecutions in the Italian Alpine valleys. Like Germany, Italy was not a nation-state until the later nineteenth century. Politically, parts of the peninsula belonged to Spain, the papal state, the republic of Venice, or the Holy Roman Empire, such as (around 1520) Savoy, Milan, Genoa, and the smaller principalities and city republics, including Mantua and Florence. However, this meant that they were virtually independent. Legally, the peninsula can be divided into three parts during the early modern period: a) the Spanish south (Naples, Sicily, Sardinia) was subject to the Spanish Inquisition and saw many trials, but few executions; b) the Germanophone north, subject partly to the Tyrolean government in Innsbruck, partly to the prince-bishoprics of Trent and Brixen, saw few trials and executions; c) much of the rest was subject from 1542 to the Roman Inquisition, which soon became as careful as its Iberian counterparts. In 1572, the last witches were burned at Rome, when the Holy Office approved four death sentences imposed by the archbishop of Naples. However, the next Pope, Gregory XIII (1502–85,

r. 1572–85), who introduced the Gregorian calendar, was reluctant to allow capital punishment in witch trials. The Holy Office, from about 1580 dominated by Cardinal Giulio Antonio Santori (?–1602), was ready to impose severe sentences against local judges instead, as in 1582, when a local judge of Parrano, north of Orvieto, was condemned to serve as a galley slave for seven years.[240] However, these attempts at calming down the excitement were not always successful, as in the case of the powerful Counter-Reforming Archbishop St Carlo Borromeo of Milan (1538–84, r. 1563–84), who authorized an as yet unknown number of burnings in his diocese.[241] Already in 1569 the Roman Inqusition recommended greater care in witch trials.[242] Even Italian-speaking valleys in the Swiss canton of Graubünden were affected by the Milanese Counter-Reformation, such as the valley of Mesolcina, where a large-scale persecution was conducted in 1583. Witch trials in the valleys of Misox, Calanca and Poschiavo led to dozens of witches being burned throughout the seventeenth century.[243] Ten witches were executed in Bologna between 1498 and 1579, nine in Milan between 1599 and 1620, and five in Siena in 1569, while executions are also known from Perugia and Mantua.[244] As had happened in the area north of the Alps, the number of trials increased after 1580, with severe panics in Genoa and Naples in 1588, both crushed by the Inquisition.[245] As far as the secular jurisdiction is concerned, the powerful analysis of the Sienese sources[246] demonstrates that our knowledge of Italy is no better than sketchy, not due to the lack of sources, but to a lack of research.

The numbers for France are a matter of dispute, largely due to 'the dismally poor level of preservation of local judicial archives across France, which are virtually non-existent for any first instance court before the later decades of the 17th century'.[247] Robert Muchembled gives estimates for many parts of Europe, even related to population numbers, but not for his own country.[248] As Alfred Soman has pointed out, his analysis of an almost complete series of appeal cases to the Parlement de Paris has to be complemented with similar research in the archives of the other courts of appeal, and the sources of the provincial courts, since control by the high courts (parlements) was not obligatory until 1625.[249] For the district of the Parlement de Paris, by far the most important court, covering about one-third of the territory of present-day France, he found 1,123 witchcraft appeals between 1564 and 1640, resulting in only 115 confirmed death sentences. Further to these executions, 52 suspects died in prison, another 130 received corporal punishments and 395 non-corporal punishments, which could still mean severe hardship, like banishment or lifelong service on the galleys. Among contemporaries these kinds of sentences were considered equal to death, since they meant at least social death. The outcome of twenty-four cases is unknown. Soman congratulates the Parlement of Paris, since the sentences of the lower

courts were indeed more unpleasant: 474 burnings, 416 corporal punishments and 233 non-corporal punishments. Had they not been
curbed, this would have amounted to a large-scale persecution.
However, there remains the problem that we do not know what these
figures actually mean, since it was up to the convicted to appeal, but
one could expect that some of those convicted accepted their sentence, while others were strongly discouraged from appealing to the
higher court, or their right was denied.[250] Monter found similarly low
numbers in the archives of the Parlements of Burgundy, Dauphiné,
Guyenne, Languedoc, Normandy and Provence, and concluded
that French courts were particularly lenient: for the core period
of 1580–1630 he identified 'only ten [executions confirmed] at
Aix-en-Provences [Languedoc], probably even fewer at Grenoble
[Dauphiné] or Rennes [Brittanny], perhaps twenty at Dijon
[Burgundy], and about two dozens apiece at de Lancre's Bordeaux
[Guyenne] or at Toulouse'. Only Rouen (Normandy) 'executed relatively large numbers of witches, about 90 in all'.[251] All in all this would
add up to something like 300 executions for witchcraft in France.

In conclusion, we know the number of appeals, but we do not know
the numbers of witch trials and executions. As in the case of the Imperial Chamber Court (see table 4.4) we can clearly see the overall
trends, but do not get exact figures. Brian Levack's estimate of 4,000
trials for the kingdom of France still sounds sensible, and these do
not include the wild lynchings in some parts of France, for instance
the killing of 300 witches in the Ardennes.[252] Legal and illegal executions taken together, we may end up with about 1,000 deaths.
However, in our survey we are not referring to the now-forgotten
borders of early modern territories, but to death penalties for witchcraft within the borders of the present existing states. The numbers
presented here for France therefore include (anachronistically) the
trials in the Dauphiné and the Artois, the Franche Comté, as well as
estimates for executions in the Alsace (with an estimated 1,000 burnings),[253] Lorraine (with an estimated 2,000 death sentences), Montbeliard, and the papal estates around Avignon, Brittany, Burgundy
and Normandy – all of which add up to at least 5,000 executions over
the whole period between 1400 and 1800.

For witchcraft and sorcery in Europe between 1400 and 1800, all
in all, we estimate something like 50,000 legal death penalties at least
half of them within the boundaries of the Holy Roman Empire.[254] The
number of trials that ended up with sentences other than capital punishment, as for instance banishment, fines, or church penance, may
have been twice as high, largely depending on the conviction rate.
The so-called trial/conviction ratio, provided by a number of scholars in order to estimate the severity of persecution, in reality does
not offer any useful information in itself. Many territories did not
accept weak accusations, and therefore arrived at a low number of

acquittals, whereas other territories would imprison literally anyone, and may have arrived at a low 'execution rate', even if they burned a substantial number of witches. Whereas careful estimates some generations ago arrived at about 100,000 victims, Levack brought this down to 60,000 executions,[255] while Monter seems to be opting for less than 40,000 in a more recent estimate.[256] This may be a bit too optimistic and does not leave much room for surprises, such as the dramatic recent figures for the Spanish Netherlands, Kurtrier, or the duchies of Holstein, Mecklenburg and Pomerania. Certainly it does not include medieval persecutions, in Russia, for example. Not all corners of Europe have been explored yet. Nevertheless, leading historians have reached a kind of consensus about an approximate figure.

Considerably higher numbers are still being circulated in popular literature and magazines, suggesting incredible numbers of people executed on Christian stakes, millions of witches, a holocaust of women, or 'gynocide', as a feminist author has claimed.[257] Some years ago I tried to trace the origin of these exaggerated numbers. It turned out that it was exclusively based upon the projection of Gottfried Christian Voigt (1740–91), who had stumbled across some twenty files of witch trials in the city archive of Quedlinburg, and started calculating in the following manner: if there were twenty trials in fifty years in Quedlinburg, this meant so-and-so many in 100 years, and accordingly so-and-so many in 1,800 years of Christian history. Quedlinburg had only so-and-so many inhabitants, compared to the whole of Europe, with so-and-so many inhabitants. Then Voigt calculated the number of victims for the whole of Europe according to the rule of three, based upon the assumption that witch-hunting had been of equal severity everywhere and at all times.[258] The imperial Abbey of Quedlinburg had joined the Reformation in 1539, fell victim to electoral Saxony in 1648, and to electoral Brandenburg/Prussia in 1697, and had presumably never had more trials than those recorded in its archive. Voigt's projection was nothing but methodological nonsense, and a result of his anti-clericalism. The calculation was adopted by the Viennese professor of Church history, Gustav Roskoff (1814–89), who included it in his authoritative *History of the Devil*, and simplified the number to an eye-catching 9 million witches.[259] During the period of the 'Kulturkampf', a conflict between the state and the Catholic Church after the Pope's decree of infallibility, Roskoff's suggestion was widely used by Protestant authors, and even dictionaries embarked on the inflation of numbers, usually ending up somewhere between 1 and 6 million. In this form the calculation was adopted by the neo-pagan movement in Germany, and furthermore by Nazi feminists, an as yet unwritten history. Eventually the 'millions of witches' were utilized by Nazi propaganda (see chapter 7), thus gaining more prominence than ever before. It is not by coincidence that after the

Second World War these numbers were carried further within the international neo-pagan and feminist movements, and it would be interesting to research the details of how they got these numbers from their German brothers and sisters. Serious feminist authors ought to be aware of the origins of the idea that up to 9 million witches were burned in Europe.[260]

Even if these extraordinary numbers cannot be confirmed, it is frightening to consider how many people were burned at the stake, many of them still alive as the fire was started. About 80 per cent of these victims were female, which corresponds with the most widespread European witch stereotype. One can only speculate how the gender distribution would have changed had the hothouses of persecution been not in Central but in Northern Europe, where witchcraft was more likely to be attributed to men, supposedly because of the shamanistic tradition in these countries, which puzzled European ethnographers in the era of the Enlightenment.[261] In Iceland for instance, about 90 per cent of the convicted were male, in Estonia 60 per cent and in Finland 50 per cent. Under the jurisdiction of the Parlement de Paris, where 1,123 appellations related to magic, sorcery and witchcraft were heard, and in some Alpine regions, the gender distribution was similarly balanced.[262] In Central Europe the witch stereotype was basically female from the beginning, and continued to be so throughout the sixteenth century. It collapsed only during the large-scale persecutions of the 1590s, due to 'crises of confidence' in individual witch-hunts,[263] and a changing climate of public opinion, as indicated by the publications of Johann Weyer and other courageous opponents of witch-hunting (see chapter 5). In the course of large-scale witch-hunts the social profile of the victims changed decisively. Old and impoverished widows from rural milieus were supplemented by wealthy urban housewives and their husbands. In the most excessive witch-hunts in the German bishoprics, the richest citizens, clergy, noblemen and members of the government, the male ruling elite, were affected disproportionately. But even there the proportion of male victims remained between 25–30 per cent. The *social mechanisms of the large-scale persecutions* have not yet really been explored, and the breakdown of the stereotype has been taken for granted. But it seems likely that the weaker victims used the witch-hunts to attack the ruling elites, either for reasons of revenge or in order to bring the persecutions to a halt.[264]

Within early modern European society it was almost proverbial that justice would never reach the rich. Indeed – very much like in our own enlightened and 'modern' societies – there were many opportunities of escape for the powerful, if they were ever accused of any crime. Except for political reasons, it was extremely rare for the clergy, the nobility or the rich urban patriciate to be tried and convicted in a formal criminal trial, with two remarkable exceptions:

the French Revolution and the great witch-hunts. Even in the nineteenth century, scholars like Soldan, Hansen or George Lincoln Burr (1857–1938) had pointed to the fact that during the great witch-hunts simple denunciation in the trials was regarded as sufficient circumstantial evidence not only for imprisonment, but also for torture. Torture, as the seventeenth-century critics had emphasized, was the very basis of the witch-hunts because under the conditions of unlimited torturing – characteristic of *crimina excepta* – almost anybody would confess anything.

More recently, scholars like Lyndal Roper have emphasized the aspect of negotiation in witch trials: the suspects could not just confess at random, but had to reconcile these stories with their life histories and their life experience, in order to make their confessions sound credible to the judges. Therefore the suspects would name primarily relatives or friends as accomplices. However true this may be, it certainly underestimates the strategies of those destined for the stake. After having confessed or officially having been convicted, it still seems hardly likely that they themselves believed their own confessions or would voluntarily condemn their closest friends to death. Rather, we should assume that they tried to involve their enemies, such as those responsible for the witch-hunts. It is true that there were a number of legal obstacles, for instance the fact that enmity could devalue accusations, and the judges obviously tried to prevent their relatives from being involved in witch-hunts by suppressing accusations. As a compromise, it seems, the convicted systematically tried to extend the persecution to the higher ranks, who were in close contact with those in charge of the witch-hunts. Only if they accused their neighbours, the wives of the judges, or the judges and councillors themselves, would it be accepted as a credible accusation. This was the case in a number of large-scale witch-hunts, where the social elite became disproportionately affected by the persecutions. A leaflet of 1629 emphasized the fact that scores of councillors had been burned, who had ruled the towns of the principality or the principality itself, and had been used to sitting at dinner with the bishop of Bamberg.[265] Even more so, we ought to acknowledge that the defenders of the witches, from Weyer to Spee, never tried to confine their protection to male witches, to lord mayors or princely councillors, but took care of exactly those women who were at the heart of the European witch-belief, and boldly attacked the witch stereotype.

That Central Europe became the *heartland of the witch craze* had a lot to do with the authorities' attitudes, the structural weakness of the states involved, the judicial system and possibly also with the prevailing kind of witch-belief, which singled out the most vulnerable members of society. It can also be related to cultural, social and ecological crises, due to the hardships of the Little Ice Age. However, nature and climate cannot serve as the sole cause, but have to be seen in combination with the organization of agriculture, transport and communication, the distribution of wealth or the existing power relations. Population density, the infrastructure of transportation, and capacities of storage – in short, *man-made conditions* – played an important role. These factors can be related to geography as well. Harvest failure in one region could potentially be balanced out by favourable harvests elsewhere. The shipping of cereals increased at an unprecedented rate in the second half of the sixteenth century. One of the reasons that England, the Netherlands, western France or Portugal were less affected by witchcraft accusations could be due to the shipping facilities along coastlines and major rivers. Starvation was not a major problem at the Western fringes of Europe, and epidemic diseases were also probably less severe. The sea climate prevented extreme frosts with all the related hardship. To improve the transport facilities in Central Europe was much more difficult, and only systematic road construction, or railroads, would eventually abolish the danger of famine.

Topography played an important role as well. Due to its sea climate England was certainly less affected by global cooling than the mountainous areas of Scandinavia, or Switzerland, where marginal soils in the highlands had to be abandoned, with a corresponding increase of social tensions. For parts of Northern and Eastern Europe, on the other hand, global cooling may have been less surprising because unfavourable climates had never been uncommon, and the Scottish Lowlands are climatically similar to northern England, but saw decisively more witch trials. The impact of the Little Ice Age was less severe in those parts of Western Europe that benefited from the Atlantic climate, and extreme climatic events were softened by the Gulf Stream. In the Mediterranean, for instance Castile, it was not coldness or increased precipitation that caused problems, but drought. The climatic deterioration was most unfavourable for the densely populated areas of Central Europe, where the infrastructure was poor, and which suffered from the negative aspects of the continental climate, prolonged harsh winters and increased precipitation. Wilhelm Abel has demonstrated that the hunger crisis of 1570 affected continental Europe, from Paris to Moscow, to a very high degree, but the effects on areas along coastlines, including England and most of Italy, were limited, or even totally absent.[266]

Another interesting aspect concerns the *structure of settlement*. Paul Baxter has pointed to the fact that suspicions of witchcraft are rare among nomads, and that 'absence makes the heart grow fonder'.[267] Jonathan Pearl has pointed out that one of the differences between colonial New England and colonial New France was that in Canada village settlements were unusual, as the settlers preferred to live in single farms, scattered throughout the woodlands. Villages served as breeding places for social tensions, which grew more intense during times of hardship, but without villages the individual disappointment could be less easily projected on to a neighbour.[268] Similar settlement structures can be found in Iceland and other parts of northern Scandinavia, with equally low rates of witch trials. Brain has pushed the argument to a higher level with his observation that generally hunters and gatherers are, like people in industrialized societies, unconcerned with witchcraft. Whereas 'sedentary small-scale agriculturalists' are tied to the land, and are forced to coexist with their fellow-villagers, with plenty of reasons for conflict, but without a safety valve for strong emotions like hatred, envy or jealousy, the life of hunters and gatherers is characterized by a high degree of personal autonomy, lack of dependence on other people and a high mobility. If tension develops, the parties can be removed from each other, an equivalent to the high rate of geographic, residential and job mobility in modern societies, where working relationships are often impersonal as well. A further similarity is that hunter-gatherers, like most people in industrial societies, are not obsessed by the dichotomy of culture and nature. Hunter-gatherers are part of both spheres, 'the bush' being part of their subsistence, and not perceived as being unstructured, disorderly and dangerous, and the antagonism is irrelevant and meaningless; those in industrial societies are too distant from agriculture to be scared by nature, which is rather welcomed as a leisure paradise. Furthermore, in both types of societies women have a role of relative equality with men, because there is no marked division of labour by sex.[269]

Furthermore the *type of agriculture* plays an important role. Fritz Byloff has emphasized that vine-growing areas were particularly affected by witchcraft accusations and persecutions.[270] In his detailed research on witch trials in Styria, Helfried Valentinitsch demonstrated that vine-growing valleys were much more affected by witch panics than valleys with different types of crops. Grapevines in northern conditions are particularly vulnerable, and the climatic deterioration during the early modern period endangered the subsistence of the vine-growing peasantry.[271] A great number of large-scale witch-hunts happened at the northern fringes of vine-growing, for instance in Styria, Franconia, Swabia, the Valais, the Alsace, Lorraine, the Mosel region or the Rhineland. It is not hard to understand that the failure of the vine harvest, like crop failure, led to social hardship, increasing tensions within families and communities, and increasing tensions within society as a whole, because the lower orders had to suffer from hunger and diseases disproportionately, whereas the merchant class and the nobility usually profited from scarcity. The prosperity of the upper classes in the decades around 1600, years of investment in architecture and art production, was paid for by the malnutrition of the majority.

Although this may not apply to every corner of Europe, and certainly not to the colonies, the *price curves of grain* can serve as a general indicator of social crises because they reflect the demand of the many, and the scarcity of supply during agrarian crises. Price peaks indicate crop failure, enhanced susceptibility to diseases and rising social tensions. As scholars have known for decades, the sixteenth century struggled not only with frequent short-term crises, but suffered from a long-term price rise. This has formerly been explained as inflation caused by the influx of American gold and silver. Economic historians nowadays assume that the increase of goods bypassed the increase of money, and relate the price rises to a rise in population numbers, causing an increasing demand for foodstuff. The drama of the period, one could say, lay in the dilemma that the most obvious reaction to this increasing demand was not feasible in a short-term reaction. During the increase in population of the High Middle Ages more and more farmland had been cleared, up to a point where marginal uphill lands or those with poor soil quality could no longer justify the increasing investment in labour. In the fourteenth century, therefore, the clearing had come to a halt, and famine and epidemics reduced the European population, first with the Great Famine, then from the Black Death.[272] From the late fifteenth century another upswing in population numbers created an increase in demand again. There was already considerable *demographic pressure* when the expanding economy was hit by climatic deterioration in the 1560s. This unexpected turn not only limited the option of clearing more farmland, but also meant that marginal farmland had to be abandoned. This added decisively to the increasing structural problem of the European economies. Growing demand for foodstuffs and a stagnating supply led to a long-term price rise, and to famine in cases of crop failure, when prices rocketed. Research into the development of the *real wages* of labourers in Augsburg has demonstrated that these non-agrarian workers must have faced substantial difficulties in sustaining their families from the 1580s.[273]

As a consequence, we can conclude that an endogenous structural crisis and an exogenous climatic deterioration interacted in the most unfavourable way. The crop failures affected an already vulnerable economy, and each sudden price rise inflicted severe hardship and caused strong social frictions. The tension between population and food production lessened only after a series of severe epidemics in the 1630s and 1640s, when *high mortality rates* – and in Central Europe extremely high mortality rates of up to 60 per cent – caused a decrease in population numbers, economic stagnation or even long-term recession. It was not until the era of the Enlightenment that the Western economies managed to improve their infrastructures by means of constructing canals and highways, and were able to achieve qualitative improvements in food production, thus escaping the Malthusian vicious circle. Although extreme climatic events still occurred, they did so less frequently, and could be considered to be isolated events, such as the Tambora Freeze of 1816, a global cooling felt for a number of years after a major volcanic eruption of Mount Tambora in Indonesia.[274]

The *psychology of the witch-hunters* is another as yet unsystematically tilled field of research. It is no exaggeration that contemporaries were already concerned about this, as can be seen by the portrayal of the zealous inquisitor by Erasmus of Rotterdam, or of the witch-hunter by Agrippa and his student Weyer. During the twentieth century a follower of Sigmund Freud, the Swiss Reformed theologian Oskar Pfister (1873–1956), tried to demonstrate with the example of Calvin how the meaning of the New Testament was overturned when Christian magistrates, among these the government of Geneva, were ready to sacrifice human lives in order to defend dogmas, rites or institutions to serve a pathological *angst* related to 'God's honour'.[275] The observation that many theologians imagined God not as a kind father but rather as a cruel fundamentalist, ready to burst into wild fury on the slightest occasion, had already been made by contemporaries like Friedrich Spee, who had claimed that this God seemed to resemble a pagan Moloch, demanding human sacrifice. The character profile of the *authoritarian personality* not only applies to Fascist or Nazi voters,[276] but also to those jurists, theologians, councillors or princes who embarked on the business of witch-hunting around 1600. The objection that such an application would be anachronistic can be tested by applying the same questions to the opponents of witch-hunting listed in the sources, or by their publications, and whose activities were often driven by compassion for the persecuted, rather than the zeal to eradicate evil, or to believe in the existence of a great conspiracy.[277] Some contemporaries recognized that witch-hunts often coincided with periods of moral campaigns, when *moral entrepreneurs*, or 'crusading reformers', as Howard S. Becker (b. 1928) has called them, succeeded in taking the initiative: 'He operates with an absolute ethic; what he sees is truly and totally evil with no qualification. Any means is justified to do away with it. The crusader is fervent and righteous, often self-righteous. It is appropriate to think of [these] reformers as crusaders because they typically believe that their mission is a holy one.'[278] It sounds almost a truism that persecutors were probably less open-minded than the defenders of the persecuted, that they felt less compassion for people, and were driven to defend authorities and dogmas instead, as suggested by Milton Rokeach (1918–88).[279]

The suppression of pogrom movements against witchcraft always moves them into illegality. Under the jurisdiction of the Parlement de Paris dozens of supposed witches were lynched by mobs, particularly in the mountainous regions of the Ardennes, because the populace was aware of the fact that the high court would not concede to their demand for persecution.[280] Illegal witch-hunts, or lynchings, are an important and yet little-explored issue. It is difficult to provide sound overall estimates for the relation between legal and illegal execution of witches, because the official records document exclusively the actions of the secular and the ecclesiastical authorities, and would refer to vigilantism only if legal action was taken. Surprisingly, this brings us to the very beginning of the European witch-hunts, when a man named Gögler was punished for accusing women of witchcraft in Lucerne in 1419. This incident was one of the first times that the German term for witchcraft – *hexereye* – was used in court.[281] During the witch craze of 1590 the imperial city of Nuremberg chose to impose capital punishment on a man who had served as a witch-finder. The former apprentice of the hangman of Eichstätt had pretended to be able to know witches by their eyes.[282] As mentioned above, lynchings are known from France, Spain, Poland and Italy, where a woman at Reggio Emilia was stoned to death in 1599 when the Inquisition had released her.[283] After witchcraft laws were repealed in Europe, witch-beliefs lingered on. From England numerous incidents of 'ducking' witches – the water test – tell us of the discrepancy between popular perception and law, very much as it had been before the start of legal witch-hunting in Europe. Then it had been Church law, and later it was secular law, that denied the capacity of supposed witches to cause harm, leaving the people alone with their misery and fear, while punishing those who dared to challenge the authorities (see chapter 6).

5

Outlawing Witchcraft Persecution in Europe

The killing of witches is nothing but a massacre of the innocents.
Johann Weyer, *De Praestigiis Daemonum*, 1563

It seems that the *disenchantment of the world* was anything but a natural development, a built-in consequence of progress, and certainly not as inevitable as Weber imagined it to be. Religion, ancestor cults or philosophy, Chinese or Greek, could discourage the attribution of misfortune to witchcraft, but a clear, definite and sustained outlawing of witch persecution was unique. Therefore it seems worthwhile to look into its historic background, and possibly redefine its foundations. Given the fact that the idea of a cumulative crime of witchcraft, developed in the fifteenth century, has been present ever since, we could ask why not much more than 50,000 people have been killed for witchcraft in Europe. The answer seems to be that there has always been considerable *scepticism* about witch-beliefs, and a dislike of fanatical inquisitors and witch-hunters with their false certainties, which cost dissenters' lives. As could be expected from the Renaissance, learned scepticism was rooted in Ancient philosophy, for instance the thought of Pyrrho of Elis (*c.*360–275 BC) or his disciple Sextus Empiricus.[1] Harsh criticism of witch-hunting was backed up throughout the early modern period by quotations from classical authors, such as Horace or Lucian.[2]

However, early Christian doubts as to the efficacy of any kind of sorcery had remained strong throughout the Middle Ages, as can be seen from the *Canon Episcopi*,[3] and were presumably the most important source of resistance. These doubts have contained the demand for persecutions, and spiritual measures absorbed more serious forms of suppression of witchcraft. It was only the authority given to inquisitors by the papacy that broke the bulwarks of tradition. This interference made it inevitable that criticism of witch-hunting became entangled with anti-clericalism and anti-Roman feelings from the beginning. The argument that there were no witches before the appearance of papal inquisitors had already begun at the start of the sixteenth century, and was widely used by intellectual critics. Some humanist opinion leaders took a definite stand against inquisitorial witch-belief in general, and the witch-hunts in particular. Nicolaus of Cusa (1401–64), who defined God mathematically as the *coincidentia oppositorum*, preached against the new inquisitorial witch pattern, and explained why two women under his jurisdiction – as prince-bishop of Brixen, Cusa ruled a territory of the Holy Roman Empire – who had confessed to flying through the air were mentally handicapped rather than minions of the devil.[4] Cusa's argument conformed to canon law, the penitentials and Gratian's decrees, but clearly there was a new dimension, since the philosopher reacted to the new challenge of the massive witch-hunts of the mid-fourteenth century. Those who knew his ideas could hardly assume that his was the viewpoint of a ninth-century abbot, and whoever wished could find his sceptical ideas in print.[5] In contrast to Germany and Austria, where persecutions were stopped immediately (see chapter 3) and the Inquisition was stripped of its rights by secular rulers, the Inquisition remained strong in Italy and its confrontation with opponents of persecution was equally fierce. The conflict was shaped by the long-standing antagonism between Dominicans and Franciscans. The Milanese philosopher and Franciscan friar Samuel de Cassinis attacked the witch-hunts in his treatise *De Lamiis, quas Strigas Vocant*. Like Cusa, Cassinis denied the reality of the witches' flight, of the witches' sabbat and of the cumulative construction of witchcraft, on the basis of the canon law in general, and the *Canon Episcopi* in particular.[6]

Such an attack, bold as it was, might have perpetuated the usual infighting between the mendicant Orders, but around 1500 the rules of the game changed decisively, and forever. It has always been argued that the ideas of the *Malleus* were disseminated by print, but the same holds true for its opponents, like Molitor or Cassinis. Critics and sceptics published their ideas in print, their treatises were sold and purchased everywhere in Europe, and they could no longer be silenced. The printing revolution created new audiences and fostered the rise of public opinion. This medium could not be controlled by the Church. Institutions of the emerging European states, such as courts, councils, academies and universities, provided platforms of discussion. And the secular necessities of state administration bred new attitudes towards spiritual affairs. Niccolò Machiavelli (1469–1527) represents the potential of Renaissance politics. In his famous writings, for instance his classic *Il Principe* (*The Prince*), religion was reduced to a tactical matter for the rational ruler.[7] In his *Discorsi*, the Florentine politician implies that religion merely serves as an instrument to frighten and discipline the populace.[8] The implications of such an attitude mark a paradigm shift in the Kuhnian sense: *politics* moves to the centre of history. Divine predestination is dismissed as irrelevant, if not non-existent, very much as in the perception of the Paduan philosopher Pietro Pomponazzi (1462–1525), who denied the immortality of the soul and the existence of hell.[9] Magic and witchcraft were not worth mentioning in such a context – they were just another invention, ridiculous to the man of virtue, the rational ruler, or the politician, who acted according to necessity and *reason of state*. Machiavelli's books, although on the 'Index librorum prohibitorum', moulded the debate about politics throughout the early modern period. Even within the confessional age, religious zealots were always complaining about Epicureans, Pyrrhonians, Libertines or Atheists, usually referring to those who did not comply with religious zeal, and rather displayed a common-sense attitude.[10]

In the middle ground between atheism and religious zeal a stratum of educated intellectuals emerged, trained beyond the standard curriculum of the seven liberal arts and the professional disciplines of theology, medicine and law, and influenced by Florentine humanism and the publications of Erasmus of Rotterdam (1466–1536). In his *Encomium Moriae* (*Praise of Folly*) the Dutch scholar dared to ridicule zealous inquisitors, who sacrificed innocent victims in order to serve their crazy theories. Without mentioning witchcraft, Erasmus ridiculed the Dominican friars for being credulous, superstitious and bloodthirsty.[11] In the debate about the 'free will' Erasmus rejected Luther's new dogmatism,[12] fostering the seemingly mild, but eventually endurable scepticism that could drive the dogmatics of the confessional age insane. Erasmus' attitude proved to be enormously influential with the spiritualist currents, radical reformers and sectarian groups, which generally despised the persecutory attitude, and denied the importance of magic and witchcraft.[13] But there were numerous mainstream admirers as well, like Andrea Alciati (1492–1550), the leading commentator of the *Corpus Juris Civilis*. In his *De lamiis et strigibus*, Alciati was the first secular author to brand the witch-hunts in the Italian Alps inhumane – in his words a *nova holocausta*, a new holocaust. Alciati created the paradigmatic interpretation that the Inquisition was not fighting against witchcraft, but was creating the witches itself – an almost Durkheimian interpretation.[14]

How influential Alciati's paradigm was can be seen from other contemporary humanists, like the German natural philosopher Agrippa. Unlike Erasmus, who spent most of his later life timidly in

Basel and Freiburg without apparent concern for the witch burnings nearby, Agrippa took action. He fought against witch burnings in the imperial city of Metz, where he courageously defended an old woman against the Inquisition of the Dominican Nicolaus Savini, whom he attacked publicly because of Savini's reliance on the ridiculous 'fantasies' of the *Malleus Maleficarum*. Agrippa repeated this bold attack on the *Malleus* and on the large-scale witch trials in Italy in his famous book *Of the Uncertainty and Vanity of the Arts and Sciences*, where he criticizes the 'art of inquisition' at length and with unprecedented vigour, labelling the witch-hunter as a 'murderous inquisitor', a 'cruel hypocrite' and a 'bloodthirsty monk', linking his defence of accused witches to Johannes Reuchlin's defence of Hebrew scholarship.[15] Agrippa was quite well informed about the debates in Italy, where politicians indeed dared to challenge the institution of the papal Inquisition. The large-scale persecution of witches in the Valcamonica, triggered by the bishop of Brescia in the summer of 1518, immediately provoked the attention of the republic of Venice, the valley's worldly overlord. The Serenissima stopped the persecution almost as soon as the news arrived. The Council of Ten summoned the inquisitors to Venice, which in turn led to a political conflict between the city republic and Pope Leo X, who tried to protect the power of the Inquisition court. The Venetian politicians, on the other hand, despised the illegal procedures of the inquisitors, and Vice-Doge Luca Tron bluntly branded all stories of flying witches as 'nonsense'. Even low-ranking citizens like the famous diarist Marino Sanudo called the executed people 'martyrs'. The conflict dragged on for more than three years, with inquisitors in the region continuing to capture 'witches', and the Venetian government immediately blocking the trials. In July 1521, however, the Venetian government utilized the beginnings of the war between France and Charles V to terminate all trials.[16]

In Italy, Austria and Germany lawyers and politicians had struggled against witch-hunting, but in Spain it was a national conference of inquisitors at Granada that decided in 1526 to dismiss the authority of the *Malleus*, and act with extreme caution in such an uncertain business as witchcraft. This decision was triggered by a witch-hunt in the kingdom of Navarre in 1525, where witch-commissioners, appointed by the government, cooperated with local witch-doctors and two ecstatic girls who claimed to recognize witches by looking into their eyes, where they could see the devil's mark.[17] As in present-day African anti-witchcraft movements, hundreds of people volunteered for the test. Many people were arrested, their livestock confiscated and an unknown number of witches were burned in five places. The procedure was so incredible that the Supreme Council of the Spanish Inquisition decided to intervene. After having gained control, the Inquisition re-examined the cases of the remaining thirty prisoners. After intensive discussions the Supreme Council issued its guidelines for witch trials in all parts of the Spanish realm. Although they asserted the reality of the crime, and even of the witches' sabbat, they recommended great caution, and forbade the employment of visionaries and witch-doctors, as well as confiscations. Regarding the reality of *maleficium*, which accounted for most of the death sentences, the council remained sceptical, and the guidelines aimed at education rather than persecution.[18] In Spain and Portugal, the only European countries where the Inquisition had been institutionalized as a permanent authority in the late fifteenth century, this institution of persecution decided to stop witch trials. Throughout the sixteenth and early seventeenth centuries the local populace and town councils in northern Spain continued trying to prosecute witches.[19] But the Spanish Inquisition had embarked on a policy of monopolizing witch trials in order to suppress them. In this respect, the Protestant ethic and the spirit of capitalism can be discounted: in Spain and Portugal, the world powers of their age, fewer witches were legally executed than in Britain, even if we include their colonies in Africa, America and Asia.[20]

Spanish and German traditions seem to have met in the legislation of Emperor Charles V (1500–58, r. 1519–57), the leading ruler of his age. Although later a fervent proponent of Catholic confessionalism, this Habsburg prince was brought up by 'Erasmian' tutors in the Netherlands. The grandson of Emperor Maximilian I was educated in the Burgundian tradition, and became duke of Burgundy in 1515. In the following year he succeeded to the throne of Spain, being crowned Carlos I, and was elected emperor three years later at the imperial diet of Augsburg, where he was named Charles V. His criminal law of 1532, promulgated as *Constitutio Criminalis Carolina*, had been negotiated long before among the imperial estates. This law, which remained virtually unchanged until the collapse of the Holy Roman Empire in 1806, completely ignored the cumulative crime of witchcraft as defined by the *Witches' Hammer*. It contained a paragraph against harmful magic (§ 109), the treatment of which was regulated scrupulously in three paragraphs on procedural law (§§ 21, 44, 52). Capital punishment was confined to cases where harmful magic could be proven beyond doubt, while non-harmful magic of any sort was left to the arbitrary judgment of the courts. The inquisitorial procedure of the *Carolina* scrupulously avoided the shortcomings of Inquisition courts, by granting clearly defined rights to the suspect, ruling out the arbitrary use of violence and granting certainty of law. Every capital sentence had to be submitted to a high court or a law faculty, in order to avoid arbitrary acts of local courts. Within the boundaries of the *processus ordinarius*, as later jurists would call it, torture could only be used as a legal means in cases of evident guilt, when the suspect already stood convicted by two independent witnesses, or in cases of clear evidence. Torture was not to be employed in order to extract confessions on the basis of mere denunciation or suspicion. Later witch-hunters would complain that under these conditions hardly anyone could be convicted of witchcraft. Indeed, this may have been the purpose of the legislation. Its main author, the Franconian baron Johann von Schwarzenberg (1463–1528), a humanist translator of Cicero who had joined the Lutheran Reformation in 1521 and was one of the first lords to forbid the Catholic rites in his territory, had been a member of Maximilian I's entourage in the late 1480s, and was presumably familiar with the discussions about the scandalous Inquisitions of Heinrich Kramer, the author of the *Malleus*. In contrast to an earlier law code designed by Schwarzenberg before the Reformation, he now eliminated the paragraphs concerning the belief in the interference of good or evil spirits, and any traces of heresy laws. The *Carolina* clearly signalled the disapproval of Inquisition courts, whose activities were no longer to be tolerated by the German estates, thus marking a clear difference from Charles's Spanish and Italian territories.[21]

The Reformation contributed to the decline of witch-beliefs in the long term because Protestant countries abandoned inquisitorial courts altogether, and reformed theologians attacked magic and supernatural agencies in general, or were at least interpreted to have done so at a later stage. In the eyes of Luther, Zwingli or Calvin, Catholic piety and Catholic rites – the veneration of saints, the expectation of miracles, the mass, the performance of pilgrimages and the use of sacramentals – were not really different from rural superstitions, and Protestant pamphlets could easily use terms like 'popish sorcery'. However, Luther, Zwingli and Calvin did not deny the existence of witchcraft and witches, and Calvinist theologians in particular, such as John Knox (1513–72) or Lambert Daneau (1530–96), perceived the witches' pact with the devil as being diametrically opposed to the believers' covenant with God. Therefore, as Larner has argued, it seemed necessary to believe in witchcraft, and to persecute witches.[22] Although the Reformation coincided with a decrease in the number of witch burnings, there seems to be no causal relation. Indeed, Protestant states were the first to start witch-hunts in the 1560s, as Johann Weyer remarked with indignation.[23]

On the other hand, it seems clear enough that the major protests against witch-hunting were published by Protestant authors, although some caution is necessary, since some concealed their confessional identity. They had good reasons for doing so, if they were not mainstream believers, like Johann Weyer,[24] Reginald Scot (1538–99), and maybe also Anton Praetorius (1555–1625), who are now believed to have been members of the 'Family of Love', a secret network of Spiritualists, who deliberately concealed their confessional identity in an age of persecution.[25] The most important criticism of witch-hunting was developed by Johann Weyer (1515–88). Weyer was born in Grave on the Meuse, 25 kilometres west of Cleves, as son of a hop merchant. At the age of fifteen, around 1530, Weyer went to study and work in the household of the famous physician and sceptical philosopher Agrippa at Bonn, capital of the archbishops of Cologne, and at Mechelen, the residence of the Holy Roman Emperor. In 1534 Weyer began to study medicine at the universities of Paris and Orléans. With his doctoral degree, Weyer became a physician, first at Arnheim (Gelderland) in 1545, where he married Judith Wintgens. In 1550 Weyer was appointed court physician, and went to Düsseldorf, the residence of Duke Wilhelm V, 'the Rich', of Jülich-Cleves (1516–92). The court and government at Düsseldorf were one of the last strongholds of Erasmianism in Europe. It was here that Weyer developed a *paradigmatic defence* of 'witches'. All subsequent demonologists argued against his *De Praestigiis Daemonum*, which provided an unprecedented wealth of arguments, drawn from every conceivable source, and included the disciplines of history, literature, theology, law and medicine. Like Cusa, Weyer tried to link his criticism to the canonical position, but it is not by coincidence that both of them were labelled as Pyrrhonians by Bodin, who clearly read their intention between the lines.[26]

At the core of Weyer's argument lay a medical consideration: since too many suspects had confessed to witchcraft already, and the witchhunters took their confessions as an irrefutable proof of the existence of the witches' conspiracy, Weyer argued that the old women were innocent even if they confessed their guilt. Weyer's diagnosis was *melancholy*, the mental illness of the period: 'So-called lamiae are indeed poor women – usually old women – melancholic by nature, feeble-minded, easily given to despondency.'[27] According to Galenic humoral medicine, the prevailing medical paradigm, melancholy was seen as a consequence of an abundance of 'black bile' in the body, a natural cause. By introducing melancholy as a medical explanation, Weyer went far beyond Cusa or Alciati and challenged the jurists with a new interpretation of unsoundness of mind, which made even confessing witches not responsible for their actions. Weyer's insanity defence has influenced subsequent generations of lawyers up to the present day.[28] Weyer received a massive response to his publication, from both supporters and enemies, and his book was frequently reprinted throughout the sixteenth century. There were at least six authorized Latin versions printed during Weyer's lifetime (Basel 1563, 1564, 1566, 1568, 1577 and 1583), three German translations by Weyer himself (Basel 1566, 1567, 1578), at least six unauthorized German versions (Basel 1565, Frankfurt 1566, again 1566, 1569, 1575 and 1586) and three unauthorized French versions (Paris 1567, 1569, Geneva 1579), adding up to almost annual prints of Weyer's book on witchcraft. This was a bestseller.[29]

Clearly Weyer's seed blossomed when in the 1580s a number of independent European intellectuals took up his arguments and added new facets, just when the persecutions were about to reach their first climax. In England, the gentleman Reginald Scot, in his ironically titled *Discoverie of Witchcraft*, blamed lack of education for the degree of superstition and credulity in which beliefs about witchcraft were rooted. Scot denied the physical qualities of demonic agents, thus removing them from the corporeal world altogether. Due to its radicality, this very effective criticism received little open support from contemporaries, but it is assumed that it gained some influence, although a lack of reprints would suggest otherwise.[30] A year later the French lawyer and nobleman Michel de Montaigne (1533–92), retired president of the Parlement de Bordeaux, articulated his scepticism against any kind of witch-belief, sarcastically remarking that the persecutors' main arguments were threats and violence. Montaigne's remarks were a thinly veiled attack on Jean Bodin, who had championed the international attack on Weyer a few years earlier: 'The witches in my neighbourhood go in danger of their lives if we follow the advice of each author who comes along and gives substance to their fantasies.'[31] Driven by compassion, the Heidelberg professor Hermann Witekind, a friend of Philip Melanchthon, attacked the witch-hunters head on, articulating the original idea that supposed witches needed love and affection, rather than punishment, in order to overcome their melancholy. Like Weyer and Scot, he did not believe in any physical effects of witchcraft. Witches could only be blamed for apostasy, a spiritual crime. But, according to Witekind, spiritual crimes were not to be punished, and anyone had the right to change his or her belief.[32]

Witekind, although a Protestant, proposed *freedom of conscience*. And he was not only the most radical, but – next to Weyer – also the most influential opponent of the witch persecutions. The Heidelberg edition was enlarged in later editions (Strasbourg 1586, Basel 1593, Speyer 1597) and reprinted frequently (Frankfurt 1586, Hamburg 1623, Basel 1627, Frankfurt 1627, Frankfurt 1654, Hamburg 1671, Nuremberg 1695).[33] Witekind found a congenial successor in Anton Praetorius (c.1560–1614), who courageously intervened in trials in the Calvinist county of Isenburg-Birstein in 1598, putting his position as court preacher at risk, and both of them finally ended up in the electoral Palatinate, a safe haven for opponents of witch-hunting. The reasons for their opposition are clearer than in Montaigne's case: Witekind and Praetorius, whose opposition to persecution was much stronger than might appear from the brief comments of Stuart Clark,[34] both bluntly denied the existence of witchcraft by means of logic, physics and the *laws of nature*, and ridiculed believers in witchcraft as being superstitious and unreasonable.[35] Witchcraft is for both of them a non-existent crime, and voluntary confessions of witchcraft are therefore worthless. Praetorius, as a Calvinist divine, still wished to punish apostasy, but for Witekind spiritual crimes were irrelevant as well. Both of them questioned the legitimacy of torture in general, not just in witch trials. Judges who issue death sentences for witch-craft should – in Praetorius' words – be considered 'blasphemers' and 'murderers'. Witekind and Praetorius published initially under pseu-donyms, but later editions were under their full names, as it became evident that the Palatine government shared their position and offered protection.[36]

Under the impact of the first great wave of persecutions an unpleasant confessional polarization took place, which has not yet been explored in depth, but is closely connected to the ongoing process of *confessionalization*.[37] It seems that a number of Catholic theologians started to refer to the *Malleus Maleficarum* during the crisis, and recognized that the main critics of the persecutions were Protestants, or were at least perceived as such. In effect, any sub-stantial denial of witchcraft was outlawed, and labelled heretical by Catholic scholars.[38] As mentioned in chapter 4, in 1592 the Catholic theologian Cornelius Loos was detained at Trier, because he had written a radical critique of the witch-hunts. Loos was forced to recant his ideas by suffragan bishop Binsfeld himself, and this recan-tation was soon after included in Martin Delrio's authoritative demonology. The discussion of witchcraft had always been difficult, but it became clear in the 1590s that Catholics had to be extremely cautious. To question the existence of witchcraft, or appear to support the witches, was considered heretical, and could even serve as cir-cumstantial evidence for witchcraft, as Delrio claimed in coining the phrase 'the witches' patrons' – those who were likely to be witches themselves.[39]

Cut off from the mainstream of criticism, Catholics therefore had to look for new methods of argumentation against the witch-hunts. They found it in the criticism of the cruel and often illegal judicial procedures in witch trials, which implied an interesting sweep across the academic disciplines. As Bodin the lawyer had argued theologi-cally, so Catholic theologians started to argue as lawyers, and referred to the teaching of the *processus ordinarius* according to the rules of the imperial law code. Ironically, however, they had again to refer to a number of Protestant authors, who had developed the criticism of the teachings of *crimen exceptum* from the 1560s. Johann Georg Goedelmann (1559–1611), law professor at the University of Rostock, had developed an efficient legal argument that made it dif-ficult to impose torture or capital punishment in cases of witchcraft. His seemingly harmless *Treatise on how the magicians, poisoners and witches can be legally recognised and punished* denied denunciations as circumstantial evidence and asked for material proof or eyewit-nesses, which – of course – could hardly ever be provided.[40] Some authors decided to disguise their religious identity completely, like the anonymous author of the pamphlet *What to Think of the Gruesome Torturings and Witch Burnings*, who branded the burnings in general as inhumane, and wished to abandon torture in criminal courts.[41] A good number of authors were calling for the abolition of torture as a consequence of the witch trials, including the Dutch Calvinist preacher Johann Greve (1584–1624), who had his *Tribunal Reformatum* printed in Hamburg.[42] A similar voice came from Cornelius Pleier (1595–?), a town physician of Kitzingen, who published anonymously a *Malleus Judicum* (*The Judges' Hammer, which means: the Hammer of Law for Merciless Judges of the Witches*), based largely upon the earlier treatise of Witekind, with his allusion to the *Malleus Maleficarum* clearly indicating whom he considered to be more dangerous.[43] But these authors remained outsiders, not quotable in law courts during the core phase of the European witch persecution.[44]

In order to look at the emergence of efficient argumentation in Catholic Germany, it is necessary to have a closer look at the situation in *Bavaria*, with Duke/Prince-Elector Maximilian being the head of the Catholic League, and Bavarian-based Jesuits spearheading the business of confessionalization. In the 1590s there was even the perception of a 'Jesuit party'. However, Bavarian politicians managed to split this party by encouraging the Tyrolean Jesuit Adam Tanner (1572–1632), a moral theologian who had succeeded at the Regensburg Colloquy in 1601, to publish his carefully designed objections against witch trials in a theological standard work.[45] The peculiarity of Tanner's argument lies in the fact that this theologian stopped arguing theologically, but emphasized the rule of law on the one hand, and compassion with the victims of the persecution on the other. According to Tanner the persecutions were clearly more dangerous than witchcraft, and he emphasized their lawlessness to the point of comparing them to the Neronian persecutions of the Christians. Tanner's relevant chapters seemed so exciting that they were reprinted separately in Cologne in 1629,[46] and they encouraged a number of Jesuits to publicly join the opposition against witch persecutions. The most famous of these was Friedrich Spee, who quoted Tanner extensively, as the only Catholic authority suited to refute the dangerous suggestions of Binsfeld and Delrio.[47]

Tanner and Spee were the leading Catholic opponents of witch-hunting in the first half of the seventeenth century, but closer analysis shows how deeply rooted their approach was in society. It is striking to see the sharp rift between two parties – zealots and moderates – within the Catholic camp in Counter-Reformation Europe. Robert Bireley dared to label a certain group of Bavarian councillors as 'extremists', because they had supported the implementation of the Edict of Restitution of 1629 at all costs, and in particular by means of war.[48] Konrad Repgen has objected to this interpretation with the argument that such phrases demonstrate a 'liberal mis-understanding' of early modern politics, since the moderate politi-cians supported the same Bavarian policy with the same arguments.[49] In a period of religious coercion and limited freedom of conscience, arguments were frequently used in a formulaic way, with both parties emphasizing their defence of God's honour, the purity of their belief and their commitment to peace. However, what seems to make a major difference is the kind of conclusions drawn from these pre-sumptions. The same politicians who represented the opposition against witch-hunting in the domestic policy suggested entering nego-tiations with Protestants, their religious enemies, in order to prevent further bloodshed in the area of foreign policy. The hawks, however, whom even Pope Urban VIII labelled as *zelanti*, would first have their enemies killed, and introduce peace afterwards. Whereas the oppo-nents of witch-hunting, the so-called *politici*, were employing the Erasmian interpretation of the parable of the wheat and the tares (Matthew 13:29), later to be adopted by the Jesuits Adam Tanner and Friedrich Spee, the zealots wished to root out the weed whatever damage this might induce, in order to prevent future heresies and crimes, and as a consequence God's revenge. It seems fair to call such an approach radical, since the idea of getting to the roots (Latin: *radix*) of crime, or of heresy, dominated their thinking, in home affairs as well as in foreign policy. The interdependence of their fantasies of eradication and the implementation of radical measures, be it un-limited torture in criminal trials or war in foreign policy, becomes as evident as the association of these ideas with a certain type of religiosity.

The striking result of an analysis of Bavarian domestic policy was the permanent struggle for power between two antagonistic factions with stable frontlines for more than a generation, labelled as *politici* and *zelanti* by contemporaries. This could be translated more neu-trally as the moderate politicians, who tried to arrive at balanced judgements in the service of their country, and the zealots, whose noblest aim was to serve the ideas of the Counter-Reformation. If we analyse the group of political hawks, the *zealous ideologues*, it turns out that most of them were pupils of the first generation of Jesuits in Germany, very much like the witch-bishops of Franconia. In Bavaria they were represented by the chancellor of the court council, Dr Johann Simon Wagnereckh (*c*.1570–1617), a social climber who, like his duke, had studied in Ingolstadt during the witch-hunt of 1590, and whose commitment to ideology would compensate for his lack of social standing within the higher ranks of the Bavarian society. Similar motivations may pertain to immigrants like Wagnereckh's ally Dr Cosmas Vagh, a northern German convert, and the secretaries of the privy council, Christian Gewold (1556–1621) and Aegidius Albertinus (1560–1620). All of them kept close contact with the Jesuit party, with Gregory of Valencia and Gretser, with the demonologist Delrio, with the princely confessors, and the Rhenish Jesuit Adam Contzen (1571–1635), as well as with the radical court preacher Jeremias Drexel SJ (1581–1638). If we analyse the careers of the zealots we can often find that they had been in touch with witch-hunts during their education. Adam Contzen, for instance, studied at the Jesuit College of Trier during Binsfeld's era. From Munich, he maintained close contacts with suffragan Förner in Bamberg. Furthermore, Gretser, Contzen and Drexel dedicated their publications to prominent witch-bishops, such as Westerstetten in Eichstätt.[50]

If we compare the social profile of the *moderate politicians*, we arrive at completely different results. During the witch-hunt of 1590 a group of councillors had already articulated their opposition, led by jurists such as the chancellor of the privy council, Dr Johann Georg Herwarth von Hohenburg (1553–1626), later chancellor of the Bavarian estates, who was succeeded as privy chancellor by his ally Dr Joachim Donnersberger (1565–1650). Both came from an urban patriciate background, Donnersberger from the Bavarian capital of Munich, and Herwarth from the imperial city of Augsburg. Both had received a solid academic education at foreign universities, a doctorate in France or Italy, and had served as lawyers at the Imperial Chamber Court. The Herwarths were a successful banker dynasty, with Protestant branches in Augsburg, France and England, while the Catholic branch had entered princely service in Bavaria, eventually joining the landed nobility and becoming leaders of the Bavarian parliament. Herwarth could recruit able officials from the Bavarian high nobility, as well as members of the aristocracy from the Holy Roman Empire, such as members of the Hohenzollern and Wolkenstein dynasties. Herwarth personified an open Catholicism, keeping international contacts within his own camp, but also contacts beyond the boundaries of confession. He supported the Protestant astronomer Johannes Kepler (1571–1630), for whom he found a job at the parliament of inner Austria in Graz, and, after the onset of the Counter-Reformation there, at the imperial court of Rudolf II in Prague. Kepler and Herwarth discussed scientific problems in a longstanding correspondence, and the Bavarian chancellor participated in the development of the logarithmic tables. He kept close contact with the Imperial Chamber Court, with Protestant jurists like Johann Georg Goedelmann (1559–1611), a supporter of the *rule of law*, strictly denying the idea that witchcraft was an exceptional crime, but also the reality of witches' flights and witches' sabbats. This link was remarkable, since Goedelmann's viewpoint was well known.[51] His publication on the legal procedure in witch trials was frequently reprinted, and was translated into the vernacular during the witch-hunt of 1590, which Herwarth had managed to end in Bavaria.[52]

The two parties clashed for the first time in 1600, when the zealots, thanks to the new government of Maximilian I, succeeded in launching an exemplary witch trial against a family of travellers.[53] In an incredibly cruel trial, the councillors Wagnereckh and Vagh, backed by the Jesuit Gretser, extracted confessions, employing unlimited torture, with Delrio's *Disquisitiones Magicae* literally on the desk beside them. Unsurprisingly, the confessions resemble those of the monk from Stavelot three years earlier, which had informed the demonologist about the rituals at the sabbat. In July, and again in December 1600, six people were burned alive in executions of unprecedented cruelty, drawing attention from all parts of the empire to Munich, with illustrated leaflets and songs being printed. Delrio did not fail to mention these executions and some accounts of the trial records in subsequent editions of his demonology.[54] This trial was meant to be the starting point of a 'national witch-hunt' the radicals were aspiring to, similar to the contemporary events in Mainz and Fulda. However, 'the cold and political Christians', as Wagnereckh labelled his opponents, the privy councillors Herwarth and Donnersberger, managed to cut the persecution short, and to launch a political debate instead. Before further torture was conceded, the case was to be considered by the university, as suggested by the imperial law code, the *Carolina*. To widespread surprise, the Ingolstadt law faculty, then dominated by Dr Joachim Denich (1560–1633) and Dr Kaspar Hell, denied the legality of torture, and criticized the trial sharply. Completely enraged, the zealots in the government suggested that the legal opinion had been commissioned by the privy council, asked for more Jesuit control at the university, namely by Gretser, accused Dr Hell of treason, and suggested that more legal opinions should be requested. As a result, Duke Maximilian ordered reports on the same cases from the universities of Freiburg, Bologna and Padua, and, on the suggestion of the zealots, from the demonologists Nicolas Rémy and Martin Delrio, as well as from some governments experienced in persecutions, like Trier and Mainz. Predictably enough, Delrio and Rémy supported the unrestricted witch-hunt, and accepted simple suspicion or denunciation as sufficient evidence for imprisonment and torture. However, the University of Bologna supported the Ingolstadt vote, and even the governments of Mainz and Trier in 1604 had become disillusioned with witch-hunting, so recommended caution. Whereas Rémy could be dismissed, Delrio's vote was taken very seriously, and even led to a correspondence between Delrio and the duke's Lorraine confessor Johannes Buslidius SJ (1554–1623), who demanded clarification on some points. Given the high esteem the Jesuits were held in, Delrio could only be beaten by another Jesuit. Now Herwarth played his final trump card: Adam Tanner.[55]

It is unnecessary to go further into the details of this Bavarian power struggle, which lasted for more than a generation, and involved almost the whole of the political and a good part of the spiritual elite. We will return later to the question of how resistance to witch-hunting could be constructed and maintained, and refer now only to some repercussions of the persecutions in Germany. The Bavarian zealots continued to sponsor their allies in other Catholic territories, but whenever they tried to launch a witch-hunt in Bavaria, they failed. During the agrarian crisis of 1608/9 they tried to exploit a panic in a small exclave territory, less tightly controlled by the government in Munich. However, after a number of executions the government became suspicious, intervened and imposed an inquiry into the conduct of the trial, which soon led to the imprisonment of the judge Gottfried Sattler (?–1613). The judge was put on trial himself and the government in Munich decided to make an example of him, by punishing his misconduct with the death penalty. The zealots in Munich fiercely opposed the sentence and even tried to raise support among the ruling family, and among the Jesuits. But the Ingolstadt law faculty twice confirmed the judgment. Sattler was decapitated in 1613, the first Catholic witch-hunter to receive such a reward, which was an important symbolic victory for the opponents of witch-hunting. Tanner mentions this capital punishment together with the trial against the Fulda witch-judge Nuss of 1618, another of the Ingolstadt law professors' successes.[56] Both death penalties proved to be extremely important because they proved the fact that Catholic witch trials could be erroneous, that severe mistakes occurred and that victims might turn out to be innocent. Spee and later opponents of witch-hunting would regularly refer to these cases, borrowing the evidence from Tanner's report.

Clearly Ingolstadt served as a bridgehead for the Bavarian moderates, lawyers as well as Jesuits. Some younger Jesuits, students of Tanner, were bold enough to challenge publicly the terrible witch-hunts of Bishop Westerstetten in Eichstätt. One of them, Professor Kaspar Hell SJ (1588–1634), attacked the prince-bishop so sharply that the Jesuit general Mutius Vitelleschi SJ (1563–1645) intervened repeatedly in favour of the dedicated Counter-Reformation prince-bishop and supporter of the Jesuit Order. The Bavarians knew only too well how to classify the Franconian events. But it had not been Tanner who had enlightened them. Jesuits like Hell and Kaspar Denich (1591–1660) were the sons of those Ingolstadt lawyers who had cut short the attempts at persecution in 1601, and their families were closely linked to the privy councillors. Some Bavarian politicians had relatives burned in Eichstätt, for instance court council Chancellor Dr Johann Christoph Abegg. When in 1620 Maria Richel, the wife of Dr Bartholomäus Richel (1580–1649), chancellor of Eichstätt, was burned, the privy councillors did not hesitate to save the rest of the family, and to evacuate them from the dangerous prince-bishopric. Richel was immediately appointed vice-chancellor in Munich.[57] In 1628 they offered a leading position to chancellor Dr Georg Haan of Bamberg, whose wife had just been burned. The episcopal government assured the prince-elector (from 1623) Maximilian of Bavaria that there was no hurry with the negotiations, and no imminent danger to the chancellor – only to burn Haan a few weeks later.[58]

The legal arguments were tested in the late 1620s, when the witch-hunts in the prince-bishoprics reached their climax. It was now that Tanner included his opinion on witchcraft, designed twenty-four years earlier,[59] in his textbook of moral theology, thus serving as an anchor for future Catholic theologians, who had been bereft of their former authorities. Tanner made the internal discussions from Munich public.[60] When Friedrich Spee published his *Judicial Reservation, or a Book about the Witch Trials*, Tanner was the only authority he could refer to, the only Catholic who relentlessly denied the legality of witch trials, without getting enmeshed in dangerous debates on the existence of witches. Spee's book is a Ciceronian masterpiece. He starts from the premise that witches undeniably exist, as all Catholic authorities confirmed, and he would therefore never return to this question. Some historians were naive enough to take this concession at face value, without taking into consideration that Spee was not contributing to a debate within a pluralistic society, but aiming to provide arguments in a situation of utmost stress and pressure, where anyone would risk his own life if he could be labelled as a 'patron of the witches'. Spee's was the classical strategy of dissimulation.[61] Nevertheless, this Jesuit began to dismantle the legal procedures against the witches so radically, and criticize every single step so effectively, filling in, hardly disguised, horrible examples from the German prince-bishoprics, that even hard-boiled contemporaries were impressed. The witch-hunters understood that this was the most dangerous enemy they had ever had. Spee made no concessions, and did not admit the guilt of the suspects in a single case. Under similar circumstances the torturers, the judges, the bishops and even the Pope would confess any crime. And at several points in his book, Spee tries to draw the readers' attention to the fact that it was not just the shocking cruelty and illegality of the horrible persecutions that worried him, but that there was another truth, too shocking to be articulated in this period of persecution. What could this additional truth be, after having torn apart every legitimation of the witch trials? The answer to anyone able to read between the lines could only be that all the executed were innocent, and the persecutors were murderers, as suggested by Tanner. The additional point, not alluded to by Tanner, was that *there were no witches at all*.[62]

It is not by coincidence that Spee adopted Tanner's comparison of the witch-hunts with the Neronian persecutions, because both of them shared the idea that the victims of the witch persecutions were

innocent, and their persecutors gruesome tyrants. Since Spee was not
interested in burning bridges, he suggested that the rulers were ignorant of what happened in their countries, deceived by corrupt and
malicious councillors, who tried to cover the deeds of greedy and
bloodthirsty witch-commissioners. This was not completely off the
point, since Spee was aiming at Prince-Elector Ferdinand of Cologne,
who was responsible for terrible witch-hunts in this prince-bishopric
and in the duchy of Westphalia, although similar events did not occur
in his other territories, the prince-bishoprics of Hildesheim, Liège,
Münster and Paderborn, where Spee's Jesuit College was located.
Clearly, the worst persecutions were produced by the government at
Bonn (Kurköln) and their witch-commissioners, such as Heinrich
Schultheis and others. Spee may have hoped that the prince-elector
might try to get rid of them, if public opinion forced him to do so.
However, this was not the case, at least not instantly. In the midst of
the Thirty Years' War the leaders of the Catholic party, and Ferdinand as the brother of Maximilian I of Bavaria counted among them,
had other problems, after King Gustav II Adolph of Sweden
(1594–1632, r. 1611–32) had entered the stage and conquered large
parts of the Holy Roman Empire, including Bavaria.

Spee published his booklet anonymously, for a number of reasons.
Presumably his superiors, or the censors, would not have allowed the
work to be published. The witch-commissioners threatened the
anonymous author of the *Cautio Criminalis* openly with torture and
execution. However, within the Jesuit Order it seems to have been
clear from the beginning who the author was. Immediately after publication, a discussion started within the Order, with some supporting
and some attacking Spee. But although Spee had vigorously challenged one of the most important protectors of the Jesuit Order in
Germany, there were no attempts to reveal his identity, or to hand
him over to the secular authorities. Spee was not even punished for
his disobedience within the Order.[63] His tiny Latin publication provoked an enormous echo outside the Order as well. In 1635 the superintendent of Thuringia, Johann Matthäus Meyfahrt (1590–1642),
published an emotional book for the use of Protestant princes, threatening them with hellfire if they did not immediately stop the burning
of witches. More than any other author on the subject, this proto-
Pietist Lutheran pastor emphasized the sufferings of supposed
witches in prison.[64] Within a few years, the *Cautio Criminalis* was
twice translated into the German vernacular, and both translators
were Protestants who tried to influence public opinion within their
camp. French and Polish translations both indicate that the witch-
hunts were still not simply a German problem, and that Spee's essay
was of wider significance. In the literature on witchcraft it has often
been argued that the criticism of the witch trials, or of witch-hunting,
was largely unsuccessful. This may seem to be the case at first glance,
if we think of the large-scale hunts around 1600, and again around

1630. However, given the fact that these persecutions were restricted to an identifiable number of territories, and the more important countries never really embarked on the business of witch-hunting, or tried it once, stopped immediately and never returned to such a policy, quite the opposite interpretation could make more sense. Even in some German territories the head-on criticism was pretty successful, for instance in the duchies of Jülich, Cleves and Berg. Another example is the Electoral Palatinate, where it was no coincidence that two sons of Johann Weyer, Dietrich Weyer and Johannes Weyer, ended up as court councillors, and whose ruling elite did not believe in the existence of witchcraft.[65] And a number of princes were deeply impressed by Spee's *Cautio Criminalis*, as Prince-Elector Johann Philipp von Schönborn (1605–1673), prince-bishop of Würzburg, Mainz and Worms, explained to the philosopher Gottfried Wilhelm Leibniz (1646–1716).

Spee had rightly pointed to the fact that far fewer witches were executed in Italy, France and Spain, than in Germany. Curiously enough, he was unable to refer more precisely to the developments in these parts of Europe, or to the conduct of the Roman Inquisition in particular. Under Cardinal Santori this authority had changed its attitude towards witchcraft decisively. Giulio Monterenzi (1550–1623), who may have been influenced by the writings of Alciati, and authored a pretty sceptical instruction for witch trials in the 1590s, became an expert in cases of witchcraft. Later one of the most influential papal politicians, governor of Rome and bishop of Faenza, he tried to interfere in witch trials as far abroad as Flanders. After Monterenzi, Inquisitor Desiderio Scaglia (1568–1639) improved the instruction, bitterly complaining in its preamble that witch trials are hardly ever conducted without the most serious errors and transgressions, to the severe disadvantage of the victims, and justice in general. This Dominican recommended the utmost caution in procedures concerning the *corpora delicti* and other circumstantial evidence, and the use of torture. He denied the value of denunciations, and urged a fair trial, with decent treatment of the suspects. Scaglia's instruction was printed in 1625 for internal use only, which explains the ignorance of a wider European public about the attitude of the Roman Inquisition towards witchcraft. It was only in 1655 that the instruction was included in a publication of Cesare Carena (1597–1659) on the Office of Inquisition, and became accessible to an educated public. Two years later it was printed separately, when Cardinal Inquisitor Francesco Albizzi (1593–1684), who quoted with approval Spee's *Cautio Criminalis*, tried to curb witch panics in Switzerland, Burgundy, France (Toulouse), Germany and Poland in the 1650s and 1660s.[66]

In France, the Parlement de Paris suggested a decree as early as 1587 that rendered the execution of witches dependent on the consent of the Parlement. Attempts by the Catholic League to introduce the *processus extraordinarius* for witchcraft were blocked after the succession of Henry IV (1553–1610, r. 1589/1594–1610). In the summer of 1601 the Parlement found the hangman of Rocroi, Jean Minard, responsible 'for the death of more than 200 persons' in Brabant (the actual number was probably even higher, because he had detected 274 people by his pricking test), and sentenced him to lifelong labour on the galleys, as he had dared to touch eight French subjects. It is striking that Jean Bodin, despite his reputation, failed to gain a significant position. Although his intellectual stature was universally recognized, his career ground to a halt, and he never rose above the position of a middle-ranking official at the sub-alternate court of Laon (in office 1575–96), where he was a minority voice, and 'apparently did not have the pleasure of convicting a single witch'.[67]

A major witch craze in the Basque territories tested the judicial systems of both Spain and France in 1609. The persecution in the French Labourd, with eighty victims inspiring the demonologist Pierre de Lancre, was brought to an end by a member of the Parlement de Bordeaux, commissioned by King Henry IV. In Spain, the Supreme Council of the Inquisition sent one of their most able inquisitors, Don Alonso Salazar Frías, to scrutinize the activities of the local authorities. Salazar interviewed about 2,000 witnesses and the imprisoned suspects, and came to the conclusion that not one of them could be convicted, that all the rumours depended on gossip, superstition or enmity, and all the suspects had to be released, even if they had already confessed. Salazar came to the conclusion that witch trials should in the future be centralized under the control of the Inquisition, and that no more death sentences should be imposed. The Supreme Council followed this advice, declared secular witch trials illegal and suppressed them vigorously in the future. Statistics reveal the impact of this surprising turn.[68] The Spanish Inquisition investigated 44,000 cases of spiritual crimes between 1540 and 1700, in nineteen tribunals on the Iberian peninsula, the Canary Islands, the Mediterranean islands, and in Latin America. About 9 per cent of all cases were dealing with magical crimes (superstition, magic, divination and witchcraft), but there were no death sentences for witchcraft. The Spanish Inquisition tried to monopolize witch trials in order to suppress them, quite contrary to the *leyenda nera*, the black legend. This does not mean of course that the Spanish Inquisition was harmless. During the same period about 775 people were convicted and executed because of crypto-Judaism, heresy (usually followers of Luther or Calvin), homosexuality or bigamy. About twice as many were convicted by the Portuguese in Europe and Brazil, and half as many by the Roman Inquisition in Italy. But none of the Iberian Inquisitions executed witches.[69]

One could argue that the Spanish Netherlands (today Belgium, Luxembourg and Northern France) suffered from severe witch-hunts because of the absence of the Spanish Inquisition in this corner of the Spanish empire. The northern Netherlands, the Protestant general estates, brought the persecutions to an end as a result of internal developments. The citizens of Amsterdam disliked witch-hunts, just like the ruling elite of cities such as Rome, Venice, Florence, Madrid, Stockholm, Paris or London. The most urbanized corner of early modern Europe was that of Holland and the northern Netherlands, with towns such as Rotterdam, Haarlem and Leiden. Hans de Waardt (b. 1952) has argued that, quite contrary to the common expectation, it was the absence of a central power in the Netherlands that allowed the abolition of witch trials, due to a consensus of the ruling elites.[70] During their struggle for freedom against the Catholic superpower of Spain, the Netherlands had turned into a safe haven for Protestant refugees from all over Europe. Their experience of persecution, and the irenic tradition of Erasmian humanism, together with the coexistence of Sephardic Jews, Calvinists, Catholics and Anabaptists, who were more likely to be sentenced to death than witches in some parts of Europe, changed the perception of this particular society. The Mennonites strictly opposed any kind of violence, including the death penalty, and they did not believe in the power of the devil, which turned witch trials into a mere absurdity. Public opinion therefore turned against witch trials from the end of the sixteenth century. The last Dutch witch burning happened in Nimwegen in 1603.[71] 'States without stakes', where witch-beliefs declined subsequently, confirmed the idea that witches were created by witch-hunting. Johan van Heemskerk (1597–1656), a Dutch traveller through the Basque territories, reported how traumatized the people were in the aftermath of a witch-hunt.[72]

When the Parlement de Paris conceded the last death sentences in 1625,[73] scepticism had taken firm roots at the French court, where the *libertins érudits* – free-thinkers who undermined accepted beliefs – began to mould a tradition of their own. Mazarin's librarian, Gabriel Naudé, launched a thinly veiled attack on witch trials with his *Defence of Famous People Accused of Magic*.[74] However, Pyrrhonian scepticism, as revived by Montaigne, ceased to appeal to the intellectuals in a period when a new generation of natural scientists attempting to gain new insights into the fabric of nature. The mechanical sciences and the world of controlled experiments fascinated the scientists, and, in contrast to the experimenters of the sixteenth century, they had stopped believing in magic, sorcery and witchcraft. Robert Fludd (1574–1637), a Rosicrucian physician and mystifying natural philosopher, was already moving in this direction,[75] and so did Pierre Gassendi (1592–1655) with his interest in Epicurus' theory of atoms.[76]

If there was a common denominator of the new philosophy, it was that leading scientists no longer bothered with scepticism, but endeavoured to arrive at new certainties in the understanding of the physical environment, while excluding mystical interference. All of them excluded spirits (angels and devils) and God from their considerations, and implicitly or explicitly ruled out the possibility of divine intervention as well. The experimental philosophy of Francis Bacon (1561–1626), as outlined in his *Novum Organon* in 1620,[77] the physics of Galileo Galilei (1564–1642), as explained in the *Dialogo* in 1632, or the rationalist philosophy of René Descartes (1596–1650), as constructed in the *Discours de la méthode*, allowed only for mechanical motion, effected by pushing and pulling, and excluded any possibility of magical flights. Since Popkins tried to link Descartes to the scandalous witch trial of Urbain Grandier,[78] it seems worth mentioning that the philosopher stayed in the winter camp of the Bavarian army at Neuburg in 1618/19 during the Thirty Years' War, so clearly he must have heard of the witch trials in neighbouring areas. Philosophy, one is tempted to say, does not exist in a vacuum,[79] and neither does science: when Galilei became involved in his lifelong struggle with the Roman Inquisition, Johannes Kepler invited him to Germany, where freedom of thought was guaranteed. There was no Inquisition and no central state, and, if the authorities were aiming at suppression, it was possible to find a friendly environment only a few miles distant. This indeed proved to be true for Kepler. His mother Katharina Kepler (1547–21), however, became involved in a witch trial between 1615–21, at Leonberg, a small market town in Württemberg, and the imperial astronomer had the greatest difficulty in securing her defence and her survival.[80]

According to the new scientists, nature should be explained exclusively in terms of measurable properties and actions, a paradigm shift usually summed up in the label 'the Scientific Revolution'. Kepler's Laws, for instance, defined the revolution of planets by means of mathematical formulae, and in his *Harmonia Mundi* there was no place for divine or demonic intervention. Leading intellectuals, such as Hector-Savinien Cyrano de Bergerac (1619–55), Baruch Spinoza (1632–77), Nicole de Malebranche (1638–1715), Gottfried Wilhelm Leibniz (1646–1716) or Pierre Bayle (1647–1706),[81] did not directly participate in debates about witchcraft, but distanced themselves in their correspondence or publications from these atrocities, and thus actively promoted the departure from a world of stakes, although none of them dared to completely deny the existence of witches.[82]

The end of witch-hunting came tacitly, since the political actors preferred to avoid provoking strange alliances between reactionary theologians and an angry populace. The governments rarely admitted that they had done injustice to all those burned at the stakes, although there were some exceptions to this rule. After the mid-seventeenth century, the tone changed completely, and it seems that this process – apart from a few exceptions such as Witekind and

Praetorius (mentioned on page 172) – started in England. Instead of defending the witches, intellectuals began to attack witch-beliefs head-on, and to ridicule and provoke its defenders publicly. Thomas Hobbes (1588–1679), one of the towering intellectuals of this period, who had met leading protagonists of the Scientific Revolution such as Galilei, Marin Mersenne (1588–1648) and Gassendi on his travels through Europe, devoted several chapters of his *Leviathan* to questions of demonology, ridiculing the 'fabulous doctrine concerning demons' in an unprecedented manner, and – in something of a travesty – portrayed the Catholic Church as the 'Kingdome of Darknesse'.[83] Although Anglicans and Presbyterians might have shared this interpretation, surely they were shocked by the notion that Hobbes might not see much of a difference between the Churches, and might lash out against them as well, as was acknowledged by the Cambridge Platonist Henry More (1614–87).[84] It was not only parish priests and their flock who still believed in devils and witches, but also high-ranking members of the Royal Society, like Joseph Glanvill, whose *Philosophical Considerations Touching the Being of Witches and Witchcraft* defended the existence of witchcraft, and therefore of witch trials.[85] The famous diarist Samuel Pepys (1633–1703) reviewed Glanvill's book as being 'well written, but not very convincing' (24.11.1666).

Even before a last series of witch trials was performed under heavy popular pressure in the early 1680s, with the last death sentence for witchcraft in England imposed on Alice Molland in Exeter in March 1685,[86] a number of intellectuals attacked Glanvill harshly. They were embarrassed by his equating disbelief in witchcraft with atheism.[87] Aggressive rebuttals, like the *Question of Witchcraft Debated*, hardly destroyed these fears, since John Wagstaffe sailed in the waters of Machiavellian or Hobbesian atheism.[88] Suddenly it was no longer the question of witchcraft alone that was being debated, but a much wider issue: *religion*. John Webster (1610–82), a Nonconformist chaplain in the Civil War, and later a medical practitioner, attacked Glanvill because of his attempt 'to defend these false, absurd, impossible, impious and bloody opinions'. Webster denied the devil's influence in the material world.[89] The 'Glorious Revolution', as in so many other areas, marked a watershed in England's attitude towards magical crimes: afterwards no more witches were executed by court sentence. Witchcraft turned into a party cause, with the Whigs generally ridiculing the belief in witchcraft, and only a few Tories still defending the cause in public, as in the case of Jane Wenham's (*c*.1642–1730) trial in 1712.[90] This former suspect became part of 'the Whig mythology of Tory superstition' after her release.[91] Due to hostility she could not return to her village, but received visits from celebrities like Hutchinson, the first English historian of witchcraft.[92] The repeal of the Witchcraft Act is seen as a machination of Prime

Minister Robert Walpole (1676–1745), who wished 'to curb high-flying churchmen'.[93] Only James Erskine, Lord Grange, who generally tried to obstruct Walpole's policy, opposed the repeal of the witchcraft legislation in 1736. His speech in parliament was greeted with laughter and scorn, and terminated the Scottish Tory's career as a politician.[94]

That the opposition was silenced does not mean that the clergy, or a majority of the population, subscribed to the abandoning of witch trials. As influential a theologian as John Wesley (1703–91), the founder of Methodism, the main revivalist movement in England, wrote in 1768 (journal entry for 25 May), 'the giving up of witchcraft is in effect giving up the Bible'.[95] With the repeal of the English and Scottish Witchcraft Acts it became impossible to prosecute witchcraft by law. Cunning folk could still be punished for fraud, but maleficient magic was no longer recognized as a crime because it was considered to be non-existent. To the dismay of the English elites, the populace cared little for the legal changes, and went on with the 'swimming' or 'ducking' of witches, with a scandalous case occurring in 1736, the very year the legislation was repealed.[96] After the outlawing of witchcraft persecution these popular gatherings could be construed as a riot, and punished according to the Riot Act of 1714, which made it a capital offence for twelve or more people to assemble tumultuously to the disturbance of the public peace. Many Justices of Peace found it difficult to enforce such laws in cases where the sympathy of the population lay with the offenders. Numerous cases of duckings are reported from the later eighteenth century, and only if the suspected witch died as a consequence of the ordeal, as Ruth Osborne did at Longmarston in 1751, did this come to the attention of a wider public. Her case was commented on in journals, newspapers and pamphlets because it was particularly embarrassing, with the mob threatening the governor (who had tried to prevent the swimming), vandalizing public buildings and threatening to set the town on fire. In the course of the nineteenth century the swimmings became more sporadic, but occurred occasionally up to 1880,[97] and as late as 1863 a suspected witch fell victim to one of these riotous duckings.[98]

The English debate swept over the continent only after another debate had excited the European public. In the 1690s the Dutch minister Balthasar Bekker (1634–98) published his attack on the powers of the devil. His *De Betooverde Wereld*, although a voluminous, cumbersome and repetitive work, was immediately translated into the main languages of the period, German, Latin, French and English, and fostered the first European debate on witchcraft since the sixteenth century.[99] With about 175 contributors, the Bekker debate counts among the most extensive of the European Enlightenment. Three out of four authors attacked Bekker vigorously, and the Calvinist Church decided to strip him of his parish, although witch burnings had stopped in the Netherlands more than three generations ago. It was the dissertation of the law professor and philosopher Christian Thomasius (1655–1728), *About the Crime of Magic,*[100] that triggered off an extensive debate, first engulfing Protestant Germany and Scandinavia, and then, after a time-lag, the Catholic South, Italy included. Thomasius had been a student of Christian Wolff (1679–1754), the champion of the early Enlightenment in the Holy Roman Empire, and became entangled in heated debates with Saxon Pietists, since he denied the importance of revelation as a source of conduct. Thomasius was forced to retire to the newly founded Prussian Reform university in Halle. As he relates in the foreword to his German translation of John Webster, he himself had almost agreed to a death sentence for witchcraft in 1694, but his colleagues at the law faculty informed him that they would not support his decision. Thomasius was an unconventional scholar, and the story of self-criticism served his legend. It was he who moved witchcraft to the centre of the early Enlightenment, by fuelling the public debate with scores of publications of his own and of his numerous students, together with translations into Latin and German, thus introducing the English debate to a wider European public.[101]

Thomasius instrumentalized *history* as a weapon of the Enlightenment, by demonstrating in the first thorough historical dissertation on the subject that witches had been legally persecuted only for a short period, and their crimes had been an invention of the inquisitors.[102] He received considerable support from theologians, as well as from lawyers, philosophers and medical doctors. The debate, which lasted for more than two decades, had much in common with earlier English debates. Like Hobbes or Wagstaffe, Thomasius was labelled an atheist, but like the Whig politicians he managed to turn the subject into a weapon against the clergy. Eventually he gained the support of Friedrich Wilhelm I of Prussia (1688–1740, r. 1713–40), who stopped further trials by a royal decree in 1714, very much like the French king about thirty years earlier. But this initiative was important, since Prussia started to crush the jurisdictions of the feudal lords, and suppressed the ongoing trials in Brandenburg, as well as in Pomerania (which had recently been annexed to Prussia). Quite unlike neighbouring Poland, where the stakes burned for another seventy years, the king managed to extinguish the fires. Three further accusations are known, the last in 1731, and all of them were dismissed.[103]

The Enlightenment, by definition, was a success story. Witch-hunting should have stopped at this point. However, this was not as simple as switching on the light, and in some cases decades of negotiating preceded the end of the burnings. Neither witch-beliefs, nor witch-hunts, stopped at the beginning of the eighteenth century. The *late legal witch burnings* have still not been thoroughly explored, and there is a strange tension between the seemingly archaic burning of witches, and the proud and distanced argumentations of the enlightened philosophers, lawyers or politicians. Even in the British Isles witches were executed as late as 1727, when the last witch was legally killed in Scotland.[104] Voltaire reported the case of the Jesuit Père Girard, who was almost put on the stake in 1730. Thirteen years later the minister Bertrand Guillaudot was burned alive at Dijon, and a further twenty-nine suspects were imprisoned in Lyon, with five of these receiving death penalties from the Parlement de Bordeaux in 1743. Although sorcery and the devil's pacts were involved, French historians exclude these cases from their considerations, as well as the legal considerations of a leading French lawyer who contemplated seriously the crime of witchcraft as late as 1780.[105] In Sweden, late trials occurred in 1742 and 1757, while a witch panic in Dalarna, where the great witch-hunts had started some decades earlier, involved thirteen women who confessed their guilt, having been imprisoned and tortured for witchcraft as late as 1763. When the governor of the province eventually stopped the local judges from continuing with the trial, the Protestant bishop of Dalarna intervened and complained about 'our free-thinking period', where authorities had become reluctant to burn confessed witches. Probably due to such voices, it took the High Court considerable time to come to a conclusion, but finally the women were released and received financial compensation, with their judges being imprisoned instead.[106] Certainly, all of these were exceptional cases, but this is true for cases of witchcraft quite generally. And of course there are many borderline cases: was it still a witch trial when a woman was executed for a devil's pact at Seville in 1781? She had confessed to intercourse with the devil, but not to harmful magic.[107]

The problems were still considerable throughout Switzerland, the southern, mostly Catholic parts of the Holy Roman Empire, and the Eastern European fringe. The prince-bishoprics were particularly affected again, although the episcopal authorities of Freising, Augsburg and Salzburg tried to conceal their witch trials under the label of *veneficium* (poisoning), clearly displaying a defensive attitude. Nevertheless, during a witch panic in Freising about sixteen young beggars were executed between 1717 and 1721, after they had confessed to the devil's pact, attendance at the witches' sabbat, and of course *maleficium* (harmful magic, or witchcraft). In the prince-bishopric of Augsburg a witch panic occurred in 1728, leading to four executions, and another execution took place in 1745. In the imperial Abbey of Obermarchthal, seven women were executed for witchcraft in 1745 and 1747 – a panic trial. In Bavaria fifteen people, mostly young beggars, were executed in the 1720s, but there was another chain of trials conducted between 1749 and 1756 in Salzburg, as well as in the provincial capitals of Burghausen, Straubing and Landshut.

In almost all of these cases accusations by children triggered the trials. The last Bavarian witch was an orphaned fourteen-year-old girl called Veronica Zerritschin (1742–56). Her stepfather had kicked her out and she had joined a children's gang, living in the streets as an itinerant beggar. Seized by distant relatives, she was put into an orphanage, where she had great difficulties fitting in. Because of her cursing, blasphemous behaviour and the theft of consecrated hosts, the orphanage consulted the Franciscans. Threatened with a beating, the girl decided to run away and seek work as a maidservant. But her employer kicked her out when she started to display signs of mental disturbance, or possession, trying to commit suicide, and to kill her employer's baby with a knife. As she was still below the age of criminal responsibility, the lord mayor of Landshut decided to send her back to the orphanage. In fact it was her 'possession' which triggered off the witch trial, although quite an unusual one. The girl confessed voluntarily that the reason for her possession was her theft of the hosts, which she had used for sorcery. The court found the hidden hosts, which had visibly been used for sorcery, so there was undeniably a *corpus delicti*, and sufficient circumstantial evidence to prove the suspicion. The girl provided extensive narratives of seduction by the devil, the witches' flight and sabbat, and harmful magic; she had also learned to act as a sorcerer, as she was able to recite a rhyming weather spell of twenty verses. The harm she claimed to have caused had indeed occurred, although her victims had not been aware of her witchcraft and had not blamed her. The judge found the case difficult to assess because this culprit had had every reason for desperation, was still quite young and cooperated willingly. But if the court would not convict this confessing witch, they would never again convict anyone for witchcraft. Therefore the girl had to be executed, as a matter of principle, as the judge indicated.[108]

Even in the second half of the eighteenth century there were still a surprising number of death penalties for witchcraft to be found in Europe. Enlightened discussions should be viewed in the light of the mass burnings still occurring in East Central Europe, in Poland, and in dominions under Habsburg rule, which were largely governed by local magnates, such as Slovakia (last execution in 1745),[109] Moravia,[110] Slovenia (last execution in 1744),[111] and Hungary. In this kingdom, which included parts of the Balkans, such as present-day Croatia, Serbia and Romania (Transylvania), witch-huntings had been suppressed during the sixteenth and early seventeenth centuries by Ottoman rule. Lynchings were the only way of hunting witches, since the Turkish authorities never accepted accusations of witchcraft in the courts. Legal trials began only after large parts of Hungary were reconquered by the Habsburgs, and reached their peak only between 1710 and 1760, not by coincidence starting after a 'year of sorrows', with drought, flooding, famine and epidemic diseases.[112] A panic trial at Szeged in 1728 was close to becoming a large-scale witch-hunt. As late as the 1750s there were 143 trials in Hungary, eventually leading to twenty-one death sentences, many of them killed in a panic trial at Arpad. In the 1760s the number of trials declined to forty-seven, but even in the 1770s eight trials were recorded, resulting in three convictions. The last Hungarian 'witch' was executed in 1777 in Késmárk, or Kezmarok, in northern Hungary.[113] The kingdom of Poland, then including present-day Lithuania and parts of the Ukraine, displays a similar pattern, but is not yet well researched. During a witch panic in Silesia five witches were executed as late as 1744 at Teppenbuden – a panic trial.[114] But there were a good number of trials in the 1750s as well. In 1756 Prussia and Austria intervened in the areas under their suzerainty, but in independent Poland witch trials went on. As late as 1774 a major witch panic occurred in the village of Doruchovo, subject to the town court of Grabowo, and claimed the lives of fourteen women. The *Sejm*, the Polish Parliament, took this as an occasion to stop all trials the following year, and to repeal the laws on witchcraft in 1775.[115]

The imperial Abbey of Kempten is famous for a very late execution. According to the legal opinion a death sentence had to be issued in 1775, and copies of the documents – the originals are missing – show that the prince-abbot Honorius Roth von Schreckenstein (r. 1760–85) signed the death sentence on 11 April, adding the words: *fiat iustitia!* A local archivist only recently found that the sentence was never executed, and the convicted witch, Maria Anna Schwägelin (1734–81) – another mentally disturbed person with an interesting life story – died some years later in prison. In his legal opinion the high judge refers to an earlier execution of a witch in 1755 as a precedent.[116] Turning to Switzerland, we can find that secular territories had problems as well. Major witch panics took place in the Catholic canton of Ticino in 1721, and in the canton of Zug in 1737, with consequences also in the cantons of Schwyz and Lucerne. But it was in the Calvinist cantons that the last 'witches' were killed. In 1779 Ursula Padrutt died in the prison of Oberhalbstein in Graubünden, a canton where the first execution for witchcraft was recorded in 1434. As late as 1782 the scandalous trial at Glarus against the maid-servant Anna Göldi (1734–82) took place. Although her indictment was *veneficium*, this was clearly a witch trial, emphasizing the devil's pact and harmful magic against her employer's children, who served as accusers. Her execution took place at Glarus on 18 June 1782, and triggered a storm of protest. Protestant intellectuals, who had imagined their camp to be morally superior, were horrified. August Ludwig Schlözer coined the term 'judicial murder' on this occasion.[117]

The final debates about witchcraft in Catholic Europe were launched after a scandalous public speech given by the Jesuit Georg

Gaar on the occasion of a witch burning in Würzburg. In 1749 the sub-prioress of the Abbey of Unterzell, Maria Renata Singerin (1678–1749), was executed, and her body burned at the stake. In the background there were, as usual, cases of possession, the group dynamics of the female convent and a mentally disturbed person who voluntarily accused herself. Among the authorities there was considerable unease about her case, since many acknowledged her disability, but again this was declared a matter of principle and the hardliners gained their victory. However, the reaction was quite unexpected, as Italian intellectuals took this as an occasion to start a major debate about witchcraft. Abbot Girolamo Tartarotti (1702–61), a member of the Imperial Academy at Rovereto, then part of the Austrian monarchy, attacked and ridiculed the barbarian Jesuit in his famous *Nocturnal Gatherings of the Witches*, where he interpreted witchcraft as an illusion.[118] More radical intellectuals were not satisfied with his attack, because Tartarotti had still made too many concessions to the Christian interpretation of magic. Scipio Maffei (1675–1755) from Verona published three voluminous books on the subject, denying the existence of magic, and therefore of witchcraft, and pleading for a complete halt to all trials.[119]

Again unexpectedly, the Franciscan provincial Benedetto Bonelli (1704–83) tried to refute Maffei's arguments, leading the conservative clergy in this Italian debate. Soon afterwards the debate swept back to Germany, when the Church historian Jordan Simon (1719–76), a former Augustinian hermit, defended Maffei's arguments in his massive book *The Great World-deceiving Nothing, or Today's Witchcraft and Art of Sorcery*.[120] The Catholic realms of the Habsburg and Wittelsbach dynasties were at this point suffering from a struggle between court and country. As in Protestant Europe, the rulers generally dismissed witchcraft as unimportant, or ridiculous, but the internal balance of power was complicated because the Jesuits were in control of higher education, the bishops controlled the book market and the religious Orders were held in high esteem by the rural population, over whom they exercised considerable influence. The greatest problems were in the relatively autonomous provinces, mostly administered by the regional higher nobility, who – often in alliance with the religious orders and the populace – tried to maintain the witch paradigm. This kind of inertia increased the developmental gap between Catholic Europe and the more advanced Protestant societies. From the second third of the eighteenth century, the privy councils therefore began to invent strategies in order to force their programmes of reform into their country's internal peripheries. As in England, witchcraft was used as a lever to break the power of conservatism. Empress Maria Theresia (1717–80, r. 1740–80) intervened directly in witch trials in Poland and Moravia (today in Slovakia) in 1756, and in Slawonia (today Croatia) in 1758.

In Bavaria, the enlightened Prince-Elector Max III Joseph (r. 1745–77), or rather his advisers, engineered a blow to the conservative clergy. They invited the Theatine Father Don Ferdinand Sterzinger (1721–86), a member of the Bavarian Academy of Science, to launch a debate on the occasion of the name-day of the prince in 1766. Sterzinger's 'Academic lecture about the Prejudice that Witchcraft can be efficient' provoked a debate that was labelled the 'Bavarian War of the Witches' by his contemporaries. It lasted for about five years and was one of the largest debates of the Enlightenment in Central Europe, with contributors from all over Germany, Austria, Bohemia, Switzerland and northern Italy. Its contributors overlapped with those of the earlier Catholic debate, and some authors had themselves participated in witch trials. It also overlapped with later debates about the exorcist Johann Joseph Gassner (1727–79), who linked all diseases to witchcraft, and Franz Anton Mesmer (1734–1815), who was considered to be a luminary in Germany, but a charlatan in France. To their displeasure, the defenders of witchcraft could not fail to notice that they were treated as the rearguard of a defeated ideology, in the same class as witches, jugglers, tellers of fairy tales and madmen. But even during the reign of enlightened Emperor Joseph II (1741–90, r. 1765/80–90), it took courage to defend the end of the witch trials. Here the Mendicant Orders remained powerful even after the dissolution of the Jesuit Order, as can be seen from Johann Pezzl's (1756–1838) satirical novel *Faustin, or the Philosophical Century*. The end of witch trials was interpreted by many contemporaries as a victory of light over darkness.[121]

Catholic Europe had managed to close the gap on Protestant Europe, where a debate about the existence of ghosts had started to test the nerves of the proponents of the Enlightenment. Emanuel Swedenborg (1688–1772) had experienced a number of revelations, and reported his encounters with the realm of spirits in his *Arcana coelestia*, which seemed to resuscitate Christian demonology.[122] This, however, invoked another great spirit, the philosopher Immanuel Kant (1724–1804), who asserted in his satire *Dreams of a Ghost Seer, Explained by Dreams of Metaphysics*, that neither the existence of ghosts, nor their non-existence could be proven scientifically. Like philosophers in a Wolffian universe, where 'aerial architects of worlds of thought are calmly inhabiting their own worlds, excluding competing dwellers', Swedenborg's 'eight volumes of nonsense' offered nothing but a 'coherent deception of the senses'. Kant's ideas about the subjectivity of human cognition and knowledge in his *Kritik der reinen Vernunft* have to be seen in the light of these ghostly discussions, where the philosopher had suggested that the task of philosophy should be to explore the 'boundaries of human reasoning'.[123]

The repeal of Witchcraft Acts in Europe has not yet been researched on a comparative level. Clearly, the formal repeal by parliamentary decision, as in the United Kingdom, was unique. The kings of France, of Russia, and of Prussia suppressed witch trials without any changes of legislation, just as the Spanish Inquisition and the Dutch general estates had done earlier. Only shortly before the French Revolution did a landslide development start. In Poland, witchcraft laws were repealed in 1776, and in Sweden in 1779. In Germany the 'judicial murder' of 1782 in Switzerland provoked action. Joseph II introduced his new criminal law for the Austrian-Hungarian monarchy in 1787, with articles on sorcery or witchcraft simply left out. In France, the laws on 'magie & sortilege' remained in place, albeit limited by the royal edict of 1682. Only after the French Revolution, in the legislation of 1791, were the *crimes imaginaires* abandoned. While some countries had never formally introduced laws on sorcery or witchcraft, and therefore did not need to remove them, most countries got rid of them during the social and political revolutions around 1800, when in the wake of general reforms new criminal law codes were introduced, often in newly created states, such as in the kingdom of Bavaria in 1813. A late repeal of witchcraft laws did not actually mean very much. It appears ironic that it was the country with the fewest executions where the legislation remained intact longest: in Ireland, where witchcraft had hardly ever been prosecuted, the Witchcraft Act of 1587 remained in place until 1821. The public debates about its abolition remind us of the fact that even in the British Isles a minority still believed in witchcraft, and was entirely convinced of the necessity of punishing witches.[124]

Interestingly enough, the decriminalization of witchcraft as a consequence of European rationalism has its counterpart in the attitudes against some other crimes. Recent research in the history of crime and punishment has demonstrated that crimes do not simply exist as such, but are constructed, or invented, according to demands of society. The crime of witchcraft – non-existent in the eyes of most Europeans after 1800 – historically has much in common with homosexuality (*sodomia*), sex with animals (*bestialitas*) and the infanticide of young mothers (*infanticidium*). After a rapid increase during the fifteenth century, their persecution climaxed around 1600, and decreased thereafter. As far as infanticide (including abortion) is concerned, it was its definition that changed considerably. Whereas it seemed to have been quite common during the Middle Ages that babies sometimes had to be abandoned, from the fifteenth century every pregnancy was monitored, and, if a mother lost her baby or a newborn suffered sudden death, the mother potentially had to face accusation. In many places more women were convicted of infanticide than of witchcraft. Similarly, crimes like blasphemy, bigamy or incest were redefined, or more closely monitored, with incest comprising degrees of kinship that would no longer be recognized as such today. It seems likely that these crimes were in particular influenced by the grand developments of the early modern period: the process of state-building on the one hand, with its tighter control and social-disciplining; and religious reform movements, Reformation and Counter-Reformation, with their emphasis on God's honour as an abstract principle, and individual responsibility for sins, on the other hand. The belief in witchcraft gradually declined during the nineteenth and twentieth centuries, among a wider population, and believers were already in the minority by the nineteenth century.

During the ages of the Industrial Revolution and of imperialism and colonial rule, the ruling and intellectual elites of Europe, and of its daughter civilizations in America and Australia, lost their interest in witchcraft. One of the main reasons may have been that they no longer felt threatened. Usually state-formation, the existence of standing armies, of effective administrations and a prospering economy are given as reasons for such a development. It may be that the intellectual properties of Reformation theology contributed decisively as well. If we believe Weber that the *Protestant ethic* has supported the rise of capitalism, by turning wealth into a sign of divine election,[125] this was certainly contrary to a traditionalist 'image of limited good', regarding wealth with envy, and interpreting it as a sign of witchcraft. The process of *modernization* in Europe changed the rules of the game altogether, and in the long run improved living conditions generally, for instance in the areas of infrastructure, agrarian production, nutrition, housing, hygiene, medical care and education. Even among the common people, where poverty prevailed and cholera or influenza remained threatening diseases throughout the nineteenth century, witchcraft beliefs became marginal. The reasons for this decline have recently been summarized by Owen Davies, who bypassed intellectual, or institutional changes, and pointed to *changing lifestyle patterns*. This refers to the breaking up of self-enclosed villages by modern media like railways, roads and coach services on the one hand, and newspapers, radio and television on the other. The shrinking importance of the agrarian sphere, the rise of mechanized farming machinery and the end of rural society have rendered traditional charges connected to the uncertainties of agrarian production meaningless. Foodstuffs like milk, butter, fruits or beer are no longer produced and consumed locally. The countryside has become part of a division of labour that transcends local, regional and even national boundaries. The introduction of insurance and the improvement of the health services has minimized risk in Western societies. The self-sufficient villages have turned into suburbs or residences of commuters, who earn their money elsewhere, and the traditional social and economic fabric has been broken up in a multitude of ways. The disappearance of neighbourhood reciprocity, the penetration of close-knit village communities by strangers, not as marginal outsiders but rather as role models, and a rising anonymity have all led to decreasing tensions of the traditional type, and therefore to a decline of witch accusations.[126]

The outlawing of witchcraft persecution has always been viewed as one of the greatest successes of European history, and we may speak of achievements in three areas. European societies are no longer angst-ridden. They have also developed a high esteem for the *rule of law*, including the abolition of torture, of extraordinary legal measures and of the death penalty. Both Europe and the USA have turned the lesson of the witchcraft persecutions into an aggressive moral weapon against tyranny. To accuse someone of conducting a *witch-hunt* is one of the most effective reproaches. It demonstrates once more how deeply impressed Europe was by its 'Age of Witch-Hunting'. And it answers the question why Europeans and Americans were so irritated when they were confronted with witch-hunts in other parts of the world, or in their own countries, after the end of witch-hunting in Europe.

6

Witch-Hunting in the Nineteenth and Twentieth Centuries

Give the Africans better nourishment, better housing, systems of pre-
ventive medicine, and adequate medical care, and then, but then only,
will they stop bothering about sorcerers, flying witches, or ancestral
spirits.

> Bronislaw Malinowski, *The Pan African*
> *Problem of Culture Contact*, 1943

Witches are modernity's prototypical malcontents. They provide – like
the grotesques of a previous age – disconcertingly full-bodied images
of a world in which humans seem in constant danger of turning into
commodities, of losing their life blood to the market and to have the
destructive desires it evokes.

> Jean and John Comaroff, *Modernity and Its Malcontents*, 1993

The European rejection of belief in witchcraft was exported in a prolonged period of European expansion, not least through ideologies
such as Marxism, Functionalism and Modernization Theory. The
Soviet rulers of Russia and China tried to crush beliefs in witchcraft,
shamanism and religion at the same time, claiming authority over
their subjects' belief like previous rulers of these empires. But in
many cases, disbelief in witchcraft was first introduced during a
period of foreign rule – colonialism – as in the Americas, Australia,
and large parts of Africa and Asia. However, modern European
legislation on witchcraft was not welcomed, or universally accepted,
and sometimes even created major problems. When Dutch legislation
was introduced in Indonesia in 1905, or British legislation in Eastern
Africa in 1922, it was misunderstood by many natives as a law that
protected the witches. Following the Christian tradition, the colonial

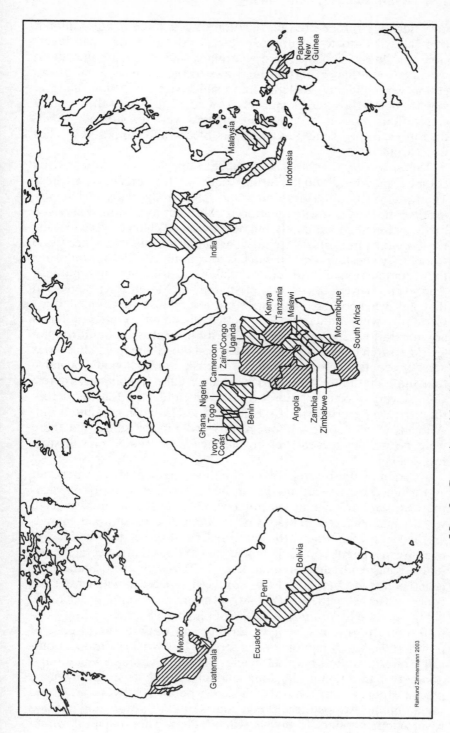

Map 3 Countries with witch-hunts between 1950 and 2000

Raimund Zimmermann 2003

laws not only forbade the persecution of evil witches, but criminal-
ized the witch-doctors. European law was experienced as an inversion of values. Since the European elites had stopped believing in
witchcraft and had exported their laws to the colonies, legal prosecution was suddenly rendered impossible, with the ritual killing of
witches being classified as murder. As a consequence of this clash of
civilizations, poison ordeals and oracles were prohibited, witch-
doctors were prosecuted as offenders of law and supposed witches
were protected.

This *inversion of norms* was unbelievable for those affected by
colonialism. Why would the foreign rulers try to protect evil witches?
The traditional authorities, chiefs and religious specialists (shamans,
ngangas, healers and witch-doctors), whose authority was challenged
by the colonial governments, but also by social change, were looking
for loopholes. In Eastern Africa, village elders tried to convince those
whom they considered to be witches to commit suicide; alternatively,
they commissioned murder, or called in foreign witch-hunters.
Audrey Richards (1899–1984), a student of Malinowski, suggested
that anti-witchcraft movements were a response to colonial rule.[1]
Certainly, witch-hunts became better documented after colonial
administrations started to produce written records, and anthropologists' research began. But witchcraft – and the killing of witches – was
a major problem *before* colonialism (see chapter 3). It would be naive
to assume that there was no social change, cultural contact, suppression, slavery, social or natural disaster or epidemic diseases before
the arrival of Europeans. As Eric Wolf (1923–99) has pointed out,
Africans were 'people without history' only in the sense that there
were no written records before the arrival of Islamic or Christian
foreigners.[2]

As soon as written records begin, there are reports of witchcraft
and witchcraft persecutions. From the seventeenth century onwards
there are reports about *poison ordeals* imposed upon suspected
witches and sorcerers in Madagascar, either directly, or upon animals
as their representatives. Recent research suggests that a decisive
increase in anxieties of bewitchment, and of poison ordeals, happened
under King Andrianampoinimerina (r. 1783–1809), who unified the
island politically. In Madagascar *mosavi* (translated as witchcraft) was
conceived as being the most anti-social crime, an essentially evil force,
being opposed to *hasina*, the ability of kings to channel positive mystical forces in order to achieve fertility and welfare, the essence of
power and political legitimacy, the force of life. Witchcraft was a political crime, as well as harmful magic. The king, who had wiped out a
number of traditional kingdoms and supported slave-trading, used
poison ordeals widely in order to detect political subversion. At the
same time he stripped traditional courts of their power, and entitled
royal commissioners to act as witch-finders. This policy of witch-

hunting was abandoned by his successor Radama I (r. 1809–28), an admirer of Napoleon, who tried to modernize the country with European support, and created a standing army. Radama abandoned the slave-trade, and tried to stifle the use of ordeals, although he did not dare to outlaw it officially. Already during his reign, the ground was prepared for the restoration of traditional customs under Queen Ranavalona I (r. 1828–61).

European influence was curbed, and a conscious attempt was made to forge a national ideology, a state religion, based upon the traditional notion of *hasina*, and the struggle against witchcraft gained central importance. Foreign as well as local observers, like the queen's private secretary Raombana, the first indigenous historian, agree on the fact that the poison ordeal was used systematically and frequently. Whole villages, towns and even regions – and in three particular years the whole island – had to perform the cleansing ritual, with the exception of children. If the tested persons were affected by the poison, they either died, a proof of their guilt, or vomited and had a chance of survival. As Raombana reported, 'a great number of them dies through this horrible test'. An English missionary calculated in the 1830s that one-tenth of the population had to take the poison at least once during their lifetime, and that a fifth of these died as a consequence. He calculated that 'a fiftieth part of the population is carried off by this most formidable instrument of destruction'. With about 2 million inhabitants, this would have amounted to tens of thousands of victims, and the worst excesses were yet to come. Later authors claim that several hundred thousand Madagascans must have died during the queen's reign. Unfortunately, administrative records do not exist to prove or disprove these assumptions. But undoubtedly the permanent witch craze, supported by the state authorities, is quite remarkable. The queen's successor, dominated by Prime Minister Rainilaiarivony (r. 1864–95), opened the island to European influence, outlawed slavery and stopped witch-hunts and ordeals, and the island finally ended up as a French colony. The notion of *mosavi* is still shared by most Madagascans.[3]

In Nigeria witch-cleansing cults are recorded from the mid-nineteenth century, well before the appearance of the first colonial agents. In Ghana traditional chiefs regularly exercised their right to judge witches, which led either to a fine, to enslavement or to the death sentence. The witch was given to the executioner, with the words: 'Take her on the path!'[4] Among the Nyoro in Uganda, 'in ancient times habitual sorcerers were tied up in dried banana leaves, which are highly flammable, and burnt to death; it is said that in Mukama Kabarega's reign, during the latter years of the 19th century, many sorcerers were despatched in this way'. Lucy Mair collects a number of quotations from anthropologists, claiming that the killings happened only 'in the past' and had been rare.[5] But this was clearly wrong. Chief Sechele of the Bechuana (Botswana) had five men executed for witchcraft in 1889, while acquitting others less guilty.[6] Among the Bakweri tribe in Cameroon 'every village had a witch-hanging tree' until the German colonial administration stopped the killings in 1894.[7] King Lobengula (1833–94) of the Ndebele presided over an average of no less than ten witch executions per month in the late nineteenth century, and among the Pondo of South Africa the estimates run at one per day on the eve of the British conquest,[8] making these events in Southern Africa, according to our definitions, two major persecutions. It seems likely that witch-hunts increased from the 1880s, when a period of favourable rainfall ended and repeated drought brought crop failure, cattle plague and famine within the next forty years, with severe epidemics of smallpox, yellow fever, cholera, meningitis and sleeping sickness. The impact of these epidemics could be compared to the Black Death in Europe.[9] Under Zulu King Shaka's nephew, Cetshwayo Ka Mpande (1826–84, r. 1857/72–84), portrayed as a bloody ruler by contemporary English South African newspapers, witches were frequently killed, particularly in times of cattle disease. However, the king was less cruel than the Anglophone press portrayed him, as he ascribed the frequency of accusations to an abundance of witch-doctors, and tried to protect the persecuted by taking them out of their environment and settling them elsewhere, not unlike the present-day South African government.[10] Although such reports were utilized for colonial propaganda, it is unlikely that they were invented. It seems rather that the reason why witchcraft was a major issue in the African colonies was that it had already been a massive problem in pre-colonial times. If it is true that the problem of witchcraft is related to settlement structure, we may assume that this had started at least from the thirteenth century, when sub-Saharan Africa, the savannas as well as the rainforests, had become more densely populated.[11]

The relation between witch-hunting and extraordinary misery, witchcraft as a 'social strain-gauge', as Marwick called it, has already been discussed in the context of the Modernization Theory (page 26). Anthony Wallace has pointed to the fact that in extreme situations *revitalization movements* are likely to occur, millenarian or nativistic movements which try to provide orientation in times of accelerated culture change and social hardship.[12] Wallace exemplified this with American examples, and in particular the case of the Longhouse religion, triggered by the Seneca prophet Handsome Lake (1735–1815). After two generations of peace and economic welfare, the equilibrium of the Iroquois cultural system had been destroyed by a series of military, political and economic disasters. In the Seven Years' War (1756–63) and the American War of Independence, the Iroquois had supported the wrong side, and their heartlands were devastated. Their leaders had to sign unfavourable contracts, depriving the tribes of their traditional lands, and of their diplomatic and military power. Exhausted by warfare, their life was first confined to concentration camps and subsequently to reservations.

The Iroquis nation fragmented, the chiefs were stripped of their legitimacy, and the men – formerly politicians, warriors and hunters – fell into unemployment and alcoholism. Being confined to the reservations, anxieties, social tensions and the fear of witchcraft mushroomed. In spring 1799 a witch was executed who was believed to be responsible for the death of a niece of Chief Cornplanter (*c.*1735–1836) of the Allegany Reservation. The chief's half-brother Handsome Lake experienced a number of trance visions. Angels appeared, dressed in old-time Indian garb, divine messengers, who urged him to abandon alcohol, return to the indigenous culture and stop the witches who were corrupting the tribe. In further ecstasies he experienced journeys through heaven and hell, and had conversations with George Washington (1732–99, r. 1789–97) and Jesus Christ, who complained of his lack of followers. Handsome Lake assumed religious leadership, and even managed to receive support from President Thomas Jefferson (1743–1826, r. 1801–9). Further visions reinforced the new moral code with the apocalyptic threat that in case of disobedience the world would be destroyed by fire. This *apocalypticism* led to the revitalization of traditional Iroquois culture, but in the first instance it triggered a considerable witch-hunt, an issue neglected in some standard accounts of these events, which attribute the prophet's ideas to Quakerism.[13] Suspected witches had to confess, and those who refused to comply were killed. The witch-hunts came to a halt after Handsome Lake ordered the killing of witches from other reserves, particularly after the accusation of some of the principal young men. Popular sentiment changed, and the prophet was criticized because of his dictatorial stance, which was not considered to be congenial to Iroquois culture. The prophet recognized that he had gone too far, and dropped the persecutory mode of handling suspected witches. Instead, he focused on cultural and political issues. Anthropologists assume that his restoration played an important part in the preservation of the Iroquois cultural heritage.[14]

The case of the Seneca was not unique, not in America and not on other continents. Bryan Wilson has shown that 'epidemics of prophetism' have swept North America since about 1760.[15] Witch-hunts against accommodationists had already been launched by earlier revivalists, like the Delaware prophet Neolin among the Ohio Valley tribes in 1762, as a prelude to Ottawa chief Pontiac's (1720–69) famous uprising against the colonial powers in North America and Canada.[16] The Shawnee, usually a peaceful agrarian society, experienced a similar prophetic movement at the beginning of the nineteenth century, when war chief Tecumseh (1768–1813), after having supported the British against their rebellious colonies, tried to unite

all American Indians under his leadership. His ambitious plan to win
back the land and to revitalize traditional culture was backed by his
brother, the shaman Tenskwatawa (*c.*1768–1834), who turned into a
millenarian prophet in 1805.[17] In order to unite the people, he chose
witches as a principal target of his warnings, and an unknown number
were burned by his followers.[18] The resistance of the Native
Americans was not just 'spirited', they were also fighting against evil
spirits and their human supporters, the witches.[19] Lucy Mair has
argued that it is 'common for the prophets of millenary cults to offer
these limited benefits in addition to the promise of the final regeneration of the world', whether the charismatic leaders fashioned
themselves as Christians or not. Furthermore, she argued that 'in any
culture area millenary, healing and witchfinding cults will be found
to have common elements of miracle, revelation and ritual'.[20] Stuart
Clark suggests that it is the witch-cleansing attitude rather than any
other goal 'that secures for these movements their popular backing',[21]
referring to the Maji-Maji rising against German colonial rule in East
Africa. Drawing on local African concepts of temporal corruption
and periodic renewal, and of anti-witchcraft cults, the people of
Matumbi and Ngindo gave their support to a traditional healer and
prophet, Kinjikitile Ngwale, who led the rebellion in 1905.[22]

In Africa revivalism and witch-hunting were particularly closely
related, and the very term 'anti-witchcraft movement' has been
coined in this context. From about 1900 onwards, these eradication
movements have repeatedly swept sub-Saharan Africa, marking the
major difference between day-to-day witchcraft accusations, which
are mainly a function of misfortune and derailed personal relationships, and the kind of collective accusations in situations of general
crises. Such movements could be invoked by a prophet, or a spirit
medium, or they could develop from a traditional anti-witchcraft
shrine, the cult of a fetish or *orisha*, which were (and are) prominent
on both sides of the Atlantic, West Africa and the Caribbean and
Brazil alike. Sometimes prophets established new shrines, for
example Marie Lalou (died 1951), the founder of a purification cult
in the French Ivory Coast. She had experienced visions after the
death of her three children, and afterwards claimed to recognize
witches on sight. These powers were sufficient to make her the object
of pilgrimages from various tribes, and the protection from witches
became the central concern of her Deíma cult. Centred around
shrines, these anti-witchcraft cults are usually more persistent than
the short-lived enthusiasm of non-institutionalized movements.
Another Ivorian cult, founded in 1946 by a visionary, was primarily
concerned with the fertility of both the fields and women, and the
restoration of old customs and practices. 'Sorcerers' and traditional
diviners had to destroy their tools, and were employed as fetish
priests. The Massa cult, with numerous temples for the fetishes, spread

Plate 9 Mask, representing a Spirit, invoked in periodical witch-finding drives of the Songe, Sankuru River area. Photo: Lucy Mair, *Witchcraft* (1969), p. 62. ©

rapidly in Western Africa and reached the French Sudan in the early 1950s. Its principal function was the abolition of witchcraft.[23] Movements could also arise from one of the numerous traditional secret societies, often busy with witch-hunting anyway, which could be transformed into a public movement. This was the case with the Ndaka Goya cult of the Nupe in Northern Nigeria, whose masked members became a witch-cleansing movement around 1920, soon to transgress boundaries of ethnicity and language. Although forbidden the following year, traces of the movement seem to have survived for decades.[24]

The transformation of the Watchtower movement, as Jehovah's Witnesses were then called, into an anti-witchcraft movement demonstrates the link to colonial suppression. Tomo Nyirenda, an African Watchtower (Kitawala) convert from Nyasaland (Malawi), started a preaching campaign after 1925 in northern Rhodesia (Zambia) and the Belgian Congo, asserting that black liberators would soon arrive and drive out the whites, stop taxation and distribute their property. At some point Nyirenda developed the idea that baptism – a common practice among Jehovah's Witnesses – was an ordeal for the detection of witches, and announced that the advent could only take place if the land was purified of witches. Soon baptism replaced the forbidden traditional ordeals, and those refusing baptism were labelled as witches. Local chiefs started calling for Nyirenda's support in destroying witchcraft. The preacher turned into a witch-finder, and his activities created a major witch panic. Chief Shaiwila of the Lala killed sixteen of his people as witches, and more people were killed in neighbouring districts. In Katanga the witch-finder indicted 176 people. Pursued by the Belgian authorities, Nyirenda returned to Rhodesia, where, despite efforts by the locals to protect them, he and Shaiwila were eventually captured, then hanged.[25]

In anti-witchcraft movements the accusations are not related to any particular misfortune, and the supposed witches are not approached in private and asked to remove their spells. Rather, the accusations are articulated publicly, and backed up by whole communities, usually driven by fears of a conspiracy of witches and aiming at the general eradication of the conspiracy, or of the conspirators, as in early modern Europe. In contrast to individual accusations, witch-cleansing movements promise not just private relief, but an *instant millennium*, the sudden beginning of a reign of peace and abundance, sometimes without labour, but always without misfortune, and without postponement of this improvement to a far-away future or the other world.[26] The leaders of the anti-witchcraft movements announce their impending arrival, and negotiate an appointment with the village elders, thus preparing the ground for their future actions, and raising the expectations and social tensions in the places to be visited. On the day of arrival, they ask the witches in proclamations or sermons to repent, to confess, to surrender their tools of sorcery and to accept punishment. Under enormous public pressure many suspects take the opportunity to confess and be purified of their supposed guilt. Their only choice is between being outlawed, or having a chance to be reintegrated into their communities. The means of sorcery – scriptures, snakes, horns, bones, pots of unguents and so on – are burned publicly. If they fail to confess, and a search of their houses reveals their guilt, more serious actions are to be taken. There seems to be no consensus as to whether anti-witchcraft movements led to increased witch killings, or rather served as valves for an already existing pressure.[27]

Recent research into the history of the Giriami people in Kenya by Cynthia Brantley emphasizes endogenous developments as determining factors. Around 1700 the Giriami suffered from oppression by the Oromo-Galla, and therefore lived in fortified villages. The village elders, who controlled the resources, were responsible for the control of witchcraft by means of secret rituals and ordeals, exercised by one of the four existing secret societies, and public trials. Witches were threatened with corporal punishment, banishment or the death penalty. After 1850 the Giriami left their villages, and started living in scattered farms. Social differentiation increased when competition set in and some farmers were more successful than others in agriculture and trading. The authority of the elders declined. Now the fears of witchcraft increased, since in the people's eyes witchcraft was controlled less effectively. Therefore there was a rise in the importance of secret societies, which could act more independently than the traditional authority of the elders. At the same time the belief in ancestral spirits lost importance, and Islam gained influence, inspiring a number of possession cases. Around 1899/1900, when a severe famine struck the country and epidemics were imminent, witchcraft and sorcery were considered to be the main reason for the uncertainty and actual misfortune. An anti-witchcraft movement was founded by a charismatic *muganga*, a medicine-man or witch-doctor, the first of many similar witch-cleansing movements recorded in that particular area. This was the situation when the British colonial administration was introduced in 1912 in 'British East Africa'. The attempt to suppress the secret societies led to the 'Giriami-uprising' of 1913. The British law courts accepted accusations of witchcraft, but always acquitted the suspected witches, and punished the accusers instead, often severely. As a result, and despite Christian education, the witch craze increased, and the secret societies organized tribunals against witchcraft. The government interpreted the organized activities against witchcraft as a political conspiracy, and never managed to take the concerns of the Giriami seriously until the end of colonial rule in 1963. After Kenya's independence, the influence of the secret societies continued. In 1965 the first post-colonial anti-witchcraft movement began. Its leader, Kajiwe, launched a campaign that was initially welcomed by the village elders. But it soon got out of control, when Kajiwe targeted Muslims as witches, started burning the Koran and blackmailing his victims for money. Eventually Kajiwe was detained, but thousands of his followers besieged the local authorities, until the police crushed the demonstrations. Kajiwe was sentenced to eighteen months in prison, but was released after a year, and resumed his activities. In 1977 the responsible district commissioner forbade a movement that had generated accusations of witchcraft. The government of President Jomo Kenyatta (1891–1978, r. 1964–78) tried to contain their activities, because they were thought to increase witch-beliefs. They were considered, just as during the colonial regime, to be a political threat.[28]

More recent surveys have shown that anti-witchcraft movements were less extraordinary events than previously assumed. The Tiv people of Nigeria, who closely associate power with supernatural forces, experienced no less than five campaigns between about 1900 and 1939, and similar movements had preceded British rule. The fifth of these recorded campaigns, the Nyambua cult, was disruptive enough to bring social and economic life to a standstill, and indigenous political power collapsed. Indeed, the anti-witchcraft movements served the function of redistributing power, and in 1939 the central shrine itself gave birth to new power structures. Among the Lele people of the Congo, where illness and death were generally attributed to witchcraft, no less than seven named campaigns occurred in the period from 1910 to 1952, some more local in character, and some part of super-regional movements, such as the Bamucapi/Mcape movement, while some were also of political significance like Kabenga-Benga, which preceded the collapse of the colonial regime.[29] Many anti-witchcraft movements have escaped the attention of anthropologists or historiographers altogether, particularly those in pre-colonial times. The well-explored examples of the Tiv and Lele may demonstrate the intensity of persecutions in the colonial period, but still a majority of the more local movements remained unrecorded. In some cases we know about campaigns, but no details, and not even a name. Some witchcraft eradication movements, however, have gained considerable attention, mostly due to their size, or their political importance, or both. They served as points of reference for contemporaries, and this is still the case in anthropological literature.

The theory that social change had caused these eradication movements, proposed by Malinowski and amplified by his students, has been modified since, due to the discovery that witches had also been killed in traditional African societies, long before the Europeans had seized power. A good number of these purification movements seem to have started in Nyasaland (now Malawi), but despite their local origins these campaigns spread rapidly over Eastern, Central and Southern Africa, notwithstanding the numerous tribes, languages, religious and cultural backgrounds, and also different colonial

Table 6.1 Witchcraft eradication movements in colonial Africa

Years	Movement	Colonies	Post-colonial countries
1905–6	Maji Maji	German	Tanzania
1920–1	Ndako Gboya	British	Nigeria
1925–8	Kitawala	British	Malawi, Zambia
		Belgian	Congo
1933–5	Bamucapi (Mcape)	British	Malawi, Zambia, Zimbabwe, Tanzania
		Portuguese	Mozambique
		Belgian	Congo
1943–4	Kamcape	British	Tanzania
1947–9	Bwanali-Mpulumutsi	British	Malawi, Zambia, Zimbabwe
		Portuguese	Mozambique
		Belgian	Congo
1950–1	Tigari/Atinga	British	Ivory Coast, Ghana, Nigeria
		French	Benin, Togo
1952–8	Kabenga-Benga	Belgian	Congo
1954	Wacilole	British	Tanzania
1962–4	Kamcape	British	Malawi, Tanzania, Zambia, Rhodesia, Zimbabwe

regimes, since these countries were under British, German (British mandate from 1920), Belgian, French and Portuguese rule in the first half of the twentieth century. Some movements were proto-religious in character, usually being founded by a charismatic leader, a wonder-performing prophet, who had constructed the basic rituals, being entitled to do so by divine vocation. Several of these leaders were said to have been resurrected after death. Bwanali, who had founded the movement of 1947, denied this in an interview with Marwick, only to add that he himself had resurrected his follower Mpulumutsi by witchcraft.[30] The founder of the Kamcape movement, Lighton Chunda, alias Chikanga, was reported by his followers to have died of witchcraft, and to have been resurrected from the dead in order to rid the world of sorcery. Again the movement had started in Nyasaland, a hothouse of charismatic leaders, and spread over large parts of East Africa, with a regular bus service transporting believers to the cult leader's village. After independence, President Hastings Banda (1906–94, r. 1966–94) summoned Chikanga in 1964 and

restricted his activities, which had disturbed the new political authorities as well as the churches.[31]

In his review of the supposed origins of the African witchcraft
eradication movements, Lee found the six prevailing concepts
wanting – namely, that they covered an anti-colonial conspiracy, that
they were a response to colonial rule, or to economic depression,
that they represented traditional religion, or were disguised neo-
Christian movements, or a means of role redefinition. According to
Lee, the purpose of these movements was nothing other than to find
a legally viable form of handling witchcraft under colonial pressure.[32]
In retrospect, it seems that the mode of organization of these anti-
witchcraft campaigns as supra-regional movements served the
purpose of exonerating the village elders from their legal responsibility, imposed by the colonial – and the post-colonial – justice administration. External witch-doctors appeared on the stage, organized the
witch-hunt and disappeared again, retiring to areas where they were
safe from prosecution.

There seems to be no consensus about the interrelation between
the different campaigns, for instance the movement amongst the
Giriami people in Kenya, the Bamucapi movement in Zambia in the
1930s, the Bwanali-Mpulumutsi movement in Malawi in the 1940s or
the Kamcape movement in Tanzania in the 1960s, although anthropologists agree on their structural similarity.[33] None of these movements was primarily aimed at killing the witches, but rather at ending
witchcraft. As in historical Europe, it is not the explosive movements
that cause the greatest toll of victims, but rather the continuous flow
of killings, where a general agreement on the belief in witchcraft and
the necessity of its eradication prevailed, as in early modern Lorraine,
Valais, Mecklenburg or Tanzanian Sukumaland. Whereas the constant killing of witches rests upon consensus, the witch-cleansing
movements had political implications as well. Willis points to the
fact that Congolese cults 'were directed against whites as well as
witches'.[34] There are obvious parallels with Latin America, for
example early modern Bolivia and Peru, where the Spanish invaders
were also interpreted in terms of witchcraft by millenarian liberation
movements, and Christian missionaries were killed as witches.[35]

Andrew Apter has recently shattered the traditional anthropologists' assumptions that collective witch-cleansings were either located
in the 'timeless world of the ethnographic present', the world of
kinship and African chiefdom, or should be interpreted as reactions
to an overall culture change. In his reinterpretation of the Atinga
movement in 1950, when thousands of women were persecuted in
the former British Gold Coast (Ghana), French Dahomey (Benin)
and British Yorubaland (Nigeria), he demonstrates that the craze was
historically linked to a dramatic rise of the cocoa price on the world
market. Apter interprets the crisis politically as a 'complicitous

assault on female power in its social, economic, and ritual domains', and the witch craze as an instrument to create new forms of domination. Although Apter does not deny that some peculiarities of attribution can be connected to structural features of Yoruba society, he emphasizes that the issue was sponsored by a new class of businessmen in order to break the power of Yoruba market women, who had traditionally dominated trade, trading associations, market networks, and banking, accumulated and controlled capital, and challenged the male position in the household. Trading capital, like the power of witchcraft, was transmitted from mother to daughter, but since capitalism had turned capital into a major resource of power, this had changed the balance of power within the families, where women were neglecting their female duties and became 'infertile'. Witchcraft could serve as a language to reinterpret economic control, and traditional male-dominated secret societies could be used for enforcing the issue, aided by the foreign cult of Atinga. The movement was wiped out in 1951 by the colonial governments, but deserves attention because the underlying anxieties were *not* triggered by economic hardship, but rather the opposite: they were triggered by sudden economic growth, which created unexpected opportunities, and caused tensions between young and old, and men and women.[36]

Witch crazes can be linked to health crises, as well as to economic, cultural or *political crises*. They accompanied the liberation of the African nations, often periods of civil unrest or civil war, of extreme spiritual and/or social uncertainty, characterized by the collapse of institutions and the tyranny of local warlords. In the Belgian Congo, where the Kabenga-Benga movement had spread in the early 1950s,[37] about 500 people were accused among the Bushong people in October 1958, shortly before independence. At least 250 people were killed in fifty-eight villages through poison ordeals, most of them women. According to our definition (p. 49), this was a massive witch-hunt.[38] In the Portuguese colony of Angola the guerrilla fighters, from 1961 onwards, aided the local population in killing witches, and practically served as an anti-witchcraft movement. After Angolan independence in 1975 the Marxist MPLA party, based in the capital Luanda, tried to stop the witch-hunts, but warriors of Jonas Savimbi's (1934–2002) US-sponsored UNITA went on killing witches in the southern parts of the country with unprecedented cruelty up to the beginning of the twenty-first century. The witches were cut with axes, guerrillas drank their blood, and spat it towards the sun, before the victims' bodies were burned. These Angolan witch burnings were staged as public rituals of violence: 'All civilians who belonged to the party had to come and watch. They had to "look happy", sing songs in praise of the party, and not even friends or relatives of the victims were allowed to cry,' as was reported in Namibian refugee camps in 1996. Most of the interviewed did not object to the execution of witches as such, but only against the abuse of these practices by the bush warriors, who launched accusations against anyone unwilling to comply with UNITA rules. 'Anyone who expressed concern about their material well-being, mentioned the harshness of life in the bush or complained about the lack of salt, soap, blankets, food, clothes, planks for burial, etc., risked being accused of treason or witchcraft and subsequently executed.'[39] There were rumours that Savimbi himself participated in witchcraft, and had engaged himself in *muti* murders and sacrificed relatives in order to gain the power of shape-shifting, and become a lion. Furthermore, it was reported that he arranged for the killing of his medicine woman, who had prepared powerful potions to protect him and make him invincible. Linda Heywood interprets the support for Savimbi in the light of the continuing importance of the tradition that the 'ruler's power was based on their control of spiritual and secular forces, the notion of centralised and decentralised power, and the concept of misuse of power through witchcraft'. Whereas supporters of Savimbi stressed his attempts at eradicating witchcraft, his opponents saw him as a witch himself.[40]

In Zimbabwe, witch-hunts reached a zenith during the war of liberation, partly due to the collapse of traditional as well as of modern institutions, partly because of the importance of spirit-mediums during the guerrilla war. They represented the legacy of the ancestral spirits, imagined to be structurally opposed to evil witch-spirits. Witch-hunting became an important issue of liberation, because the spirit-mediums and *ngangas* supported the persecution, whereas the white rulers – whether colonial, Rhodesian or representatives of the Apartheid system – protected them. Witch-hunting became an act of liberation in itself. The traditional healers and spirit-mediums therefore became natural allies of the new nationalist leaders, even if they were not political supporters of the Zimbabwe African National Union (ZANU), later president Robert Mugabe's (1925–, r. 1980–) state party. Witch-finding became one of the 'techniques used by the guerrillas to gain support'. The warriors could soon rely on their reputation, and often the villagers reported on their arrival who they suspected of being witches. One of the comrades of the ZANU reported:

> When we entered a village we didn't ask people where the witches are. We waited until people complained about a person, and then we went to interrogate them. If that person continued to deny he was a witch we left him alone. But if he admitted it we asked the people what sort of punishment he should be given and we carried it out. He could be set free, if this was what they wanted, but also he could be killed.

In many cases, however, the comrades did not wait for denunciations, as another ex-warrior reported: 'During the war ZANU used to travel round with that medium called Chivere. He told them who all the witches are. It's very good to kill all those witches.' Political liberation and witch-hunting, it seems, were perceived as almost identical at the grassroots of the movement: 'The guerillas' explicit and aggressive policy against witches was the final turn of the key in the lock. The doorway to legitimate political authority was opened wide.'[41] This road to success must have inspired some African leaders. During the election campaign of 2002 Mugabe threatened the supporters of the opposition openly with witchcraft at a pre-election rally in Manicaland.[42]

Freed from colonial jurisdiction, a popular demand for the eradication of evil seems to have exploded in many African countries, particularly where anti-witchcraft movements had flourished earlier. A good example is Malawi, ruled for decades by Hastings Kamuzu Banda, a firm believer in witchcraft, who had managed to seize power in the turmoil of a witch craze. Although Banda curbed the activities of a witch-hunting prophet, he actively encouraged the youth league of his state party to engage in violent anti-witchcraft activities, and danced publicly with the masks of a male secret society, well-known for their abilities to shape-shift and persecute witches in the shape of wild animals. Banda eventually became fascinated by a young female diviner, who turned public meetings into manifestations of witchcraft eradication, not unlike the earlier Kamcape movement.[43] Witchcraft eradication became a vital issue in the Zambia of President Kenneth Kaunda (1924–91, r. 1964–91), as well as in Congo Leopoldville (Kinshasa), soon to be renamed Zaire during a campaign for African authenticity by President Mobutu Sese Seko (1930–97, r. 1965–97), whose wearing of a leopard's skin presumably signalled his abilities to shape-shift and his properties as a human leopard. Secret societies of witch-hunters use leopard attributes as signs of their ability to shape-shift.[44] By initiation all men symbolically become wild animals, predators and carnivores, but the power of the chief implies deeper knowledge of secret rituals, and it is not by coincidence that ritual murders and human sacrifices are frequently attributed to the powerful in Africa. Power and witchcraft are as closely related as wealth and witchcraft.

The rising importance of witchcraft from the 1970s occurred also in countries of peaceful transition, like French and British West Africa, or Tanzania. Only more recently has it been argued that this was due less to former colonialism, or modernization, than to economic crisis and ecological catastrophe. The economic boom of the 1950s, due to late colonial capital investment in infrastructure and mining, and the integration into the world market, had clearly raised expectations. African nationalists suspected that colonialism retarded the economic development, and they drew confidence from their rapid political success. Economic growth did indeed continue in the 1960s, and the new states benefited from relatively small public debts, ample land, and free peasants who extended their plantations and produced cash-crops. The rapid population growth was seen as a corresponding sign of hope and improvement. However, in the 1970s, colonization was by necessity driven into marginal lands, growing poor crops even in good years, and multiplying the number of potential famine victims during drought. The prices on the world market became unfavourable for African products, and expanding existing services to provide millions of young children with food, housing, medicine and education absorbed the surplus. A downward spiral of *economic decline* started, with declining investment, a deteriorating infrastructure, deteriorating public services in health and education, the delegitimization of the state and disintegration of political authority, as well as corruption, all contributing to the crisis. *State contraction* opened the gates to vigilantism, fragmentation along the lines of ethnicity or religion, tribal wars, attempts at secession, and genocidal civil wars as in Rwanda and the Congo.[45]

Ecological catastrophes – sometimes beyond political control, like the droughts of the early 1980s – combined with a rapidly rising population, paving the way for malnutrition, famine and epidemic diseases, like smallpox and tuberculosis, or new diseases, like AIDS. Drugs against malaria, sleeping sickness and yellow fever became unavailable for the impoverished. All these developments, exacerbated by political unrest and warfare, added up to a rapid increase of uncertainty and hardship. Witchcraft fears proliferate amidst insecurity and encourage the revival of protection cults, witch-finding and persecution. And the dimension of a hyper-acute generational conflict is added by a young generation – with considerable weight in the age pyramid – bred by rapid demographic growth and mass urbanization, with high expectations of Western-style consumerism, propelled by new media like television, who face economic decay, unemployment and increasing uncertainty.[46] Youth violence fuels fundamentalism in Northern Africa, but fuels crime, vigilantism and anti-witchcraft movements in the sub-Saharan parts of the continent. Age hierarchies are dramatically inverted when the established elders are labelled witches, and the young radicals – or, where politics is involved, young 'comrades' – set the agenda. Revolution is translated into the African 'languages' of fundamentalism and witchcraft,[47] and the transformation of traditional societies does not seem to pose a major obstacle: 'Witchcraft rumours easily integrate modern technology, party politics, and the state's legal and administrative practices. They bridge easily the distance between village and city; and . . . they increasingly acquire transnational dimensions.'[48]

Witch-hunting reached gruesome dimensions in Tanzania, where anti-witchcraft movements had already been active in pre-colonial and colonial times. According to Simeon Mesaki, an anthropologist from the University of Dar-es-Salaam, between 1970 and 1984 about

3,692 persons were killed as witches in Tanzania, 69 per cent of them female. In this Swahili-speaking country, the Bantu-people of Sukuma, living under traditional conditions in the northern provinces of Mwanza and Shinyanga, were particularly affected, with 2,246 witch killings in the area of Sukumaland alone, and another 826 lynchings between 1985 and 1988, 'giving a grand total of 3,072 from 1970 to 1988 for the area'. According to Mesaki, the 'witch-killing in Sukumaland' could be interpreted as an indirect outcome of the villagization programme imposed by the socialist government of Julius Kambarage Nyerere (1922–99, r. 1961–85, party leader until 1987). It was meant to stop nomadism in Tanzania's northern provinces, and to force the people to settle down in *Ujamaa* (freedom) villages. However, villagization led to the weakening of traditional structures (ancestor cults, chiefdom), an increase of ecological problems (soil exhaustion, decreasing field ratios) and of social tensions. Formerly, the tribes had split in cases of disagreement, but now they were tied together in artificial villages. As a result, tensions and witchcraft accusations soared, and killings were commissioned. The local criminal courts, and the representatives of Nyerere's TANU party, tolerated the killings. But in 1988, after Nyerere's resignation, a special commission was set up by the central government, and some local leaders were punished.[49] The heroic period of the liberation wars is already part of a distant history, long-forgotten by those young men who are presently killing witches. According to a study of the Tanzanian Ministry of Family, another 5,000 people were killed in witch-hunts in only five years between 1994 and 1998. The Association of Tanzanian Media Women reports that in the region adjacent to Lake Victoria, an average of nine people are *presently* killed every month for suspected witchcraft.[50]

More complicated were the developments in the republic of South Africa, where political independence was replaced by the apartheid system. The practice of *necklacing*, supported by Winnie Mandela, gained worldwide attention in 1985, when a Dutch television team managed to film the punishment of collaborators of the apartheid regime in a black township. Necklacing basically means 'placing a tyre soaked in petrol around the victim's neck and setting it alight'. However, Joanna Ball managed to demonstrate that the burning of political traitors was grounded in the public punishment of anti-social people more generally, which had started with the burning of fourteen witches in Lebowa in December 1976 and January 1977. They were either locked in their huts and burned alive, or thrown onto a pile of wood and burned. By 1983/4, when burning had become 'the standard means of disposing of witches', necklacing had already become a common variant. Burning, as in Europe, implied the complete destruction of the culprit in order to wipe out his or her memory, prevent the return of 'shades' and break the link with the ancestors. However, after the extra-legal burning of witches had resumed, 'spies and puppets of the Apartheid regime' were equated with them and treated in the same way, obviously because their crime was perceived as equally anti-social and evil. Subsequently, necklacing was extended to ritual murderers and those who commit treason or sexual crimes like sodomy, bestiality, incest or rape. It is worth remembering that in historical Europe witchcraft, treason and some sexual offences had been likewise treated as interchangeable crimes since the Middle Ages. However, even in the decade between 1984–93, when the burning of 'traitors' peaked in South Africa, 60 per cent of the victims of necklacing remained witches, and an additional 7.5 per cent of people who had actually committed *muti*-murders had killed someone in order to get hold of certain body parts (head, heart, hands, genitals and so on) for the purpose of preparing magic potions.[51]

The statistical data provided by the Ralushai Commission indicates that within the ten years before publication, 312 'witchcraft related killings' were recorded by the police of Lebowa, before and after the end of the apartheid regime. However, Lebowa is a small district, and even there it is suggested that killings were not usually recorded. The police were reluctant to investigate even reported cases, and refused to cooperate with the government commission.[52] Niehaus suggests that the figures are 'obviously vast underestimates' because the report refers only to some areas, while more than seventy-three people were killed as witches in 1994 alone, according to Lebowa police reports.[53] Having listed witchcraft murders and *muti* cases treated in the courts of Lebowa, Venda and Gazankulu,[54] the Ralushai Report emphasizes 'the continued frequency of witchcraft murders, if not their increase'.[55] There seems to be agreement on the fact that the misery of everyday life was ultimately responsible for the rise in witch killings, although the contributing factors are not evaluated. The late apartheid system is named, as well as rising unemployment and AIDS, but no reasons are given why the killings increased after Nelson Mandela was elected president. There is agreement on the fact that the killings are usually committed by young male 'comrades', but disagreement whether they were commissioned by village elders, chiefs or traditional healers, or whether the latter only agreed to 'sniff out' the witches because they were threatened with death by the comrades, as the Ralushai Commission suggests. The killings were committed by males, but accusations were launched by similar numbers of men and women (49 per cent female). In litigations against the accusers the complainants were overwhelmingly women (78 per cent).[56]

The Institute for Multi-Party Democracy in Durban has calculated 587 witch killings, with an additional 432 violent attacks against suspected witches in South Africa's northern province in the 1990s. In

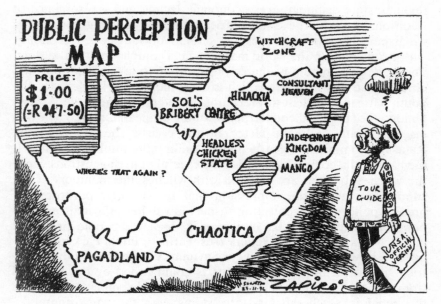

Plate 10 South Africa's northern province as 'Witchcraft Zone':
Public Perception Map from *The Sowetan*, 9 July 1997. ©

2000, the story of one of the murders committed by ANC activists,
the killing of Abraham Madibeng Phasha (1941–93) and his brother
Moses in the village of Mahlabela, was heard by South Africa's Truth
Commission. His nephew Michael Morudi Phasha (b. 1961), then
twenty-five, one of the leaders of those who had stoned Abraham to
death and mutilated the body of Moses, begged for pardon. According to the murderer, the murder had been necessary because his uncle
had been detected by the witch-doctor as an evil sorcerer, a *muti* murderer who had intended to obstruct the work of the ANC. As an
activist of the ANC Youth League it was his duty to kill his uncle,
because it was politically necessary. The Truth Commission was confronted with the delicate task of reassessing the crimes of thirty-four
detainees, who had killed twenty-six witches at the beginning of the
1990s, still under the apartheid regime, and had received prison sentences of between twelve years and life. All of them claimed to have
been members of the ANC. In most of the cases the Truth Commission, by now under president Thabo Mbeki (1942–, r. 1999–), granted
amnesty on the grounds that the murderers had been driven by traditional belief in witchcraft.[57]

   In contrast to Europe, where state-formation, economic improvement and the development of rational thought led to a decline in
anxieties, many African countries are characterized by corrupt

regimes, state disintegration, economic decline and a resurgence of traditional beliefs. The South African case is terrifying because its witch persecutions occur despite a relatively developed economy, with strong links to the world market, and a complex political system. The ANC government is unable or unwilling to take a clear position on the issue of witchcraft, which is even more regrettable since the South African president was recently elected president of the 'African Union', the supposed counterpart of the European Union. The existing law seems to be neglected by the courts. The report of the Ralushai Commission clearly aims at ending the public lynchings. It seems that the commission had to be careful in its suggestions. Since the witches' patrons are equated with witches, the members of the commission avoid the impression that this is their purpose. The present policy of concentrating suspected witches in 'witch camps' – or according to South African newspeak 'displaced people' protected in 'witch sanctuaries' like Helena Trust Farm, or Phola Park in Acornhoek, Tshitwi Village in Venda, or Savuanu Village in the Giyani district – or at certain police stations, is commended by the Ralushai Commission,[58] although the observation that policemen usually share the belief in witchcraft, and are 'siding with the witch-hunters',[59] might give cause for concern.

Given the sheer number of people involved in present-day witch killings in sub-Saharan Africa, it is quite surprising how little we know about the particular circumstances of these cases. Anthropologists have difficulties in uncovering such actions, even if they wish to do so. Informants keep silent, since they know that most anthropologists share Western values.[60] But anthropologists themselves prefer to research social structures and belief systems rather than scrutinize cases of lynchings and murder, which could spoil their relations with local authorities. We know about many killings only from local newspaper reports, where freedom of the press is in place, or through brief remarks in the literature, for example, regarding witch-hunts among the Mijekenda in coastal Kenya in the 1980s.[61] Thorough research, such as that by Peter Geschiere in Cameroon or Isak Niehaus in South Africa, is still the exception. As a consequence, it seems that we know more about historical European witch-hunts than about contemporary ones in Africa or other parts of the world. But although our knowledge is limited, it is certain that some major outbreaks of persecution were linked to the traditional perception of unusual disease being caused by mystical forces. Exceptional health crises, particularly when children are involved, still have the potential to trigger witch-hunts. The persecution in Benin in the late 1970s was linked to a tetanus epidemic, and the witch-hunts in Ghana in 1997 to meningitis. The protests of a human rights organization against the lynchings caused the government of Jerry Rawlings (1947–, r. 1981–2001) to allocate four camps, or 'sanctuaries', for the protection of suspected witches in October 1997, following the example of South Africa. The Gambaga camp sheltered 123 women, the Kukuo camp 450 women, the Kpatinga camp 42 women, and the Nagani camp 193 women and 13 men. These 821 inmates of the Ghanaian witch camps were aged between thirty-five and ninety. Despite these measures, lynchings continued into the following year.[62] More recently, HIV-infection (AIDS) is a major cause of concern. The witch-hunts in Mozambique and Kenya at the beginning of the twenty-first century are reported to be linked to this new disease. But the persecutions mentioned in recent newspaper reports are presumably only the tip of the iceberg. It is impossible to make overall estimates of the size of the witch-hunts, particularly given the horrors of the civil wars in several parts of sub-Saharan Africa. But the figures for the Tanzanian Sukumaland give a clue as to what we can expect. Among all the other catastrophes – including war, famine, AIDS, civil war and genocide – the fear of witchcraft and witch-hunts have a firm place.

Post-colonial witch persecutions are not restricted to Africa. In India several thousand people have been killed for witchcraft since independence, including in urban metropolises such as Bombay.[63] This is perhaps unsurprising if we consider that similar rates have been reported for pre-colonial northern India around 1800.[64] Witch-hunts had also erupted when colonial rule was weakened briefly during the uprising of 1857, and may even have been connected to the rebellion. In the Bengal presidency a local tribe started a systematic persecution, with hunters going from house to house during the night and killing the supposed witches and their families, as was reported in the English Parliament some years later.[65] In New Zealand, witch killings occurred among the native Maori people in the early 1860s. In one of the lynchings a retired British judge was involved.[66] Under Burmese kings, witchcraft was considered to be punishable by law, particularly if murder was involved, but it seems that even in colonial times and afterwards witches have occasionally been killed, with an instance reported from 1963.[67] On the Solomon Islands, one of the Pacific paradises of the European imagination, 'death was the usual penalty for witchcraft'.[68] In countries like Papua New Guinea, a hotspot of witch-belief, witches are killed on a regular basis to the present day, with few of them ever reported to the outside world. Remoteness and the prevailing animism do not seem to be the main reasons, since similar things also happen in south-east Asian countries with an Islamic background, such as Malaysia or Indonesia. Newspaper reports about mob lynchings have increased in the late 1980s in Java, as well as in Papua New Guinea, but it is uncertain whether this reflects an upsurge of local panics or merely a rising public concern at the national level. Judicial records are not helpful for researching the subject because the lynchings are treated as murder cases, and witchcraft comes to the fore only if the suspects refer to it in order to excuse their crimes.[69] Much of our knowledge depends on reports in local newspapers, and this may be one of the reasons why we hear little about witchcraft from Islamic countries, where the freedom of the press is more limited. The isolated report of a Syrian condemned for witchcraft in Saudi Arabia in 1998 indicates that there may be more to be found than is assumed.[70]

Central America is another hothouse of persecution in the twentieth century. In the community of Amatenango, a district inhabited by Tzeltal Maya in the Chiapas highlands of Mexico, on average every second month a man was murdered as a witch when anthropologists were collecting evidence there in the 1950s. Because the witches were supposed to be powerful, the killing always took place in an ambush, committed by groups of men, friends or kinsmen of the bewitched. This however does not imply that these killings were secret or lawless, according to native ideas of justice. Within the Maya communities it was public knowledge who had committed the murders. In a formal trial, an indigenous court attempted to establish whether the victim was indeed commonly perceived as a witch, in which case the slaying was to be accepted as justified. Subjects like the victim's ability as a healer (*curandero*), the power of his *nagual*, his animal alter ego, and indeed the suspicion of witchcraft were discussed within the indigenous community. If in this discourse the witch's relatives publicly redefined their relation, and excluded the possibility of revenge, the killing was commonly accepted as a necessary execution. When the Mexican police turned up to investigate the murder case, they received a detailed description of the outward evidence (time, location and so on), but no information on a suspect. The Maya kept silent about the executioners' names, and of course the reasons for the execution: the official records would not contain any hint of witchcraft.[71] The complex task of finding a consensus after the killing is clearly prohibitive, but the strong belief in witchcraft nevertheless allowed for a steady flow of accusations, and executions. There is little doubt that killings took place in other Maya communities in Mexico and Guatemala with similar frequency, and may still take place. June Nash formulated as a general rule that whenever a community passes through a period of crisis, 'the number of persons murdered as witches rises far above the norm'.[72] And witch killings are not confined to tribal people. In 1981 a Mexican mob stoned a woman to death after her husband accused her of using witchcraft to incite the assassination attempt on Pope John Paul II in Rome.[73]

Witch killings are reported from South America as well. Among the Jivaro Indians (Shuara) of Ecuador, legendary for their poisoned arrows and shrunken heads, misfortune and illness were frequently explained by witchcraft, and death generally so. The culprits were to be identified by the shaman, supported by his animal spirit. Usually witchcraft is attributed to shamans of neighbouring groups, who are the natural target of retaliation. The Jivaros had managed to fight back the Inca in 1455, and the Spaniards in 1699, and maintained independence until the second half of the nineteenth century. Only in the 1960s did a majority become Christian, at which time the continuous warfare for the purpose of retaliation stopped. But at the same time the status of the shamans rose, since retaliation now had to be enacted spiritually. It was never customary to boast of witch killings, because this would lead to revenge, and revealed a capital offence according to the laws of Ecuador and Peru.[74]

On the occasion of a witch scare in Chipaya, a village in the Bolivian highlands, the French anthropologist Nathan Wachtel traced back some of the suspicions and discovered that a generation ago, in the 1950s, the grandfather of one of the suspects had been slain as a witch, and the whole family had a long-standing fame of hereditary witchcraft, of extracting blood and selling it to foreigners. In 1983 a village resident of Orinoca (near Lake Poopo in the Bolivian highlands), a 'rich' businessman who could afford a van, was formally convicted by the village assemby of having made a contract with the devil and of having conducted harmful magic (*kharisiri*) in order to sell the body parts. The man was burned and his ashes dispersed in the winds. When the regular judges attempted to intervene, they encountered a wall of silence.[75] In the 1980s a sorcery scare accompanied the activities of the indigenous guerrilla movement *Sendero Luminoso* (the Shining Path) in Peru. People employed night patrols in order to prevent witches from extracting human fat or organs and selling them to the industrialized world. The indigenous liberation movement possibly tried to exploit popular anxieties in order to gain support from the villagers, very much like their African counterparts. The Peruvian panics reached a peak in 1987 when a young merchant from Huancayo was lynched as a *pishtako* by locals near the town of Ayacucho. Among those threatened with lynching for supposed organ-trading were also three French tourists. Similar witch panics occurred during 1982–3 in the northern Potosí region of Bolivia in the context of a national economic crisis, aggravated by successive droughts, famine and epidemics.[76]

Witch killings occur in societies where witchcraft is not punishable in court, for instance in Native American reservations in the USA.[77] But the witch killings were again not confined to the Native Americans. In Texas a Mexican couple, both citizens of the United States, attributed the husband's incurable disease to a Mexican woman in a neighbouring village. In February 1860, his father, one of the wealthiest Mexican landowners in the area, hired a party of men to kidnap the witch, Antonia Alanis. They killed one of her daughters, who had tried to protect her mother, wounded another, 'lassoed' the suspected witch and 'dragged her on the ground' towards the village of Camargo (Nueva Villa). There she was illegally kept prisoner over a period of two weeks, and repeatedly beaten. Since the bewitched man's health failed to improve, a witch-doctor suggested that the witch had to be burned.[78] Witch-hunting was not confined to the Catholic population either. Another lynching was reported from Arkansas, where a widow named Hill was murdered together with a slave woman, and her house was burned down in order to conceal the murder. The *New York Tribune* reported that a slave was forced by means of severe torture to confess to the murders in November 1859. And although he was subsequently burned at the stake, the metropolitan newspaper strongly suggested that he was innocent, and the instant execution had been staged to protect the true culprits.[79]

A killing among the Pueblo people caused considerable uneasiness in 1854 because the Indians were thought to be subject to the law of New Mexico, and the murderers were put on trial according to the law of the USA. In their eyes, however, they had merely executed the decision of the Council of the Pueblo, who had always governed themselves and were still doing so. The witch killing thus became a test case for the relations between the USA and the Pueblo nation, and for the kind of law that was to be applied in court. The 'governor of the tribe' – as a newspaper happened to label the Pueblo chief – testified as a witness in a US court that the executioners had acted on his command:

> It was the duty of the prisoners to execute the orders of the Pueblo ... The deceased men had been detected in the act of witchcraft, they confessed they had been guilty of witchcraft and sorcery; they had eaten up the little children of the Pueblo; it has always been the custom to put a stop and check bad acts; we have not exercised this custom of killing the witches since the Americans came here, because there had not been such bad doings before. We have always governed ourselves as an independent community.[80]

The Pueblo case was anything but unusual. Among the Navaho of New Mexico, even major witch persecutions occurred. From 1875 onwards 'many were killed', and US authorities had to intervene 'to prevent wholesale slaughter of "witches"'.[81] How substantial these persecutions must have been becomes clear from the fact that Chief Manuelito commissioned the execution of more than forty witches in 1884 alone. It seems the Navaho leader managed to reverse the usual pattern, since he utilized the witch-hunt to curb a nativistic movement, and to get rid of troublemakers who wished to introduce the Ghost Dance among the Navaho and start a liberation war against the USA.[82]

Under the theocratic rule of a group of Zuni shamans, witch-hunting had become the most prominent task of the medicine society of the Bow Priests, from at least the 1880s. In common with some

African examples, this secret society had adopted the task of purify-
ing their community of witchcraft, after their traditional tasks of
support for hunting and war had evaporated. However, when the
young Zuni Nick Tumaka was arrested for suspected witchcraft in
1900, he managed to send his father to the nearby garrison at Fort
Wingate. Commissioned by the Agency for Indian Affairs in Santa
Fe, US troops immediately suppressed the witch craze. The Bow
Priests were arrested, and the Indian authorities stripped of their
power. Troops remained there for more than a year, and an Agency
for Indian Affairs was moved to a nearby town.[83] Kluckhohn scatters
evidence of killings among the Navaho throughout his text and foot-
notes, for instance the report from 'about twenty years ago' of the
'shooting of a woman "werewolf"'.[84] Although he disguised names
and dates, the recorded answers of his interviewees do not provide
the impression that the killings were over. The reports of catching,
torturing and killing of (mostly male) witches are detailed and
colourful, along the lines of: 'They tied witches down and made them
confess. Kill the ones that never tell.'[85] In 1942 the young Native
American Custer Badoni 'took the lives of a young Navaho man and
wife, and fatally wounded an elderly Navaho man, and then blew off
the top of his own head'. The elderly man, Gray Horse, had been the
father-in-law of the murdered George Nice, a railway worker, whose
wife was pregnant. The murderer had recently lost two children from
tuberculosis, one of whom died the night before the murder took
place. Custer Badoni had suspected witchcraft, and a female Navaho
witch-doctor had directed his suspicion towards the nearby family.[86]
The situation seems to have been similar in Arctic societies of
Canada, where witches were killed infrequently, but whenever necessary. Witchcraft was closely related to murder, and therefore
required severe punishment.[87] In the 1920s and 1940s, when indigenous prophets, possession cases, exorcism and millenarianism held
a grip on the Inuit of Quebec, 'sorcery accusations were common, and
summary executions were not rare',[88] and on several occasions the
Royal Canadian Mounted Police had to intervene to prevent further
killings.

Witch-hunts were frequently reported from Eastern Europe in the
second half of the nineteenth century. In Bosnia and Montenegro,
then still under Turkish rule, witches were still illegally stoned to
death after 1860, and there is an enigmatic case where Ottoman
police officers beat four women to death in Kosovo.[89] In Russia, with
elites educated in the spirit of European Enlightenment, Czar Peter
I (1672–1725, r. 1682/9–1725) and Catherine the Great (1729–96,
r. 1762–96) had tried to curb witch trials, but the belief in witchcraft
remained strong among the peasants. Killings were mostly linked to
crop failure, drought, epidemics, lack of milk, or love magic, particularly in the 1880s, with four known killings in 1880 alone. The

lynchings often included a swimming test, severe beating and mutilating the corpse of the deceased.[90]

Researchers have collected more than 100 cases of lynching, from a random sample of ethnographic, juridical, psychiatric and newspaper reports, reaching from urban areas in the Ukraine to remote rural areas in European Russia. The measures against witchcraft included disinterring the bodies of suspected witches and transporting their dangerous remains to remote forests. The craze was fuelled by cases of demonic possession (*klikushestvo*), which could be seen as a Russian anti-witchcraft movement, since the 'shrieker's' aim was to identify witches.[91] The reported killings represent only the tip of the iceberg. Witch-hunts without lethal consequences were less likely to be reported, although there were exceptions. The governor of the Caucasian region mentioned in 1811 that villagers in Georgia had subjected thirteen women to a water ordeal, observing a well-established Caucasian tradition. The women were suspected of withholding the rain, but all of them passed the test. In the Ukraine women were rounded up in cases of severe droughts as well. Several multiple swimming tests took place in the 1830s, with others in the late 1850s, in 1872 and in 1885. As a consequence of the pogrom in May 1872 several of those thrown into the water became seriously ill, and the ringleaders of the villagers were punished with imprisonment.[92] It may well be that witch killings went on even after the Bolshevik Revolution, since remote rural areas were hardly under Communist control, particularly during the hunger crisis of the 1920s. But the issue of witchcraft in the Soviet Union has not yet been explored. The wave of esotericism after its collapse may have contributed to a resurgence of witch-beliefs. In 1997 a woman was killed, and another woman and five children injured, in an attack on an alleged witch in the village of Terekhovo near Kursk. The police officer in charge remarked: 'You can go anywhere in Russia these days, and witchcraft is a daily part of life.'[93]

Not even Western Europe remained unaffected. The fear of witches repeatedly led to witch mobbings, when excited crowds attacked suspected witches. In 1808 villagers of Great Paxton, Cambridgeshire, broke into the cottage of Ann Izzard, restrained her husband from protecting her, dragged her out of bed, threw her naked into the yard, scratched her arms with pins and beat her stomach, breasts and face with a length of wood. The parish constable refused to help her, but a compassionate neighbour, Anne Russel, gave her shelter. On hearing this the villagers returned and, by arguing that 'the protectors of witches are as bad as a witch, and deserve the same treatment', they attacked the widow as a harbourer of witches. Anne Russel died as a consequence a few days later. The mob threatened Izzard with ducking, but the fifty-six-year-old woman managed to flee from the village, and subsequently was able to sue her attackers. The murderers received short prison sentences, and the constable remained unpunished.[94] From England we know a number of maltreatments, and a suspected witch was killed by a riotous mob in 1863.[95] In Dorset a young farmer, John Bird, was tried as late as 1871 for severely beating Charlotte Griffin, an eighty-five-year-old woman. Bird believed she was bewitching him and 'hag-riding' him at night. A surgeon dismissed Bird as 'simple, weak-minded, mono-maniac'. The hospitals and asylums of that period would have been bursting with inmates if all believers of witchcraft were diagnosed as insane. In 1875 Ann Tennant was killed in Warwickshire with a pitchfork because a man, James Haywood, believed that she had bewitched him. The killer defended himself by claiming that he had not intended to kill the old woman, but just 'to draw her blood in order to break her power over him'. On a different occasion he said that he felt it his duty to kill the witches, and that there were fifteen more in his village. Haywood was charged with murder, but a surgeon considered him insane, and the jury acquitted him on those grounds.[96]

In Denmark, a group of ten villagers in Jutland killed Dorte Jensdatter (c.1670–1722), who was held responsible for diseases of cattle and children. Under the leadership of her neighbour Karen Thatcher, they tied her to the main barn of her hut, questioned her for several hours, tortured her, and finally set the house on fire, burning the 'witch' alive. Although the Danish supreme court sentenced the ringleaders of the mob to death at the stake, in a reversed witch trial, there were further witch killings in Denmark until 1800, and cases of physical violence until 1921.[97] In 1976 some villagers tried to kill Elisabeth Hahn, an elderly spinster, living in a small village in Germany. Neighbours shunned her, threw stones at her, threatened to beat her to death and eventually set fire to her house, badly burning her and killing her animals, which were supposed to be familiars.[98] In 1977 two brothers succeeded in murdering a village sorcerer near Alençon (France), who was suspected of collecting harmful potions and who was known to throw salt on people's gardens.[99] It is obvious that this is an incomplete list, since murderers usually conceal their deeds, not to mention their motives.

The recent witch killings described so far in this chapter are illegal acts according to the state law. Some African countries, however, have begun to *legalize* witch persecution. In Uganda the new independent state introduced legislation in 1965 that replaced the colonial witch-craft ordinance by an 'Act to Make Provision for the Prevention of Witchcraft and the Punishment of Persons Practising Witchcraft'. This Act lays considerable emphasis on 'repute' as valid evidence. Abrahams suggests that this repeal may have encouraged the witch-hunts in northern Uganda in subsequent years, launched in the home region of President Milton Obote (1924–, r. 1962–71, 1980–5) during a time of political difficulty, when the president had decided to

destroy the traditional Bugandan monarchy and to introduce socialist reforms. His supporters took the Five Year Economic Plan of
1966/7 as a model for a 'five year anti-sorcery plan', and started
rounding up suspected witches, many of them educated or wealthy.[100]
In Cameroon and Malawi diviners are admitted to court in order to
testify against suspected witches. It has become acceptable for courts
to judge cases of suspected witchcraft with the aid of occult practices,
like divination, resulting in physical punishment and prison sentences
for the accused. It is no longer necessary to kill witches clandestinely,
since they may be officially accused and tried. During the presidency
of Ahmadou Ahidjo (1924–?, r. 1960–82) in Cameroon, from the late
1970s the official tribunal of the eastern province, the home of the
Maka people, regularly sentenced accused witches, sometimes even
without their admission of guilt. Traditional healers, the *nganga*,
testify to the witches' guilt by means of their mystical knowledge, and
on such a basis the courts issue sentences of up to ten years in prison,
the maximum sentence according to the penal code of 1965. The
interesting thing here is that the law is still very similar to the English
Witchcraft Act of 1736, and to colonial law codes which were meant
to punish witch-doctors. However, legal practice turned this meaning
upside down. The first new legal sentences against witches were
pronounced in Bertoua, the capital of Cameroon's northern province,
and these trials have attracted much attention in other parts of
Africa.[101]

Geschiere has researched the character of these trials in the
archives of the Bertoua Court of Appeals, where thirty files related
to witchcraft trials are recorded for the period 1981–4. The confession of a young man called Nkal before the Court of First Instance
of Abong-Mbang, proves revealing: Nkal declared himself a member
of a secret society of sorcerers, who performed *la sorcellerie de la nuit*
(night witchcraft). A group of four pupils went to their teacher's
house, took out his heart mystically, and ate it, which was supposed
to cause his death. The teacher accused the four alleged witches, and,
although three of them denied the accusations, the court condemned
two of them to five years in prison, one of them to four, and the
youngest one to two years. Furthermore, they had to pay heavy fines
in compensation to the teacher, and the expenses of the trial. These
severe verdicts were confirmed by the Court of Appeals at Bertoua
in November 1983.[102] The witch panic subsequently spread to southern Cameroon, where the authorities have not yet met the villagers'
expectations. In 1991 an elderly man was dragged to court because
of suspected witchcraft. But the man was released by the state prosecutor a few days later, due to the lack of tangible proof. Several
months later the villagers set fire to the man's house, and he perished
in the flames. The prosecutor who had to deal with the seventeen
arrested young killers articulated his unease, because this trial would

confirm the suspicion that even the post-colonial state is still inclined to act in favour of the witches.[103]

The proposal to introduce traditional African methods of proving witchcraft in court, in order to curb 'necklacing' or other forms of lynching, evokes exactly the kind of problems European courts had to face during the early modern period. By definition witchcraft is an occult crime, and only the guilty can know what he or she has done. The evidential essence of culpability is forever hidden from view, as the author of the *Malleus* had already recognized, because there will never be hard evidence such as an eyewitness account. In a period of modern statecraft, the era of human rights and the rule of law, this poses insurmountable problems in the judicial management of witch-craft. Legal torture is no longer available for forcing confessions, and the testimony of witch-doctors or diviners can hardly meet the stand-ards of verifiable evidence. This kind of knowledge is not open to corroboration in the manner typically required by modern jurispru-dence.[104] The South African government's wavering position is also regrettable, because sharp measures can seemingly stop the witch-hunts. In Venda, where witch-hunting had started in about 1988, when the political situation was 'quite volatile, and the intention of the lib-eration forces was to make the country ungovernable . . . to politicise the rural communities, the revolutionary forces chose witchcraft and ritual killing to destabilise these communities'. In 1991 the Supreme Court began to impose harsh sentences. The Ralushai Report sug-gests that this 'played a significant role in curbing these killings', with only one isolated case afterwards.[105]

One of the unpleasant aspects of the revival of witchcraft perse-cutions in Africa is the involvement of churches and political parties, another reminder of European history. Some of the anti-witchcraft movements resemble churches, or proto-churches. Evangelical, Revivalist or Pentecostal Churches, such as the Zionist Churches in South Africa's northern province, take witchcraft seriously, and actively focus their members' attentions on witchcraft, encouraging them to act out their shocking fantasies. Led by a charismatic prophet, male or female, as in the church of Alice Lenshina in Zambia, who is said to have died and been resurrected, and to be informed by visions,[106] these churches provoke cases of possession, and offer exorcisms, with consequences similar to those in sixteenth-and seventeenth-century Europe, when the possessed frequently launched accusations of witchcraft, if this was conceded by the bishops. In meetings of the *African Churches*, where reconciliation rather than capital punishment is the purpose, 'witches' frequently confess in front of the enthusiastic believers, usually emphasizing that they had been unaware of their power of witchcraft, but confirming the belief system. One of the reasons for the rapid growth of African Churches in Nigeria, Cameroon, Ghana, Zambia, Zimbabwe or the republic of South Africa seems to be that they are willing to take the threat of evil spirits seriously, and to actively combat witchcraft. An early analyst, who coined the generic term 'Zionist Churches', argued that witch-hunting is not just a by-product of these African Christian Churches, but that they are 'modern movements of witch-finders'.[107]

The political emphasis on African values seems to lead to an increased importance of witch-beliefs, and therefore witch-hunts, as markers of African self-consciousness in a post-colonial setting. The liberation movements were already infected by this attitude, and after independence the *state parties*, in countries like Tanzania or Benin, brought it to new prominence. The depth to which these parties are penetrated by witch-beliefs can be seen from the fact that in South Africa the second generation, the activists of the ANC youth movement, took a leading role in local witch-hunts, in order to secure political hegemony.[108] Geschiere, who had previously assumed that the omnipresence of witchcraft rumours in modern African states should be related to the authoritarianism of their regimes, is now inclined to admit that democratization under the auspices of 'the concomitant uncertainties offered new scope for rumours on the decisive role of witchcraft in politics. Apparently, witchcraft notions easily invade such new and more open types of public spaces.'[109] Understandably enough, anthropologists are not eager to emphasize the involvement of contemporary politicians. Given the acceptance of witch-beliefs in sub-Saharan Africa, one could argue that these parties simply represent their constituencies. Despite the education of the African elite in France, the United Kingdom or the USA, whose universities still attract a good number of students from the future African ruling class, it seems likely that more African countries will change their witchcraft legislation in the future.

It is difficult to provide a survey of countries afflicted by severe witch-hunts during the second half of the twentieth century (see table 6.2). Mostly we can only glean from the literature that there were severe problems over a number of years, but only rarely has an attempt been made to assess the numbers of witch-related killings, as in the case of Tanzania and – less reliably – India. In a number of cases we only know that witches were killed on a regular basis at a certain point, but do not know what happened after the last publication on the subject. In some cases we know about the killings only from newspaper reports. In any case the allocation of responsibility is – with the possible exception of Jonas Savimbi – extremely difficult, if not impossible. In Mexico, as in other American countries, the killings are an affair of the *indígenas*, who do not recognize the authority of the modern state. In Papua New Guinea the killings occur among traditional tribes in remote areas. It is likely that the conditions in the Indonesian province Irian Jaya were similar to those in Papua New Guinea, but reports are lacking. A similar lack of infor-

Table 6.2 Countries with severe witch-hunts between 1950 and 2000

Country	Period	Politically in charge
Uganda	1965–8	Milton Obote
Angola	1975–2000	UNITA, Jonas Savimbi
Benin	1975–8	Mathieu Kérékou
Ghana	1997–8	Jerry Rawlings
India	1948–80	Jawaharlal Nehru, Indira Ghandi
Indonesia?		Suharto
Kenya	1965–2001	Jomo Kenyatta, Daniel Arap Moi
Malawi	1966–94	Hastings Banda
Mexico	1950–2000	PRI
Papua New Guinea	1950–2000	Commonwealth
South Africa	1985–2000	ANC
Tanzania	1960–88	TANU, Julius Nyerere
Zaire/Congo	1965–2000	Mobutu Sese Seko
Zimbabwe	1980–2000	ZANU, Robert Mugabe

mation applies to a number of African and south-east Asian states, where killings in remote rural areas might be frequent. However, in countries like India or South Africa, witches are also killed in major towns. A number of African rulers can be directly linked to belief in witchcraft, including Banda, and possibly Mobuto and Mugabe, who deliberately used intensive killings during the wars of liberation to raise support among the rural population. But there are also some political leaders whom few would like to see on such a pillory, such as Nyerere or Mandela. However, their party youth organizations were clearly involved in witch-hunting, and even if the ANC leadership tried to curb the persecutions, a president is still politically in charge. It may appear unfair to put elected presidents on a list of those responsible for witch-hunts if they had never personally sponsored these occurrences. But we have to keep in mind that we do exactly the same with political leaders of early modern Europe, many of whom were not personally frightened by supposed witches, and did not themselves encourage witch-hunting, but merely failed to suppress it effectively, for whatever reasons. The allocation of political responsibility may serve as a reminder that someone has to take responsibility for these atrocities, and naturally this should be the government.

The persecution of witchcraft has never been a success story. African courts will be facing exactly the kind of difficulties European courts had to struggle with in their period of witch persecution. However, it is mainly in African witch-cleansing campaigns that we can find similarities to the European hunts. The politically responsible, the presidents of the newly independent republics, ruling by means of their state parties, are apparently not the driving forces. It seems that none of the African rulers has seized leadership of an eradication movement, in order to maintain power or to restore order, with the unhappy exceptions of two Madagascan kings in the nineteenth century, and the Marxist government of Benin, where this seems to have happened in the 1970s. However, persecutions organized by the populace are tolerated by a number of regimes, and some leaders even make clear their sympathies with witch-hunters, such as Hastings Banda, or threaten their political opponents, such as Mugabe.

Those anthropologists who have more recently begun exploring the philosophical and moral dimensions of witch-beliefs are carefully avoiding the subject of the witch killings. Maybe this is just another example of the tension between purity and danger, since the amount of blood shed in the ongoing persecutions of our time would presumably spoil the pleasures of reasoning to a certain degree. However, as in historical Europe, the persecutions are substantial, and are – like the belief in witchcraft – triggered by conditions of spiritual or cultural uncertainty with social and economic crises. In early modern Europe these were premodern subsistence crises, aggravated by inter-state and civil war. However, crop failure or dearth do not inevitably cause witch-hunts, and witches can be persecuted without the background of major social crises. Human relations can always fail, and 'unnatural' diseases and misfortune may happen without any link to general economic conjunctures. Malinowski's prophecy that better health care would stop African beliefs in witchcraft sounds like a bold assumption from our present perspective. Individual illness, spirit possession, love magic, arson or an escalation of neighbourhood conflicts are as independent from meteorology as the appearance of a 'moral entrepreneur', a fanatical preacher or judge. Most historians would agree that a number of factors are necessary to create a witch-hunt, and the most important pre-condition seems to be a kind of consensus between the rulers and the ruled. If the rulers or the ruling elite stop tolerating witch trials, the witch-hunts stop – if the rulers have the institutional power to stop them. Or to turn it the other way round, quoting an American in Paris: 'Prolonged witch-hunting is as good a barometer as any for measuring weakness in a state.'[110]

7

Old and 'New Witches'

The Belief in occult forces provides the link into at least four domains, with their different analytic perspectives: the cognitive and the philosophical; the ideological and the hegemonic; the experiential and behavioral; and the domain of praxis, resistance, and protest.

George Clement Bond/Diane M. Ciekawy,
Witchcraft Dialogues, 2001

Occultism is the metaphysics of the blokes.

Theodor W. Adorno, *Minima Moralia*, 1951

People's anxieties can be minted into different currencies, for political power as well as for economic gain. There are few subjects as powerful and ambivalent as witchcraft, which can be used for almost any purpose, as long as a number of people believe in it, and even more so if a majority does. Moral entrepreneurs,[1] rule-creators and rule-enforcers such as the author of the *Witches' Hammer* could, although interested in the content of the rules, increase either their own personal power or that of their Order. Lawyers like Jean Bodin could plead for a strengthening of the state, as he did in his famous *Six livres de la République*, as well as in his demonology. Calvinist Reformers like John Knox could emphasize the importance of their covenant with God, as being opposed to the witches' pact; or Counter-Reformers like Carlo Borromeo could equate witchcraft with Protestantism. Witchcraft could be used in cases of political factionalism. We know of a number of cases where the law-and-order party tried to identify their political opponents with witchcraft, and in Bamberg they succeeded in sending their enemies to the stake. However,

witchcraft in Europe changed its meaning, and although Scottish sep-
aratists used the subject to reconfirm their identity within the United
Kingdom, the Whigs were much more successful in identifying witchcraft with backwardness and crushing the Tories.

Certainly the multitude of petty healers, witch-doctors, diviners
and cunning folk earned a living from curing harmful magic, selling
(harmful) counter-magic, and discovering those responsible for diseases and other misfortune, namely the witches. This business was
flourishing in fifteenth-century Rhineland, in sixteenth-century
England, and supposedly everywhere in early modern Europe,
although with decreasing popular support from the seventeenth-
century in much of Europe.[2] Occasionally, the day-to-day handling of
supposed bewitchment seemed insufficient, and professional witch-
hunters seized the opportunity to profit from the persecutions, in
early modern Europe as well as in present-day Africa. Nativistic and
millenian movements gained support by promising the eradication
of witchcraft, and with surprising frequency these energies were
mobilized in order to forge a rebellion, or – from their point of view
– a liberation war. Churches like the movement of Alice Lenshina in
Zambia and the charismatic African Churches in general benefit from
the persistent fears of bewitchment, and we may assume that the
same was true for the Church in early modern Europe. Furthermore,
it was possible to turn the subject of witchcraft into a profitable business without being interested in magic or bloodshed. In the prince-
bishopric of Münster there were noblemen who allowed their fishing
ponds to be used for duckings, in order to make money from the
crowd attracted to such exciting events. Almost always the suspects
proved to be heavier than water, and therefore innocent, and in the
warm summer months witch swimmings were scheduled frequently,
on a weekly basis, providing relief and fun in one.[3] The little town of
Oudewater in the Netherlands sold certificates to suspected witches,
proving that they were heavier than air, according to their famous
town scales, and therefore could not fly. Women would travel from
far away to Oudewater, because the weighing procedure appeared to
be safer than the Westphalian duckings. In their footsteps follow
curious tourists today, who are of course eager to buy a certificate
themselves, as well as all kinds of souvenirs – ties, socks or whatever
the latest round of merchandizing has invented.[4]

Cultural production, one must admit, was stimulated by the fantasies of witchcraft at least from about 1500 (the starting point of
Europe's 'modern period', by the way). Early printers or publishers
like Anton Koberger (1440–1513), who reprinted the *Witches'*
Hammer several times, or Nikolaus Basse, who commissioned the
Theatrum de Veneficis, managed to turn the demand for information
into commercial success at the book fairs. Artists benefited from the
subject early on. Woodcuts illuminated many demonologies, begin-

ning with Ulrich Molitor's *De Laniis at Phitonicis Mulieribus* in the last decade of the fifteenth century and climaxing in the extensive series of illustrations for Guazzo's *Compendium Maleficarum*. Witchcraft became a subject for famous painters like Albrecht Dürer (1471–1528) and his student Hans Baldung Grien (1484–1545), who toyed with aspects of contemporary demonology,[5] without necessarily believing in witchcraft. Given their close relationship with the *'Godless Painters of Nuremberg'*, who denied any metaphysical interference in worldly affairs, even by Mary, Christ, or God, it seems likely that these artists merely used the subject to portray nude women or sexual fantasies and enjoyed themselves in illustrating the horrors of their period with 'grotesque humour', or portraying a 'dirty joke', as Baldung did with his lascivious depiction of carnal lust between witch and devil.[6] Internationally renowned painters like Albrecht Altdorfer (1480–1538), Lukas Cranach (1472–1553) and Pieter Brueghel (1525–69) utilized witchcraft to experiment with modes of illustrating fantastical nightmares. During the seventeenth century, some Dutch painters even specialized in pictures of witchcraft, for instance David Teniers the Younger (1610–90).[7]

A definite break with the past, and a creative reinterpretation, occurred in the period of Romanticism. Between the French Revolution (1789) and the Congress of Vienna (1815), most of the old monarchies crumbled, including the Holy Roman Empire, and new nation-states were constructed. Francisco Goya (1746–1828), court painter to Charles IV of Spain (1748–1819, r. 1788–1808) and director of the Academy of Arts, demonstrated the dangers arising from a new emphasis on fantasy over reason in his *capriccios* (caprices) of 1797, the humour of which is always overshadowed by nightmare, as for instance in his famous *Reason's Sleep Generates Monsters*.[8] This observation links well with the reinterpretation of the witches by intellectuals of the period. Jacob Grimm, founding father of international language studies and academic romanticism, whose influence can still be felt in collections of fairy tales all over Europe, in 1835 redefined witches as *wise women*, conserving the age-old wisdom of their peoples, their tradition, and of the 'Germanic tradition' in particular.[9] The wise woman had emerged from Grimm's head like Athena from Zeus, and Grimm became the creator of the *Romantic paradigm* in the interpretation of historical witchcraft.[10] His nationalistic myth construction, in a period when German politicians had not yet succeeded in assembling all the tiny principalities into a nation, was met by overwhelming applause from the educated. But after 1871 dire derision would follow, when hundreds of well-paid folklorists continued to collect evidence for Germanic glory. The language scholar Moriz Haupt (1808–74) ridiculed the activities of the *Altertumsvereine* and suggested that no stinking he-goat or red rooster could pass by any longer without running the risk of being interpreted as a Germanic god. Other nations developed their own obsessions. Jules Michelet (1798–1874), another fervent nationalist, constructed an interpretation of the French nation based on the French Revolution, and transformed Grimm's notion of the wise women into female 'doctors of the people', fighters against feudal suppression, ruthlessly persecuted and crushed by a conspiracy of princes and lawyers, theologians and academic physicians. Witches, therefore, were nothing other than the forerunners of the French Revolution, or the French nation. In Michelet's eyes the witches should also stand unforgotten as a source of power in an ever-lasting fight for freedom.[11]

The examples of Grimm and Michelet demonstrate the political agenda of the nineteenth century. Witchcraft gained new importance in the increasing conflicts between the European nation-states and the universal Catholic Church. The tensions increased when Pope Pius IX (1792–1878, r. 1846–78) condemned Rationalism and Liberalism in his *Syllabus*, and Catholic political parties tried to implement papal policies within some of the new nation-states. This conflict gained momentum when the Pope declared himself infallible during the First Vatican Council in 1870. Now the subject of witchcraft gained importance as circumstantial evidence against the *dogma of infallibility*. Large parts of the literature on witchcraft, and on witchcraft persecutions in particular, were written in subsequent years, or rather by the generation moulded by the conflict between Church and State, the *Kulturkampf*.[12] Even Joseph Hansen, protagonist of the *Rationalist paradigm* in the historiography of witchcraft, felt obliged to articulate his political comment: 'The elements of the craze, leading to witch persecution, are almost without exception still part of the Christian teachings in all denominations. This is why our historical research is of particular actuality'.[13] American scholars, like Henry Charles Lea (1825–1909) and Burr (1857–1938) had their own political agenda. This group of historians, all in close contact with Hansen, emphasized the guilt of Church and State for the persecutions. Andrew Dickson White (1832–1918), president of Cornell University in Ithaca, New York, was deeply annoyed by the attempts of religious fundamentalists at his university to restrict the freedom of science, and to control the curriculum. Therefore he included a long chapter on the European 'witch craze' in his utterly polemical *History of Warfare of Science with Theology and Christendom*.[14]

Quite a different usage of witchcraft was being developed in the context of a rising *occultist movement*, which flourished at the *fin de siècle* in European cities like London, Paris and Vienna. Abundance and ennui created strange combinations of life reform, theosophy, spiritualism, early communism, the early feminist movement, vegetarianism and anti-vivisectionism, but also anti-Semitism, clearly a sign of unrest in these exploding centres of industrial capitalism. The son of a beer brewer, Edward Alexander (1875–1947), founded a satanic order under the pseudonym of 'Aleister Crowley'. This 'Thelema' club – a term alluding to a group of free-thinkers in Rabelais' _Gargantua_ – served as a meeting point for all kinds of sinister figures, such as Ron L. Hubbard, a member of the American branch of Alexander's movement before founding his own group, later to be called the 'Scientology Church'.[15] Another of Alexander's students was Gerald B. Gardner (1884–1964), who became the founder of a _new religion of witchcraft_. Gardner made use of one of the most irritating publications, Margaret Murray's (1863–1963) _Witch Cult in Western Europe_, imagining the persistence of an age-old pagan fertility cult,[16] where wise men and women ritually adored a horned god, 'the God of the witches', who was, of course, misinterpreted by the Christian Church as the devil.[17]

Murray must have been amazed by the success of her story, which turned her into a celebrity, with applause even from fascinated academic historians, including eminent scholars like Christopher Hill and Sir Stephen Runciman, and an odd resonance in the _Encyclopedia Britannica_, whose entry on witchcraft was based upon Murray's work between 1929 and 1968. Murray had used the demonologies uncritically, and had remained unaffected by any knowledge of the existing secondary literature as well as of the sources. As an old lady – shortly before publishing her autobiography _My First Hundred Years_ – she came into contact with the 'new witches' movement. She even contributed a foreword to Gardner's _Witchcraft Today_, the first trace of the new religion of witchcraft, constructed neatly according to the guidelines of Murray's fantasies.[18] Gardner's _Wicca coven_ grew quickly in England, and soon moved over to the USA, mostly by way of emigration, as Doreen Valiente (1922–99), one of Gardner's 'High Priestesses' admitted.[19] Dissent and factionalism within the movement led to its split into several neo-pagan and feminist factions from the 1960s onwards.[20]

Neo-paganists today try to present themselves as an alternative to the Christian Church, with numerous sects all over the USA and Europe. However, the roots of the movement are not as pure as some members assume, because they point back to Nazi Germany. The very term _neo-pagan_ was coined by Nazi authors, as a neo-pagan Wiccan priestess from Manhattan recently found out: 'We can't deny it; we can only mourn and rage.'[21] It is not by coincidence that the Nazis used a (neo)-pagan symbol, the swastika, adopted shortly after the First World War, since this points back to their 'occult roots'.[22] During the early years of the Weimar Republic, when the Nazis were still an unimportant political sect, witches were used for tourist purposes in Weimar Germany, for instance in Lemgo, where a major witch-hunt had taken place in the seventeenth century. Public lectures were organized, alongside an exhibition, processions and guided tours. After

Plate 11   Witches' dance, enacted by 'new witches'.
Photo: Russels. ©

the Nazi's seizure of power they used the already existing infrastructure, with its attraction to an unpolitical public. Chief ideologue Alfred Rosenberg (1893–1946), executed as a war criminal in 1946, launched a major anti-clerical attack. He interpreted the witch persecutions as an attempt by the Christian Church to eradicate Germanic traditions, locating his witches somewhere between Grimm and Michelet, and seeing the Roman Catholic Church driven by 'Syrian', which in fact meant Jewish, ideas.[23] Rosenberg tried to politicize the witch subject, and witchcraft became a major issue of Nazi folklore. 'Witch groups' were established in order to welcome Nazi celebrities with 'Germanic witch dances' on their arrival, these groups serving in a way as neo-pagan cheerleaders. Authors such as Mathilde Ludendorff (1877–1966), wife of a First World War general and early follower of Hitler, and herself a leader of the neo-pagan movement in the 1930s, wrote in her pamphlet *Christian Cruelties on German Women* that the Christians had taught the 'witch craze, made witch persecutions a religious duty, and had instigated these crimes against women'. The results were these 'gruesome torturings and burnings of nine million "witches" [. . .], killed by the Christians'. Like the cruelties of the Soviet regime for Marxism, witch persecutions should be considered 'a yardstick of the teachings which caused them'.[24]

Quite surprisingly, it was not only neo-paganism that flourished in Nazi Germany, but also a form of *radical feminism*, often combined with racism and anti-Semitism. Nazi feminists considered women to be the superior gender, and Aryan women the superior gender of a superior race. Friederike Müller-Reimerdes, an otherwise unknown author, explains in her pamphlet *The Christian Witch Craze. Thoughts Considering the Religious Fight for Freedom of the German Women* that 'Jewish thinking, liberalist rootlessness, and the mental and intellectual laws of the Christian church, dominated by priests and dogma, foreign to the race' had cut 'the deepest and bloodiest wounds to the dignity of the German women'. Christianity, a 'world view foreign to the race', had caused a 'degeneration of German manliness', which had lost its 'specific heroism, which once could only tolerate women of equal standing, and has changed into oriental manhood'. For more than a thousand years, the Nazi feminist suggested, German women had 'suffered under an unworthy position in the people's life, shaped by men', and the Church had tried systematically to wipe out 'blonde women and mothers, bearing the racial characteristics of the Nordic race'. Men were burned during the witch-hunts merely in order 'to conceal the eradication of women' (*Frauenausrottung*). Therefore, the modern sisterhood of women should face the challenge of the Church, 'this most consequent of all male collectives', and solemnly vow: 'I shall be an avenger of my martyred sisters!'[25]

During the upswing of post-Second World War feminism, similar ideas gained momentum, despite or because of a longing for ideological purity.[26] In 1968 – a symbolic year in many ways – an organization nicely called 'Women's International Conspiracy from Hell', abbreviated as WITCH, was formed in New York, drawing heavily in its programmatic manifesto from romantic fantasies, assuming that witchcraft had been the religion of pre-Christian Europe, and had persisted as a secret religion afterwards. Its suppression in early modern times was interpreted as the suppression of an alternative culture by the ruling elite. Again, of course, 'nine million witches' were put to death, courageous and independent women, and modern women needed to become powerful witches again to liberate themselves from patriarchal oppression.[27] Since the middle of the 1970s, demonstrations on the night of 1 May have been performed under the motto 'the witches are back', and the 'regaining of female power of spirituality' has become a major issue.[28] In Mary Daly's (b. 1928) *Gyn/Ecology*, the figure of the witch is central to the narrative. She recasts witch-hunting as 'women-hunting', and the 'eradication of women' as *gynocide*, articulating the odd idea 'that women have suffered more than any victims of racism and genocide'.[29] These dark dreams of women's suffering and omnipotence have recently been rejected by the leading gender historian Merry Wiesner,[30] and were masterfully deconstructed by the feminist language scholar Diane

Purkiss, who argues that it makes no sense to inflate the victims of witch persecutions, because 'seeing yourself as eternally oppressed is not really liberating'. Purkiss concludes that these fantasies are rather 'silencing early modern women anew'. She rightly attacks the attitude of identification of feminists with witches: 'Daly casts herself as a witch, ensuring that anyone who disagrees with her can be cast as an inquisitor.' Purkiss is not willing to accept the matronizing attitude, and comes to the conclusion: 'Daly wants us to see her as the embodiment of the Hag, but sometimes she sounds more like Kramer', the Dominican inquisitor and author of the *Witches' Hammer*.[31]

It was presumably not by coincidence that the notion of the historical witch-hunts as more terrible than the Holocaust of the European Jewry emerged at the interface of neo-paganism and feminism, where scientific research is replaced by feeling and believing. Although many feminist authors display a leftist attitude, the extremism of the right does not seem far away. Daly's German translator Erika Wisselinck, for instance, quotes Mathilde Ludendorff as an authority in her own publication on witchcraft, where she criticizes historians because of their lack of imagination and their forgeries of history. The 'nine million witches' killed by a conspiracy of male priests and judges also resurfaces in this blending of new feminism and neo-paganism.[32] The closeness of Nazi feminism and the post-war feminist movement has bothered more than one author since. Anja Malanowski and Anne-Bärbel Köhle complain in their book on *The Witches' Power*: 'However, it appears somehow problematic when Neo-Nazi skinheads and spiritual women are sweating up the same magic steps, in order to celebrate Whitsun. Unfortunately the places of spiritual power are attracting black witches as well as wise women with their universal fascination.'[33] As if this were not enough, some Wicca covens in the USA are tracing their roots back to the '(magical) power of the old Germans'. Within the American New Age movement this affiliation has caused considerable irritation, since educated feminists like Rosemary Ruether have criticized the deliberately biased account of history by the New York 'witch' Miriam Simos (b. 1951), alias 'Starhawk', presently the most successful of the 'new witches' on the book market,[34] and have acknowledged the roots of the movement in Romanticism, Nationalism and Nazism.[35]

The number of 'new witches' in the USA was calculated at a quarter of a million around 1990, but may have doubled since. In some American states their movement is acknowledged as a religion. Obviously, the 'new witches' can live without historical research because their self-stigmatizing identity is related to an archetype, adequately symbolizing their dissidence against Western religions as well as against modern science, or the state. Sociological research among the 'new witches' in the mid-1990s has demonstrated that the majority are middle-class people, with a disproportionate share of women of North and Western European origins, looking for a new meaning in life. According to Shelley Rabinovitch, many are attracted to witch-craft in personal conversations, at meeting places like health shops, vegetarian dinners, women's circles or ecology activists' meetings, with related media and literature.[36] During the past ten years more books have been published and bought on esoteric cults and witch-craft than during past centuries. Everyone can assemble the individ-ual set of rituals he or she likes most. Some scholars assume that such movements should be interpreted as forms of compensation, and are mainly attracting lonely people with a lack of self-confidence,[37] but one may ask how significant such a judgement actually is, if the same profile could be claimed of those who are attending mainstream Christian Church services, pop concerts or political party meetings. Rather than just for the esoteric milieu, it seems to be characteristic of a society where many individualists wish to be spared from ide-ologies in their leisure time, while traditional institutions are losing their attraction and have ceased to satisfy the religious desire. Some have argued that this should be interpreted as a response to the crisis of modernity, and have tried to place the 'new witches' in the context of postmodernism.[38]

Some of the most intriguing analyses of neo-pagan witchcraft have asked how these new identities were forged. They are coming to the conclusion that the invention of the Wicca movement could well be seen as a paradigmatic case of *invention of tradition*. Several authors have scrutinized the way that Gardner assembled the rituals in the 1950s, and have compiled a fine selection of quotations from earlier authors like Crowley or Murray, as well as folklore dictionaries, and ascertained that no 'witch cult' had existed before. All the 'new witches' therefore depend on Gardner, with Murray and the famous folklorist James George Frazer (1854–1941) in the background.[39] Since the 1960s, and particularly since this movement has spread to North America, a rapid process of proliferation has led to a wide spectrum of neo-pagan groups, and, as a sub-species, groups who are defining themselves as 'new witches'.

Hierarchical 'Gardnerian' witchcraft has shrunk to a minority posi-tion because, from its 1960s origins, the movement has been swept by the political ideas of the decade, for instance political egalitarianism, feminism and all kinds of psychological approaches. According to the variety of social and intellectual backgrounds, and the fact that ever more groups, or even individuals, were tailoring their beliefs and rituals according to their individual needs, the variety of sources is stunning. It could of course be expected that folklore collections and fairy tales still play a role, but it is surprising that TV programmes have turned into a constant source of inspiration: The *Discovery Channel* provides information with ethnographic films about African peoples like the Yoruba, Australian Aborigines or Native Americans.

Science-fiction programmes, such as *Star Trek* and its subsequent serials (*The Next Generation*; *Deep Space Nine*), are also favoured by neo-pagans, and the customs and rituals of 'aliens' attract particular attention. But even advertisements have an impact, when consumer products are presented with fitting material, for instance plastic troll dolls. From the 1980s, neo-pagan festivals, regional or international, began to play an increasing role as marketplaces for the transmission of ideas, rituals and techniques. The new 'religion', it seems, has become basically eclectic, as Sabina Magliocco reports: 'To my question about the sources for ritual materials, a Neo-Pagan from Illinois replied: "Anything that doesn't run away fast enough is a potential source." '[40]

Recent research into neo-pagan groups, or among 'new witches' – carried out with increasing frequency by academics as participant observers who are perfectly aware of the fact that the belief is fabricated – demonstrates that these groups are not merely temporary phenomena, but are consolidating. The playing with beliefs is interpreted as a positive process of emancipation, and their own *bricolage* is deliberately seen in contrast to the prefabricated ideologies of orthodox religions or political parties, and well in line with intellectual relativism, or postmodernism.[41] This claim has recently been corroborated by anthropologists: 'Whatever "postmodernism" may mean, it is about disappointment in the modernist scheme with its unilineal certainties – hence it concerns bringing to light the inconsistencies and ambiguities of the "modern". That is, of course, precisely what stories about witchcraft and the occult have the potential to do.'[42] From the 1990s, the witchcraft religion has experienced a new experimental stage, with a generation of children born into these circles and educated in their spirit. Helen Berger, who addresses these changes, tries to portray the 'new witches' as 'an outgrowth of globalism', in contrast with face-to-face religious communities, a religious movement in close contact with modern media, communicating their ideas – at least from an American perspective – worldwide. Although the neo-pagans became more evenly distributed in North America during the 1990s, with members in many states, their preferred breeding grounds are still California, New York and Massachusetts.[43]

Nachman Ben-Yehuda has pointed to the fact that the occultist revival is to a certain degree a media event. Superstition in grubby fairground booths, or in *Yellow Pages* ads, has been replaced by middle-class New Age seminars, and the illusory world of TV talkshows. Astrology has turned into big business, and the film industry makes millions of dollars through non-Christian metaphysics. Even if this pot-pourri has primarily entertaining functions, there is something beyond fun in the booming belief in the supernatural. In respect of the ever growing attraction of regional, national or even international fairs for esoteric articles and teachings, such as a 'World Congress of Witchcraft' in Bogotá (Colombia) in 1975, it seems fair to conclude that the demand for salvation beyond the established Church is tremendous, and the number of believers seems to be growing rapidly. In Africa, the Zionist Christian Churches try to satisfy the people's demands by dealing with the traditional anxieties of witchcraft; in the West, magic as a resource is actively explored. However, the stock of ideas is limited. The return of well-known ideas, in new combinations, with changing accentuation and in ever more glamorous wrapping, are characteristic of the *magic market*. Exotic folk medicines are being used by the esoteric industry to redefine witchcraft with a positive spin, and to separate it from previous demonological interpretations. Shamanism has again been burdened with a leading role, and it seems that in addition to numerous charlatans some Third World religious specialists are eventually receiving their share of the cake.

The public interest in all kinds of aspects of witchcraft has evoked a new intensity of marketing since the 1980s. Salem Village has been turned into a major event, popping up on numerous web pages, and serving as a modern pilgrimage. An increasing number of exhibitions are inviting the public to learn about witchcraft, and it may pass as a curiosity that two major exhibitions opened on the same day, 1 May, in 1987, in order to mark the 500th anniversary of the *Witches' Hammer* (although it was published in 1486 and had nothing at all to do with May Day). What was striking was the difference in attitude. The Austrian exhibition was staged at one of the most theatrical castles of Styria, the Riegersburg, where witch trials had indeed taken place in the past. The event received the patronage of parliament and the president of Styria, and was opened, curiously enough, by a Catholic bishop, who celebrated Mass on Sunday afternoon. The exhibition in Saarbrücken, on the other hand, organized by Richard van Dülmen (1937–2004) and Eva Labouvie (b. 1957), took place in the postmodern building of the City Art Gallery, and was opened at midnight with a witches' dance around an open bonfire, the music being provided by a feminist rock band. To be fair, although dressed up by exhibition designers, both exhibitions had been prepared by academic historians.

Clearly, academic scholars, too, are fascinated by the subject and play their part in serving the demands of an interested public, at the same time riding their magical hobby horses. Exhibitions are nowadays besieged by an increasing *witchcraft folklorism*, comprising imaginative combinations of herbal teas, liquids, liquors, pills and ointments. Songs are being composed, plays written and performed, and monuments erected, usually in honour of the innocent victims of the persecution, but sometimes alluding to their particular qualities.

Witchcraft became part of a new 'event culture' and was neatly integrated in redesigned concepts of tourism, with organized bus tours to the exhibitions, theatres or monuments, or simply to traditional witches' mountains, like the Blocksberg, or places like Oudewater or Salem. Witchcraft tourism, of course, has to be supported by the production of souvenirs, stickers, children's toys, key-fobs, car stickers or witch dolls. Fantasy seems to be unlimited, as far as merchandizing is concerned.

Traditional fears of bewitchment survive in the more traditional settings of Western societies, and the Catholic Church retains much of its demonological ballast, despite Pope John Paul II's apology in the year 2000 for the Church's responsibility for the historical witch persecutions. But the 'culture industry' is placing ever more emphasis on the positive aspects of witchcraft, as fascinated by the bounty of fantastical elements as artists since the beginning of the 'modern age' 500 years ago. Constructors of feminist fairy worlds, like Marion Zimmer Bradley (b. 1930), or authors exploiting the potential of witch-lore, like J. K. Rowling, are better known today than Jacob Grimm or Jules Michelet, who invented this 'romantic interpretation' of witchcraft. Whereas Walt Disney's (1901–66) adaptation of the witch figure still retained an idea of the danger inherent in maleficient magic, children's books like *The Little Witch* combine the rebellious potential of childhood with fantasies of omnipotence, and are likely to transform the image of witchcraft. According to a bon mot of Marcello Truzzi, a confessing witch today is less likely to be burned at the stake than to be invited to a party.[44] Certainly, it is true that the 'new witches' are largely tolerated, and that Wicca is even acknowledged as a new religion in some states of the USA. Nevertheless, it seems to be an exaggeration to speak of a 're-enchantment of the World' in this context.[45]

'New witches' would be surprised at how much traditional witchcraft is still alive, not as a tourist attraction – although there is room for misunderstanding. In Bali, well known to tourists for its beauty and elaborate Hindu ritual dances, one of the plays represents the evil witch Rangda, who is believed to devour children and to induce misfortune, illness and death. Rangda, the mythical widow, is different from other monsters of Hindu mythology, since her symbolism relates not only to the multiple aspects of life, but also to mundane everyday life. Formerly, widowhood was a monstrous condition in Hinduism, where good wives were supposed to follow their deceased husbands to the underworld. In one of the ritual dances, the witch is defeated by the monster Barong, which defends the Balinese against the evil. In another dance, however, Rangda has human disciples, who learn the art of witchcraft. In order to break their spell, a witch-finder is employed, who detects the witch during a trance. This dance is more than just a tourist attraction. It is performed on ritually significant days, but also when a village is afflicted by misfortune, and sickness in particular. The ritual dance expresses the people's desire: its essence is the destruction of the witch.[46]

Traditional witchcraft is not just a party gimmick, and is not only alive in the jungles of the rainforest, or Third World capitals like Bombay or Mexico City. In September 2001 a child's torso was found on the embankment of the Thames in London, the head and limbs chopped off and missing. The young male's body was dressed in orange shorts of a type only sold at branches of Woolworth in Germany. A first guess at child abuse with subsequent murder was soon superseded by another, equally gruesome suspicion. Specialists in African witchcraft explained that the ritual murder of innocent children, who have to be sacrificed in order to get hold of parts of their bodies, was necessary for certain types of black magic in South and West Africa. The case of 'Adam', as the police named the boy, aged between five and seven, will probably prove to be exemplary. Scotland Yard promised a reward of £50,000, but the seriousness with which this event has been taken is emphasized by the fact that the former president of the republic of South Africa, Nelson Mandela, intervened with a public announcement in support of the investigation. According to the South African police, hundreds of children have been sacrificed recently for similar *muti* murders, to produce effective 'medicine'. Police authorities suppose that African witchcraft has been imported by immigrants to Europe and the USA. Investigations into 'old witchcraft' ritual murders are presently being held in France, Greece, Italy and the United States of America. Bone fragments found in the boy's stomach were analysed by specialists in New York. In July 2002, in Glasgow, Scotland Yard arrested a thirty-year-old married woman from West Africa in connection with the 'Adam' murder case. She was bailed and later returned to her home country, Nigeria. Her estranged husband, who had fled Germany after being convicted for a number of crimes, was arrested in Dublin in July 2003. Scotland Yard suspects that the boy had been brought to London from Nigeria to be the victim of a ritual sacrifice. Nwankwo Kanu, the Nigerian football star of Arsenal, London, made a TV appeal for information about the boy, whose murder has involved liaison between police on three continents.[47]

8

Epilogue

Perhaps my neighbour...would adopt the position, commonplace
now in anthropological studies, that talk of witchcraft is not an index
of primitive ignorance and superstition but an idiom through which
other realities are expressed, realities such as social stress and strain,
unemployment, capitalist globalisation, the collective fantasizing of
popular culture, and so on.

Adam Ashforth, *Madumo*, 2000

One branch of esotericism that does not claim similarities to witchcraft has more in common with traditional witchcraft fantasies than
is usually assumed: the community of UFO believers, dreaming of
encounters with extraterrestrials possessing supernatural capacities,
of being kidnapped by them, transported to foreign places and being
abused as sexual objects. After their raptures, scars of surgical oper-
ations confirm their experiences, like the witches' mark after a
meeting with the devil. Some of them believe they have received
superior knowledge of secrets inaccessible to their neighbours.[1]
Without being forced to do so, the UFO believers develop ideas that
are useless in our societies, and stigmatize themselves as outsiders,
driven by their fantasies, which seem so real to them that they are
ready to sacrifice their normal life. Their fantasies of raptures have
something in common with shamanistic rituals, but also with otherworld journeys in near-death experiences.[2] It is in no way clear yet
how assumptions of Western psychology about a collective subconscious, or of possible archetypes, if they exist at all beyond Jungian
fantasies,[3] relate to the belief systems of a wider world. To understand
the witches' dreams, it seems, could eventually lead into the border

zones of physiology and psychology, the cerebral space, where physical stimuli are translated into emotions and pictures, whose interpretation counts among the duties of religious specialists in traditional societies. Medieval European theologians were successful in their attempt to ban witch-beliefs to the realm of dreams. But for large parts of the European population, as for non-European peoples, witches represented the menace of inimical forces, which threaten individuals as well as their kin and neighbours, and sometimes whole societies, in their material and metaphysical existence. Wherever witch-beliefs persist, persecution is a potential consequence, however legal or illegal this is deemed to be by law or the ruling elites. Witch-hunting was and is an attempt to get rid of *evil* by means of self-help, beyond the institutions of Church and State.

The explosiveness of the historical witch-hunts in Europe was based on the fact that for a limited period the agents of Church and State felt obliged not to stop, but rather to lead witch-cleansing movements. But even during the so-called era of the witch persecutions, this was the case only in certain areas, and for a limited number of years. Quite surprisingly, a general and long-standing witch-hunt has never taken place in Europe, and less women and men fell victim to the European persecutions than is usually assumed. The more we become aware of witch-hunts in a wider world, we must conclude that persecutions in Africa, America or Asia are comparable to the European persecutions in size and structure. In no case is it possible to speak of a holocaust, although the term was indeed used by contemporaries at that time, such as Alciati or Weyer. But since then the term has changed its meaning, and clearly the witch persecutions cannot be equated with genocides of the twentieth century, systematically organized and enforced by modern state administrations and political parties, as in Turkey in the 1920s, Nazi Europe in the 1940s, Cambodia under the Khmer Rouge in the 1970s or Rwanda in 1994. Some witch-hunters aimed at a more systematic extermination, but witches were after all not a coherent social, ethnic or religious group, and the idea that women could have been eradicated systematically in a *gynocide*, is a twentieth-century horror fiction.[4] Every man had a mother, and many had sisters, wives and daughters, and in traditional societies, as well as in early modern Europe, to accuse a woman meant attacking the honour of a family, foremost the head of the household, usually the father. Witch-hunting therefore was not woman-hunting, despite the fact that a majority of those convicted were women in many, but not all, societies.

Large-scale witch-hunts were not confined to Europe. We have seen that there were massive witch-hunts in Ancient Rome, and certainly major persecutions in Inca Peru, Aztec Mexico, Russia, China, India, and in some Bantu empires of Africa, to mention just a few examples. Given the worldwide distribution of witch-hunts we should assume that they happened in illiterate societies as well, long before contact with literate civilizations. Observations of the past 300 years suggest that tribal societies on all continents resorted to the persecution of evildoers in times of crisis, and that major crises were frequently related to conspiracies of witches, sorcerers or evil shamans. In Europe fewer people were executed for witchcraft than is usually assumed. The sheer number of victims cannot serve as a yardstick for the importance of the subject. The witchcraft paradigm has the potential of spreading an atmosphere of fear, to cause witch panics, as in Savoy in the 1430s, Italy in the 1480s, Scotland in the 1590s, Germany in the 1620s, England in the 1640s, Madagascar in the 1830s, Mexico in the 1950s, Bolivia in the 1980s or sub-Saharan Africa at the beginning of the twenty-first century. Societies without killings can be ravaged by fears of bewitchment, and related social mechanisms. The belief in witchcraft is *universal*, because it links misfortune to basic human (negative, or 'evil') emotions, like envy. The vanishing point of witch-belief, however, is violence, if anxieties are not counterbalanced by tradition, or the belief in science, that is, if acceptable social and economic conditions with functioning legal and political institutions are lacking in periods of spiritual crisis. The diversity of anxiety-ridden fantasies of witchcraft relates to their character as a construct, according to Monica Wilson (1908–82) a *standardized nightmare*,[5] which renders a key to the understanding of society because it embodies the inversion of social values.

Most civilizations have developed methods to minimize the impact of the witchcraft paradigm, and it seems that China, Japan and the Islamic civilization(s) were and are particularly successful in doing so. The European idea of the witch figure became ambivalent during the period of the witch-hunts. Opponents of witch-hunting moulded a completely new image, not of the witches, but of those convicted for witchcraft: they construed them as innocent victims. Their virginity, as far as guilt is concerned, might be related to the idea of the virgin mother Mary, at least in the perception of Jesuits like Tanner and Spee, but it served as a strategy to pull women out of the trials. Unlikely as it seems, this proved to be a successful strategy. However, as historians can recognize from the surviving sources, many of the accused women were indeed involved in superstitious activities, divination, magical cures, the wearing of amulets or the casting of horoscopes. Many could memorize magical spells, or prayers, and some were practising magicians as well. According to contemporary law, as well as to demonology, this could be interpreted as circumstantial evidence for sorcery or witchcraft, very much as in contemporary African societies, where house searches reveal plenty of magical devices, which of course can easily be acquired in the markets. The 'innocent victim' was just another construct, far from the reality of a society entrenched in magic.

It is most worrying that it has never been possible to stop a 'witch craze', or witch-beliefs, with medical, sociological or psychological arguments. The doctrine of the physical power of evil spirits invalidates any reasonable argumentation. Discourses on magic and witchcraft coexisted and will continue to coexist with the scientific discourse developed in early modern Europe. How central the subject of witchcraft was to European culture can be gauged from the fact that this was the only civilization where a rationalistic philosophy was developed, which excludes any kind of occult forces from scientific explanation, accepting purely mechanical causation, restricting God to laws of nature and mathematical equations, denying supernatural intervention in the course of nature, and eliminating any theoretical basis for demonic power. The Baconian philosophy of progress can serve as an example of wishful thinking, or, one could also argue, of a self-fulfilling prophecy, because real improvements – the victory over famine, the decrease of epidemic diseases and mortality crises, improved social security, scientific discoveries, technical innovations and new cultural attractions – proved to be sufficiently convincing, or at least entertaining and distracting, to prevent witch-hunts.[6]

However, this was not the end of the story. Refashioned into an anti-type of patriarchal society in the period of Romanticism, the witch could easily be converted into a symbol of women's liberation. This transformation was rooted in the traditional stereotype of the *powerful female outsider*, as well as in the fact that women had been disproportionately affected by the persecutions. Scientific interpretations have been determined by these perceptions of witchcraft, labelled the 'Romantic' and the 'Rational' interpretation.[7] Some historians were more inclined to find innocent victims and cruel persecutors, while others were more interested in the witches themselves, their social position, magical activities and heterodox religious ideas. And more recently some preferred to construct *abstract interpretations*, distancing themselves as far as possible from any involvement with either side, or the subject itself. At least in this respect the 'social-scientific' approach is not far from postmodernism. But even those who consider witchcraft to be a social or cultural construct agree on its relevance for understanding society.[8]

Witchcraft, one could conclude, is a subject of importance for all humanity, but for different reasons at the present time than historically. Traditionally, it was important because it allows for a direct response to conditions of uncertainty, as well as offering an explanation for misfortune with hope for individual agency beyond the laws of nature. By analysing trial records, we get plenty of information about individual and collective sorrows and aspirations, patterns of interpretation and modes of behaviour. Trial records, more than normative sources, or even autobiographies and correspondences,

Plate 12   Francisco Goya, *Reason's Sleep Generates Monsters*.
Capriccio, 1797

introduce us intimately to individuals and the problems of their time. By analysing these sources, whether from Europe, Africa or elsewhere, we can look at everyday life, human feelings and anxieties, contemporary attitudes towards nature, gender relations, problems of truth-finding in court, cultural barriers between common folk and the educated elite, and the dynamics of stereotypes, particularly in periods of crises; but they also bring to light the fragility of scientific hypotheses, and the danger of moral entrepreneurs in politics, science, law courts, at universities and in the neighbourhood.

The management of misfortune has improved and the disappearance of previous horrors allowed for the creation of new myths in Europe and its daughter civilizations. However, 'new witches' should beware of travelling to those parts of the world where more traditional malcontents of modernity are still dominant.[9] Geschiere argues that the persistence of witch-beliefs and witch-hunts in underdeveloped countries demonstrates the *modernity of witchcraft*.[10] Modernity, that is, in the sense of adapting an ancient, extremely flexible system of beliefs – originally tied to traditional social relations – to new situations, rather than as 'a meta-commentary on the ill-doings of capitalism and globalization'.[11] Western rationalism has not extinguished the integrating power of religion, and it seems that neither rationalism nor religion will be able to destroy the attractiveness of magic and of the witchcraft paradigm in a globalized world, where many are excluded from the benefits of the 'multiple modernities'.[12] However, anthropologists should not be too ready to excuse the beliefs in witchcraft they are confronted with, and comfort the believers, because there is no indication that the witchcraft paradigm is likely to improve their situation. It is pointless, patronizing and too polite to concede relevance to the interpretation of AIDS as being caused by *isidliso*, or by poverty, as President Mbeki claimed in 1999. Postmodern permissiveness and denial of reality fail to repay. The ANC spokesman who had to defend Mbeki's interpretation died of an AIDS-related illness soon after.[13]

Some Africanists are presently trying to reframe witchcraft in terms of an African philosophy:

> Witchcraft is more than a mere social construction; it is about power and inequality, individual and collective interests, the parameters of belief and action, the conditions of knowing, and the criteria of knowledge. It is about the manner in which people apprehend the world and the way in which they attempt to interpret and explain it.[14]

The witchcraft paradigm may be deeply rooted in cosmology and customs, and serve immediate demands in African cultures, but it adds to the misery on a micro-level as well as in global competition.[15] Not by coincidence have the more successful civilizations abandoned the belief in witchcraft, together with the habit of scapegoating other people for misfortune. In the still irritating definition of Kant, Enlightenment is not a matter of education, or of scientific progress, but the achievement of understanding that mankind has to blame *itself* for dependence ('self-imposed immaturity'), to get rid of it.[16] Science may be as much an illusion as religion or the belief in witchcraft, but it is a more helpful one. And the case of early modern Europe demonstrates that a witch-ridden society can manage to throw off the yoke of witch-belief, and its consequences. Renaissance Europe may have been entrenched in witch-belief, but eminent figures like Machiavelli or Jacob Fugger did not waste a word on it. They had already found their 'occult' forces in the form of power and money, as could be expected in a period of successful state-formation and early capitalism. As Cassius says in *Julius Caesar*: 'The fault, dear Brutus, lies not in the stars, but in ourselves.'[17]

However, at the beginning of the new millennium it does not require divinatory power to foresee that 'new witches' and traditional (belief in) witchcraft will continue to be attractive to many, in all parts of the world, so that they will coexist in different spheres and even mingle to a certain degree. The very reason why belief in the occult and magical practices has not died out will guarantee their survival. Beyond the legitimate demand for entertainment and enchantment with cute fantasy stories, fundamental uncertainties and an uneven distribution of wealth persist. So, too, does the stock of human feelings and anxieties, and the demand for simple explanations. Where states disintegrate, room for immediate action emerges. And since the belief in witchcraft potentially generates persecutions, whether we like the idea or not, there will be a continuing concern with witches and witch-hunts.

Notes

Chapter 1   Introduction

1   Isak Niehaus et al., *Witchcraft, Power and Politics*, London/Cape Town 2001, 156–66.
2   Victor Ralushai, *Report of the Commission of Inquiry into Witchcraft*, Pietersburg 1996, 45.
3   William David Hammond-Tooke, *The Bantu-Speaking Peoples*, London 1974, 336ff.
4   Norman Cohn, *Europe's Inner Demons*, London 1975.
5   Hugo G. Nutini/John M. Roberts, *Bloodsucking Witchcraft*, Tucson/London 1993, 15.
6   Gabor Klaniczay, *The Uses of Supernatural Power*, Cambridge 1990.
7   Ernest Jones, *On the Nightmare*, London 1949.
8   Hugh R. Trevor-Roper, *The European Witch-Craze*, Harmondsworth 1969.
9   Stuart Clark, Witchcraft and Magic in Early Modern Culture, in *AHWME*, 4 (2002), 113.
10   Peter Geschiere, *The Modernity of Witchcraft* (1997), 215–21.
11   Edgar E. Evans-Pritchard, *Witchcraft, Oracles and Magic*, Oxford 1937, 21ff, 387.
12   Claude Lévi-Strauss, The Sorcerer and His Magic (1949), in Middleton (1967), 23–41.
13   Robert Redfield, *The Folk Culture of Yucatan*, Chicago 1941, 303–36.
14   Roy Ellen, Introduction, in Watson/Ellen (1993), 1–25.
15   For other positions: Bryan R. Wilson (1973), 76ff.
16   St Augustine, *De Doctrina Christiana*, II, 30–40.
17   Corrector Burchardi, in *Decretorum Libri Viginti*, in *PL* 140, col. 491–1090.
18   *Malleus Maleficarum*, Speyer 1486, book 1.

19　Johann Weyer, *De Praestigiis Daemonum*, Basel 1563, preface.
20　Abermaliger Justizmord in der Schweiz, in A. L. Schlözer, *Stats-Anzeigen*, Bd. 2 (1783), 273–7.
21　Jacob Grimm, *Deutsche Mythologie*, Heidelberg (1835), trans 1883.
22　Jules Michelet, *La Sorcière*, Paris 1862.
23　William Monter, The Historiography of European Witchcraft, in *JIH*, 2 (1971/72), 435–53.
24　Wilhelm Gottlieb Soldan, *Geschichte der Hexenprozesse*, Darmstadt 1843.
25　Joseph Hansen, *Zauberwahn, Inquisition und Hexenprozeß im Mittelalter*, Munich 1900.
26　Eric J. Hobsbawm, Introduction, in: *The Invention of Tradition*, Cambridge 1983, 1–14.
27　Sigmund Freud, *The Interpretation of Dreams*, Vienna 1900.
28　Émile Durkheim, *The Division of Labour in Society* (1893), New York 1933.
29　Max Weber, *The Protestant Ethic and the Spirit of Capitalism* (1904/1905), London 1985.
30　Bronislaw Malinowski, *Magic, Science and Religion*, London 1954.
31　Bronislaw Malinowski, Culture [1948], in *IESS*, vol. 4 (1968), 621–45.
32　Lucien Lévy-Bruhl, *Primitive Mentality*, London 1923.
33　Claude Lévi-Strauss, The Sorcerer and his Magic (1949), in Middleton (1967), 23–41.
34　Peter Geschiere, *The Modernity of Witchcraft*, Virginia University Press 1997.
35　Roy Ellen, Introduction, in Watson/Ellen (1993), 1–25.
36　Morton Smith, *Jesus, the Magician*, London 1978.
37　Sigmund Riezler, *Geschichte der Hexenprozesse*, Stuttgart 1896, 1–6.
38　Geschiere, *The Modernity of Witchcraft* (1997), 187ff.
39　H. C. Erik Midelfort, Recent Witch Hunting Research, in *The Papers*, 62 (1968), 373–420.
40　Bond/Ciekawy, Introduction, in Bond/Ciekawy, *Witchcraft Dialogues* (2001), 1–38.
41　Stuart Clark (ed.), *Languages of Witchcraft*, London 2001.
42　Lynn Thorndike, *History of Magic and Experimental Science*, 8 vols, New York 1923–58.
43　Kirsten Hastrup, The Challenge of the Unreal, in *Culture and History*, 1 (1986), 50–62.
44　Stuart Clark, *Thinking with Demons*, Oxford 1996.
45　William Perkins, *A Discourse of the Damned Art of Witchcraft*, Cambridge 1608.
46　Johann Jacob Wecker, Hexen-Büchlein, Colmar 1575, cap. 20; ed. Behringer (2001), 339.
47　Max Weber, *The Methodology of the Social Sciences,* New York 1949, 50–112.
48　Bruno Bettelheim, *The Uses of Enchantment*, Harmondsworth 1978.
49　Marion Zimmer Bradley, *The Mists of Avalon*, New York 1983.
50　Diane Purkiss, *The Witch in History*, London 1996, 38.

Chapter 2   The Belief in Witchcraft

1   George M. Foster, Peasant Society, in *AA*, 67 (1965), 293–315.
2   Fischer Weltalmanach. *Zahlen, Daten*, Fakten 1999; Frankfurt/Main 1998.
3   Tamara Multhaupt, *Hexerei und Antihexerei in Afrika*, Munich 1989, 231ff.
4   *La lutte contre la sorcellerie* (*Forces du Mal*), Benin 1977.
5   Parrinder (1958), 125–35.
6   Melford E. Spiro, *Burmese Supernaturalism*, Englewood Cliffs 1967, 26ff.
7   Laura de Mello e Souza, Witchcraft in Colonial Brazil, in Klaniczay/Pócs (1994), 243–56.
8   Marwick (1982), 12ff.
9   Frederick H. Cryer/Marie-Louise Thomson, Biblical and Pagan Societies (*AHWME* vol. 1), London 2001.
10   Bronislaw Malinowski, Culture (1948), in *IESS*, vol. 4 (1968), 621–45.
11   Vladimir Propp, *Morphology of the Folk Tale*, New York 1968.
12   Edgar E. Evans-Pritchard, *Witchcraft, Oracles and Magic among the Azande*, Oxford 1937.
13   Max Marwick, *Sorcery in its Social Setting*, Manchester 1965.
14   Gluckman (1965), 91.
15   Susan Rasmussen, Betrayal or Affirmation? in Moore/Sanders (2001), 136–59.
16   Clyde Mitchell, Perception of the Causes of Disease, in Marwick (1982), 401–21.
17   Homepage 'Sports Talk' of BBC Sports, 8 April 2002.
18   C. Bawa Yamba, Witchfinding and AIDS in Chiawa, Zambia, in *Africa*, 67 (1997), 200–23.
19   Adam Ashforth, Reflections on Spiritual Insecurity, in *ASR*, 41(3) (1998), 36–67.
20   Adam Ashforth, *Aids, Witchcraft and the Problem of Power*, 2001, 1ff., 7ff.
21   John S. Mbiti, *African Religion and Philosophy*, New York 1970, 9ff.
22   Ralushai (1996), 12ff.
23   Isaac Schapera, Sorcery and Witchcraft in Bechuanaland, in *African Affairs*, 51 (1952), 41–52.
24   Jane Parish, Anti-witchcraft Shrines, in Moore/Sanders (2001), 118–35.
25   Ray Abrahams (ed.), *Witchcraft in Contemporary Tanzania*, Cambridge 1994.
26   Victor Ralushai, *Report of the Commission of Inquiry into Witchcraft*, Pietersburg 1996.
27   Bronislaw Malinowski, *Argonauts of the Western Pacific*, London 1922.
28   Arthur M. Hocart, Witchcraft in Eddystone of the Solomons, in *JRAI*, 55 (1925), 229–70.
29   Reo F. Fortune, *Sorcerers of Dobu*, London 1932.
30   Adolphus Peter Elkin, *Aboriginal Men of High Degree* (1945), Queensland University Press 1994.

31   Shirley S. Lindenbaum/Mary Zelienetz (eds), *Sorcery and Social Change*, Adelaide 1981.
32   C. W. Watson/Roy Ellen (eds), *Understanding Witchcraft in Southeast Asia*, Honolulu 1993.
33   Melford E. Spiro, *Burmese Supernaturalism*, Englewood Cliffs 1967, 21–32.
34   Nancy E. Levine, Nyinba Women's Witchcraft, in *Man*, 17 (1982), 259–74.
35   Bruce Kapferer, *The Feast of Sorcerer*, London 1997.
36   Philip A. Kuhn, *Soulstealers*, Cambridge/Mass. 1990.
37   Kwang-Ching Liu, World-View and Peasant Rebellion, in *JAS*, 40 (1981), 297ff.
38   Ann S. Anagnost, Politics and Magic in China, in *Modern China*, 13 (1987), 40–61.
39   Sohaila Kapur, *Witchcraft in Western India*, Hyderabad 1983.
40   Ronnie Nitibaskara, Sorcery in Java, in Watson/Ellen (1993), 123–34.
41   Clyde Kluckhohn, *Navaho Witchcraft*, Boston 1944, 122ff.
42   Günter Lanczkowski, *Götter und Menschen im alten Mexiko*, Olten 1984, 118ff.
43   Iris Gareis, 'Hexen' im alten Peru, in *Münchner Beiträge*, 4 (1991), 265–91.
44   George M. Foster, Nagualism, in *Acta Americana*, 2 (1944), 85–102.
45   Wilhelm Georg Soldan, *Geschichte der Hexenprozesse*, Berlin 1911, vol. 2, 381ff.
46   William Madsen/Claudia Madsen, *Mexican Witchcraft*, Mexico City 1992.
47   Henry A. Selby, *Zapotec Deviance*, Austin/Texas 1974, appendix 1.
48   Nathan Wachtel, *Gods and Vampires*, Chicago 1994, 52ff., 81ff.
49   Deward E. Walker (ed.), *Witchcraft of the American Native Peoples*, Moscow/Idaho 1989.
50   Asen Balikci, Netsilik, in *HNAI*, vol. 5, Washington 1984, 425.
51   Inge Kleivan, West Greenland before 1950, in *HNAI*, vol. 5, Washington 1984, 618ff.
52   Laura de Mello e Souza, Witchcraft in Colonial Brazil, in Klaniczay/Pócs (1994), 243–58.
53   Institut für Demoskopie, Allensbach, opinion poll 1973.
54   Forsa-Institut, opinion poll 1986.
55   Institut für Demoskopie, Allensbach, opinion poll 1989; Wickert Institut, opinion poll 1991.
56   Opinion poll 1976.
57   Gallup Institute, opinion poll 1988.
58   Donald O'Brien, Satan Steps out from the Shadows, in *Africa*, 70 (2000), 520–5.
59   *FAZ*, 12 Feb. 2003, p. 9.
60   Thomas Hauschild, *Der böse Blick*, Berlin 1982.
61   Marie-Louise Thomsen, The Evil Eye in Mesopotamia, in *JNES*, 51 (1992), 19–32.
62   Susan Rasmussen, Betrayal or Affirmation? in Moore/Sanders (2001), 136–59.
63   Brian Spooner, The Evil Eye in the Middle East, in Douglas (1970), 311–19.

64 Willem de Blécourt, *Termen van Toverij*, Nijmegen 1990.
65 Edgar E. Evans-Pritchard, *Witchcraft, Oracles and Magic*, Oxford 1937, 65ff.
66 Lucien Lévy-Bruhl, *Primitive Mentality*, London 1923, 50.
67 Jean Piaget, *The Child's Conception of Physical Causality*, London 1930.
68 Judith Green, *Risk and Misfortune. The Social Construction of Accidents*, London 1997.
69 Edgar E. Evans-Pritchard, *Witchcraft, Oracles and Magic*, Oxford 1937.
70 Keith Thomas, History and Anthropology, in *Past & Present*, 24 (1963), 3–24.
71 Thomas (1971), *Religion and the Decline of Magic*, 494ff.
72 Sharpe (2001), 36–42.
73 Alan Macfarlane, *Witchcraft in Tudor and Stuart England*, London 1970.
74 Alan Macfarlane, *The Origins of English Individualism*, Oxford 1979, 1ff., 59.
75 George M. Foster, The Anatomy of Envy, in *CA*, 13 (1972), 165.
76 Henry A. Selby, *Zapotec Deviance*, Austin/Texas 1974, 108.
77 Rainer Walz, *Hexenglaube und Magische Kommunikation im Dorf*, Paderborn 1993.
78 Geschiere (1997), 219.
79 Ibid., 188.
80 Neil J. Smelser, Toward a Theory of Modernization, in Etzioni/Etzioni (1973), 268–84.
81 Bronislaw Malinowski, Reflections on Witchcraft, in *The Dynamics*, New Haven 1945, 95–9.
82 David J. Silverman, Native American Witchcraft, in *GEW* (2004).
83 Clyde Kluckhohn, *Navaho Witchcraft*, Boston 1944, 114–18.
84 Wilson (1973), 70–101.
85 Nathan Wachtel, *Gods and Vampires*, Chicago 1994, 74ff.
86 Iris Gareis, 'Hexen' im alten Peru, in *Münchner Beiträge*, 4 (1991), 265–91.
87 Jack Goody, Anomy in Ashanti, in *Africa*, 27 (1957), 356–63.
88 Max Marwick, Witchcraft, in *Australian Journal of Science*, 26 (1964), 263–8.
89 Niehaus (2001), 83.
90 Adam Kuper, Enemies of the People, in *TLS*, 8 June 2001, 5–6.
91 George M. Foster, Peasant Society, in *AA*, 67 (1965), 293–315.
92 Johannes Harnischfeger, Unverdienter Reichtum, in *Sociologus*, 47 (1997), 129–56.
93 Comaroff/Comaroff (1993), xxxviii ff.
94 Philipp Mayer, *Witches*, Grahamstown 1954.
95 Sergej M. Shirokogoroff, *Psychomental Complex of the Tungus*, London 1935.
96 Mircea Eliade, *Le chamanisme*, Paris 1951.
97 Ake Hultcrantz, Mythology and Religious Concepts, in *HNAI*, vol. 11 (1986), 630–40.
98 Asen Balikci, Netsilik, in *HNAI*, vol. 5, Washington 1984, 425ff.
99 Carlo Ginzburg, *I Benandanti*, Turin 1966; *The Night Battles*, Baltimore 1983.
100 Maja Boskovic-Stulli, Kresnik-Krsnik, in *Fabula*, 3 (1960), 275–98.

101   Gábor Klaniczay, *The Uses of Supernatural Power*, Cambridge 1990, 129–50.
102   Ginzburg (1991), 207–312.
103   Alex Scobie, Strigiform Witches, in *Fabula*, 19 (1978), 74–101.
104   Cohn (1975), 206ff.
105   Hansen (1900), 58ff.
106   Hansen (1900), 58–61.
107   Edward Peters, The Medieval Church and State, in Jolly/Raudvere/Peters (2002), 202.
108   Mansi, vol. 2, 522.
109   Regino von Prüm, *Libri Duo de Synodalibus Causis*, II, cap. 371.
110   Kors/Peters (1972), 29ff.
111   Corrector Burchardi, cap. V, §§ 70, 90.
112   Corrector Burchardi, §§ 170–1.
113   Hansen (1901), 76ff.
114   Byloff (1934), 26.
115   Giuseppe Bonomo, *Caccia alle Streghe*, Palermo 1959.
116   Dieter Harmening, *Superstitio*, Berlin 1979.
117   Hansen (1901), 48.
118   Luisa Muraro, *La Signora del Gioco*, Milan 1976.
119   Nicolai Cusae, *Cardinalis Opera*, II, Paris 1514, fol. 170 verso–172 recto.
120   Hans Peter Duerr, *Dreamtime*, Oxford 1985.
121   Antti Aarne/Stith Thompson, *The Types of the Folktale*, 2nd edn, Helsinki 1964.
122   Vladimir Propp, *Morphology of the Folk Tale*, New York 1968.
123   Georg Luck, *Magie und andere Geheimlehren der Antike*, Munich 1990, 147–51.
124   Marie Theres Fögen, *Die Enteignung der Wahrsager*, Frankfurt 1997, 223–2.
125   Henry Chadwick, *Priscillian of Avila*, Oxford 1976.
126   Dieter Harmening, *Superstitio*, Berlin 1979, 303–8.
127   Deward E. Walker (ed.), *Witchcraft and Sorcery*, Moscow/Id. 1989.
128   Robert W. Hefner (ed.), *Conversion to Christianity*, Berkeley 1993.
129   Jörg Haustein, *Luthers Stellung zum Zauber- und Hexenwesen*, Stuttgart 1990, 69.
130   Karen Jolly, Medieval Magic, in Jolly/Raudvere/Peters (2002), 21.
131   Baluze (ed.), *Capitularia regum francorum*, Paris 1677, vol. 1, col. 150–2.
132   Thomas Aquinas, *Summa Theologiae* (*c.*1270), London 1964–6, II, 96.
133   Bernard Gui, *Practica Inquisitionis Haereticae Pravitatis*, part V, ch. VI.
134   Kors/Peters (1972), 84–92.
135   Charles Webster, *From Paracelsus to Newton*, Cambridge 1982.
136   Brian Easlea, *Witch Hunting, Magic, and the New Philosophy*, Brighton 1980.
137   Marcel Mauss, Théorie générale de la Magie, in *Année Sociologique*, 7 (1903), 1–146.
138   Ernesto de Martino, *Italie du Sud et Magie*, Mailand 1959.
139   Margaret Aston, *England's Iconoclasts*, Oxford 1988.
140   Carol F. Karlsen, *The Devil in the Shape of a Woman*, New York 1987, xiii.
141   *Malleus Maleficarum*, Speyer 1486, fol. 20–1.

142   Agrippa von Nettesheim, *De Nobilitate et Praecellentia Foeminei Sexus*, 1509.
143   Alexander Roberts, *A Treatise of Witchcraft*, London 1616; Sharpe (2001), 108ff.
144   Kirsten Hastrup, Iceland, in Ankarloo/Henningsen (1990), 383–402.
145   William Monter, The Male Witches of Normandy, 1564–1660, in *FHS*, 20 (1997), 563–95.
146   William Madsen/Claudia Madsen, *A Guide to Mexican Witchcraft*, Mexico City 1992.
147   Manning Nash, Witchcraft as Social Process, in *America Indígena*, 20 (1961), 121–6.
148   Elizabeth Colson, The Father as Witch, in *Africa*, 70 (2000), 333–58.
149   Siegfried F. Nadel, Witchcraft in Four African Societies, in *AA*, 54 (1952), 18–29.
150   Gluckman (1956), 98ff.
151   Andrew Apter, Atinga Revisited, in Comaroff/Comaroff (1993), 111–28.
152   Esther Goody, Legitimate and illegitimate Aggression, in Douglas (1970), 207–43.
153   Larner (1981), 94ff.
154   Carol F. Karlsen, *The Devil in the Shape of a Woman*, New York 1987.
155   Heide Wunder, Hexenprozesse im Herzogtum Preußen, in Degn (1983), 197–203.
156   Robert Muchembled, *La sorcière au village*, Paris 1979.
157   Gottlieb/Buckley (eds), *Blood Magic*, Berkeley/Cal. 1988.
158   Claude Lévi-Strauss, The Sorcerer and his Magic [1949], in Middleton (1967), 23–41.
159   James L. Brain, Witchcraft and Development, in *African Affairs*, 81 (1982), 371–84.
160   Monica Blöcker, Wetterzauber, in Francia (1982), 117–31.
161   Larner (1981), 102.
162   Roper (1994), 1–27.
163   Ibid., 232.
164   Melanie Klein, *The Psychoanalysis of Children*, London 1989.
165   Roper (1994), 202ff.
166   Ibid., 210ff.
167   Sigmund Freud. *Briefe an Wilhelm Fliess*, Frankfurt/M. 1986, 237, 240 (January 1897).
168   Sigmund Freud, Eine Teufelsneurose, in *Studienausgabe*, VIII, Frankfurt 1982, 283–322.
169   Paul Parin/et al., *Psychoanalyse und Gesellschaft*, Frankfurt 1971, 309.
170   Roper (1994), 205ff.
171   Jonathan Durrant, *Witchcraft, Gender and Society*, London 2002, 294.
172   Iliffe (1995), 89ff.
173   Marianne Hester, *Lewd Women and Wicked Witches*, London 1992.
174   Clark (1997), 116ff.
175   Walter Stephen, *Demon Lovers. Witchcraft, Sex, and the Crisis of Belief*, Chicago 2002.
176   Theodor W. Adorno et al., *The Authoritarian Personality*, New York 1950.

177 Sigmund Freud, *Das Ich und die Abwehrmechanismen*, Vienna 1936.
178 Erving Goffman, *Stigma*, Englewood Cliffs/NJ 1963.
179 Howard S. Becker, *Outsiders*, New York 1963.
180 Robert K. Merton, *Social Theory and Social Structure*, New York 1968.
181 Henry A. Selby, *Zapotec Deviance*, Austin/Texas 1974, 128.
182 Walter B. Cannon, Voodoo Death, in *AA*, 44 (1942), 169–81.
183 Elliot P. Currie, Crimes without Criminals, in *Law and Society Review*, 3 (1968), 7–28.
184 Ralushai Report (1996), 51–6.
185 David Lan, *Guns and Rain*, London 1985, 140.
186 Ralushai Report (1996), 56ff.
187 Ibid., 4.
188 *HNAI*, vol. 5 (Arctic), Washington 1984, 355, 366ff., 425, 455, 504, 615, 618ff., 632.
189 Clark (1997), 3–10.
190 Paul Turner, Witchcraft as Negative Charisma, in *Ethnology*, 9 (1970), 366–72.
191 Gluckman (1965), 93.
192 Krige/Krige, *The Realm of the Rain Queen*, London 1943, 168.
193 Mary Douglas, *Purity and Danger*, London 1966.
194 Ashforth (2000), 132.

Chapter 3   The Persecution of Witches

1 Marie-Louise Thomsen, Witchcraft in Ancient Mesopotamia, in *AHMWE* (2001), 25ff.
2 Tzvi Abusch, *Babylonian Witchcraft Literature. Case Studies*, Atlanta 1987.
3 Frederick H. Cryer, Magic in the Old Testament, in *AHWME*, vol. 1 (2001), 97–152.
4 Herodotus, *The Histories*, book 4, chs 67–9.
5 Richard Gordon, Imagining Greek and Roman Magic, in *AHWME*, vol. 2 (1999), 243–52.
6 Fritz *Graf, Gottesnähe und Schadenzauber*, Munich 1996, 58–61.
7 Livy, *Roman History*, book 8, ch. 18.
8 Richard Gordon, Imagining Greek and Roman Magic, in *AHWME*, vol. 2 (1999), 254.
9 Livy, *Roman History*, book 39, ch. 41.
10 Ibid., book 40, ch. 43.
11 Midelfort (1972), 9.
12 Monter (1976), 89.
13 Larner (1981), 60ff.
14 Ibid., 80ff.
15 Behringer (1997), xviii–xxiii, 60–5.
16 Fritz Graf, *Gottesnähe und Schadenzauber*, Munich 1996, 147ff.
17 J. Ferrary, Lex Cornelia de sicariis et veneficiis, in *Athenaeum*, 69 (1991), 417–34.
18 Marie Theres Fögen, *Die Enteignung der Wahrsager*, Frankfurt 1997, 157ff., 168, 183.

19 Ammianus Marcellinus, *The Later Roman Empire*, book 16, ch. 8.
20 Ibid., book 19, ch. 12.
21 Ibid., book 26, ch. 3.
22 Ibid., book 28, ch. 1.
23 Ibid., book 29, chs 1–2.
24 Bernardino de Sahagun, *Historia general de las cosas de Nueva Espania* (1956), book 12, ch. 1.
25 Iris Gareis, 'Hexen' im alten Peru, in *Münchner Beiträge*, 4 (1991), 265–91.
26 Kwang-Ching Liu, World-View and Peasant Rebellion, in *JAS*, 40 (1981), 297ff.
27 Iliffe (1995), 87.
28 Rosalind Shaw, The Production of Witchcraft, in *American Ethnologist*, 24 (1997), 856–76.
29 Gerald W. Hartwig, The Evolution of Sorcery among the Kerebe, in *AHS*, 4 (1971), 505–24.
30 C. R. Harrington (ed.), *The Year without a Summer? World Climate in 1816*, Ottawa 1992.
31 Andrew Sanders, *A Deed without a Name*, Oxford 1995, 137.
32 Iliffe (1995), 173ff.
33 Ashforth (2000), 129.
34 Hansen (1900), 3–122.
35 Hansen (1900), 63ff.
36 Hansen (1900), 55ff.
37 Cecil L'Estrange Ewen, *Witchcraft and Demonianism*, London 1933, 26.
38 Hansen (1900) 387; Behringer (2001), 64–7.
39 Ibid., 283ff.
40 Vita Hludovici, in *MGH, Scriptores*, II, 639.
41 *MGH, Scriptores*, I, 414.
42 Hansen (1900), 116–19.
43 Cohn (1975), 153.
44 Ibid., 149.
45 *Laxdaela Saga*, chs 35–8, ed. Magnus Magnusson, Harmondsworth 1969.
46 *Orkneyinga Saga*, chs 55, 78, ed. H. Palsson/Paul Edwards, Harmondsworth 1981.
47 Hansen (1900), 116–19.
48 Davies (1999), 87.
49 Cecil L'Estrange Ewen, *Witchcraft and Demonianism*, London 1933, 28.
50 Hansen (1900), 381.
51 Hansen (1900), 354ff., 360–5, 386–96, Ginzburg (1991), 91ff.
52 Gregory of Tours, *The History of the Franks*, trans. L. Thorpe, New York 1974.
53 Agobard von Lyon, Contra Insulsam Vulgi Opinionem de Grandine, in *PL*, vol. 104, Sp. 147–58.
54 Hansen (1900), 96.
55 *MGH, Scriptores*, XIII, 52.
56 Byloff (1934), 19.
57 Ryan (1999), 411ff.
58 Russell Zguta, The Ordeal by Water, in *Slavic Review*, 36 (1977), 220–30.
59 Ibid., 223.
60 Cohn (1975), 160.

61   M. K. Hughes/H. F. Diaz (eds), *The Medieval Warm Period*, Dordrecht 1994.
62   William Chester Jordan, *The Great Famine*, Princeton 1996.
63   Jean M. Grove, The Onset of the Little Ice Age, in Jones/et al. (2001), 153–87.
64   Hansen (1901), 2–8.
65   Umberto Eco, *The Name of the Rose*, trans W. Weaver, London 1984.
66   L. S. Davidson/J. O. Ward, *The Sorcery Trial of Alice Kyteler*, Binghamton 1993.
67   H. A. Kelly, English Kings and the Fear of Sorcery, in *Medieval Studies*, 39 (1977), 206–38.
68   Cecil L'Estrange Ewen, *Witchcraft and Demonianism*, London 1933, 38ff.
69   Cohn (1975), 126–46.
70   Richard Kieckhefer, *European Witch-Trials*, London 1976.
71   Hansen (1901), 64–5.
72   Winfried Trusen, Der Inquisitionsprozeß, in *ZRGKA*, 74 (1988), 168–230.
73   Edward Peters, *Torture*, Philadelphia 1985.
74   Ginzburg (1991), 33–88.
75   Frantisek Graus, *Pest – Geißler – Judenmorde*, Göttingen 1987.
76   John Aberth, *From the Brink of the Apocalypse*, New York 2001.
77   Kirsten A. Seaver, *The Frozen Echo*, Stanford/CA 1996, 153ff.
78   Russell Zguta, The Ordeal by Water, in *Slavic Review*, 36 (1977), 226.
79   Hansen (1900), 381–98.
80   Köbler (1989), 480ff.
81   Robert Muchembled, *Le roi et la sorcière*, Paris 1993, 76–80.
82   Massimo Centini, *I Processi di stregoneria in Piemonte*, Cuneo 1995.
83   Hansen (1900), 18ff.
84   Wolfgang Behringer, Detecting the Ultimate Conspiracy, in Swann/Coward (2004).
85   *Errores Gazariorum*, in Hansen (1900), 118–22; Ostorero (1999), 267–354.
86   Gabriel Audisio, Les Vaudois, Turin 1989.
87   Ginzburg (1991), 33–53.
88   Arno Borst, *Die Katharer*, Stuttgart 1953.
89   Bernardo Rategno, *Tractatus de Strigiis* (1508), ch. 4; Hansen (1901), 282.
90   Johannes Nider, *Formicarius* (1437), in Hansen (1901), 94.
91   Chantal Ammann-Doubliez, La première chasse aux sorciers en Valais, in Ostorero (1999), 77ff.
92   Johannes Franck, Geschichte des Wortes Hexe, in Hansen (1901), 614–70.
93   Hansen (1901), 16ff.
94   Ibid., 17.
95   Ibid., 17.
96   Ostorero (1999), 330–4.
97   Ibid., 23–98.
98   Fründ's report, in Hansen (1901), 533–7; Behringer (2001), 80–2.
99   Chantal Ammann-Doubliez, La première chasse aux sorciers en Valais, in Ostorero (1999), 63–98.

100 *Errores Gazariorum*, ed. Hansen (1901), 118–22.
101 *Errores Gazariorum*, ed. and commented by Ostorero (1999), 267–354.
102 Glaser (2001), 68, 86.
103 Hansen (1901), 536.
104 Chantal Ammann-Doubliez, La première chasse aux sorciers en Valais, in Ostorero (1999), 80–98.
105 Briggs (1996), 402.
106 Catherine Chène, L'inquisiteur d'Autun, in Ostorero et al. (1999), 231ff.
107 Catherine Chène, Le juge Pierre, in Ostorero et al. (1999), 223–30.
108 Thomas Middleton, *A Tragicomedy Called The Witch* (1615).
109 Johann Nider, *Formicarius*, in Hansen (1901), 88–98; Ostorero et al. (1999), 99–266.
110 Pierette Paravy, *De la chrétienté romaine à la réforme en Dauphiné*, Rome 1993, 333–79.
111 Claude Tholosan, *Ut Magorum, 1436*, in Blauert (1990), 145; Ostorero (1999), 355–438.
112 Andreas Blauert, *Frühe Hexenverfolgungen*, Hamburg 1989, 118ff.
113 Franco Mormando, *The Preacher's Demons. Bernardino da Siena*, Chicago 1999, 52–108.
114 Bernardino da Siena, *Prediche volgare sul campo di Siena*, 2 vols, Milan 1989, 1007.
115 Candida Peruzzi, Un processo di stregoneria a Todi nel '400, in *Lares* 21 (2) (1955), 1–17.
116 Nikolaus Schatzmann, *Verdorrende Bäume*, Zürich 2002, 226.
117 Michael D. Bailey, *Battling Demons*, Pennsylvania University Press, Philadelphia, 2003, 15.
118 Martin Le Franc, *Le Champion des Dames*, in Hansen (1900), 103; Hansen (1901), 441.
119 Byloff (1934), 31.
120 Wolfgang Behringer, Climatic Change and Witch-Hunting, in *Climatic Change*, 43 (1999), 335–51.
121 Hansen (1901), 17ff.
122 Martin le Franc, *Le Champion des Dames*, livre IV, in Ostorero (1999), 439–508.
123 Gabriel Audisio, *Les Vaudois*, Turin 1989.
124 Alfonsus Tostatus (1440), in Hansen (1901), 105–9.
125 Nicolas Jacquier, *Flagellum haereticorum fascinariorum* (1458), in Hansen (1901), 133–44.
126 Girolamo Visconti, An strie sint velut heretice iudicande (1460), in Hansen (1901), 200–6.
127 Jens C. V. Johansen, Hexen auf mittelalterlichen Wandmalereien, in Blauert (1990), 217–40.
128 Vincenc Rajsp, Hexenprozesse in Slowenien, in Klaniczay/Pócs (1992), 51–66.
129 Gluckman (1965), 103.
130 *Malleus Maleficarum*, Speyer 1486.
131 Andreas Schmauder (ed.), *Frühe Hexenverfolgung in Ravensburg*, Konstanz 2001.
132 Summis desiderantes affectibus (1484), in Hansen (1901), 24–7.

133   Wolfgang Behringer/Günter Jerouschek, Introduction, in *Malleus* (2000), 58–69.
134   Ibid., 23ff.
135   All discussed in detail, in Ibid., 64–9.
136   *Malleus* (2000), 803.
137   Ulrich Molitor, *De laniis et phitonicis mulieribus* (Konstanz 1489).
138   Jane P. Davidson, *The Witch in Northern European Art, 1450–1750*, Freren 1987.
139   Charles Zika, Fears of Flying, in *Australian Journal of Art*, 8 (1989/90), 19–47.
140   Hartmut H. Kunstmann, *Zauberwahn in der Reichsstadt Nürnberg*, Nuremberg 1970.
141   Wolfgang Behringer/Günter Jerouschek, Introduction, in *Malleus* (2000), 82.
142   Ibid., 31–40.
143   Bryan R. Wilson, *Magic and the Millennium*, London 1973.
144   *Malleus Maleficarum*, Speyer 1486, Apologia.
145   Behringer (2001), 112.
146   Decker (2003), 50.
147   Monter (2002), 44.
148   Bernardo [Rategno] da Como, *Lucerna Inquisitorum* (1508), Mailand 1546.
149   Bartolomeo de Spina, *De strigibus et lamiis*, Venice 1523, ch. 13; Hansen (1901), 331.
150   Decker (2003), 67.
151   Giuseppe Bonomo, *Caccia alle Streghe*, Palermo 1959, 74–84.
152   Giovanni Francesco Pico della Mirandola, *Strix*, s.l. (Bologna) s.d. (1523).
153   Silvester Prierias, *De strigimagarum libri tres*, Rome 1521; Hansen (1901), 317–23.
154   Paulus Grillandus, *Tractatus de hereticis et sortilegiis* (1525), Lyon 1536.
155   Gary K. Waite, *Heresy, Magic and Witchcraft in Early Modern Europe*, London 2003.
156   Byloff (1934), 38ff.
157   Johann Weyer, *De Praestigiis Daemonum*, Basel 1563, preface.
158   Misty L. Bastian, Witchcraft in the Nigerian Popular Press, in Comaroff/Comaroff (1993), 129–66.
159   *Ein erschröckhlich geschicht Vom Tewfel und einer unhulden*, s.l. (Nuremberg) 1533.
160   Wilde (2003), 158ff.
161   Jörg Haustein, *Luthers Stellung zum Zauber- und Hexenwesen*, Stuttgart 1990, 141ff.
162   William G. Naphy, *Plagues, Poisons and Potions*, Manchester 2002.
163   Mair (1969), 39ff.
164   William Monter, *Witchcraft in France and Switzerland*, Ithaca/London 1976, 42–66.
165   *Ein erschröckliche Geschicht [. . .] von dreyen Zauberin*, Nuremberg 1555.
166   Ingrid Evers, Maaslandse heksenprocessen, in de Blécourt/Gijswijt-Hofstra (1986), 95ff.

167 Gustav Henningsen, *Fra heksejagt til heksekult, 1484–1984*, Copenhagen 1984, 30ff.
168 Decker (2003), 78ff.
169 Gustav Henningsen, *The Witches' Advocate*, Reno/Nevada 1980.
170 José Pedro Paiva, Portugal, in *GEW* (2004).
171 James M. Stayer, Anabaptism, in *OER*, vol. 1 (1996), 31–5.
172 Gary K. Waite, Anabaptists, in: *Essays Presented to James Stayer*, Ashgate 1999, 120–40.
173 Bartholomäus Anhorn, *Magiologia* (Basel) 1675, ch. 1.

Chapter 4   The European Age of Witch-Hunting

1 Warhafftige und Erschreckhenliche Thatten der 63 Hexen (1563), in Behringer (2001), 138–40.
2 Monter (2002), 21.
3 Midelfort (1972), 34–63.
4 Sharpe (2001), 99ff.
5 William Monter, The Male Witches of Normandy, 1564–1660, in *FHS*, 20 (1997), 594.
6 Lawrence Norman/Gareth Roberts, *Witchcraft in Early Modern Scotland*, Exeter 2000, 17.
7 Wolfgang Behringer, *Mit dem Feuer vom Leben zum Tod*, Munich 1988, 57–61.
8 Theophrastus Bombastus von Hohenheim (Paracelsus), *De sagis et earum operibus*, 1538.
9 Jean M. Grove, *The Little Ice Age*, London/New York 1988.
10 Christian Pfister/et al. (eds), *Climatic Change*, 43 (Special Issue), Dordrecht 1999.
11 Christian Pfister, *Klimageschichte der Schweiz 1525–1860*, Bern/Stuttgart 1988.
12 Glaser (2001), 116.
13 Johann Weyer, *Of Witchcraft* (1566/1583), Asheville 1998, 269.
14 Wolfgang Behringer, Climatic Change and Witch-Hunting, in *Climatic Change*, 43 (1999), 335–51.
15 *Summa etlicher Predigen vom Hagel und Unholden*, Stuttgart 1562.
16 Johannes Brenz, *Sermon von Hagel und Ungewitter*, Stuttgart 1562.
17 The debate of 1564/65 is published in Johann Weyer, *De Praestigiis Daemonum*, Basel 1563; Frankfurt 1586.
18 Erik Midelfort, *A History of Madness*, Stanford/Cal. 1999, 196.
19 Johann Weyer, *De Praestigiis Daemonum* (1563), Frankfurt 1586, preface.
20 Monter (2002), 21.
21 Gustav Henningsen/John Tedeschi (eds), *The Inquisition*, Dekalb/Ill. 1986.
22 Oscar di Simplicio, *Inquisizione, stregoneria, medicina*, Siena 2000, 21ff.
23 William Monter, Alsace, in *GEW* (2004).
24 Wilde (2003), 28–34, 168ff.

25   Heinrich Bullinger, Von Hexen (1571), in *Theatrum de Veneficis*, Frankfurt 1586, 298–306.

26   Lambert Daneau, *Les Sorciers*, Lyon 1572; *A Dialogue of Witches*, London 1575.

27   Jean Bodin, *De la Démonomanie des Sorciers*, Paris 1580.

28   Zwo Newe Zeittung, *Was man für Hexen und Unholden verbrendt hat*, s.l. 1580.

29   *Warhafftige und glaubwirdige Zeyttung*, Strasbourg 1583.

30   Decker (2003), 84ff.

31   Alan Macfarlane, *Witchcraft in Tudor and Stuart England*, London 1970, 20, 57, 60ff.

32   George Gifford, *The Subtill Practises of Devilles by Witches*, London 1587.

33   John H. M. Salmon, *Society in Crisis*, London 1975, 76ff.

34   Alfred Soman, The Parlement of Paris and the Great Witch Hunt, in *SCJ*, 9 (1978), 31–44.

35   Denis Crouzet, *Les Guerriers de Dieu*, 2 vols, Paris 1990, vol. 2, 340ff.

36   Monter (1976), 89.

37   Peter Kamber, La chasse aux sorciers, in: *Revue Historique Vaudoise*, 90 (1982), 21–33.

38   Sharpe (1997), 92.

39   Johann Linden, *Gesta Treverorum*, ed. Hugo Wyttenbach/M. F. J. Müller, vol. 3, Trier 1839.

40   Peter Binsfeld, *Tractatus de Confessionibus Maleficorum et Sagarum*, Trier 1589 (196 pages).

41   Peter Binsfeld, *Tractat von Bekantnuß der Zauberer und Hexen*, Munich 1591.

42   Peter Binsfeld, *Tractatus*, Trier 1591 (364 pages); *Tractatus*, Trier 1596 (405 pages).

43   Rita Voltmer, Hexenverfolgungen, in *JWLG*, 27 (2001), 37–107.

44   Rosemarie Beier-de-Haan/Rita Voltmer/Franz Irsigler (eds), *Hexenwahn*, Berlin 2002.

45   Cornelius Loos, *De vera et ficta [falsa] magia*, Cologne 1592.

46   *Theatrum Diabolorum*, Frankfurt 1569.

47   Johannes Trithemii zu Spanheim Antwortt, in *Theatrum de Veneficis*, Frankfurt 1586, 355–66.

48   *Historia von D. Johann Fausten*, Frankfurt/Main 1587.

49   Henricus Cornelius Agrippa von Nettesheim, *De Occulta Philosophia*, Antwerp 1531.

50   Girolamo Cardano, *De Propria Vita*, Milan 1575.

51   Giovanni Battista della Porta, *Magia Naturalis*, Naples 1589; *Natural Magick*, London 1658.

52   Peter French, *John Dee. The World of an Elizabethan Magus*, New York 1972.

53   Christopher Marlowe, *The Tragical History of Doctor Faustus*, London 1592.

54   Erweytterte Unholden Zeyttung, s.l. 1590, ed. in Behringer (2001), 218–23.

55   James VI of Scotland, *Daemonologie*, Edinburgh 1597.

56   [James Carmichael] *News from Scotland*, Edinburgh 1591.

57 Ludovicus a Paramo, *De officii Sancti Inquisitionis*, Madrid 1598, 296.
58 Nicolas Rémy, *Daemonolatria*, Lyon 1595 (Frankfurt 1598), preface.
59 Briggs (1996).
60 Monter (2002), 36.
61 Rosemarie Beier-de-Haan/Rita Voltmer/Franz Irsigler (eds), *Hexen-wahn*, Berlin 2002.
62 Denis Crouzet, *Les Guerriers de Dieu*, Paris 1990, vol. 1, 93.
63 Ibid., vol. 2, 340.
64 Rita Voltmer/Franz Irsigler, Hexenverfolgungen, in Beier-de-Haan (2002), 30–45, esp. 35.
65 Peter George Maxwell-Stuart, Introduction, in Delrio, *Investigations into Magic*, Manchester/New York 2000, 4.
66 Martin Delrio SJ, *Disquisitionum Magicarum libri sex*, Louvain 1599/1600.
67 Robert Filmer, *An Advertisement to the Jurymen of England*, London 1653, 3ff.
68 Sharpe (1997), 95ff.
69 Jean Fraikin, Eine Seite in der Geschichte der Hexerei, in Franz/Irsigler/Biesel (1995), 417–34.
70 Martin Delrio SJ, *Disquisitionum Magicarum libri sex*, Louvain 1599/1600, lib. II, q. 16.
71 M.-L. Polain, *Recueil des Ordonnances de la Principauté de Stavelot*, Brussels 1984, 77.
72 Martin Delrio SJ, *Disquisitionum Magicarum libri sex*, Louvain 1599/1600, lib. V, sect. 1.
73 Zauberey, in Zedler, *Universal-Lexicon*, vol. 61, Leipzig 1749, col. 62–142.
74 Wolfgang Behringer, Climatic Change and Witch-Hunting, in *Climatic Change*, 43 (1999), 335–51.
75 Shanaka L. de Silva/Gregory A. Zielinski, Global Influence, in *Nature*, 393 (1998), 455–8.
76 Glaser (2001), 152ff.
77 Henri Boguet, *Discours des Sorciers*, Lyon 1602.
78 Monter (1976), 67–87.
79 Brigitte Rochelandet, *Sorcières, diables et bouchers en Franche-Comté*, Besançon 1997.
80 William Monter, *Witchcraft in France and Switzerland*, Ithaca/London 1976, 69–74.
81 *Compendium Maleficarum*, Milan 1608, lib. II, ch. 13; Summers ed., p. 130.
82 H. C. Erik Midelfort, *Mad Princes*, Charlottesville/Va. 1994, 148ff.
83 Communication by Robin Briggs.
84 Francesco Maria Guazzo, *Compendium Maleficarum*, Milan 1608.
85 Pierre de Lancre, *Tableau de l'Inconstance des mauvais Anges et Démons*, Paris 1612.
86 Pierre de Lancre, *L'incrédulité et mescréance du sortilège*, Paris 1622.
87 De Lancre analyses the difference in: *Tableau* (1612), 382ff. (book 5, disc. 3).
88 Diego de Landa, *Historia de las Cosas de Yucatan* (1566), Merida 1990.
89 José de Acosta, *Historia Natural e Moral de las Indias*, Seville 1590.

90   William Monter, *Ritual, Myth and Magic in Early Modern Europe*, Brighton 1983, 87.

91   Herbert Pohl, *Hexenverfolgung im Kurfürstentum Mainz*, Bielefeld 1998.

92   Gerhard Schormann, *Der Krieg gegen die Hexen*, Göttingen 1991, 115–20.

93   Peter Oestmann, *Hexenprozesse am Reichskammergericht*, Wien 1997, 438–46.

94   Friedrich Förner, *Panoplia armaturae Dei*, Ingolstadt 1625.

95   Midelfort (1972), 98–112.

96   Jonathan Durrant, *Witchcraft, Gender and Society*, London 2002, 287.

97   Wolfgang Mährle, Hexenverfolgungen in Ellwangen, in Dillinger (1998), 325–500.

98   Britta Gehm, *Die Hexenverfolgungen des Hochstifts Bamberg*, Hildesheim 2000, 149–61.

99   Herbert Pohl, *Hexenverfolgung im Kurfürstentum Mainz*, Bielefeld 1998, 19ff.

100 Wolfgang Mährle, Hexenverfolgungen in Ellwangen, in Dillinger (1998), 381–92.

101 Wolfgang Behringer, Climatic Change and Witch-Hunting, in *Climatic Change*, 43 (1999), 335–51.

102 Wolfgang Behringer, Weather, Hunger and Fear, in *German History*, 13 (1995), 1–27.

103 Britta Gehm, *Die Hexenverfolgungen des Hochstifts Bamberg*, Hildesheim 2000, 118ff.

104 Christian Pfister, *Klimageschichte der Schweiz 1525–1860*, Bern 1988, 140.

105 Neue Zeitung von sechshundert Hexen, s.l. 1629; ed. in Behringer (2001), 261–4.

106 Diane Ciekawy/Peter Geschiere, Containing Witchcraft, in *ASR*, 41 (1998), 4.

107 Harald Schwillus, *Kleriker im Hexenprozeß*, Würzburg 1992.

108 'Es wird Wirtzbürgisch werck werden . . .': Behringer (2001), 265.

109 Gerhard Schormann, *Der Krieg gegen die Hexen*, Göttingen 1991, 169ff.

110 Lucy S. Davidowitz, *Der Krieg gegen die Juden, 1933–45*, Wiesbaden 1979.

111 Thomas Becker, Hexenverfolgung in Kurköln, in *AHVN* 195 (1992), 202–14.

112 [Friedrich Spee], *Cautio Criminalis*, s.l. (Rinteln) 1631.

113 Heinrich von Schultheis, *Ausführliche Instruction*, Cologne 1634.

114 Map 3: Ecclesiastical Territories in Central Europe, in *OER*, vol. 4, 333.

115 Marc Forster, *The Counter-Reformation in the Villages*, Ithaca 1992.

116 Götz von Pölnitz, *Julius Echter von Mespelbrunn*, Munich 1934.

117 Friedrich Spee, *Cautio Criminalis*, Rinteln 1631.

118 Karl Mannheim, Das Problem der Generationen, in *Kölner Vierteljahreshefte für Soziologie*, 7 (1928), 157ff.

119 Robert Bireley, *Maximilian von Bayern*, Göttingen 1975, 226.

120 Gregory of Valencia S.J., *Commentariorum theologicorum tomi IV*, Ingolstadt 1591–7.

121 Behringer (1997), 115–93.

122   Johannes Dillinger, *Hexenverfolgungen*, Trier 1999.
123   Manfred Tschaikner, *Damit das Böse ausgerottet werde*, Bregenz 1992.
124   Johannes Dillinger, *Hexenverfolgungen*, Trier 1999.
125   Walter Niess, *Hexenprozesse in der Grafschaft Büdingen*, Büdingen 1982.
126   Gerhard Schormann, *Der Krieg gegen die Hexen*, Göttingen 1991, 144ff.
127   Larner (1981), 60–88.
128   James VI of Scotland, *Daemonologie*, Edinburgh 1597.
129   [James Carmichael], *News from Scotland*, Edinburgh 1591.
130   Lawrence Normand/Gareth Roberts, *Witchcraft in Early Modern Scotland*, Exeter 2000, 56.
131   William Monter, *Ritual, Myth and Magic*, Brighton 1983, 53.
132   Larner (1981), 80.
133   Katrin Moeller, Hexenverfolgungen, in Beier-de-Haan (2002), 96–107.
134   Rolf Schulte, *Hexenverfolgung in Schleswig-Holstein*, Heide 2001.
135   Roland Füssel, *Hexenverfolgung in Thüringen*, Erfurt 1998.
136   Heinrich Kaak, Brandenburg, in *GEW* (2004).
137   Wilde (2003), 142–53.
138   Nils Hemmingsen, *Admonitio de superstitionibus magicis vitandis*, Copenhagen 1575.
139   Rita Voltmer/Franz Irsigler, Hexenverfolgungen, in Beier-de-Haan (2002), 30–45, esp. 35.
140   Schmidt (2000), 80–361.
141   Thomas Erastus, *Disputatio de lamiis seu strigibus*, Basel 1572.
142   Sharpe (1997), 107–11.
143   William Monter, The Male Witches of Normandy, 1564–1660, in *FHS*, 20 (1997), 594.
144   H. C. Erik Midelfort, *Mad Princes*, Charlottesville/Va. 1994, 73–143.
145   Anton Praetorius, *Gründlicher Bericht von Zauberey und Zauberern*, Lich 1598.
146   Manfred Tschaikner, Graubünden, in *GEW* (2004).
147   Manfred Tschaikner, *Damit das Böse ausgerottet werde*, Bregenz 1992.
148   Otto Seger/Peter Putzer, *Hexenprozesse in Liechtenstein*, Wien 1987.
149   Trevor Aston (ed.), *Crisis in Europe 1560–1660*, London 1965.
150   Albert L. Beier, *Masterless Men*, London 1985.
151   Henry Kamen, *The Iron Century, 1550–1650*, London 1971.
152   Hartmut Lehmann, The Persecution of Witches, in *CEH*, 21 (1988), 107–21.
153   Theodore K. Rabb, *The Struggle for Stability*, Princeton 1975.
154   Hugh Redwald Trevor-Roper, *Princes and Artists*, London 1976.
155   Vaughan Hart, *Art and Magic in the Court of the Stuarts*, London 1994.
156   Robert J. Evans, *Rudolf II and His World*, Oxford 1973.
157   Geoffrey Parker/L. M. Smith (eds), *The General Crisis*, London 1978.
158   Trevor Aston (ed.), *Crisis in Europe 1560–1660*, London 1965.
159   Robin Briggs, France, in *GEW* (2004).
160   Briggs (1996), 193ff.
161   B. Capp, Godly Rule and English Millenarianism, in *PP*, 52 (1971), 106–17.
162   Mathew Hopkins, *The Discoverie of Witches*, London 1647.

163   John Stearne, *A Confirmation and Discovery of Witchcraft*, London 1648, A2 verso.
164   Ibid., 11.
165   Guilelmus Scribonius, *De sagarum natura et potestate*, Marburg 1588.
166   John Stearne, *A Confirmation and Discovery of Witchcraft*, London 1648, 18.
167   Ibid., 61.
168   Ibid., p. A2 verso (preface), and on p. 11; pp. 10, 15ff., 20ff., 29, 40, 57; pp. 11, 15ff., 38.
169   Francis Hutchinson, *An Historical Essay Concerning Witchcraft*, London 1718.
170   Sharpe (1997), 128–47, cit. p. 145.
171   Robert Poole (ed.), *The Lancashire Witches*, Manchester 2002.
172   Sharpe (1997), 126ff.
173   Alison Findley, Sexual and Spiritual Politics in the Events of 1633/34, in Poole (2002), 159ff.
174   Thomas Potts, *The Wonderfull Discoverie of Witches*, London 1613.
175   Thomas Heywood/Richard Broome, *The Late Lancashire Witches*, London 1634.
176   Peter Corbin/Douglas Sedge (eds), *Three Jacobean Witchcraft Plays*, Manchester 1986.
177   Herbert Berry, The Globe Bewitched, in *Drama in England*, 1 (1984), 215.
178   Behringer (2001), 414–20.
179   Peter Oestmann, *Hexenprozesse am Reichskammergericht*, Wien 1997, 531–602.
180   Robin Briggs, France, in *GEW* (2004).
181   Jürg Luterbacher, The Late Maunder Minimum, in Jones/Ogilvie/Davies/Briffa 2001, 29–54.
182   Bengt Ankarloo/Gustav Henningsen (eds), *Early Modern European Witchcraft*, Oxford 1990.
183   Levack (1987), 191.
184   Bengt Ankarloo, *Trolldomsprocesserna i Sverige*, Lund 1971, 326–34.
185   Bengt Ankarloo, Sweden: The Mass Burnings (1668–76), in Ankarloo/Henningsen (1990), 367–82.
186   Maia Madar, Estonia I: Werewolves and Poisoners, in Ankarloo/Henningsen (1990), 257–72.
187   Joseph Glanvill, *Sadducismus Triumphatus*, London 1681.
188   George Sinclair, *Satan's Invisible World*, Edinburgh 1685.
189   Cotton Mather, *Memorable Providences, Relating to Witchcraft and Possessions*, Boston 1689.
190   Balthasar Bekker, *De betoverde Weereld*, 4 vols, Amsterdam 1691–3, part 4, ch. 39.
191   Behringer (1997), 336–44.
192   Rolf Schulte, *Hexenmeister*, Frankfurt/Main 1999.
193   Gábor Klaniczay, Hungary, in Ankarloo/Henningsen (1990), 219–56.
194   Mircea Eliade, *Shamanism*, Princeton 1964.
195   Byloff (1934), 55.
196   Michel de Certeau, *La Possession de Loudon*, Paris 1971.
197   *Newer Tractat von der verführten Kinder Zauberey*, Aschaffenburg 1629.

198 Bernhard Duhr, *Geschichte der Jesuiten*, 4 vols, Freiburg 1906–27.
199 Wolfgang Behringer, Kinderhexenprozesse, in *ZHF*, 16 (1989), 31–47.
200 Robert Walinski-Kiehl, The Devil's Children, in *Continuity and Change*, 11 (1996), 171–90.
201 Hans Sebald, *Witch-Children*, New York 1995.
202 Florence H. Ellis, Isleta Pueblo, in *HNAI*, vol. 9, Washington 1979, 351–65.
203 Joe S. Sando, The Pueblo Revolt, in *HNAI*, vol. 9, Washington 1979, 194–7.
204 M. J. Westerkamp, *Women and Religion in Early America, 1600–1850*, London New York 1999.
205 David D. Hall (ed.), *Witch-Hunting in Seventeenth-Century New England*, Northeastern University Press 1999.
206 Paul Boyer/Stephen Nissenbaum (eds), *Salem Witchcraft Papers*, 1978.
207 Kai T. Erikson, *Wayward Puritans*, New York 1966.
208 Paul Boyer/Stephen Nissenbaum, *Salem Possessed*, Harvard 1974.
209 Carol F. Karlsen, *The Devil in the Shape of a Woman*, New York 1987.
210 Cotton Mather, *The Wonders of the Invisible World*, Boston 1693.
211 Cotton Mather, *Memorable Providences*, Boston 1689.
212 William Monter, *Ritual, Myth and Magic*, Brighton 1983, 107ff.
213 Frank Wesley Pitman, Fetishism, in *Journal of Negro History*, 11 (1926), 650–68.
214 Bengt Ankarloo/et al. (ed.), *Early Modern European Witchcraft*, Oxford 1990.
215 Francisco Bethencourt, Portugal, in Ankarloo/Henningsen (1990), 403–24.
216 José Pedro Paíva, Portugal, in *GEW* (2004).
217 Henry Kamen, *The Phoenix and the Flame*, New Haven 1993.
218 Monter (2002), 47.
219 Henry Kamen, Spain, in *GEW* (2004).
220 Francisco Fajardo Spinola, *Hechicería y brujería en Canarias*, Las Palmas 1992.
221 Raymond Gille, Ireland, in *GEW* (2004).
222 Marijke Gijswijt-Hofstra/Willem Frijhóff (eds), *Witchcraft in the Netherlands*, Rotterdam 1991.
223 The numbers are usually from *GEW* (2004).
224 [Friedrich Spee], *Cautio Criminalis*, Rinteln 1631.
225 Köbler (1995), introduction.
226 Wolfgang Behringer, *Im Zeichen des Merkur*, Göttingen 2003.
227 Otto Seger/Peter Putzer, *Hexenprozesse in Liechtenstein*, Wien 1987.
228 Hans Eyvind Naess, Norway, in Ankarloo/Henningsen (1990), 367–82.
229 Rune Hagen, The Witch-Hunt in Early Modern Finnmark, in *Acta Borealia* (1999), 43–62.
230 Ryan (1999), 412ff.
231 Natallia Slizh, Lithuania, in *GEW* (2004).
232 Parsla Petersone, Latvia, in *GEW* (2004).
233 Janusz Tazbir, Hexenprozesse in Polen, in *ARG*, 71 (1980), 280–307.
234 Trpimir Vedris, Croatia, in *GEW* (2004).
235 Trpimir Vedris, Balkans, in *GEW* (2004).

236   Janusz Tazbir, Hexenprozesse in Polen, in *ARG*, 71 (1980), 280–307.
237   Monter (2002), 12ff.
238   Karen Lambrecht, *Hexenverfolgung in den schlesischen Territorien*, Cologne 1995, 345ff.
239   Ibid., 130–92.
240   Decker (2003), 81–92.
241   Marina Montesano, Milan, in *GEW* (2004).
242   Giovanni Romeo, *Inquisitori, esorcisti e streghe*, Florence 1990, 49.
243   Manfred Tschaikner, Graubünden, in *GEW* (2004).
244   Monter (2002), 46ff. (without references).
245   Decker (2003), 87ff.
246   Oscar di Simplicio, *Inquisizione, stregoneria, medicina*, Siena 2000.
247   Robin Briggs, France, in *GEW* (2004)
248   Robert Muchembled, *Le roi et la sorcière*, Paris 1993, 74ff.
249   Alfred Soman, The Parlement of Paris and the Great Witch Hunt, in *SCJ*, 9 (1978), 31–44.
250   Ibid., 33–8.
251   Monter (2002), 39–44.
252   Levack (1987), 181.
253   William Monter, Alsace, in *GEW* (2004).
254   Wolfgang Behringer, Neun Millionen Hexen, in *GWU*, 49 (1998), 684ff.
255   Levack (1987), 21.
256   Monter (2002), 13.
257   Mary Daly, Gyn/Ecology. *The Metaethics of Radical Feminism*, Boston 1978.
258   G. C. Voigt, Etwas über die Hexenprozesse, in *BM*, 3 (1784), 297–311.
259   Gustav Roskoff, *Geschichte des Teufels*, Leipzig 1869.
260   Wolfgang Behringer, Neun Millionen Hexen, in *GWU*, 49 (1998), 664–85.
261   Gloria Flaherty, *Shamanism and the Eighteenth Century*, Princeton/New Jersey 1992.
262   Rolf Schulte, *Hexenmeister*, Frankfurt/Main 1999.
263   Midelfort (1972), 121–63.
264   Behringer (1997), 183–205.
265   *Neue Zeitung von sechshundert Hexen*, s.l. 1629, ed. Behringer (2001), 261–4.
266   Wilhelm Abel, *Massenarmut und Hungerkrisen*, Hamburg/Berlin 1974.
267   Paul Baxter, Absence Makes the Heart Grow Fonder, in Gluckman (1973), 163–91.
268   Jonathan L. Pearl, Witchcraft in New France, in *Historical Reflections*, 4 (1977), 191–206.
269   James L. Brain, Witchcraft and Development, in *African Affairs*, 81 (1982), 380ff.
270   Fritz Byloff, *Hexenverfolgung in den österreichischen Alpenländern*, Berlin 1934.
271   Helfried Valentinitsch (ed.), *Hexen und Zauberer*, Graz 1987, 297–316.
272   William Chester Jordan, *The Great Famine*, Princeton 1996.
273   Henry Phelps-Brown/Sheila Hopkins, Seven Centuries, in *Economica*, 23 (1956), 296–314.

274 C. R. Harrington (ed.), *The Year Without a Summer? World Climate in 1816*, Ottawa 1992.
275 Oskar Pfister, *Das Christentum und die Angst*, Zürich 1944.
276 Theodor W. Adorno/et al., *The Authoritarian Personality*, New York 1950.
277 Wolfgang Behringer, Falken und Tauben, in Hsia/Scribner (1997), 219–61.
278 Howard S. Becker, *Outsiders*, New York 1963, 147–63, esp. 148.
279 Milton Rokeach, *The Open and the Closed Mind*, New York 1960.
280 Alfred Soman, Les procès de sorcellerie au Parlement de Paris, in *AESC*, 32 (1977), 790–812.
281 Hansen (1901), 528.
282 Behringer (1997), 148.
283 Giuliana Zanelli, *Streghe e societa nell'Emilia e Romagna*, Ravenna 1992.

Chapter 5   Outlawing Witchcraft Persecution in Europe

1 Richard H. Popkin, *The History of Scepticism*, Assen 1960, 1–67.
2 Georg Luck, *Magie und andere Geheimlehren der Antike*, Munich 1990, vols 6–7, 27, 42.
3 Regino von Prüm, *Libri duo de synodalibus causis*, II, cap. 371 (see ch. 1).
4 Carlo Ginzburg, The Philosopher and the Witches, in Klaniczay/Pócs (1994), 283–93.
5 Nicolai Cusae *Cardinalis Opera*, II, Paris 1514, fol. 170 verso–172 recto.
6 Samuel de Cassinis, *De Lamiis, Quas Strigas Vocant*, Milan 1505; Hansen (1901), 262–72.
7 Niccolò Machiavelli, *Il Principe* (1513), 1532.
8 Niccolò Machiavelli, *Discorsi*, 1532.
9 Pietro Pomponazzi, *De immortalitate animae* (1516), Rome 1925.
10 Gerhard Schneider, *Der Libertin*, Stuttgart 1970.
11 Erasmus of Rotterdam, *Praise of Folly* (1515), London 1971, 122–5.
12 Richard H. Popkin, *The History of Scepticism*, Assen 1960, 5ff.
13 Gary K. Waite, *Heresy, Magic and Witchcraft in Early Modern Europe*, London 2003.
14 Andrea Alciati, *De lamiis seu strigibus* (1515), in Hansen (1901), 310–12.
15 Agrippa of Nettesheim, *De incertitudine et vanitate scientarum* (1526), Cologne 1544, ch. 46.
16 Decker (2003), 55–66.
17 Maria Tausiet, *Ponzonia en los Ojos*, Zaragoza 2000.
18 Florencio Idoate, *La Brujería en Navarra y sus documentos*, Pamplona 1967.
19 Julio Caro Baroja, *The World of the Witches*, London 1964, 143–55.
20 Henry Kamen, Spain, in *GEW* (2004).
21 Friedrich Merzbacher, Schwarzenberg, in *Fränkische Lebensbilder*, 4 (1971), 173–85.

22   Christina Larner, *Witchcraft and Religion*, Oxford 1984.
23   Johann Weyer, *De Praestigiis Daemonum*, Basel 1563, preface.
24   Hans de Waardt, paper given at the conference 'Witchcraft in Context', York 2002.
25   Perez Zagorin, *Ways of Lying*, Cambridge/Mass. 1990.
26   Jean Bodin, *Démonomanie*, Paris 1580, preface, and book 5.
27   Johann Weyer, *On Witchcraft* (1566/1583), Asheville/NC 1998, 268.
28   H. C. Erik Midelfort, *A History of Madness*, Stanford/Calif. 1999.
29   Johann Weyer, *On Witchcraft*, Asheville/NC 1998, xli–xliii.
30   Reginald Scot, *The Discoverie of Witchcraft*, London 1584.
31   Michel de Montaigne, *Essais*, Paris 1588, lib. 3, cap. 11.
32   [Herman Witekind], *Christlich Bedencken und Erinnerung von Zauberey*, Heidelberg 1585.
33   Schmidt (2000), 206ff.
34   Clark (1997), 326, 562ff.
35   [Anton Praetorius], *Gründlicher Bericht von Zauberey und Zauberern*, Lich 1598.
36   Schmidt (2000), 205–41 (Witekind), 296–311 (Praetorius).
37   Midelfort (1972), 30–66.
38   Behringer (1997), 214ff.
39   Martin Delrio, *Disquisitionum magicarum libri sex*, Louvain 1599/1600.
40   Johann Georg Goedelmann, *Tractatus de magis, veneficis et lamiis*, Nuremberg 1584.
41   *Was von gräulichen Folterungen und Hexenbrennen zu halten ist*, s.l. 1608.
42   Johann Greve, *Tribunal reformatum*, Hamburg 1624.
43   [Cornelius Pleier], *Malleus Judicum*, s.l. 1628.
44   Clark (1997), 211ff.
45   Adam Tanner SJ, *Theologia scholastica*, 4 vols, Ingolstadt 1626/1627, vol. 3, col. 981–1022.
46   Adam Tanner SJ, *Tractatus theologicus de processu adversus crimina excepta*, Cologne 1629.
47   Friedrich Spee, *Cautio Criminalis*, Rinteln 1631.
48   Robert Bireley, The Thirty Years' War as Germany's Religious War, in Repgen (1988), 85–106.
49   Konrad Repgen (ed.), *Krieg und Politik, 1618–1848*, Munich 1988.
50   Jacob Gretser, *De festis christianorum*, Ingolstadt 1612, preface.
51   Johann Georg Goedelmann, *Tractatus de magis, veneficis, et lamiis*, Nuremberg 1584.
52   Johann Georg Goedelmann, *Von Zauberern und Unholden*, Frankfurt/Main 1592.
53   Michael Kunze, *Highroad to the Stake*, Chicago 1987.
54   Martin Delrio SJ, *Disquisitionum Magicarum libri sex*, Mainz 1603.
55   Behringer (1997), 239–69.
56   Adam Tanner SJ, *Theologia Scholastica*, vol. 3, Ingolstadt 1627, col. 1005.
57   Behringer (1997), 244ff.
58   Britta Gehm, *Die Hexenverfolgungen des Hochstifts Bamberg*, Hildesheim 2000, 149–61.
59   Adam Tanner SJ, *Theologia Scholastica*, vol. 3, Ingolstadt 1627, col. 981.
60   Ibid., col. 981–1022.

61 Perez Zagorin, *Ways of Lying*, Cambridge/Mass. 1990.
62 [Friedrich Spee], *Cautio Criminalis*, Rinteln 1631.
63 Gunther Franz (ed.), *Friedrich Spee*, Trier 1991.
64 Johann Matthäus Meyfahrt, *Christliche Erinnerung*, Schleusingen 1635.
65 Schmidt (2000), 140–3.
66 Decker (2003), 93–107.
67 Alfred Soman, Decriminalizing Witchcraft, in *CJH*, 10 (1989), 11.
68 Gustav Henningsen, *The Witches' Advocate*, Reno/Nevada 1980; see ch. 4.
69 Jaime Contreras/Gustav Henningsen, Forty-four Thousand Cases, in Henningsen/Tedeschi (1986), 100–29.
70 Hans de Waardt, Rechtssicherheit, in Lorenz/Bauer (1995), 129–52.
71 Marijke Gijswijit-Hofstra/Willem Frijhoff (eds), *Witchcraft in the Netherlands*, Rotterdam 1991.
72 Jan van Heemskerk, *Batavische Arcadia*, Amsterdam 1639.
73 Alfred Soman, The Parlement of Paris and the Great Witch Hunt, in *SCJ*, 9 (1978), 31–44.
74 Gabriel Naudé, *Apologie pour les grands Hommes*, Paris 1625.
75 Frances Amelia Yates, *The Rosicrucian Enlightenment*, London 1972.
76 Richard Popkin, *History of Scepticism*, Assen 1960, 100–8.
77 Paolo Rossi, *Francis Bacon. From Magic to Science*, London 1968.
78 Richard Popkin, *History of Scepticism*, Assen 1960, 185.
79 Behringer (2001), 403.
80 Berthold Sutter, *Der Hexenprozeß gegen Katharina Kepler*, Weil der Stadt 1979.
81 Pierre Bayle, Response (1703), in Kors/Peters (1972), 360–8.
82 Paul Hazard, *La Crise de la Conscience Européenne*, 3 vols, Paris 1935.
83 Thomas Hobbes, *Leviathan*, London 1651, chs 44–7.
84 Henry More, *An Antidote against Atheisme*, London 1653.
85 Joseph Glanvill, *Some Philosopical Considerations*, London 1665.
86 Sharpe (2001), 75.
87 Joseph Glanvill, *A Blow at Modern Sadducism*, London 1668.
88 John Wagstaffe, *The Question of Witchcraft Debated*, London 1669.
89 John Webster, *The Displaying of Supposed Witchcraft*, London 1677, 36.
90 F[rancis] B[ragge], *Witchcraft Farther Display'd*, London 1712.
91 Bostridge (1997), 135.
92 Francis Hutchinson, *An Historical Essay Concerning Witchcraft*, London 1718, 130.
93 Sharpe (2001), 87.
94 Bostridge (1997), 184–95.
95 John Wesley, *The Journal*, 8 vols, ed. N. Curnock, London 1909–16.
96 Joseph Juxon, *A Sermon upon Witchcraft*, London 1736.
97 Davies (1999), 86–100.
98 *The Times*, 24 September 1863.
99 Balthasar Bekker, *De betoverde Weereld*, 4 vols, Amsterdam 1691–3.
100 Christian Thomasius, *De crimine magiae*, Halle 1701.
101 Johann Reiche (ed.), *Unterschiedliche Schrifften von Unfug des Hexen-Processes*, Halle 1703.
102 Christian Thomasius, *De origine processus inquisitorii contra sagas*, Halle 1712.

103   Heinrich Kaak, Brandenburg, in *GEW* (2004).
104   Bostridge (1997), 21–37.
105   Ibid., 205–31.
106   Kurt Baschwitz, *Hexen und Hexenprozesse*, Munich 1963, 327.
107   Hansen (1900), 532.
108   Behringer (1997), 344–54.
109   Petr Kreuz, Slovakia, in *GEW* (2004).
110   Petr Kreuz, Moravia, in *GEW* (2004).
111   Matevz Kosir, Slovenia, in *GEW* (2004).
112   W. Gregory Monahan, *Year of Sorrows*, Columbus/Ohio 1993.
113   Gabor Klaniczay, Hungary, in Ankarloo/Henningsen (1990), 219–56.
114   Karen Lambrecht, *Hexenverfolgung*, Cologne 1995, 515.
115   Brian Levack, Witch Hunts, Decline, in *GEW* (2004).
116   Wolfgang Behringer, *Hexen*, Munich 2002, 85ff.
117   Ibid.
118   Girolamo Tartaroti, *Del congresso notturno delle lammie*, Rovereto 1749.
119   Scipione Maffei, *L'arte magica distrutta*, Trient 1750.
120   Jordan Simon, *Das große weltbetrügende Nichts*, s.l. 1762.
121   Wolfgang Behringer, Der 'Bayerische Hexenkrieg', in Lorenz/Bauer (1995), 287–314.
122   Emanuel Swedenborg, *Arcana Coelestia*, 8 vols, London 1749–56.
123   Immanuel Kant, *Träume eines Geistersehers*, Königsberg 1766.
124   Bostridge (1997), 196–201.
125   Max Weber, *The Protestant Ethic and the Spirit of Capitalism* (1904/1905), London 1985.
126   Davies (1999), 278–93.

Chapter 6   Witch-Hunting in the Nineteenth and Twentieth Centuries

1   Audrey Richards, A Modern Movement of Witchfinders, in *Africa*, 8 (1935), 448–61.
2   Eric Wolf, *Europe and the People without History*, Berkeley/Calif. 1982.
3   Stephen Ellis, Witch-Hunting in Central Madagascar, 1828–1861, in *PP*, 175 (2002), 90–123.
4   Esther Goody, Legitimate and Illegitimate Aggression, in Douglas (1970), 207–43.
5   Mair (1969), 140ff.
6   Parrinder (1958), 125.
7   Edwin Ardener, Witchcraft, in Douglas (1970), 141–60, esp. 145.
8   Ronald Hutton, The Global Context, in Goodare (2002), 22ff.
9   Iliffe (1995), 208ff.
10   R. L. Cope, Written in Characters of Blood? in *JAH*, 36 (1995), 247–69.
11   Iliffe (1995), 62–127.
12   Anthony F. Wallace, Revitalization Movements, in *AA*, 58 (1956), 264–81.
13   Vittorio Lanternari, *The Religions of the Oppressed*, London 1963, 114–23.

14   Anthony F. Wallace, Origins of the Longhouse Religion, in *HNAI*, vol. 15 (1978), 442–8.
15   Wilson (1973), 221–36.
16   David Silverman, Native American Witchcraft, in *GEW* (2004).
17   David R. Edmunds, *The Shawnee Prophet*, Lincoln/Nebraska 1983.
18   Wilson (1973), 229–36.
19   Gregory Evans Dowd, *A Spirited Resistance*, Baltimore 1992.
20   Lucy P. Mair, Independent Religious Movements, in *CSSH*, 1 (1958/59), 113–36.
21   Clark (1997), 378.
22   M. Adas, *Prophets of Rebellion*, Chapel Hill 1979, 102–5.
23   Wilson (1973), 152–6.
24   Parrinder (1958), 168–71.
25   Wilson (1973), 83ff.
26   Roy G. Willis, Instant Millennium, in Douglas (1970), 129–39.
27   Audrey Richards, A Modern Movement of Witchfinders, in *Africa*, 8 (1935), 448–61.
28   Cynthia Brantley, Giriama and Witchcraft Control, in *Africa*, 49 (1979), 112–33.
29   Wilson (1973), 86–9.
30   Max Marwick, Another Modern Anti-Witchcraft Movement, in *Africa*, 20 (1950), 100–12.
31   Alison Redmayne, Chikanga, in Douglas (1970), 103–28.
32   A. Lee, Ngoja and Six Theories of Witchcraft Eradication, in *Ufahamu*, 6 (1976), 101–17.
33   Roy G. Willis, Kamcape, in *Africa*, 38 (1968), 1–15.
34   Roy G. Willis, Instant Millennium, in Douglas (1970), 132.
35   Nathan Wachtel, *Gods and Vampires*, Chicago 1994, 78ff.
36   Andrew Apter, Atinga Revisited, in Comaroff/Comaroff (1993), 111–28.
37   Wilson (1973), 86ff.
38   Jan Vansina, The Bushong Poison Ordeal, in Douglas/Kaberry (1969), 246.
39   Inge Brinkman, Ways of Death, in *Africa*, 70 (2000), 15.
40   Linda M. Heywood, Modern Political Ideology in Africa, in *JMAS*, 36 (1998), 151.
41   David Lan, *Guns and Rain*, London 1985, 167ff.
42   Mugabe Resorts to Witchcraft, in *www.Africawoman.net/politics/ Mugabewitchcraft.html* (24 July 2002).
43   Rijk van Dijk, La guérisseuse du docteur Banda, in *Politique Africaine*, 52 (1992), 145–50.
44   Parrinder (1958), 149–55.
45   Ray Abrahams, *Vigilant Citizens*, Cambridge 1998.
46   Iliffe (1995), 246–70.
47   Elizabeth Colson, The Father as Witch, in *Africa*, 70 (2000), 333–58.
48   Diane Ciekawy/Peter Geschiere, Containing Witchcraft, in *ASR*, 41 (1998), 5.
49   Simeon Mesaki, Witch-Killing in Sukumaland, in Abrahams (1994), 47–60.
50   Ruth F. Hoffmann, Amnestie für Hexenmörder, in *Die Zeit* (2000).
51   Joanna Ball, *The Ritual of the Necklace*, Johannesburg 1994.

52   Ralushai Report (1996), 31ff.
53   Niehaus et al., *Witchcraft* (2001), 210.
54   Rulashai Report (1996), 121–267.
55   Ibid., 57.
56   Ibid., 268.
57   Ruth F. Hoffmann, Amnestie für Hexenmörder, in *Die Zeit* (2000).
58   Ralushai Report (1996), 15.
59   Ibid., 62.
60   C. W. Watson/Roy Ellen (eds), *Understanding Witchcraft in Southeast Asia*, Honolulu 1993.
61   Mark Auslander, Open the Wombs!, in Comaroff/Comaroff (1993), 191.
62   Jani Farrell Roberts (2002), after Africa News Service 1997, and Reuters 1998.
63   Sohaila Kapur, *Witchcraft in Western India*, Hyderabad 1983.
64   Ronald Hutton, The Global Context, in Goodare (2002), 22ff.
65   *The Times*, 2 Aug. 1861, p. 9.
66   Ibid., 22 Dec. 1865, p. 9.
67   Melford E. Spiro, *Burmese Supernaturalism*, Englewood Cliffs 1967, 29–32.
68   Arthur M. Hocart, Witchcraft in Eddystone of the Solomons, in *JRAI*, 55 (1925), 230.
69   Hermann Slaats/Karen Portier, Law in Modern Indonesia, in Watson/Ellen (1993), 135–48.
70   Jani Farrell Roberts, *The Seven Days of My Creation*, London 2002 (website).
71   Manning Nash, Witchcraft as Social Process, in *America Indígena*, 20 (1961), 121–6.
72   June Nash, Death as a Way of Life, in *AA*, 69 (1967), 455–70.
73   *Newsweek*, 25 May 1981, quoted from Levack (1987), 229.
74   Mark Münzel, *Jibaro-Indianer in Südamerika*, Frankfurt 1977.
75   Nathan Wachtel, *Gods and Vampires*, Chicago 1994, 53ff.
76   Ibid., 83–6.
77   Deward E. Walker/Carrasco (eds), *Witchcraft of the American Native Peoples*, Moscow/Id. 1989.
78   *The Times*, 17 April 1860, p. 12.
79   *The New York Tribune*, quoted in *The Times*, 17 April 1860, p. 12.
80   *The Times*, 22 June 1854.
81   Clyde Kluckhohn, *Navaho Witchcraft*, Boston 1944, 120.
82   Richard van Valkenburgh, *A Short History of the Navaho People*, Window Rock 1938, 47, 232.
83   Fred Eggan/T. N. Pandey, Zuni History, 1850–1970, in *HNAI*, vol. 9 (1979), 474–81.
84   Clyde Kluckhohn, *Navaho Witchcraft*, Boston 1944, 241.
85   Ibid., 196, and many examples pp. 193–8.
86   J. C. Morgan, Navaho Witchcraft, in Kluckhohn (1944), 252–4.
87   Eugene Y. Arima, Caribou Eskimo, in *HNAI*, vol. 5, Washington 1984, 455.
88   Bernard Saladin d'Anglure, Inuit of Quebec, in *HNAI*, vol. 5, Washington 1984, 504.

89　Trpimir Vedris, Balkans, in *GEW* (2004).
90　Stephen P. Frank, Popular Justice, 1870–1900, in *RR*, 46 (1987), 240, 261–4.
91　Christiane D. Worobec, Witchcraft, in *RR*, 54 (1995), 167.
92　Russell Zguta, The Ordeal by Water, in *Slavic Review*, 36 (1977), 225, 228ff.
93　*International Herald Tribune*, 7 April 1997, p. 2; Ryan (1999), 427.
94　Ibid., p. 111ff.
95　*The Times*, 24 September 1863.
96　Ibid. 41ff.
97　Gustav Henningsen, Die Fortsetzung der Hexenverfolgung, in Lorenz/Bauer (1995), 315–28.
98　Hans Sebald, *Witchcraft*, New York 1978, 223.
99　Levack (1987), 229.
100　Ray Abrahams, A Modern Witch-Hunt, in *Cambridge Anthropology*, 10 (1985), 32–45.
101　Cyprian F. Fisiy, *Palmtree Justice in the Bertoua Court of Appeal*, Leiden 1990.
102　Geschiere (1997), 171–4.
103　Ibid., 184ff.
104　Adam Ashforth, *Aids, Witchcraft and the Problem of Power*, 2001, 15.
105　Ralushai Report (1996), 270.
106　Wilson (1973), 94–100.
107　Bernhard Sundkler, *Bantu Prophets in South Africa*, London/New York 1961, 109, 238ff.
108　Isak Niehaus, *Witchcraft, Power and Politics*, London 2001.
109　Geschiere (1997), 205.
110　Alfred Soman, Decriminalizing Witchcraft, in *CJH*, 10 (1989), 17.

Chapter 7　Old and 'New Witches'

1　Howard S. Becker, *Outsiders*, New York 1963, 147–64.
2　Oscar di Simplicio, A Parting of Ways?, in Behringer/Sharpe (2004).
3　Gudrun Gersmann, *Wasserprobe und Prozeß*, Munich 1999.
4　Hans de Waardt, Oudewater, in *Westfälische Zeitschrift*, 144 (1994), 249–63.
5　Charles Zika, Fears of Flying, in *Australian Journal of Art*, 8 (1989/90), 19–47.
6　Linda Hults, Baldung and the Witches of Freiburg, in *JIH*, 18 (1987), 249–76.
7　Jane P. Davidson, *The Witch in Northern European Art, 1450–1750*, Freren 1987.
8　Francisco Goya, *El sueno de la razon produce monstruos*, Madrid 1797 (see table 12).
9　Jacob Grimm, *Teutonic Mythology*, trans. J. Stallybrass, London 1883.
10　Mircea Eliade, Some Observations, in *History of Religions*, 14 (1975), 149–72.
11　Jules Michelet, *La Sorcière*, Paris 1862.

12   Jörg Haustein, *Luthers Stellung*, Stuttgart 1990, 17–29.
13   Hansen (1900), vii.
14   Andrew Dickson White, *The Warfare of Science with Christendom*, New York 1913.
15   Ellic Howe, *The Magicians of the Golden Dawn*, London 1972.
16   Margaret Murray, *The Witch Cult in Western Europe*, Oxford 1921.
17   Margaret Murray, *The God of the Witches*, London 1931.
18   Gerald B. Gardner, *Witchcraft Today*, London 1954.
19   Doreen Valiente, *The Rebirth of Witchcraft*, Custer 1989.
20   James W. Baker, White Witches: Historic Fact and Romantic Fantasy, in Lewis (1996), 171–92.
21   Judy Harrow, The Contemporary Neo-Pagan Revival, in Lewis (1996), 9–24, 15.
22   Nicholas Goodrick-Clarke, *The Occult Roots of Nazism*, New York 1992.
23   Alfred Rosenberg, *Der Mythus des 20. Jahrhunderts*, Berlin 1930.
24   Mathilde Ludendorff, *Christliche Grausamkeit an Deutschen Frauen*, Munich 1934.
25   Friederike Müller-Reimerdes, *Der christliche Hexenwahn*, Leipzig 1935.
26   Barbara Ryan, Ideological Purity and Feminism, in *Gender and Society*, 3 (1989), 239–57.
27   Roland Hutton, *The Triumph of the Moon*, Oxford 1999, 341.
28   Charlene Spretnak (ed.), *The Politics of Women's Spirituality*, New York 1982.
29   Mary Daly, *Gyn/Ecology*, Boston 1978. 4th edn 1987, 178–222.
30   Merry Wiesner, *Witchcraft and Gender in Early Modern Europe*, Cambridge 1993, 218–38.
31   Diane Purkiss, *The Witch in History*, London 1996, 13–19.
32   Erika Wisselinck, *Hexen*, Munich 1986, 10ff.
33   Anja Malanowski/Anne-Bärbel Köhle, *Hexenkraft*, Munich 1996.
34   [Miriam Simos] Starhawk, *The Spiral Dance*, San Francisco 1979.
35   Rosemary Ruether, Goddesses and Witches, in *Christian Century* (1980), 843–4.
36   Shelley Rabinovitch, Categorizing Modern Neo-Pagan Witches, in Lewis (1996), 75–92.
37   Inge Schöck, *Hexenglaube in der Gegenwart*, Tübingen 1978.
38   Adrian Ivakhiv, The Resurgence of Magical Religion, in Lewis (1996), 237–68.
39   James W. Baker, White Witches, in Lewis (1996), 171–92.
40   Sabina Magliocco, Ritual is My Chosen Art Form, in Lewis (1996), 75–92.
41   Tanya M. Luhrmann, *Persuasions of the Witch's Craft*, Oxford 1989, 307–56.
42   Diane Ciekawy/Peter Geschiere, Containing Witchcraft, in *ASR*, 41 (1998), 2.
43   Helen A. Berger, *A Community of Witches*, Columbia/SC 1999.
44   Marcello Truzzi, The Occult Revival, in *Sociological Quarterly*, 13 (1972), 130–40.
45   Morris Berman, *The Reenchantment of the World*, Ithaca/NY 1981.

46 Mair (1969), 72–5.
47 dpa, London, 10 July 2002.; FAZ, 11 July 2002, p. 7.; the *Guardian*, 3 July 2003, p. 5.

Chapter 8   Epilogue

1 Ulrich Magin, *Von Ufos entführt*, Munich 1991.
2 Carol Zaleski, *Otherworld Journeys*, New York 1987.
3 Carl Gustav Jung, *Archetypes and the Collective Unconscious*, London 1968.
4 Mary Daly, *Gyn/Ecology*, Boston 1978.
5 Monica Wilson, Witch Beliefs and Social Structure, in *AJS*, 56 (1951), 313.
6 Max Marwick, Is Science a Form of Witchcraft?, in *New Scientist*, 63 (1974), 578–81.
7 William Monter, The Historiography of European Witchcraft, in *JIH*, 2 (1971/72), 435–53.
8 Diane Purkiss, *The Witch in History*, London 1996.
9 Jean Comaroff/John Comaroff (eds), *Modernity and Its Malcontents*, Chicago 1993.
10 Peter Geschiere, *The Modernity of Witchcraft*, Virginia University Press 1997.
11 Henrietta L. Moore/Todd Sanders, Introduction, in Moore/Sanders (2001), 14.
12 Shmuel N. Eisenstadt, Multiple Modernities, in *Daedalus*, 129 (2000), 1–29.
13 Adam Ashforth, *Aids, Witchcraft and the Problem of Power* (2001), 2.
14 Bond/Ciekawy (2001), Introduction, in Bond/Ciekawy (2001), 25.
15 James L. Brain, Witchcraft and Development, in *African Affairs*, 81 (1982), 371–84.
16 Immanuel Kant, *Beantwortung der Frage: Was ist Aufklärung?*, Berlin 1784.
17 William Shakespeare, *Julius Caesar* (1604), I, 2.

Bibliography

1 Dictionaries, Handbooks, Source Editions

Aarne, Antti/Thompson, Stith, *The Types of the Folktale*, 2nd edn, Helsinki 1964.

Ankarloo, Bengt/Clark, Stuart (eds), *The Athlone History of Witchcraft and Magic in Europe* (= *AHWME*), 6 vols, London 1999–2002.

Bächtold-Stäubli, Hanns (ed.), *Handwörterbuch des Deutschen Aberglaubens*, 10 vols, 1927–42.

Behringer, Wolfgang (ed.), *Hexen und Hexenprozesse in Deutschland*, 5th edn Munich 2001.

Boyer, Paul/Nissenbaum, Stephen (eds), *Salem Witchcraft Papers*, 1978.

Brady, Thomas A./Oberman, Heiko A./Tracy, James D. (eds), *Handbook of European History 1400–1600. Late Middle Ages, Renaissance and Reformation*, 2 vols, Leiden 1994.

Burr, George Lincoln (ed.), *Narratives of the Witchcraft Cases, 1648–1706*, New York 1914.

Corbin, Peter/Sedge, Douglas (eds), *Three Jacobean Witchcraft Plays: The Tragedy of Sophonisba [1606]. The Witch [1620]. The Witch of Edmonton [1621]*, Manchester 1986.

Eliade, Mircea (ed.), *The Encyclopedia of Religion*, 16 vols, New York 1987.

Gibson, Marion (ed.), *Early Modern Witches. Witchcraft Cases in Contemporary Writing*, London 2000.

Golden, Richard M. (ed.), *Encyclopedia of Witchcraft. The Western Tradition* (= *GEW*), 4 vols, Austin/Texas 2004.

Hall, David D. (ed.), *Witch-Hunting in Seventeenth-Century New England. A Documentary History, 1638–1693*, Northeastern University Press 1999.

Hansen, Joseph (ed.), *Quellen und Untersuchungen zur Geschichte des Hexenwahns und der Hexenverfolgung im Mittelalter*, Bonn 1901.

Hillerbrand, Hans J. (ed.), *The Oxford Encyclopedia of the Reformation*, 4 vols, Oxford 1996.

Köbler, Gerhard, *Historisches Handbuch der deutschen Länder*, Munich 1995.

Köbler, Gerhard, *Lexikon der Europäischen Rechtsgeschichte*, Munich 1997.

Kors, Alan Charles/Peters, Edward (eds), *Witchcraft in Europe, 400–1700. A Documentary History*, 2nd edn, rev. by Edward Peters, Philadelphia 1972; 2001.

Kuper, Adam/Kuper, Jessica (eds), *The Social Science Encyclopedia*, London 1985.

Lea, Henry Charles, *Materials toward a History of Witchcraft*, 3 vols, Philadelphia 1939; repr. New York 1957.

Luck, Georg, *Magie und andere Geheimlehren der Antike. Mit 112 neu übersetzten und einzeln kommentierten Quellentexten*, Munich 1990.

de Martino, Ernesto (ed.), *Magia e civiltà. Un antologia critica fondamentale per lo studio del concetto di magia nella civiltà occidentale*, Mailand 1962.

Maxwell-Stuart, Peter George (ed.), *The Occult in Early Modern Europe. A Documentary History*, London 1999.

Monter, William (ed.), *European Witchcraft*, New York 1969.

Normand, Lawrence/Roberts, Gareth, *Witchcraft in Early Modern Scotland. James VI's 'Demonology' and the North Berwick Witches*, Exeter 2000.

Oliver, R./Fage, J. D. (eds), *The Cambridge History of Africa*, 8 vols, Cambridge 1975–86.

Ostorero, Martine/Bagliani, Agostino Parvicini/Tremp, Kathrin Utz/Chène, Catherine (eds), *L'Imaginaire du Sabbat. Édition critique des textes les plus anciens*, Lausanne 1999.

Rabinovitch, Shelley/Lewis, James (eds), *The Encyclopedia of Modern Witchcraft and Neo-Paganism*, New York 2002.

Robbins, Harold, *Encyclopedia of Witchcraft and Demonology*, New York 1959.

Senn, Matthias (ed.), *Die Wickiana. Johann Jacob Wicks Nachrichtensammlung aus dem 16. Jahrhundert*, Zurich 1975.

Sharpe, James, *Witchcraft in Early Modern England*, London 2001.

Sharpe, James (ed.), *English Witchcraft, 1560–1730*, 6 vols, London 2003.

Sills, David Lawrence (ed.), *International Encyclopedia of the Social Sciences* (= *IESS*), 18 vols, repr. New York 1968–79.

Sturtevant, William C. (ed.), *Handbook of North American Indians* (= *HNAI*), 20 vols, Washington 1978.

Thompson, Stith, *Motif-Index of Folk-Literature*, 6 vols, Copenhagen 1955–8.

Thorndike, Lynn, *History of Magic and Experimental Science*, 8 vols, New York 1923–58.

Wakefield, Walter L./Evans, Austin P. (eds), *Heresies of the High Middle Ages. Selected Sources*, translated and annotated, New York 1969.

Zedler, Johann Heinrich (ed.), *Großes vollständiges Universal-Lexicon aller Wissenschaften und Künste*, 64 vols, Halle/Leipzig 1732–54.

2 Demonologies and Literature before 1800

Abermaliger Justizmord in der Schweiz, in August Ludwig Schlözer (ed.), *Stats-Anzeigen*, vol. 2 (1783), 273–7.

de Acosta, José, *Historia Natural e Moral de las Indias*, Seville 1590.

Ady, Thomas, *A Candle in the Dark, or, a Treatise Concerning the Nature of Witches*, London 1656.

Agobard of Lyon, *Contra Insulsam Vulgi Opinionem de Grandine et Tonitruis*, in *Patrologia Latina 104*, col. 147–58.

Agricola, Franciscus, *Gründtlicher Bericht, Ob Zauberey die argste und grewlichste sünd auff Erden sey*, Cologne 1597.

Agrippa of Nettesheim, Henricus Cornelius, *De Occulta Philosophia*, Antwerp 1531.

Agrippa of Nettesheim, Henricus Cornelius, *De Incertitudine et Vanitate Scientarum* [1526], Cologne 1544.

Alber, Matthäus/Bidembach, Wilhelm, *Ein Summa etlicher Predigen vom Hagel und Unholden, gethon in der Pfarrkirch zuo Stuotgarten im Monat Augusto Anno CLXII [. . .] sehr nützlich und tröstlich zuo diser Zeit zuo lesen*, Tübingen 1562.

Albrecht, Bernhard, *Magia, das ist: christenlicher Bericht von Zauberey und Hexerey*, Augsburg 1628.

Alciati, Andrea, *De Lamiis seu Strigibus* [1515], in *Parergon Juris* [1530], lib. 8, cap. 22, in *Opera*, Bd. IV, Basel 1582, lib. 8, cap. 22, col. 498, reprinted in Hansen (1901), 310–12.

Anhorn, Bartholomäus, *Magiologia Das ist: Christlicher Bericht Von dem Aberglauben und Zauberey. Der Welt/ohne einige Passion der Religionen/ fürgestellt*, Basel 1675.

Aquinas, Thomas (St), *Quaestiones Disputatae de Malo* (c.1270), in *Opera Omnia*, vol. 15, Parma 1855.

Aquinas, Thomas (St), *Summa contra Gentiles*, in A. C. Pegis (ed.), *The Basic Writings of Saint Thomas Aquinas*, 2 vols, New York 1945, II, 3–224.

Aquinas, Thomas (St), *Summa Theologiae* (c.1270), London 1964–6.

Augustine (St), *De Doctrina Christiana*, in *PL*, 34.

Augustine (St), *The City of God*, London 1968.

Bacon, Francis, *The Essays* (1597, 1612, 1625), ed. John Pitcher, Harmondsworth 1985.

Bacon, Francis, *Novum Organon*, London 1620.

Baxter, Richard, *The Certainty of the World of Spirits. Fully Evinced by the Unquestionable Histories of Apparitions, Witchcraft, Voices, etc.* London 1691.

Bekker, Balthasar, *De Betoverde Weereld*, 4 vols, Amsterdam 1691–3; *Die Bezauberte Welt*, 4 vols, Amsterdam 1693; *Le monde enchanté*, Amsterdam 1694; *The World Bewitched*, London 1695.

de Bergerac, Cyrano, Lettre contre les sorciers [1654], in Frederic Lachevre (ed.), *Les Oeuvres Libertines de Cyrano de Bergerac*, vol. 2, Paris 1912, 211–18 [Monter (1969), 113–20].

Bernard, Richard, *A Guide to Grande-Iury Men*, London 1627.

Bernardino da Siena (St), *Prediche Volgare sul Campo di Siena*, 2 vols, Milan 1989.

Bernardo da Como, see: Rategno.

Bernardo Gui, *Practica Inquisitionis Haereticae Pravitatis* [1324]; Part V, *Description of Heresies*, in Wakefield/Evans (1969), 375–445.

Bernardo Gui, *Interrogatoria ad Sortilegos et Divinos et Invocatores Demonum* (1315), in Hansen (1901), 47–8.

Binsfeld, Peter, *Tractatus de Confessionibus Maleficorum et Sagarum*, Trier 1589; Trier 1591; Trier 1596; 4th Latin edn Cologne 1623; *Tractat von Bekanntnuß der Zauberer und Hexen*, trans. Bernhard Vogel, Munich 1591; Munich 1592.

Bodin, Jean, *De la Démonomanie des Sorciers*, Paris 1580. *De Magorum Daemonomania libri IV*, Basel 1581. *Vom Außgelasenen wüttigen Teuffelsheer*, trans. by Johann Fischart, Strasbourg 1591. *On the Demon-Mania of Witches*, trans. R. A. Scott, ed. by Jonathan Pearl, Toronto 1995.

Boguet, Henry, *Discours execrable des Sorciers*, Lyons 1602; *An Examen of Witches*, trans. by E. A. Ashwin, ed. by Montague Summers, London 1929.

Boulton, Richard, *The Possibility and Reality of Magick, Sorcery, and Witch-craft, Demonstrated. Or, a Vindication of a Complete History of Magick, Sorcery and Witchcraft. In Answer to Dr. Hutchinson's Historical Essay*, 2 vols, London 1722 (ed. Sharpe 2003, vol. 6).

B[ragge], F[rancis], *Witchcraft Farther Display'd*, London 1712.

Brenz, Johannes, *Homilia de Grandine*, in: *Pericopiae Evangeliorum quae Usitato More in Praecipius Festis Legi Solent*, Frankfurt 1557. *Ein Predig von dem Hagel und Ungewitter*, in: *Evangelien der fürnembsten Fest- und Feyertagen [. . .]*, Frankfurt 1558; *Predigt vom Hagel, Donner und allem Ungewitter*, 1564.

Brenz, Johannes, *Sermon von Hagel und Ungewitter*, Stuttgart, 1562.

Bruno, Giordano, *De Magia*, in *Opera Latine Conscripta*, 4 vols, ed. F. Fiorentino, Naples 1879–91, vol. 3, 395–454.

Bullinger, Heinrich, Von Hexen und Unholden. Wider die schwartzen Künst, aberglaubig segnens, unwarhafftigs Warsagen und andere dergleichen von Gott verbottne Künst [1571], in *Theatrum de Veneficis*, Frankfurt 1586, 298–306.

Burchard von Worms, *Decretorum Libri Viginti*, in *PL*, 140, Paris 1880, col. 491–1090.

Burton, Richard, *The Anatomy of Melancholy*, 3 vols, Oxford 1628.

Cardano, Girolamo, *De Rerum Varietate*, Basel 1557.

Cardano, Girolamo, *Opera Omnia*, 10 vols, Lyon 1663.

[Carmichael, James], *News from Scotland, Declaring the Damable Life and Death of Doctor Fian, a Notable Sorcerer, who was Burned at Edinburgh in January Last, 1591* (Edinburgh 1591), in Normand/Roberts (2000), 309–26.

Casaubon, Meric, *Of Credulity, and Incredulity of Things, Natural, Civil, and Divine*, London 1682.

de Cassinis, Samuel, *De Lamiis, Quas Strigas Vocant*, Milan 1505; repr. in Hansen (1901), 262–73.

Celichius, Andreas, *Notwendige Erinnerung von des Sathans letztem Zorn-sturm*, Wittenberg 1594.

Compendium Maleficarum, see: Guazzo.

Contzen SJ, Adam, *Methodus Civilis Doctrina, seu Abissini Regis Historia*, Cologne 1628.

Cooper, Thomas, *The Mystery of Witchcraft*, London 1617.

Cotta, John, *Triall of Witch-craft*, London 1616.

Cusae, Nicolai, *Cardinalis Opera*, II, Paris 1514.

Daneau, Lambert, *Les Sorciers. Dialogue tres-utile et necessaire pour ce temps: auquel ce qui se dispute auiourdhui des Sorciers & Eriges, est traité bien amplement & resolu*, Geneva 1574; *A Dialogue of Witches*, London 1575.

Delrio, Martin, *Disquisitionum Magicarum Libri Sex*, Louvain 1599/1600; 3rd edn Mainz 1603 (partly trans.: *Investigations into Magic*, trans. and ed. by Peter George Maxwell-Stuart, New York 2000).

Ein erschröckliche Geschicht/so zu Derneburg [Derenburg] in der Graffschaft Reinsteyn [Regenstein]/am Harz gelegen/von dreyen Zauberin und zwayen Mannen/In ettlichen Tagen deß Monats Octobris Im 1555. Jare ergangen [. . .], Nuremberg (Jörg Merckel), 1555.

Ellinger, Johann, *Hexen Coppel*, Frankfurt/Main 1629.

Erasmus, Desiderius, *Praise of Folly* [1515], trans. by Betty Radice, Penguin Books, London 1971.

Erastus, Thomas, *Disputatio de Lamiis seu Strigibus. De Strigibus Liber*, Basel 1572; *Repetitio de Lamiis seu Strigibus; in qua Plene, Solide et Persique de Arte, Potentate Itemque Poena Disceptatur*, Basel 1577; *Deux dialogues touchant le pouvoir des sorciers et de la punition qu'elles meritent*, in *Histoires, disputes et discours des illusions et impostures des diables*, Geneva 1579.

Ewich, Johann, *De Sagarum [. . .] Natura*, Bremen 1584; repr. in *Theatrum de Veneficis*, Frankfurt/Main 1586, 325–55.

Eymericus, Nicolaus, *Directorium Inquisitorum* (MS Avignon 1376), Avignon 1503.

Fairfax, Edward, *Daemonologia: A Discourse on Witchcraft, as it was Acted in the Family of Mr. Edward Fairfax, in the County of York, in the Year 1621*, Harrogate 1882.

Ficino, Marsilio, *De Theologia Platonica*, Florence 1482.

Filmer, Robert, *An Advertisement to the Jurymen of England Touching Witches*, London 1653.

Fludd, Robert, *Utriusque Cosmi Historia*, London 1617.

Förner, Friedrich, *Panoplia Armaturae Dei, Adversus Omnem Superstitionem, Divinationem, Excantationem, Daemonolatriam, et Universas Magorum, Veneficorum & Sagarum*, Ingolstadt 1625.

Le Franc, Martin, *Le Champion des Dames*, 3 vols, Paris 1530, in Hansen (1900; 1901).

Freudius, Michael, *Gewissens-Fragen von Processen wider die Hexen, insonderheit denen Richtern hochnöthig zu wissen*, Güstrow 1667.

Frisius, Paulus, *Des Teuffels Nebelkappen*, Frankfurt/Main 1583.

Gaule, John, *Select Cases of Conscience Touching Witches and Witchcrafts*, London 1646.

Geiler von Kaisersberg, Johann, *Die Emeis. Dies ist das Buch von der Omeissen*, Strasbourg 1516.

Gifford, George, *A Discourse of the Subtill Practises of Devilles by Witches and Sorcerers*, London 1587.

Gifford, George, *A Dialogue Concerning Witches and Witchcraftes*, London 1593.

Glanvill, Joseph, *Some Philosophical Considerations Touching the Being of Witches and Witchcraft*, London 1665.

Glanvill, Joseph, *A Blow at Modern Sadducism*, London 1668.

Glanvill, Joseph, *Sadducismus Triumphatus, or Full and Plain Evidence Concerning Witches and Apparitions*, London 1681; 3rd edn 1689.

Goedelmann, Johann Georg, *Tractatus de Magis, Veneficis et Lamiis, Recte Cognoscendis et Puniendis*, Nuremberg 1584; Frankfurt/Main 1591.

Goedelmann, Johann Georg, *Von Zauberern und Unholden Warhafftiger und wolgegründter Bericht*, Frankfurt/Main 1592.

Graeter, Jacob, *Hexen oder Unholden Predigten*, Tübingen 1589.

Graminaeus, Dietrich, *Inductio sive Directorium*, Cologne 1594.

Gregory of Tours, *The History of the Francs*, trans. L. Thorpe, New York 1974.

Gregory of Valencia SJ, *Commentariorum Theologicorum Tomi Quatuor*, Ingolstadt 1591–7.

Greve, Johann, *Tribunal Reformatum*, Hamburg 1624.

Grillandus, Paulus, *Tractatus de Hereticis et Sortilegiis* (1525), Lyon 1536.

Guazzo, Francesco Maria, *Compendium Maleficarum*, Milan 1608, trans. E. A. Ashwin, ed. Montague Summers, London 1929.

Hemmingsen, Nils, *Admonitio de Superstitionibus Magicis Vitandis*, Copenhagen 1575.

Herodotus, *The Histories*, new edn, trans. Aubrey de Sélincourt, rev. by John Marincola, Harmondsworth 1972.

Heywood, Thomas/Broome, Richard, *The Late Lancashire Witches*, London 1634 (ed. Laird H. Barber, New York/London 1979).

Hobbes, Thomas, *Leviathan*, London 1651.

Holland, Henry, *A Treatise against Witchcraft, or, a Dialogue, wherein the Greatest Doubts Concerning that Sinne, are Briefly Answered*, Cambridge 1590 (Sharpe 2003, vol. 1).

van Hoogstraaten, Jacob, *Tractatus Magistralis Declarans quam Graviter Peccent Querentes Auxilium a Maleficis*, Cologne 1510.

Hopkins, Mathew, *The Discoverie of Witches*, London 1647 (ed. Sharpe 2003, vol. 3).

Hutchinson, Francis, *An Historical Essay Concerning Witchcraft*, London 1718 (ed. Sharpe 2003, vol. 6).

Jacquier, Nicolas, *Flagellum Haereticorum Fascinariorum*, Frankfurt/Main 1581.

James VI of Scotland, *Daemonologie, in Forme of a Dialogue*, Edinburgh 1597 (repr. in Normand/Roberts (2000), 327–426).

Jordanaeus, Johannes, *Disputatio Brevis et Categorica de Proba Stigmatica Utrum Scilicet et Licita sit, necne*, Cologne s.d. (1630).

Juxon, Joseph, *A Sermon upon Witchcraft, Occasion'd by a Late Illegal Attempt to Discover Witches by Swimming*, London 1736.

Kant, Immanuel, *Träume eines Geistersehers, erläutert durch Träume der Metaphysik*, Königsberg 1766.

Kant, Immanuel, *Beantwortung der Frage: Was ist Aufklärung?*, Berlin 1784.

Knox, John, *The First Blast of the Trumpet against the Monstrous Regiment of Women*, s.l. (Geneva) 1558.

[Kramer, Heinrich/Institoris], *Malleus Maleficarum*, Speyer 1486; Facsimile edn, ed. Günter Jerouschek, Hildesheim 1992; *Malleus Maleficarum*, English trans. Montague Summers, London 1928; Heinrich Kramer (Institoris), *Malleus Maleficarum. Kommentierte Neuübersetzung* (new German trans. from Latin) by Wolfgang Behringer, Günter Jerouschek and Werner Tschacher, with an introduction by Wolfgang Behringer and Günter Jerouschek, ed. by Günter Jerouschek/Wolfgang Behringer, Munich 2000.

de Lancre, Pierre, *Tableau de l'Inconstance des mauvais Anges et Démons. Ou il est amplement traicté de la Sorcelerie & Sorciers [. . .]*, Paris 1612; *On the Fickleness of Demons*. English trans. by Gerhild Scholz Williams (forthcoming).

de Lancre, Pierre, *L'incrédulité et mescréance du sortilège pleinement convaincue, où est amplement et curieusement traicté de la verité ou illusion du sortilège*, Paris 1622.

de Landa, Diego, *Historia de las Cosas de Yucatan* (1566), Merida 1990.

Laxdaela Saga, ed. Magnus Magnusson, Harmondsworth 1969.

Laymann SJ, Paul, *De Processu Juridico contra Sagas et Veneficos*, Cologne 1629.

Leib, Johann, *Consilia, Responsa ac Deductiones Juris Variae [. . .], wie und welcher Gestalt der Process wider die Zauberer und Hexen anzustellen*, Frankfurt/Main 1666.

Livy, *Roman History*, Harmondsworth (Penguin: various edns).

Löher, Hermann, *Hochnöthige unterthanige wemütige Klage der Frommen Unschültigen*, Amsterdam 1676.

Loos, Cornelius, *De Vera et Ficta [falsa] Magia*, Cologne 1592.

Ludovicus a Paramo, *De Origine ac Progressu Officii Sancti Inquisitionis Eiusque Dignitate et Utilitate*, Madrid 1598.

Lutz, Reinhard, *Warhafftige Zeitung von gottlosen Hexen* [1571], in *Theatrum de Veneficis*, Frankfurt 1586, 1–11.

Machiavelli, Niccolò, *Il Principe*, Florence 1532.

Machiavelli, Niccolò, *Discorsi*, Florence 1532.

Maffei, Scipione, *L'arte Magica Distrutta*, Trient 1750.

Magnus, Olaus, *Historia de Gentibus Septentrionalibus*, Rome 1555.

de Malebranche, Nicolas, *Des Sorciers par imagination, et des Loups-Garoux*, in *De la Recherche de la vérité [. . .]*, 3 vols, Paris 1674–8, vol. 2, part 3, ch. 6, 337ff.; *Oeuvres Complètes* (ed. A. Robinet), vol. 1, Paris 1962, 370–6. [Monter (1969), 121–6].

Malleus Judicum, see: Pleier.

Malleus Maleficarum, see: Kramer.

Marcellinus, Ammianus, *The Later Roman Empire (AD 354–378)*, trans. Walter Hamilton, Harmondsworth 1986.

Marlowe, Christopher, *The Tragical History of Doctor Faustus*, London 1592.

Mason, James, *The Anatomie of Sorcerie*, London 1612.

Mather, Cotton, *Memorable Providences, Relating to Witchcraft and Possessions*, Boston 1689; ed. in Burr (1914), 89–143.

Mather, Cotton, *The Wonders of the Invisible World*, Boston 1693.

Mather, Increase, *Cases of Conscience Concerning Evil Spirits Personating Men*, Boston 1693.

Meder, David, *Acht Hexen-Predigten von der Hexen schrecklichen Abfall und üblthatten*, Leipzig 1605.

Meyfahrt, Johann Matthäus, *Christliche Erinnerung an gewaltige Regenten [. . .], wie das abscheuliche Laster der Hexerey mit Ernst auszurotten*, Schleusingen 1635.

Michaelis, Sébastien, *Pneumologie ou Discours des Esprits*, Paris 1587.

Middleton, Thomas, *A Tragicomedy called The Witch* (1615), in Peter Corbin/Douglas Sedge (eds), *Three Jacobean Witchcraft Plays*, Manchester 1986, 85–142.

Milichius, Ludwig, *Der Zauber Teuffel*, 1563.

Molitor, Ulrich, *De Laniis et Phitonicis Mulieribus, Teutonice unholden vel hexen*, s.l. [Constance] s.d. [1489].

de Montaigne, Michel, *Essais*, Paris 1588.

More, Henry, *An Antidote against Atheisme, or an Appeal to the Natural Faculties of the Minde of Men, whether There Be not a God*, London 1653.

Naudé, Gabriel, *Apologie pour tous les grands personnages, qui ont esté sopconnez de magie*, Paris 1625.

Neue Zeitung von sechshundert Hexen, Zauberern und Teufelsbannern, welche der Bischof von Bamberg hat verbrennen lassen, s.l. 1629.

Neuwaldt, Hermann, *Bericht von Erforschung/prob und erkentnis der Zauberinnen durchs kalte Wasser/Inn welchem Wilhelm Adolph Scribonii meinung widerleget*, Helmstedt 1584.

Newer Tractat von der verführten Kinder Zauberey, Aschaffenburg 1629.

Neydecker, Johannes, *Disputatio Juridica de Maleficis*, Ingolstadt 1629.

Nider, Johannes, *Formicarius* (1435), Cologne 1475.

Orkneyinga Saga, ed. Hermann Palsson/Paul Edwards, Harmondsworth 1981.

de Ossuna, Francesco, *Flagellum Diaboli*, Munich 1602.

Paracelsus, Theophrastus Bombastus von Hohenheim, *De Sagis et Earum Operibus* (1538), in *Sämtliche Werke*, ed. Karl Sudhoff, vol. 14, Munich/Berlin 1933, 5–27.

Pererius, Benedictus, *Adversus Fallaces et Superstitiosas Artes, id est, de Magia, de Observatione Somniorum, et de Divinatione Astrologica*, Ingolstadt 1591.

Perkins, William, *A Discourse of the Damned Art of Witchcraft*, Cambridge 1608.

Picatrix, *The Latin Version of the Ghayat Al-Hakim*, ed. David Pingree, London 1988.

Pico della Mirandola, Giovanni, *De Imaginationibus*, Bologna 1496.

Pico della Mirandola, Giovanni Francesco, *Dialogus in Tres Libros Divisus, Cuius Titulus est Strix, sive de Ludificatione Daemonum*, n.p. [Bologna] n.d. [1523].

Plantsch, Martin, *Opusculum de Sagis Maleficis*, Pforzheim 1507.

[Pleier, Cornelius], *Malleus Judicum, das ist: Gesetzhammer der unbarmherzigen Hexenrichter*, s.l. 1627 (ed. in Reiche (1701), 1–48).

Pomponazzi, Pietro, *De Immortalitate Animae* (1516), Rome 1925.

Pomponazzi, Pietro, *De Naturalium Effectuum Admirandorum Causis, sive de Incantationibus*, 1520.

Ponzinibius, Johannes Franciscus, *Tractatus de Lamiis*, Frankfurt/Main 1592.

della Porta, Giambattista, *Natural Magick*, London 1658.

Potts, Thomas, *The Wonderfull Discoverie of Witches in the Countrie of Lancaster. With the Arraignement and Triall of Nineteene Notorious Witches*, London 1613.

Praetorius, Anton, *Gründlicher Bericht von Zauberey und Zauberern*, Lich 1598; Lich 1602; Heidelberg 1613; Frankfurt/Main 1629.

Prierias, Silvester, *De Strigimagarum Libri Tres*, Rome 1521.

[Rategno] da Como, Bernardo, *Tractatus de Strigiis* (*c.*1508), in *Lucerna Inquisitorum Haereticae Pravitatis*, Mailand 1546.

Regino, von Prüm, *Libri Duo de Synodalibus Causis et Disciplinis Ecclesiasticis* [*c.*906], ed. F. G. A. Wasserschleben, Leipzig 1840.

Reiche, Johann (ed.), *Unterschiedliche Schrifften von Unfug des Hexen-Processes*, Halle 1703.

Rémy, Nicolas, *Daemonolatriae Libri Tres*, Lyon 1595; *Daemonolatria. Das ist von Unholden und Zauber Geistern*, Frankfurt/Main 1598; *Daemonolatry*, trans. Montague Summers, London 1930.

Roberts, Alexander, *A Treatise of Witchcraft*, London 1616.

Rowley, William/Dekker, Thomas/Ford, John, *The Witch of Edmonton* (London 1621), in Peter Corbin/Douglas Sedge (eds), *Three Jacobean Witchcraft Plays*, Manchester 1986, 143–209.

Rüdiger, Johannes, *De Magia Illicita Decas Concionum. Zehen nuetzliche Predigten von der Zauber- und Hexenwerck*, Jena 1630.

de Sahagun, Bernardino, *Historia General de las cosas de Nueva Espania* (*c.*1555), 4 vols, Mexico City 1956.

Sawr, Abraham, *Eine kurtze und trewe Warnung, Anzeige und Underricht, ob auch zu dieser unserer Zeit unter uns Christen Hexen, Zauberer und Unholden vorhanden: und was sie ausrichten können*, Frankfurt/Main 1584; repr. *Theatrum de Veneficis*, Frankfurt 1586, 202–14.

Sawr, Abraham (ed.), *Theatrum de Veneficis*, Frankfurt/Main 1586.

Schaller, Daniel, *Zauber Händel in viii Predigten*, Magdeburg 1611.

von Schultheis, Heinrich, *Ausführliche Instruction, wie in Inquisition Sachen des grewlichen Lasters der Zauberey zu procedieren*, Cologne 1634.

Scot, Reginald, *The Discoverie of Witchcraft*, London 1584; 3rd edn London 1665.

Scribonius, Guilelmus, *De Sagarum Natura et Potestate*, Marburg 1588.

Simon, Jordan, *Das große weltbetrügende Nichts, oder die heutige Hexerey und Zauberkunst*, s.l. 1762.

Sinclair, George, *Satan's Invisible World*, Edinburgh 1685.

[Spee, Friedrich] *Cautio Criminalis seu de Processibus contra Sagas Liber [. . .], auctore Incerto Theologo Romano*, Rinteln 1631.

Spina, Bartolomeo, *De Strigibus et Lamiis*, Venice 1523.

Stearne, John, *A Confirmation and Discovery of Witchcraft [. . .]. Together with the Confessions of Those Executed since May 1645*, London 1648 (Facsimile repr. Exeter 1973).

Stubs, Philip, *The Witchcraft of the Scriptures. A Sermon Preach'd on a Special Occasion*, London 1736.

Swedenborg, Emanuel, *Arcana Coelestia, quae in Scriptura Sacra, seu Verbo Domini sunt, detecta . . . Una cum Mirabilibus quae Visa sunt in Mundo Spiritum et in Coelo Anglorum*, 8 vols, London 1749–56.

Tanner SJ, Adam, *Theologia Scholastica*, 4 vols, Ingolstadt 1626/27.

Tanner SJ, Adam, *Tractatus Theologicus de Processu Adversus Crimina Excepta ac Speciatim Adversus Crimen Veneficii*, Cologne 1629.

Tartaroti, Girolamo, *Del Congresso Notturno delle Lammie*, Robereto 1749.

Theatrum Diabolorum, Frankfurt/Main 1569.

Theatrum de Veneficis, Frankfurt/Main 1586, see: Sawr.

Tholosan, Claude, *Ut Magorum et Maleficorum Errores* (1436), in Blauert (1990), 143–59.

Thomasius, Christian, *De Crimine Magiae*, Halle 1701.

Thomasius, Christian, *Disputatio Juris Canonici de Origine ac Progressu Processus Inquisitorii contra Sagas*, Halle 1712.

Trithemius, Johannes, *Von den Gottlosen hexen und zauberern*, Ingolstadt 1555.

Trithemius, Johannes, *Antipalus Maleficorum* (MS von 1508), in *Paralipomena Opusculorum [. . .] Joannis Trithemii*, Mainz 1605, 273–426.

Vairius, Leonardus, *De Fascino*, Paris 1583; Venice 1589.

Vallick, Jacob, *Von Zäuberern, Hexen und Unholden*, in Sawr (1586), 54–69.

Visconti, Girolamo, *Lamiarum sive Striarum Oposcula*, Milan 1490.

Voigt, Gottfried Christian, *Etwas über die Hexenprozesse in Deutschland*, in *Berlinische Monatsschrift*, Dritter Band, Berlin 1784, 297–311.

Wagstaffe, John, *The Question of Witchcraft Debated. Or a Discourse against Their Opinion that Affirm Witches*, London 1669 (ed. Sharpe 2003, vol. 4).

Wahrhafftige und glaubwirdige Zeyttung. Von Hundert und vier und dreyssig Unholden/ so um ihrer Zauberey halben/ verbrennet worden, Strasbourg 1583, ed. in Behringer (2001), 167–9.

Webster, John, *The Displaying of Supposed Witchcraft*, London 1677.

Wecker, Johann, *Hexen-Büchlein, das ist: Ware entdeckung und erklärung [. . .] der Zauberey, und was von Zauberern, Unholden und Hengsten [!], Nachtschaden, Schützen, auch der Hexen händel, art, thun, lassen, wesen, artzeney [. . .] zu halten sey*, Colmar 1575. Theatum de Veneficis, Frankfurt/Main 1586, 306–24.

Weyer, Johann, *De Praestigiis Daemonum*, Basel 1563; partly trans., *On Witchcraft*, ed. by Benjamin G. Kohl/H. C. Erik Midelfort, Asheville/NC 1998.

Weyer, Johann, *De Lamiis Liber*, Basel 1577.

Witches' Hammer, see: Kramer.

Witekind, Herman, *Christlich Bedencken und Erinnerung von Zauberey*, Heidelberg 1585.

Yupanqi, Titu Kusi, Inca, *Relación de la conquista del Peru* (c.1570), Lima 1973.

Zehner, Joachim, *Fünff Predigten von Hexen, ihren Anfang, Mittel und End in sich haltend und erklärend*, Leipzig 1613.

Zeittung, Zwo Newe, *was man für Hexen und Unholden verbrendt hat*, 1580, in: Behringer (2001), 159–61.

3 Witchcraft Monographs

Abusch, Tzvi, *Babylonian Witchcraft Literature. Case Studies*, Atlanta 1987.

Ankarloo, Bengt, *Trolldomsprocesserna i Sverige*, Lund 1971.

Apps, Lara/Gow, Andrew, *Male Witches in Early Modern Europe*, Manchester 2003.

Ashforth, Adam, *Madumo. A Man Bewitched*, Chicago/London 2000.

Bader, Guido, *Hexenprozesse in der Schweiz*, Zurich 1945.

Bailey, Frederick George, *Witch Hunt in an Indian Village, or the Triumph of Morality*, New Delhi 1997.

Bailey, Michael D., *Battling Demons. Witchcraft, Heresy, and Reform in the Late Middle Ages*, Pennsylvania University Press 2003.

Baroja, Julio Caro, *The World of the Witches* (Madrid 1961), London 1964.

Barstow, Ann Llewellyn, *Witchcraze. A New History of the European Witch Hunts*, New York 1994.

Baschwitz, Kurt, *Hexen und Hexenprozesse*, Munich 1963.

Basso, Keith H., *Western Apache Witchcraft*, Tucson/Arizona 1969.

Behringer, Wolfgang, *Mit dem Feuer vom Leben zum Tod. Hexengesetzgebung in Bayern*, Munich 1988.

Behringer, Wolfgang, *Witchcraft Persecutions in Bavaria. Popular Magic, Religious Zealotry and Reason of State in Early Modern Europe*, Cambridge 1997.

Behringer, Wolfgang, *Shaman of Oberstdorf. Chonrad Stoeckhlin and the Phantoms of the Night*, trans. H. C. Erik Midelfort, Charlottesville/Va. 1998.

Behringer, Wolfgang, *Hexen. Glaube, Verfolgung, Vermarktung*, 3rd edn Munich 2002.

Bethencourt, Francisco, *O imaginarío da magia: Feiticeiras, saludadores e nigromantes no século 16*, Lisbon 1987.

Biesel, Elisabeth, *Hexenjustiz, Volksmagie und soziale Konflikte im lothringischen Raum*, Trier 1997.

Blauert, Andreas, *Frühe Hexenverfolgungen. Ketzer-, Zauberei- und Hexenprozesse des 15. Jahrhunderts*, Hamburg 1989.

de Blécourt, Willem, *Termen van Toverij. De veranderende beteke-nis van toverij in Nordoost-Nederland tussen de 16de en 20ste eeuw*, Nijmegen 1990.

Bongmba, Elias, *African Witchcraft and Otherness. A Philosophical and Theological Critique of Intersubjective Relations*, Charlottesville/Va. 2001.

Bonomo, Giuseppe, *Caccia alle Streghe*, Palermo 1959.

Bostridge, Ian, *Witchcraft and its Transformations, c.1650–c.1750*, Oxford 1997.

Boyer, Paul/Nissenbaum, Stephen, *Salem Possessed. The Social Origins of Witchcraft*, Harvard 1974.

Brauner, Sigrid, *Fearless Wives and Frightened Shrews. The Construction of the Witch in Early Modern Germany*, Massachusetts 1995.

Briggs, Robin, *Witches and Neighbours. The Social and Cultural Context of European Witchcraft*, London 1996.

Byloff, Fritz, *Hexenglaube und Hexenverfolgung in den österreichischen Alpenländern*, Berlin/Leipzig 1934.

Cassar, Carmel, *Witchcraft, Sorcery and the Inquisition. A Study of Cultural Values in Early Modern Malta*, 1996.

Centini, Massimo, *Streghe, roghi e diavoli. I Processi di stregoneria in Piemonte*, Cuneo 1995.

de Certeau, Michel, *La Possession de Loudon*, Paris 1971.

Cervantes, Fernando, *The Devil in the New World. The Impact of Diabolism in New Spain*, New Haven/London 1994.

Chavunduka, G., *Witches, Witchcraft and the Law in Zimbabwe*, Harare 1982.

Clark, Henry A., *Policeman's Narrative of Witchcraft and Murder in Zimbabwe*, Melbourne 1985.

Clark, Stuart, *Thinking with Demons. The Idea of Witchcraft in Early Modern Europe*, Oxford 1997.

Cohn, Norman, *Europe's Inner Demons: An Enquiry Inspired by the Great Witch-Hunt*, London 1975.

Crawford, John R., *Witchcraft and Sorcery in Rhodesia*, London 1967.

Davidson, Jane P., *The Witch in Northern European Art, 1450–1750*, Freren 1987.

Davidson, L. S./Ward, J. O., *The Sorcery Trial of Alice Kyteler*, Binghamton 1993.

Davies, Owen, *Witchcraft, Magic and Culture, 1736–1951*, Manchester 1999.

Deacon, Richard, *Mathew Hopkins. Witch Finder General*, London 1976.

Debrunner, Hans W., *Witchcraft in Ghana. A Study of the Belief in Destructive Witches and its Effect on the Akan Tribe*, Kumasi 1959.

Decker, Rainer, *Die Hexen und ihre Henker. Ein Fallbericht*, Freiburg/Br. 1994.

Decker, Rainer, *Die Päpste und die Hexen*, Darmstadt 2003.

Demos, John Putnam, *Entertaining Satan. Witchcraft and the Culture of Early New England*, Oxford 1983.

Devlin, Judith, *The Superstitious Mind*, New Haven 1987.

Dillinger, Johannes, *'Böse Leute'. Hexenverfolgungen in Schwäbisch Österreich und Kurtrier im Vergleich*, Trier 1999.

Dinzelbacher, Peter, *Heilige oder Hexen. Schicksale auffälliger Frauen in Mittelalter und Frühneuzeit*, Zurich 1995.

Duhr, Bernhard, *Die Stellung der Jesuiten in den deutschen Hexenprozessen*, Cologne 1900.

Durrant, Jonathan, *Witchcraft, Gender and Society in the Early Modern Prince-Bishopric of Eichstätt*, Ph.D., University of London 2002 (MS).

Durston, Gregory, *Witchcraft and Witch Trials. A History of English Witchcraft and its Legal Perspectives, 1542–1736*, Chichester 2000.

Easlea, Brian, *Witch Hunting, Magic, and the New Philosophy*, Brighton 1980.

Elkin, Adolphus Peter, *Aboriginal Men of High Degree. Initiation and Sorcery in the World's Oldest Tradition* (1945), 3rd edn, Queensland University Press, St Lucia/Australia 1994.

Erikson, Kai T., *Wayward Puritans*, New York 1966.

L'Estrange Ewen, Cecil, *Witch Hunting and Witch Trials. The Indictments for Witchcraft from the Records of 1373 Assizes Held for the Home Circuit, AD 1559–1736*, London 1929.

L'Estrange Ewen, Cecil, *Witchcraft and Demonianism. A Concise Account Derived from Sworn Depositions and Confessions Obtained in the Courts of England and Wales*, London 1933.

Evans-Pritchard, Edgar Evan, *Witchcraft, Oracles and Magic among the Azande*, Oxford 1937.

Favret-Saada, Jeanne, *Les mots, la mort, les sorts*, Paris 1977; *Deadly Words. Witchcraft in the Bocage*, Cambridge 1980.

Fisiy, Cyprian F., *Palmtree Justice in the Bertoua Court of Appeal. The Witchcraft Cases*, Leiden 1990.

Flint, Valerie I. J., *The Rise of Magic in Early Medieval Europe*, Oxford 1991.

Fögen, Marie Theres, *Die Enteignung der Wahrsager. Studien zum kaiserlichen Wissensmonopol in der Spätantike*, Frankfurt/Main 1997.

Fortune, Reo F., *Sorcerers of Dobu*, London 1932.

French, Peter, *John Dee. The World of an Elizabethan Magus*, New York 1972.

Freuler, Kaspar, *Anna Göldi, die Geschichte der letzten Hexe der Schweiz*, Glarus 1987.

Füssel, Roland, *Hexenverfolgung in Thüringen*, Erfurt 1998.

Gehm, Britta, *Die Hexenverfolgungen des Hochstifts Bamberg und das Eingreifen des Reichshofrates zu ihrer Beendigung*, Hildesheim 2000.

Gentilcore, David, *From Bishop to Witch. The System of the Sacred in Early Modern Terra d'Otranto*, Manchester 1992.

Gersmann, Gudrun, *Wasserprobe und Prozeß. Hexenverfolgung und adelige 'Hexenpolitik' im frühneuzeitlichen Fürstbistum Münster, Diss. habil.* Munich 1999.

Geschiere, Peter, *The Modernity of Witchcraft. Politics and the Occult in Postcolonial Africa*, Virginia University Press 1997.

Ginzburg, Carlo, *I Benandanti. Stregoneria e culti agrari tra cinquecento e seicento*, Turin 1966; *The Night Battles*, Baltimore 1983.

Ginzburg, Carlo, *Storia notturna. Una decifrazione del Saba*, Turin 1989; *Ecstasies. Deciphering the Witches' Sabbath*, New York 1991.

Graf, Fritz, *Gottesnähe und Schadenzauber. Die Magie in der griechischrömischen Antike*, Munich 1996 (= *Magic in the Ancient World*, trans. F. Philip, Cambridge/MA 1997).

Habiger-Tuczay, Christa, *Magie und Magier im Mittelalter*, Munich 1992.

Hansen, Joseph, *Zauberwahn, Inquisition und Hexenprozeß im Mittelalter und die Entstehung der großen Hexenverfolgung*, Munich 1900.

Harmening, Dieter, *Superstitio*, Berlin 1979.

Hauschild, Thomas, *Der böse Blick*, Berlin 1982.

Haustein, Jörg, *Luthers Stellung zum Zauber- und Hexenwesen*, Stuttgart 1990.

Heinemann, Evelyn, *Hexen und Hexenglauben. Eine historisch sozialpsychologische Studie über den europäischen Hexenwahn des 16. und 17. Jahrhunderts*, Frankfurt u.a. 1986.

Henningsen, Gustav, *The Witches' Advocate. Basque Witchcraft and the Spanish Inquisition (1609–1614)*, Reno/Nevada 1980.

Henningsen, Gustav, *Fra heksejagt til heksekult, 1484–1984*, Copenhagen 1984.

Hester, Marianne, *Lewd Women and Wicked Witches. A Study of the Dynamics of Male Domination*, London 1992.

Hart, Vaughan, *Art and Magic in the Court of the Stuarts*, London 1994.

Idoate, Florencio, *La Brujería en Navarra y sus documentos*, Pamplona 1967.

Jensen, Karsten Sejr, *Trolldom i Danmark, 1500–1588*, Copenhagen 1982.

Jerouschek, Günther, *Die Hexen und ihr Prozeß. Die Hexenverfolgung in der Reichsstadt Esslingen*, Sigmaringen 1992.

Johansen, Jens C. V., *Da Djaevelen var du . . . Troldom i det 17. Arhundredes Danmark*, Odense 1991.

Kapferer, Bruce, *The Feast of Sorcerer: Practices of Consciousness and Power*, London 1997.

Kapur, Sohaila, *Witchcraft in Western India*, Hyderabad 1983.

Karlsen, Carol F., *The Devil in the Shape of a Woman. Witchcraft in Colonial New England*, New York 1987.

Kauertz, Claudia, *Wissenschaft und Hexenglaube. Die Diskussion des Zauber- und Hexenwesens an der Universität Helmstedt (1576–1626)* (*Hexenforschung*, vol. 6), Bielefeld 2001.

Kieckhefer, Richard, *European Witch-Trials. Their Foundation in Popular and Learned Culture, 1300–1500*, London 1976.

Kilpatrick, Alan, *The Night has a Naked Soul. Witchcraft and Sorcery among the Western Cherokee*, Syracuse/New York 1997.

King, Leonard W., *Babylonian Magic and Sorcery. Being 'The Prayers of the Lifting of the Hand'. The Cuneiform Texts of a Group of Babylonian and Assyrian Incantations and Magical Formulae*, London 2000.

Kittredge, George Lyman, *Witchcraft in Old and New England*, Cambridge/Mass. 1929.

Klaits, Joseph, *Servants of Satan. The Age of the Witch Hunts*, Bloomington 1985.

Klaniczay, Gábor, *The Uses of Supernatural Power. The Transformation of Popular Religion in Medieval and Early Modern Europe*, Cambridge 1990.

Kluckhohn, Clyde, *Navaho Witchcraft*, Boston 1944.

Knauft, Bruce M., *Good Company and Violence. Sorcery and Social Action in a Lowland New Guinea Society*, Berkeley/Cal. 1985.

Kuhn, Philip A., *Soulstealers. The Chinese Sorcery Scare of 1768*, Cambridge/Mass. 1990.

Kunstmann, Hartmut H., *Zauberwahn und Hexenprozeß in der Reichsstadt Nürnberg*, Nuremberg 1970.

Kunze, Michael, *Highroad to the Stake. A Tale of Witchcraft*, Chicago 1987.

Labouvie, Eva, *Zauberei und Hexenwerk. Ländlicher Aberglaube in der frühen Neuzeit*, Frankfurt/M. 1991.

Lambek, Michael, *Knowledge and Practice in Mayotte. Local Discourses of Islam, Sorcery and Spirit Possession*, Toronto 1993.

Lambrecht, Karen, *Hexenverfolgung und Zaubereiprozesse in den schlesischen Territorien*, Cologne 1995.

Larner, Christina, *Enemies of God. The Witch-Hunt in Scotland*, London 1981.

Larner, Christina, *Witchcraft and Religion. The Politics of Popular Belief*, edited and with a foreword by Alan Macfarlane, Oxford 1984.

Levack, Brian P., *The Witch-Hunt in Early Modern Europe*, London/New York 1987.

Lewis, Ioan M., *Ecstatic Religion. A Study of Shamanism and Spirit Possession*, 2nd edn, London 1989.

Lieban, Richard W., *Cebuano Sorcery. Malign Magic in the Philippines*, Berkeley/Los Angeles 1967.

Lindenbaum, Shirley, *Kuru Sorcery. Disease and Danger in the New Guinea Highlands*, Palo Alto 1979.

Luck, Georg, *Arcana Mundi. Magic and the Occult in the Greek and Roman Worlds*, Baltimore 1985.

Lüking, Rolf-Michael, *Vom Unwesen der Magie. Annäherung an das Fremde über den sogenannten Todeszauber im Südwestpazifik*, Münster/Hamburg 1993.

Macfarlane, Alan, *Witchcraft in Tudor and Stuart England. A Regional and Comparative Study*, London 1970; 2nd edn by J. Sharpe, Cambridge 1999.

Madsen, William/Madsen, Claudia, *A Guide to Mexican Witchcraft. With a Commentary by Gonzalo Aguire Beltrán*, Mexico City, 10th edn 1992.

Mair, Lucy P., *Witchcraft*, London 1969.

Martin, Ruth, *Witchcraft and the Inquisition in Venice, 1550–1650*, Oxford/New York 1989.

de Martino, Ernesto, *Sud e Magia*, Mailand 1959.

Marwick, Max, *Sorcery in its Social Setting. A Study of the Northern Rhodesian Cewa*, Manchester 1965.

Maxwell-Stuart, Peter George, *Witchcraft in Europe and the New World, 1400–1800*, Basingstoke 2001.

Melland, Frank Hulme, *In Witchbound Africa*, London 1923.

Meyer, Birgit, *Translating the Devil. Religion and Modernity among the Ewe in Ghana*, Trenton/NJ 1999.

Michelet, Jules, *La Sorcière*, Paris 1862.

Midelfort, H. C. Erik, *Witch-Hunting in South-Western Germany, 1582–1684. The Social and Intellectual Foundations*, Stanford/Calif. 1972.

Monter, William, *Witchcraft in France and Switzerland. The Borderlands during the Reformation*, Ithaca/London 1976.

Morris, Katherine, *Sorceress or Witch? The Image of Gender in Medieval Iceland and Northern Europe*, New York/London 1991.

Muchembled, Robert, *La sorcière au village*, Paris 1979.

Muchembled, Robert, *Le roi et la sorcière. L'Europe des buchers XVe–XVIIIe siècle*, Paris 1993.

Multhaupt, Tamara, *Hexerei und Antihexerei in Afrika*, Munich 1989.

Muraro, Luisa, *La Signora del Gioco. Episodi della Caccia alle Streghe*, Milan 1976.

Naess, Hans Eyvind, *Trolldomsprosessene i Norge pa 1500–1600-tallet. En retts- og sosialhisttorisk undersokelse*, Oslo 1982.

Niehaus, Isak/Mohlala, Eliazaar/Kally, Shokane, *Witchcraft, Power and Politics. Exploring the Occult in the South African Lowveld*, London/Cape Town 2001.

Niess, Walter, *Hexenprozesse in der Grafschaft Büdingen*, Büdingen 1982.

Notestein, Wallace, *A History of Witchcraft in England from 1558 to 1718*, London 1911.

Oestmann, Peter, *Hexenprozesse am Reichskammergericht*, Wien 1997.

Offiong, Daniel A., *Witchcraft, Sorcery, Magic and Social Order among the Ibibio of Nigeria*, Enugu/Nigeria 1991.

Omoyajowo, Justus Akinwale, *Witches? A Study of the Belief in Witchcraft and of Its Future in Modern African Society*, University of Ibadan (Nigeria) 1965; 3rd edn 1974.

Ostorero, Martine, *Folatrer avec le Démon. Sabbat et chasse aux sorciers à Vevey (1448)*, Lausanne 1998.

Paravy, Pierette, *De la chrétienté romaine à la réforme en Dauphiné: Éveques, fidèles et déviants (vers 1340–vers 1530)*, 2 vols, Rom 1993.

Parin, Paul/Morgenthaler, Fritz/Parin-Matthey, Goldy, *Fürchte deinen Nächsten wie dich selbst. Psychoanalyse und Gesellschaft am Modell der Agni in Westafrika*, Frankfurt am Main 1971.

Parrinder, Geoffrey, *Witchcraft. A Critical Study of the Belief in Witchcraft from the Records of Witch Hunting in Europe Yesterday and Africa Today*, Harmondsworth 1958.

Pearl, Jonathan, *The Crime of Crimes. Demonology and Politics in France, 1560–1620*, Waterloo/Ont. 1999.

Peters, Edward, *The Magician, the Witch, and the Law*, Pennsylvania University Press 1982.

Pintschovius, Joska, *Zur Hölle mit den Hexen. Abschied von den weisen Frauen*, Berlin 1991.

Pócs, Eva, *Fairies and Witches at the Boundaries of South-Eastern and Central Europe*, Helsinki 1989.

Pócs, Eva, *Between the Living and the Dead. A Perspective on Witches and Seers in the Early Modern Age*, Budapest 1998.

Pohl, Herbert, *Hexenglaube und Hexenverfolgung im Kurfürstentum Mainz. Ein Beitrag zur Hexenfrage im 16. und beginnenden 17. Jahrhundert*, Wiesbaden 1988; 2nd edn (*Hexenforschung*, vol. 3) Bielefeld 1998.

Purkiss, Diane, *The Witch in History. Early Modern and Twentieth Century Representations*, London 1996.

Quaife, Geoffrey Robert, *Godly Zeal and Furious Rage. The Witch in Early Modern Europe*, London 1987.

Ralushai, Victor/et al., *Report of the Commission of Inquiry into Witchcraft, Violence and Ritual Murders in the Northern Province of the Republic of South Africa*, Pietersburg 1996.

Rapley, Robert, *A Case of Witchcraft: The Trial of Urbain Grandier*, Manchester 1998.

Reis, Elizabeth, *Damned Women. Sinners and Witches in Puritan New England*, Ithaca 1997.

Rochelandet, Brigitte, *Sorcières, diables et bouchers en Franche-Comté*, Besançon 1997.

Romeo, Giovanni, *Inquisitori, esorcisti e streghe nell'Italia della Controriforma*, Florence 1990.

Rowlands, Alison, *Narratives of Witchcraft in Early Modern Germany. Fabrication, Feud and Fantasy*, Manchester 2002.

Rummel, Walter, *Bauern, Herren und Hexen. Studien zur Sozialgeschichte sponheimischer und kurtrierischer Hexenprozesse, 1574–1664*, Göttingen 1991.

Ryan, Willam F., *The Bathhouse at Midnight. An Historical Survey of Magic and Divination in Russia*, London 1999.

Sanders, Andrew, *A Deed without a Name. The Witch in Society and History*, Oxford 1995.

Schatzmann, Nikolaus, *Verdorrende Bäume und Brote wie Kuhfladen. Hexenprozesse in der Leventina 1431–1459 und die Anfänge der Hexenverfolgung auf der Alpensüdseite*, unpublished Ph.D., Zurich 2002.

Schmidt, Jürgen Michael, *Glaube und Skepsis. Die Kurpfalz und die abendländische Hexenverfolgung, 1446–1685* (*Hexenforschung*, vol. 5), Bielefeld 2000.

Schöck, Inge, *Hexenglaube in der Gegenwart. Empirische Untersuchungen in Südwestdeutschland*, Tübingen 1978.

Schönhuth, Michael, *Das Einsetzen der Nacht in das Recht des Tages. Hexerei im symbolischen Kontext afrikanischer und europäischer Weltbilder*, Münster/Hamburg 1992.

Schormann, Gerhard, *Hexenprozesse in Deutschland*, Göttingen 1981.

Schormann, Gerhard, *Der Krieg gegen die Hexen. Das Ausrottungsprogramm des Kurfürsten von Köln*, Göttingen 1991.

Schulte, Rolf, *Hexenmeister. Die Verfolgung von Männern im Rahmen der Hexenverfolgungen von 1530–1730 im Alten Reich*, Frankfurt/Main 1999.

Schulte, Rolf, *Hexenverfolgung in Schleswig-Holstein vom 16.–18. Jahrhundert*, Heide 2001.

Schwillus, Harald, *Kleriker im Hexenprozeß. Geistliche als Opfer der Hexenprozesse des 16. und 17. Jahrhunderts in Deutschland*, Würzburg 1992.

Sebald, Hans, *Witchcraft*, New York 1978.

Sebald, Hans, *Witch-Children. From Salem Witch-Hunts to Modern Courtrooms*, New York 1995.

Seger, Otto/Putzer, Peter, *Hexenprozesse in Liechtenstein und das Salzburger Rechtsgutachten von 1682*, Wien 1987.

Sharpe, James, *Instruments of Darkness. Witchcraft in England 1550–1750*, London 1997.

Sharpe, James, *The Bewitching of Anne Gunther. A Horrible and True Story of Football, Witchcraft, Murder, and the King of England*, London 1999.

Silverblatt, Irene, *Moon, Sun and Witches. Gender Ideologies and Class in Inca and Colonial Peru*, Princeton 1987.

Simmons, Marc, *Witchcraft in the Southwest. Spanish and Indian Supernaturalism on the Rio Grande*, Nebraska University Press 1980.

Simons, Manuel, *Heilige, Hexe, Mutter. Der Wandel des Frauenbildes durch die Medizin im 16. Jahrhundert*, Berlin 1993.

Smith, Morton, *Jesus, the Magician*, London 1978.

Soldan, Wilhelm Gottlieb, *Geschichte der Hexenprozesse*, Darmstadt 1843.

Soldan, Wilhelm Gottlieb/Heppe, Heinrich/Bauer, Max, *Geschichte der Hexenprozesse*, 2 vols, Berlin 1911.

di Simplicio, Oscar, *Inquisizione, stregoneria, medicina. Siena e il suo stato (1580–1721)*, Monteriggione/Siena 2000.

Sörlin, Per, *Wicked Arts. Witchcraft and Magic Trials in Southern Sweden, 1635–1754*, Leiden 1998.

Spinola, Francisco Fajardo, *Hechicería y brujería en Canarias en la Edad Moderna*, Las Palmas 1992.

Spiro, Melford E., *Burmese Supernaturalism. A Study in the Explanation and Reduction of Suffering*, Englewood Cliffs 1967.

Stephen, Walter, *Demon Lovers. Witchcraft, Sex, and the Crisis of Belief*, Chicago 2002.

Sterly, Joachim, *Kumo. Hexer und Hexen in Neu-Guinea*, Munich 1987.

Stoller, Paul, *In Sorcery's Shadow. A Memoir of Apprenticeship among the Songhay of Niger*, Chicago University Press 1989.

Summers, Montague, *The History of Witchcraft and Demonology*, London 1926.

Tausiet, Maria, *Ponzonia en los Ojos. Brujería y superstición en Aragon en el siglo XVI*, Zaragoza 2000.

Taussig, Michael, *The Magic of the State*, New York 1997.

Thomas, Keith, *Religion and the Decline of Magic. Studies in Popular Beliefs in Sixteenth and Seventeenth Century England*, London 1971.

Trachtenberg, Joshua, *The Devil and the Jew*, New Haven 1943.

Trevor-Roper, Hugh R., *The European Witch-Craze of the Sixteenth and Seventeenth Centuries*, Harmondsworth 1969.

Tschaikner, Manfred, *'Damit das Böse ausgerottet werde'. Hexenverfolgungen in Vorarlberg im 16. und 17. Jahrhundert*, Bregenz 1992.

de Waardt, Hans, *Toverij en Samenleving. Holland 1500–1800*, Rotterdam 1991.

Wachtel, Nathan, *Gods and Vampires. Return to Chipaya*, trans. by Carol Volk, Chicago 1994.

Waite, Gary K., *Heresy, Magic and Witchcraft in Early Modern Europe*, London 2003.

Walker, Daniel Pickering, *Spiritual and Demonic Magic from Ficino to Campanella*, London 1958.

Walker, Daniel Pickering, *Unclean Spirits. Possession and Exorcism in France and England in the Late Sixteenth and Early Seventeenth Centuries*, London 1981.

Walz, Rainer, *Hexenglaube und Magische Kommunikation im Dorf der frühen Neuzeit. Die Verfolgungen in der Grafschaft Lippe*, Paderborn 1993.

Whiting, Beatrice, *Paiute Sorcery*, New York 1950.

Wilde, Manfred, *Die Zauberei- und Hexenprozesse in Kursachsen*, Cologne/Weimar 2003.

Williams, Gerhild Scholz, *Defining Dominion. The Discourses of Magic and Witchcraft in Early Modern France and Germany*, Ann Arbor 1995.

Willis, Deborah, *Malevolent Nurture. Witch-Hunting and Maternal Power in Early Modern England*, Ithaca/London 1995.

Worobec, Christine D., *Possessed: Women, Witches and Demons in Imperial Russia*, Northern Illinois University Press 2001.

Zanelli, Giuliana, *Streghe e societa nell'Emilia e Romagna del cinqueseicento*, Ravenna 1992.

4   Essay Collections

Abrahams, Ray (ed.), *Witchcraft in Contemporary Tanzania*, Cambridge 1994.

Ahrendt-Schulte, Ingrid/Bauer, Dieter/Lorenz, Sönke/Schmidt, Jürgen Michael (eds), *Geschlecht, Magie und Hexenverfolgung* (*Hexenforschung*, vol. 7), Bielefeld 2002.

Anglo, Sidney (ed.), *The Damned Art. Essays in the Literature of Witchcraft*, London 1977.

Ankarloo, Bengt/Henningsen, Gustav (eds), *Early Modern European Witchcraft. Centres and Peripheries*, Oxford 1990.

Ankarloo, Bengt/Clark, Stuart/Monter, William, *Magic and Witchcraft in Europe: The Period of the Witch Trials* (*AHWME*, vol. 4), London 2002.

Barry, Jonathan/Hester, Marianne/Roberts, Gareth (eds), *Witchcraft in Early Modern Europe. Studies in Culture and Belief*, Cambridge 1997.

Bauer, Dieter R./Behringer, Wolfgang (eds), *Fliegen und Schweben. Annäherung an eine menschliche Sensation*, Munich 1997.

Behringer, Wolfgang/Sharpe, Jim (eds), *Witchcraft in Context*. The Third York Cultural History Conference, forthcoming.

Beier-de-Haan, Rosemarie/Voltmer, Rita/Irsigler, Franz (eds), *Hexenwahn. Ängste der Neuzeit. Begleitband zur gleichnamigen Ausstellung*, Berlin 2002.

Ben-Yehuda, Nachman (ed.), *Deviance and Moral Boundaries. Witchcraft, the Occult, Science Fiction, Deviant Sciences and Scientists*, Chicago 1985.

Blauert, Andreas (ed.), *Ketzer, Zauberer, Hexen. Die Anfänge der europäischen Hexenverfolgungen*, Frankfurt/M. 1990.

de Blécourt, Willem/Gijswijt-Hofstra, Marijke (eds), *Kwade Mensen. Toverij in Nederland*, Amsterdam 1986 (= *Volkskundig Bulletin*, 12, 1).

de Blécourt, Willem/Hutton, Ronald/La Fontaine, Jean, *Witchcraft and Magic in Europe: The Twentieth Century* (*AHWME*, vol. 6), London 1999.

Bond, George Clement/Ciekawy, Diana M. (eds), *Witchcraft Dialogues. Anthropological and Philosophical Exchanges*, Athens/Ohio 2001.

Ciekawy, Diane/Bond, George Clement (eds), *Envisioning and Revisioning 'Witchcraft'. New Directions in African Philosophy and Anthropology*, Athens/Ohio 2000.

Clark, Stuart (ed.), *Languages of Witchcraft. Narrative, Ideology and Meaning in Early Modern Culture*, London 2001.

Cohen, Jeremy (ed.), *From Witness to Witchcraft. Jews and Judaism in Medieval Christan Thought*, Wiesbaden 1996.

Comaroff, Jean/Comaroff, John (eds), *Modernity and Its Malcontents. Ritual and Power in Postcolonial Africa*, Chicago 1993.

Cryer, Frederick H./Thomson, Marie-Louise, *Witchcraft and Magic in Europe: Biblical and Pagan Societies* (*AHWME*, vol. 1), London 2001.

Degn, Christian/Lehmann, Hartmut/Unverhau, Dagmar (eds), *Hexenprozesse. Deutsche und skandinavische Beiträge*, Neumünster 1983.

Dillinger, Johannes/Fritz, Thomas/Mährle, Wolfgang, *Zum Feuer verdammt. Die Hexenverfolgungen in der Grafschaft Hohenberg, der Reichsstadt Reutlingen und der Fürstpropstei Ellwangen* (= *Hexenforschung*, vol. 2), Stuttgart 1998.

Douglas, Mary (ed.), *Witchcraft. Confessions and Accusations*, London 1970.

van Dülmen, Richard (ed.), *Hexenwelten*, Frankfurt/Main 1987.

Edwards, Kathryn A., *Werewolves, Witches, and Wandering Spirits. Traditional Belief and Folklore in Early Modern Europe*, Kirksville/Missouri 2002.

Eiden, Heribert/Voltmer, Rita (eds), *Hexenprozesse und Gerichtspraxis*, Trier 2002.

Eliade, Mircea, *Occultism, Witchcraft, and Cultural Fashions*, Chicago 1976.

Flint, Valerie/Gordon, Richard/Luck, Georg/Ogden, Daniel, *Witchcraft and Magic in Europe: Ancient Greece and Rome* (*AHWME*, vol. 2), London 1999.

Franz, Gunther (ed.), *Friedrich Spee. Dichter, Seelsorger, Bekämpfer des Hexenwahns (1591–1635)*, Trier 1991.

Franz, Gunther/Irsigler, Franz/Biesel, Elisabeth (eds), *Hexenglaube und Hexenprozesse im Raum Rhein-Mosel Saar*, Trier 1995.

Gijswijt-Hofstra, Marijke/Frijhoff, Willem (eds), *Witchcraft in the Netherlands from the Fourteenth to the Twentieth Century*, Rotterdam 1991.

Gijswijt-Hofstra, Marijke/Levack, Brian P./Porter, Roy, *Witchcraft and Magic in Europe: The Eighteenth and Nineteenth Centuries* (*AHWME*, vol. 5), London 1999.

Goodare, Julian (ed.), *The Scottish Witch-Hunt in Context*, Manchester 2002.

Hallen, Barry/Sodipo, J. O. (eds), *Knowledge, Belief, and Witchcraft. Analytic Experiments in African Philosophy*, London 1986.

Jolly, Karen/Raudvere, Catharine/Peters, Edward, *Witchcraft and Magic in Europe: The Middle Ages* (*AHWME*, vol. 3), London 2002.

Joralemon, Donald/Sharon, Douglas (eds), *Sorcery and Shamanism. Curanderos and Clients in Northern Peru*, Salt Lake City 1993.

Kiev, Ari (ed.), *Magic, Faith and Healing. Studies in Primitive Psychiatry*, London 1964.

Klaniczay, Gábor/Pócs, Eva (eds), *Witch-Beliefs and Witch-Hunting in Central and Eastern Europe*, Budapest 1994.

Lehmann, Arthur C./Myers, James E. (eds), *Magic, Witchcraft and Religion. An Anthropological Study of the Supernatural*, Palo Alto 1985.

Lehmann, Hartmut/Ulbricht, Otto (eds), *Vom Unfug des Hexen-Processes. Gegner der Hexenverfolgung von Johann Weyer bis Friedrich Spee*, Wiesbaden 1992.

Lorenz, Sönke (ed.), *Hexen und Hexenverfolgung im deutschen Südwesten. Katalog der Ausstellung*, Ostfildern 1994.

Lorenz, Sönke/Bauer, Dieter R. (eds), *Das Ende der Hexenverfolgung* (*Hexenforschung*, vol. 1), Stuttgart 1995.

Lorenz, Sönke/Bauer, Dieter R./Behringer, Wolfgang/Schmidt, Jürgen Michael (eds), *Himmlers Hexenkartothek. Das Interesse des National-sozialismus an der Hexenverfolgung* (*Hexenforschung*, vol. 4), Bielefeld 1999.

Lorenz, Sönke/Wandel Uwe Jens (eds), *Hexen und Hexenverfolgung in Thüringen*, Bielefeld 2002.

Malinowski, Bronislaw, *Magic, Science and Religion, and other Essays*, London 1954.

Malinowski, Bronislaw, *Culture* (1948), in *IESS*, vol. 4 (1968), 621–45.

Marwick, Max (ed.), *Witchcraft and Sorcery. Selected Readings*, London/New York 1970; enlarged 2nd edn, 1982; repr. 1990.

Middleton, John/Winter E. H. (eds), *Witchcraft and Sorcery in East Africa*, London 1963.

Middleton, John (ed.), *Magic, Witchcraft and Curing*, Austin/Texas 1967.

Moore, Henrietta L./Sanders Todd (eds), *Magical Interpretations, Material Realities. Modernity, Witchcraft and the Occult in Postcolonial Africa*, New York 2001.

Muchembled, Robert (ed.), *Magie et Sorcellerie en Europe du Moyen Age à nos jours*, Paris 1994.

Nutini, Hugo G./Roberts, John M., *Bloodsucking Witchcraft. An Epistemo-logical Study of Anthropomorphic Supernaturalism in Rural Tlaxcala*, Tucson/London 1993.

Opitz, Claudia (ed.), *Der Hexenstreit. Frauen in der frühneuzeitlichen Hexenverfolgung*, Freiburg 1995.

Poole, Robert (ed.), *The Lancashire Witches. Histories and Stories*, Manchester 2002.

Roper, Lyndal, *Oedipus and the Devil*, London/New York 1994.

Schmauder, Andreas (ed.), *Frühe Hexenverfolgung in Ravensburg und am Bodensee*, Konstanz 2001.

Segl, Peter (ed.), *Der Hexenhammer. Entstehung und Umfeld des Malleus Maleficarum von 1487*, Cologne/Berlin 1988.

Soman, Alfred, *Sorcellerie et Justice Criminelle. Le Parlement de Paris (16e–18e siècles)*, Hampshire 1992.

Stephen, Michele (ed.), *Sorcerer and Witch in Melanesia*, Melbourne 1987.

Valentinitsch, Helfried (ed.), *Hexen und Zauberer*, Graz 1987.

Walker, Deward E./Carrasco David (eds), *Witchcraft and Sorcery of the American Native Peoples*, Moscow/Idaho 1989.

Watson C. W./Ellen Roy (eds), *Understanding Witchcraft and Sorcery in Southeast Asia*, Honolulu 1993.

Willis, Roy G. (ed.), *Witchcraft and Healing*, Edinburgh 1969.

Zelenietz, Mary/Lindenbaum, Shirley S. (eds), *Sorcery and Social Change in Melanesia* (= *Social Analysis*, 8, special issue), Adelaide 1981.

5   Articles on Witchcraft

Abrahams, Ray, A Modern Witch-Hunt among the Lango of Uganda, in *Cambridge Anthropology*, 10 (1985), 32–45.

Ammann-Doubliez, Chantal, La première chasse aux sorciers en Valais, in Ostorero (1999), 63–98.

Anagnost, Ann S., Politics and Magic in Contemporary China, in *Modern China*, 13 (1987), 40–61.

Andenmatten, Bernard/Utz-Tremp Kathrin, De l'hérésie à la sorcellerie: L'inquisiteur Ulric de Torrenté OP (vers 1420–1445) et l'affermissement de l'inquisition en Suisse romande, in *ZSKG*, 86 (1992), 69–119.

Andersson, Jens A, Sorcery in the Era of 'Henry IV': Kinship, Mobility and Mortality in Buhera District, Zimbabwe, in *Journal of the Royal Anthropological Institute*, 8 (2002), 425–48.

Ankarloo, Bengt, Witch-Trials in Northern Europe, 1450–1700, in *AHWME*, vol. 4 (2002), 53–96.

Apter, Andrew, Atinga Revisited: Yoruba Witchcraft and the Cocoa Economy, 1950–1951, in Comaroff/Comaroff (1993), 111–28.

Ardener, Edwin, Witchcraft, Economics and the Continuity of Belief, in Douglas (1970), 141–60.

Ashforth, Adam, Reflections on Spiritual Insecurity in a Modern African City (Soweto), in *ASR*, 41, 3 (1998), 36–67.

Ashforth, Adam, Aids, Witchcraft and the Problem of Power in Post-Apartheid South Africa, *Occasional Papers of the Institute for Advanced Study*, 10, May 2001.

Auslander, Mark, 'Open the Wombs!' The Symbolic Politics of Modern Ngoni Witchfinding, in Comaroff/Comaroff (1993), 167–92.

Austen, Ralph, The Moral Economy of Witchcraft. An Essay in Comparative History, in Comaroff/Comaroff (1993), 89–110.

Ball, Joanna, The Ritual of the Necklace (Occasional Paper, Centre for the Study of Violence and Reconciliation), Johannesburg 1994.

Bastian, Misty L., 'Bloodhounds Who Have No Friends.' Witchcraft and Locality in the Nigerian Popular Press, in Comaroff/Comaroff (1993), 129–66.

Baxter, Paul, Absence Makes the Heart Grow Fonder: Some Suggestions Why Witchcraft Accusations are Rare among East African Pastoralists, in Gluckman (1972), 163–91.

Becker, Thomas, Hexenverfolgung in Kurköln. Kritische Anmerkungen zu Gerhard Schormanns 'Krieg gegen die Hexen', in *Annalen des Historischen Vereins für den Niederrhein*, 195 (1992), 202–14.

Behringer, Wolfgang, Erträge und Perspektiven der Hexenforschung, in *HZ*, 249 (1989), 619–40.

Behringer, Wolfgang, Kinderhexenprozesse. Zur Rolle von Kindern in der Geschichte der Hexenverfolgungen, in *ZHF*, 16 (1989), 31–47.

Behringer, Wolfgang, 'Allemagne, Mère de tant des sorcières'. Au Coeur des Persécutions, in Muchembled (1994), 59–98.

Behringer, Wolfgang, Zur Geschichte der Hexenforschung, in Lorenz (1994), 93–146.

Behringer, Wolfgang, Der 'Bayerische Hexenkrieg'. Die Debatte am Ende der Hexenprozesse in Deutschland, in Lorenz/Bauer (1995), 287–314.

Behringer, Wolfgang, Weather, Hunger and Fear. The Origins of the European Witch Persecution in Climate, Society and Mentality, in *German History*, 13 (1995), 1–27.

Behringer, Wolfgang, Neun Millionen Hexen. Entstehung, Tradition und Kritik eines populären Mythos, in *GWU*, 49 (1998), 664–85.

Behringer, Wolfgang, Climatic Change and Witch-Hunting. The Impact of the Little Ice Age on Mentalities, in *Climatic Change*, 43 (1999), 335–51.

Behringer, Wolfgang, Detecting the Ultimate Conspiracy, or How Waldensians Became Witches, in Swann/Coward (2003).

Berndt, Ronald M., A Devastating Disease Syndrome: Kuru Sorcery in the Eastern Central Highlands of New Guinea, in *Sociologus*, 8 (1958), 68–82.

Berry, Herbert, The Globe Bewitched and 'El hombre fiel', in *Medieval and Renaissance Drama in England*, 1 (1984), 211–30.

Bethencourt, Francisco, Portugal: A Scrupulous Inquisition, in Ankarloo/Henningsen (1990), 403–24.

Blöcker, Monica, Wetterzauber. Zu einem Glaubenskomplex des frühen Mittelalters, in Francia (1982), 117–31.

Boskovic-Stulli, Maja, Kresnik-Krsnik, ein Wesen aus der kroatischen und slowenischen Volksüberlieferung, in *Fabula*, 3 (1960), 275–98.

Brain, James L., Witchcraft and Development, in *African Affairs*, 81 (1982), 371–84.

Brantley, Cynthia, A Historical Perspective of the Giriama and Witchcraft Control, in *Africa*, 49 (1979), 112–33.

Brinkman, Inge, Ways of Death. Accounts of Terror from Angolan Refugees in Namibia, in *Africa*, 70 (2000), 1–24.

Burr, George Lincoln, The Literature of Witchcraft, in *Papers of the American Historical Association*, 4, 4 (1889/1890), 37–66.

Cannon, Walter B., Voodoo Death, in *AA*, 44 (1942), 169–81.

Ciekawy, Diane/Geschiere, Peter, Containing Witchcraft: Conflicting Scenarios in Postcolonial Africa, in *ASR*, 41 (1998), 1–14.

Clark, Stuart, Witchcraft and Magic in Early Modern Culture, in *AHWME*, vol. 4 (2002), 97–170.

Colson, Elizabeth, The Father as Witch, in *Africa*, 70 (2000), 333–58.

Contreras, Jaime/Henningsen, Gustav, Forty-four Thousand Cases of the Spanish Inquisition (1540–1700): An Analysis of a Historical Data Bank, in Henningsen/Tedeschi (1986), 100–29.

Cope R. L., Written in Characters of Blood? The Reign of King Cetshwayo Ka Mpande (1872–9), in *JAH*, 36 (1995), 247–69.

Cryer, Frederick H., Magic in Ancient Syria-Palestine – and in the Old Testament, in *AHWME*, vol. 1 (2001), 97–152.

Currie, Elliot P., Crimes without Criminals. Witchcraft and Its Control in Renaissance Europe, in *Law and Society Review*, 3 (1968), 7–28.

van Dijk, Rijk, La guérisseuse du docteur Banda au Malawi, in *Politique Africaine*, 52 (1992), 145–50.

Eliade, Mircea, Some Observations on European Witchcraft, in *History of Religions*, 14 (1975), 149–72.

Ellis, Stephen, Witch-Hunting in Central Madagascar, 1828–1861, in *PP*, 175 (2002), 90–123.

Ennen, Edith, Zauberinnen und fromme Frauen – Ketzerinnen und Hexen, in Segl (1988), 7–22.

Evers, Ingrid, Maaslandse Heksenprocessen, in de Blécourt/Gijswijt-Hofstra (1986), 77–110.

Ferrary J., Lex Cornelia de sicariis et veneficiis, in *Athenaeum*, 69 (1991), 417–34.

Findley, Alison, Sexual and Spiritual Politics in the Events of 1633/34 and 'The Late Lancashire Witches', in Poole (2002), 146–65.

Fisiy, Cyprian F., Containing Occult Practices: Witchcraft Trials in Cameroon, in *ASR*, 41 (1998), 143–63.

Fisiy, Cyprian F./Geschiere, Peter, Witchcraft, Development and Paranoia in Cameroon. Interactions between Popular, Academic, and State Discourse, in Moore/Sanders (2001), 226–46.

Foster, George M., Nagualism in Mexico and Guatemala, in *Acta Americana*, 2 (1944), 85–102.

Fraikin, Jean, Eine Seite in der Geschichte der Hexerei in den Ardennen und im Moselraum. Die Affäre um Jean de Vaulx, Mönch in Stablo (1592–1597), in Franz/Irsigler/Biesel (1995), 417–34.

Franck, Johannes, Geschichte des Wortes Hexe, in Hansen (1901), 614–70.

Frank, Stephen P., Popular Justice, Community and Culture among the Russian Peasantry, 1870–1900, in *RR*, 46 (1987), 239–65.

Frigerio, Pierangelo/Pisoni, Carlo Alessandro, Un brogliacco dell'Inquisizione milanese (1418–1422), in *Libri & Documenti. Rivista Quadragesimale* (Milano), 21 (3) (1995), 46–65.

Fuge, Boris, Das Ende der Hexenverfolgungen in Lothringen, Kurtrier und Luxemburg im 17. Jahrhundert, in Beier-de-Haan/Voltmer/Irsigler (2002), 164–72.

Gareis, Iris, 'Hexer' und 'Hexen' im alten Peru: Trugbild und Wirklichkeit in den historischen Quellen, in *Münchner Beiträge zur Völkerkunde*, 4 (1991), 265–91.

Geschiere, Peter/Fisiy, Cyprian F., Domesticating Personal Violence: Witchcraft, Courts and Confessions in Cameroon, in *Africa*, 64 (1994), 323–41.

Gijswijt-Hofstra, Marijke, Six Centuries of Witchcraft in the Netherlands: Themes, Outlines, and Interpretations, in Gijswijt-Hofstra/Frijhoff (1991), 1–36.

Ginzburg, Carlo, The Philosopher and the Witches: An Experiment in Cultural History, in Klaniczay/Pócs (1994), 283–93.

Glover, Jessy R., The Role of the Witch in Gurung Society, in *Eastern Anthropology*, 25 (1972), 221–6.

Gluckman, Max, The Logic of Witchcraft, in Gluckman (1956), 81–108.

Goodare, Julian, The Scottish Witchcraft Panic of 1597, in Goodare (2002), 51–72.

Goody, Esther, Legitimate and Illegitimate Aggression in a West African State, in Douglas (1970), 207–43.

Goody, Jack, Anomy in Ashanti, in *Africa*, 27 (1957), 356–63.

Gooneratne, Dandris de Silva, On Demonology and Witchcraft in Ceylon, in *Journal of the Ceylon Branch, Royal Asiatic Society*, 4 (1866), 1–117.

Gordon, Richard, Imagining Greek and Roman Magic, in *AHWME*, vol. 2 (1999), 159–276.

Green, Maia, Witchcraft Suppression Practices and Movements: Public Politics and the Logic of Purification, in *CSSH*, 39 (1997), 319–45.

Hagen, Rune, The Witch-Hunt in Early Modern Finnmark, in *Acta Borealia* (1999), 43–62.

Hammond-Tooke, William David, Urbanization and the Interpretation of Misfortune. A Quantitative Analysis, in *Africa*, 40 (1970), 25–39.

Harnischfeger, Johannes, Unverdienter Reichtum über Hexerei und Ritualmorde in Nigeria, in *Sociologus*, 47 (1997), 129–56.

Harnischfeger, Johannes, Witchcraft and the State in Africa, in *Anthropos*, 95 (2000), 99–112.

Hartwig, Gerald W., Long-Distance Trade and the Evolution of Sorcery among the Kerebe, in *AHS*, 4 (1971), 505–24.

Henningsen, Gustav, Das Ende der Hexenverfolgungen und die Fortsetzung der populären Hexenverfolgung, in Lorenz/Bauer (1995), 315–28.

Heywood, Linda M., Towards an Understanding of Modern Political Ideology in Africa: The Case of the Ovimbundu in Angola, in *JMAS*, 36 (1998), 139–67.

Hocart, Arthur M., Medicine and Witchcraft in Eddystone of the Solomons, in *JRAI*, 55 (1925), 229–70.

Hoffmann, Ruth F., Amnestie für Hexenmörder, in *Die Zeit* (2000).

Honigman, John, Witch-fear in Post-contact Kaska Society, in *AA*, 49 (1947), 222–42.

Hultcrantz, Ake, Mythology and Religious Concepts, in *HNAI*, 11 (1986), 630–40.

Hults, Linda, Baldung and the Witches of Freiburg. The Evidence of Images, in *JIH*, 18 (1987), 249–76.

Hutton, Ronald, The Global Context of the Scottish Witch-Hunt, in Goodare (2002), 16–32.

Jahoda, Gustav, Social Aspirations, Magic, and Witchcraft in Ghana, in P. C. Lloyd (ed.), *The New Elites of Tropical Africa*, London 1966, 199–212.

Johansen, Jens C. V., Hexen auf mittelalterlichen Wandmalereien. Zur Genese der Hexenprozesse in Dänemark, in Blauert 1990, 217–40.

Jolly, Karen, Medieval Magic: Definitions, Beliefs, Practices, in Jolly/Raudvere/Peters (2002), 1–71.

Kamber, Peter, La chasse aux sorciers et aux sorcières dans le pays de Vaud. Aspects quantitativ (1581–1620), in *Revue Historique Vaudoise*, 90 (1982), 21–33.

Kelly H. A., English Kings and the Fear of Sorcery, in *Medieval Studies*, 39 (1977), 206–38.

Klaniczay, Gábor, Hungary: The Accusations and the Universe of Popular Magic, in Ankarloo/Henningsen (1990), 219–56.

Kuper, Adam, Enemies of the People. Where Witches – and Witch-Hunters – Still Ride, in *Times Literary Supplement*, 8 June 2001, 5–6.

Lee A., Ngoja and Six Theories of Witchcraft Eradication, in *Ufahamu*, 6 (1976), 101–17.

Lehmann, Hartmut, The Persecution of Witches as Restoration of Order: The Case of Germany, 1590s–1650s, in *CEH*, 21 (1988), 107–21.

Levack, Brian, The Great Scottish Witch-Hunt of 1661–62, in *Journal of British Studies*, 20 (1980), 90–108.

Levine, Nancy E., Belief and Explanation in Nyinba Women's Witchcraft, in *Man*, 17 (1982), 259–74.

Lévi-Strauss, Claude, The Sorcerer and His Magic [1949], in *Structural Anthropology*, New York 1963, 161–80; repr. in Middleton (1967), 23–41.

Mährle, Wolfgang, 'O wehe der armen seelen.' Hexenverfolgungen in der Fürstpropstei Ellwangen (1588–1694), in Dillinger/et al. (1998), 325–500.

Malinowski, Bronislaw, Reflections on Witchcraft, in *The Dynamics of Culture Change*, New Haven 1945, 95–9.

Marwick, Max, Another Modern Anti-witchcraft Movement in East Central Africa, in *Africa*, 20 (1950), 100–12; abridged repr. in Marwick (1982), 213–17.

Marwick, Max, Is Science a Form of Witchcraft? in *New Scientist*, 63 (1974), 578–81.

Marwick, Max, Witchcraft as a Social Strain-Gauge, in Marwick (1982), 300–13.

Mauss, Marcel/Hubert, Henri, Esquisse d'une théorie générale de la Magie, in *Année Sociologique*, 7 (1902/1903), 1–146.

Mavhungu, Khaukanani, Heroes, Villains and the State in South Africa's Witchcraft Zone, in *The African Anthropologist*, 7 (2000), 114–29.

Mayer, Philipp, Witches, in Marwick (1982), 54–70.

de Mello e Souza, Laura, Witchcraft and Magic Practices in Colonial Brazil, in Klaniczay/Pócs (1994), 243–56.

Mesaki, Simeon, Witch-Killing in Sukumaland, in Abrahams (1994), 47–60.

Midelfort, Erik, Recent Witch Hunting Research, or Where Do We Go from Here?, in *The Papers of the Bibliographical Society of America*, 62 (1968), 373–420.

Midelfort, Erik, Heartland of the Witchcraze: Central and Northern Europe, in *History Today*, 31 (1981), 27–31.

Mitchell, Clyde/Flagg-Mitchell, Hilary, Social Factors in the Perception of the Causes of Disease, in Marwick (1982), 401–21.

Moeller, Katrin, 'Es ist ein überaus gerechtes Gesetz, dass die Zauberinnen getötet werden'. Hexenverfolgungen in Mecklenburg, in Beier-de Haan/Voltmer/Irsigler (2002), 96–107.

Monter, William, The Historiography of European Witchcraft: Progress and Prospects, in *JIH*, 2 (1971/72), 435–53.

Monter, William, Toads and Eucharists. The Male Witches of Normandy, 1564–1660, in *FHS*, 20 (1997), 563–95.

Monter, William, Witch-Trials in Continental Europe, 1560–1660, in *AHWME*, vol. 4 (2002), 1–52.

Morgan J. C., Navaho Witchcraft has Significance in Navaho Life, in *Times Hustler* (Farmington, New Mexico), 18 September 1942 (repr. Kluckhohn (1944), 252–4).

Musambachime M. C., The Impact of Rumour: The Case of the Banyama (Vampire Men) Scare in Northern Rhodesia, 1930–1964, in *IJAHS*, 21 (1988), 201–17.

Nadel, Siegfried Ferdinand, Witchcraft in Four African Societies, in *AA*, 54 (1952), 18–29.

Nitibaskara, Ronnie, Observations on the Practice of Sorcery in Java, in Watson/Ellen (1993), 123–34.

O'Brien, Donald B. Cruise, Satan Steps out from the Shadows. Religion and Politics in Africa, in *Africa*, 70 (2000), 520–5.

Paravy, Pierette, A propos de la genèse médiévale des chasses aux sorcières: le traité de Claude Tholosan, juge dauphinois (vers 1436), in *Mélanges de l'école francaise de Rome. Moyen Age/Temps Modernes*, 91 (1979), 322–79.

Parish, Jane, Black Market, Free Market. Anti-witchcraft Shrines and Fetishes among the Akan, in Moore/Sanders (2001), 118–35.

Pearl, Jonathan L., Witchcraft in New France in the Seventeenth Century: The Social Aspect, in *Historical Reflections. Réflexions historiques*, 4 (1977), 191–206.

Pels, Peter, The Magic of Africa. Reflections on a Western Commonplace, in *ASR*, 41 (1998), 193–209.

Peruzzi, Candida, Un processo di stregoneria a Todi nel '400, in *Lares*, 21, 2 (1955), 1–17.

Peters, Edward, The Medieval Church and State on Superstition, Magic and Witchcraft: From Augustine to the Sixteenth Century, in Jolly/Raudvere/Peters (2002), 173–245 (*AHWME*, vol. 3).

Pitman, Frank Wesley, Fetishism, Witchcraft, and Christianity among the Slaves, in *Journal of Negro History*, 11 (1926), 650–68.

Priester P./Barske A., Vervolging van tovenaars(en) in Groningen, 1547–1597, in de Blécourt/Gijswijt-Hofstra (1986), 50–76.

Rajsp, Vincenc, Hexenprozesse in Slowenien, in Klaniczay/Pócs (1992), 51–66.

Rasmussen, Susan, Betrayal or Affirmation? Transformations in Witchcraft Technologies of Power, Danger, and Agency among the Tuareg of Niger, in Moore/Sanders (2001), 136–59.

Redmayne, Alison, Chikanga. An African Diviner with an International Reputation, in Douglas (1970), 103–28.

Richards, Audrey, A Modern Movement of Witchfinders, in *Africa*, 8 (1935), 448–61.

Roeck, Bernd, Christlicher Idealstaat und Hexenwahn, in *Historisches Jahrbuch*, 108 (1988), 379–405.

Rutherford, Blair, To Find an African Witch: Anthropology, Modernity and Witch-Finding in North-West Zimbabwe, in *Critique of Anthropology*, 19 (1999), 89–109.

Saler, Benson, Nagual, Witch and Sorcerer in a Quiché Village, in Middleton (1967), 69–99.

Schapera, Isaac, Sorcery and Witchcraft in Bechuanaland, in *African Affairs*, 51 (1952), 41–52.

Scobie, Alex, Strigiform Witches in Roman and Other Cultures, in *Fabula*, 19 (1978), 74–101.

Seler, Eduard, Zauberei und Zauberer im alten Mexiko, in *Veröffentlichungen aus dem Königlichen Museum für Völkerkunde*, 4 (1899), 29–57.

Shaw, Rosalind, The Production of Witchcraft/Witchcraft as Production: Memory, Modernity, and the Slave Trade in Sierra Leone, in *American Ethnologist*, 24 (1997), 856–76.

di Simplicio, Oscar, A Parting of Ways? From Witchcraft Accusations to a New Culture of Misfortune: The Sienese Case 1580–1721, in Behringer/ Sharpe (2004).

Slaats, Hermann/Portier, Karen, Sorcery and the Law in Modern Indonesia, in Watson/Ellen (1993), 135–48.

Soman, Alfred, Les procés de sorcellerie au Parlement de Paris (1565–1640), in *AESC*, 32 (1977), 790–812.

Soman, Alfred, The Parlement of Paris and the Great Witch Hunt (1565–1640), in *SCJ*, 9 (1978), 31–44.

Soman, Alfred, Decriminalizing Witchcraft: Does the French Experience Furnish a European Model?, in *CJH*, 10 (1989), 1–22.

Spanos, Nicholas P., Witchcraft in Histories of Psychiatry: A Critical Analysis and an Alternative Conceptualization, in *Psychological Bulletin*, 85 (1978), 417–39.

Spindler, Louise, Witchcraft in Menominee Acculturation, in *AA*, 54 (1952), 393–402.

Spooner, Brian, The Evil Eye in the Middle East, in Douglas (1970), 311–19.

Stadler J. J., Witches and Witch-Hunters: Witchcraft, General Relations and the Life-Cycle in a Lowveld Village, in *African Studies*, 55 (1996), 87–110.

Steadman L., The Killing of Witches, in *Oceania*, 56 (1985), 106–23.

Strathern, Andrew, Witchcraft, Greed, Cannibalism and Death. Some Related Themes from the New Guinea Highlands, in Maurice Bloch/ J. Parry (eds), *Death and the Regeneration of Life*, Cambridge University Press 1982, 111–33.

Tait, David, A Sorcery Hunt in Dagomba, in *Africa*, 33 (1963), 136–46.

Tazbir, Janusz, Hexenprozesse in Polen, in *ARG*, 71 (1980), 280–307.

Thomsen, Marie-Louise, The Evil Eye in Mesopotamia, in *JNES*, 51 (1992), 19–32.

Thomsen, Marie-Louise, Witchcraft and Magic in Ancient Mesopotamia, in *AHWME*, vol. 1 (2001), 1–95.

Todorov, Tsetvan, Le discours de la magie, in *L'Homme*, 4, 13 (1973), 38–65.

Trusen, Winfried, Der Inquisitionsprozeß, in *ZRGKA*, 74 (1988), 168–230.

Turner, Paul, Witchcraft as Negative Charisma, in *Ethnology*, 9 (1970), 366–72.

Turner, Victor, Witchcraft and Sorcery: Taxonomy versus Dynamics, in *The Forest of Symbols: Aspects of Ndembu Ritual*, Ithaca/NY 1967, 112–27.

Vincent, Jeanne-Françoise, Le Mouvement Croix-Koma: une nouvelle forme de lutte contre la sorcellerie en pays Congo, in *Cahiers d'Études Africaines*, 6, 4 (1966).

Voltmer, Rita, Zwischen Herrschaftskrise, Wirtschaftsdepression und Jesuitenpropaganda. Hexenverfolgungen in der Stadt Trier (15.–17. Jahrhundert), in *Jahrbuch für westdeutsche Landesgeschichte*, 27 (2001), 37–107.

Voltmer, Rita/Irsigler, Franz, Die europäischen Hexenverfolgungen der Frühen Neuzeit – Vorurteile, Faktoren und Bilanzen, in Beier-de-Haan/Voltmer/Irsigler (2002), 30–45.

de Waardt, Hans, Oudewater. Eine Hexenwaage wird gewogen – oder: Die Zerstörung einer historischen Mythe, in *Westfälische Zeitschrift*, 144 (1994), 249–63.

de Waardt, Hans, Rechtssicherheit nach dem Zusammenbruch der zentralen Gewalt. Rechtspflege, Obrigkeit, Toleranz und wirtschaftliche Verhältnisse in Holland, in Lorenz/Bauer (1995), 129–52.

Waite, Gary K., Between the Devil and the Inquisitor: Anabaptists, Diabolical Conspiracies and Magical Beliefs in the Sixteenth-century Netherlands, in Werner O. Packull (ed.), *Radical Reformation Studies. Essays presented to James Stayer*, Ashgate 1999, 120–40.

Walinski-Kiehl, Robert, 'The Devil's Children'. Child Witch-trials in Early Modern Germany, in *Continuity and Change*, 11 (1996), 171–90.

Walinski-Kiehl, Robert, Pamphlets, Propaganda and Witch-Hunting in Germany c.1560-c.1639, in *Reformation*, 6 (2000), 51–74.

Walker, Deward E., Nec Percé Sorcery, in *Ethnology*, 6 (1967), 66–96.

Willis, Roy G., Kamcape: An Anti-sorcery Movement in South-west Tanzania, in *Africa*, 38 (1968), 1–15.

Willis, Roy G., Instant Millennium. The Sociology of African Witch-Cleansing Cults, in Douglas (1970), 129–39.

Wilson, Monica Hunter, Witch Beliefs and Social Structure, in *AJS*, 56 (1951), 307–13.

Worobec, Christiane D., Witchcraft Beliefs and Practices in Prerevolutionary Russian and Ukrainian Villages, in *RR*, 54 (1995), 165–87.

Wunder, Heide, Hexenprozesse im Herzogtum Preußen während des 16. Jahrhunderts, in Degn (1983), 197–203.

Yamba, Bawa C., Cosmologies in Turmoil: Witchfinding and AIDS in Chiawa, Zambia, in *Africa*, 67 (1997), 200–23.

Zelenietz, Mary, Sorcery and Social Change. An Introduction, in Zelenietz/Lindenbaum (1981), 3–15 (= *Social Analysis*, 8 (1981), 3–15).

Zguta, Russell, The Ordeal by Water (Swimming of Witches) in the East Slavic World, in *Slavic Review*, 36 (1977), 220–30.

Zika, Charles, Fears of Flying: Representations of Witchcraft and Sexuality in Early Sixteenth-Century Germany, in *Australian Journal of Art*, 8 (1989/90), 19–47.

6   Occultism, Esotericism and 'New Witches'

Adler, Margot, *Drawing down the Moon. Witches, Druids, Goddess-Worshippers, and Other Pagans in America Today*, 2nd edn New York 1986.

Adorno, Theodor W., Thesen gegen den Okkultismus, in *Minima Moralia. Reflexionen aus dem beschädigten Leben*, Frankfurt/Main 1951, 321–9.

Adorno, Theodor W., *The Stars Down to Earth, and Other Essays on the Irrational in Culture*, ed. Stephen Crock, London 2002.

Baker, James W., White Witches: Historic Fact and Romantic Fantasy, in Lewis (1996), 171–92.

Berger, Helen A., *A Community of Witches. Contemporary Neo-Paganism and Witchcraft in the United States*, Columbia/South Carolina University Press 1999.

Billig, Otto, *Flying Saucers – Magic in the Skies. A Psychohistory*, Cambridge/Mass. 1982.

Blavatsky, Helena Petrowna, *Isis Unveiled*, New York 1875.

Bradley, Marion Zimmer, *The Mists of Avalon*, New York 1983.

Brandon, Ruth, *The Spiritualists. The Passion for the Occult in the Nineteenth and Twentieth Centuries*, London 1983.

Christ, Carol, *Rebirth of the Goddess. Finding Meaning in Feminist Spirituality*, New York 1997.

Crabtree, Adam, *From Mesmer to Freud. Magnetic Sleep and the Roots of Psychological Healing*, New Haven 1993.

Daly, Mary, *Gyn/Ecology. The Metaethics of Radical Feminism*, Boston 1978.

Darnton, Robert, *Mesmerism and the End of Enlightenment in France*, Cambridge 1968.

Dworkin, Andrea, *Woman Hating. A Radical Look at Sexuality*, New York 1974.

Ehrenreich, Barbara/English, Deirdre, *Witches, Midwives and Nurses. A History of Women Healers*, New York 1973.

Galbreath, Robert, Traditional and Modern Elements in the Occultism of Rudolf Steiner, in *Journal of Popular Culture*, 3 (1969), 451–67.

Galbreath, Robert, The History of Modern Occultism: A Bibliographical Survey, in *Journal of Popular Culture*, 5 (1971), 726–54.

Gardner, Gerald B., *Witchcraft Today*, London 1954.

Garrett, Clarke, *Spirit Possession and Popular Religion from the Camisards to the Shakers*, Baltimore 1987.

Goodrick-Clarke, Nicholas, *The Occult Roots of Nazism. Secret Aryan Cults and Their Influence on Nazi Ideology. The Ariosophists of Austria and Germany, 1890–1935*, New York 1992.

Goodrick-Clarke, Nicholas, *Black Sun. Aryan Cults, Esoteric Nazism, and the Politics of Identity*, New York 2002.

Graves, Robert, *The White Goddess*, New York 1948.

Harrow, Judy, The Contemporary Neo-Pagan Revival, in Lewis (1996), 9–24.

Hart E., *Hypnotism, Mesmerism and the New Witchcraft*, London 1898.

Howe, Ellic, *Urania's Children*, London 1967.

Howe, Ellic, *The Magicians of the Golden Dawn*, London 1972.

Hume, Lynn, *Witchcraft and Paganism in Australia*, Melbourne 1997.

Hutton, Roland, *The Triumph of the Moon. A History of Modern Pagan Witchcraft*, Oxford 1999.

Ivakhiv, Adrian, The Resurgence of Magical Religion as a Response to the Crisis of Modernity, in Lewis (1996), 237–68.

Jencson, Linda, Neopaganism and the Great Mother Goddess: Anthropology as Midwife to a New Religion, in *Anthropology Today*, 5 (1989), 2–4.

Jung, Carl Gustav, *Psychologie und Okkultismus*, Olten 1971.

Kapferer, Bruno (ed.), *Beyond Rationalism. Sorcery, Magic and Ritual in Contemporary Realities*, New York 2003.

Lewis, James R. (ed.), *Magical Religion and Modern Witchcraft*, New York 1996.

Ludendorff, Mathilde, *Christliche Grausamkeit an Deutschen Frauen*, Munich 1934.

Luhrmann, Tanya M., *Persuasions of the Witch's Craft. Ritual Magic and Witchcraft in Present-day England*, Oxford 1989.

Magin, Ulrich, *Von Ufos entführt. Unheimliche Begegnungen der vierten Art*, Munich 1991.

Magliocco, Sabina, Ritual is My Chosen Art Form: The Creation of Ritual as Folk Art among Contemporary Pagans, in Lewis (1996), 75–92.

Malanowski, Anja/Köhle, Anne-Bärbel, *Hexenkraft*, Munich 1996.

Marty, Martin, The Occult Establishment, in *Social Research*, 37 (1970), 212–30.

Melton, John Gordon, *Magic, Witchcraft and Paganism in America. A Bibliography*, New York 1982.

Möller, Helmut/Howe, Ellic, *Merlin Peregrinus. Vom Untergrund des Abendlandes*, Würzburg 1986.

Müller-Reimerdes, Friederike, *Der christliche Hexenwahn*, Leipzig 1935.

Murray, Margaret, Organization of Witches in Great Britain, in *Folk-Lore*, 28 (1917), 228–58.

Murray, Margaret, *The Witch-Cult in Western Europe*, Oxford 1921.

Murray, Margaret, *The God of the Witches*, London 1931.

M[urray], M[argaret] A[lice], Witchcraft, in *Encyclopaedia Britannica*, vol. 23, Chicago/London/Toronto 1959, 686–8.

Oppenheim, Janet, *The Other World. Spiritualism and Psychical Research in England, 1850–1914*, Cambridge 1985.

Price, Harry, *Poltergeist over England*, London 1945.

Rabinovitch, Shelley, Spells of Transformation: Categorizing Modern Neo-Pagan Witches, in Lewis (1996), 75–92.

Roberts, Jani Farrell, *The Seven Days of My Creation. Tales of Magic, Sex and Gender*, London 2002.

Roszak, Theodore, *The Making of a Counter Culture*, Garden City/NY 1969.

Ruether, Rosemary, Goddesses and Witches. Liberation and Counter-Culture Feminism, in *Christian Century* (1980), 843–4.

Ruether, Rosemary, *Gaia and God. An Ecofeminist Theology of Earth Healing*, San Francisco 1992.

Russell, Jeffrey Burton, *A History of Witchcraft. Sorcerers, Heretics, and Pagans*, London 1980.

Spretnak, Charlene (ed.), *The Politics of Women's Spirituality. Essays on the Rise of Spiritual Power within the Feminist Movement*, New York 1982.

Starhawk, [Miriam Simos], *The Spiral Dance. A Rebirth of the Ancient Religion of the Great Goddess*, San Francisco 1979.

Summers, Montague, *History of Witchcraft*, London/New York 1926.

Surette, Leon/Tryphonopoulos, Demetres (eds), *Literary Modernism and the Occult Tradition*, Orono/Me. 1996.

Tiryakian, Edward A., Towards the Sociology of Esoteric Culture, in *AJS*, 78 (1972), 491–512.

Tiryakian, Edward A. (ed.), *On the Margin of the Visible: Sociology, the Esoteric, and the Occult*, New York 1974.

Truzzi, Marcello, The Occult Revival as Popular Culture: Some Random Observations on the Old and Nouveau Witch, in *Sociological Quarterly*, 13 (1972), 130–40.

Truzzi, Marcello, Towards a Sociology of Modern Witchcraft, in Zaretsky/Leone (1974), 628–45.

Valiente, Doreen, *The Rebirth of Witchcraft*, London 1989.

Webb, James, *The Flight from Reason*, London 1971 (= *The Occult Underground*, La Salle/Ill. 1974).

Wiesendanger, Harald, *In Teufels Küche. Jugendokkultismus: Gründe, Folgen, Hilfe*, Düsseldorf 1992.
Wisselinck, Erika, *Hexen*, Munich 1986.
Zaretsky, Irving I./Leone, Mark P. (eds), *Religious Movements in Contemporary America*, Princeton 1974.

7 General Standard Works

Abel, Wilhelm, *Massenarmut und Hungerkrisen im vorindustriellen Europa*, Hamburg/Berlin 1974.
Abel, Wilhelm, *Agricultural Fluctuations in Europe*, London 1980.
Aberth, John, *From the Brink of the Apocalypse: Confronting Famine, War, Plague and Death in the Later Middle Ages*, New York 2001.
Abrahams, Ray, *Vigilant Citizens. Vigilantism and the State*, Cambridge 1998.
Adas, Michael, *Prophets of Rebellion. Millenarian Protest Movements against the European Colonial Order*, Chapel Hill 1979.
Adorno, Theodor W./Frenkel-Brunswik, Else/Levinson, Daniel J./Sanford, R. Nevitt, *The Authoritarian Personality*, New York 1950.
Arens, William, *The Man-eating Myth. Anthropology and Anthropophagy*, Oxford 1979.
Arima, Eugene Y., Caribou Eskimo, in *HNAI*, vol. 5, Washington 1984, 447–62.
Aston, Margaret, *England's Iconoclasts. Laws against Images*, Oxford 1988.
Aston, Trevor (ed.), *Crisis in Europe 1560–1660*, London 1965.
Audisio, Gabriel, *Les Vaudois*, Turin 1989.
Balikci, Asen, Netsilik, in *HNAI*, vol. 5, Washington 1984, 447–62.
Barlow, Lisa K./et al., Interdisciplinary Investigations of the End of the Norse Western Settlement in Greenland, in *The Holocene*, 7 (1997), 489–500.
Beattie, John, *Other Cultures*, London 1964.
Becker, Howard S., *Outsiders. Studies in the Sociology of Deviance*, New York 1963.
Behringer, Wolfgang, Falken und Tauben, in Hsia/Scribner (1997), 219–61.
Behringer, Wolfgang, *Im Zeichen des Merkur. Reichspost und Kommunikationsrevolution in der Frühen Neuzeit*, Göttingen 2003.
Beier, Albert L., *Masterless Men. The Vagrancy Problem in England, 1560–1640*, London 1985.
Benedict, Ruth, The Vision in Plains Culture, in *AA*, 24 (1922), 1–23.
Berman, Morris, *The Re-enchantment of the World*, Ithaca 1981.
Bettelheim, Bruno, *The Uses of Enchantment. The Meaning and Importance of Fairy Tales*, Harmondsworth 1978.
Bireley, Robert, The Thirty Years' War as Germany's Religious War, in Repgen (1988), 85–106.
Bloch, Marc, *The Royal Touch*, trans. J. E. Anderson, London 1973.
Boas, Francis, *The Mind of Primitive Man*, New York 1931.
Bockie, Simon, *Death and the Invisible Powers. The World of Kongo Belief*, Bloomington/Indiana 1993.
Borst, Arno, *Die Katharer*, Stuttgart 1953.

Briffa, Keith R./et al., Influence of Volcanic Eruptions on Northern Hemisphere Summer Temperature over the Past 600 Years, in *Nature*, 393 (1998), 450–5.

Brown, Peter, *Religion and Society in the Age of St. Augustine*, London 1972.

Burke, Peter, *History and Social Theory*, Cambridge 1992.

Buckley, Thomas/Gottlieb, Alma (eds), *Blood Magic. The Anthropology of Menstruation*, Berkeley/Ca. 1988.

Capp, B., Godly Rule and English Millenarianism, in *PP*, 52 (1971), 106–17.

Chadwick, Henry, *Priscillian of Ávila. The Occult and the Charismatic in the Early Church*, Oxford 1976.

Chayanov, Aleksandr, *The Theory of Peasant Economy*, Manchester 1989.

Clark, Peter (ed.), *The European Crisis of the 1590s*, London 1985.

Cohn, Norman, *The Pursuit of the Millennium*, London 1957.

Comaroff, Jean/Comaroff, John, *Of Revelation and Revolution*, Chicago 1991.

Crouzet, Denis, *Les Guerriers de Dieu*, 2 vols, Paris 1990.

Delumeau, Jean, *Sin and Fear. The Emergence of a Western Guilt Culture, 13th–18th Centuries*, trans. Eric Nicholson, New York 1990.

Dirks, R., Social Responses during Severe Food Shortages and Famine, in *CA*, 21 (1980), 1–44.

Douglas, Mary, *Purity and Danger*, London 1966.

Douglas, Mary, *Natural Symbols. Explorations in Cosmology*, London 1973.

Douglas, Mary/Kaberry, Philip (eds), *Man in Africa*, London 1969.

Dowd, Gregory Evans, *A Spirited Resistance. The North American Indian Struggle for Unity, 1745–1815*, Baltimore 1992.

Duerr, Hans Peter, *Dreamtime*, trans. Felicitas Goodman, Oxford 1985.

Duhr, Bernhard, *Geschichte der Jesuiten in den Ländern deutscher Zunge*, 4 vols, Freiburg 1906–1927.

Dunning, Chester, Who was Tsar Dmitrii?, in *Slavic Review*, 60 (2001), 705–29.

Durkheim, Émile, *The Division of Labour in Society* (1893), New York 1933.

Durkheim, Émile, *Les formes élémentaires de la vie religieuse*, Paris 1912.

Edmunds, David R., *The Shawnee Prophet*, Lincoln/Nebraska 1983.

Eggan, Fred/Pandey T. N., Zuni History, 1850–1970, in *HNAI*, vol. 9 (1979), 474–81.

Eisenstadt, Shmuel N., Multiple Modernities, in *Daedalus*, 129 (2000), 1–29.

Eliade, Mircea, *Shamanism: Archaique Techniques of Ecstasy* (1951), Princeton 1964.

Elias, Norbert, *The Civilizing Process*, 2 vols (1939), Oxford 1978/1982.

Ellis, Florence H., Isleta Pueblo, in *HNAI*, vol. 9 (1979), 351–65.

Elsas, Moritz John, *Umriß einer Geschichte der Preise und Löhne vom ausgehenden Mittelalter bis zum Beginn des 19. Jh.*, 2 vols, Leiden 1936/1949.

Escobar, A., *Encountering Development. The Making and Unmaking of the Third World*, Princeton 1995.

Etzioni-Halevy, Eva/Etzioni, Amitai (eds), *Social Change*, New York 1973.

Evans, Robert J., *Rudolf II. and His World*, Oxford 1973.

Farmer, Paul, *Aids and Accusation. Haiti and the Geography of Blame*, Los Angeles 1992.

Fields, Karen E., *Revival and Rebellion in Colonial Central Africa*, Princeton 1985.

Flaherty, Gloria, *Shamanism and the Eighteenth Century*, Princeton/NJ 1992.

Forster, Marc, *The Counter-Reformation in the Villages. Religion and Reform in the Bishopric of Speyer, 1560–1720*, Ithaca 1992.

Foster, George M., Peasant Society and the Image of Limited Good, in *AA*, 67 (1965), 293–315.

Foster, George M., The Anatomy of Envy: A Study in Symbolic Behavior, in *CA*, 13 (1972), 165–202.

Frazer, James George, *The Golden Bough*, 12 vols, London 1907–1915.

Frenzel, Burkhard (ed.), *Climatic Trends and Anomalies in Europe 1675–1715*, Stuttgart 1994.

Freud, Sigmund, *Das Ich und die Abwehrmechanismen*, Vienna 1936.

Freud, Sigmund, *Die Traumdeutung*, Vienna 1900; *The Interpretation of Dreams*, London 1950.

Freud, Sigmund, *Complete Psychological Works*, ed. J. Strachey, 24 vols, London 1953–1974.

Freud, Sigmund, Eine Teufelsneurose, in *Studienausgabe*, VIII, Frankfurt 1982, 283–322.

Freud, Sigmund, *Briefe an Wilhelm Fliess 1887–1904*, ed. J. M. Masson; German edn by M. Schröter, Frankfurt/M. 1986.

Gareis, Iris, *Die Geschichte der Anderen. Zur Ethnohistorie am Beispiel Perus (1532–1700)*, Berlin 2003.

Gaskill, Malcolm, *Crime and Mentalities in Early Modern England*, Cambridge 2000.

Gay, Peter, *The Enlightenment. An Interpretation*, 2 vols, New York 1969/1970.

Geertz, Clifford, *The Interpretation of Cultures*, New York 1973.

Gellner, Ernest, *Postmodernism, Reason and Religion*, New York 1992.

van Gennep, Arnold, *The Rites of Passage* (1909), Chicago 1960.

Gentilcore, David, *Healers and Healing in Early Modern Italy*, Manchester 1998.

Giddens, Anthony, *The Constitution of Society*, Cambridge 1984.

Glaser, Hubert, *Klimageschichte Mitteleuropas*, Darmstadt 2001.

Gluckman, Max, *Custom and Conflict in Africa*, Oxford 1956.

Gluckman, Max (ed.), *The Allocation of Responsibility*, Manchester 1973.

Goffman, Erving, *Stigma. Notes on the Management of Spoiled Identity*, Englewood Cliffs/NJ 1963.

Goody, Jack, *The Domestication of the Savage Mind*, Cambridge/Mass. 1977.

Graus, Frantisek, *Pest – Geißler – Judenmorde*, Göttingen 1987.

Green, Judith, *Risk and Misfortune. The Social Construction of Accidents*, London 1997.

Grimm, Jacob, *Teutonic Mythology*, trans. J. Stallybrass, London 1883.

Grove, Jean M., *The Little Ice Age*, London/New York 1988.

Grove, Jean M., The Onset of the Little Ice Age, in Jones/et al. (2001), 153–87.

Hammer C. U./Clausen H. B./Dansgaard W., Past Volcanism and Climate Revealed by Greenland Ice Cores, in *Journal of Volcanology*, 11 (1981), 3–10.

Hammond-Tooke, William David, *The Bantu-Speaking Peoples of Southern Africa*, London 1974.

Harrington C. R. (ed.), *The Year Without a Summer? World Climate in 1816*, Ottawa 1992.

Harris, Grace Gredys, *Casting out Anger. Religion among the Taita of Kenya*, Cambridge 1978.

Hazard, Paul, *La Crise de la Conscience Européenne*, 3 vols, Paris 1935.

Heald, Suzette, *Controlling Anger. The Sociology of Gisu Violence*, Manchester 1989.

Hefner Robert W. (ed.), *Conversion to Christianity. Historical and Anthropological Perspectives on a Great Transformation*, Berkeley 1993.

Henningsen, Gustav/Tedeschi, John (eds), *The Inquisition in Early Modern Europe. Studies on Sources and Methods*, Dekalb/Il. 1986.

Hobsbawm, Eric J., The General Crisis of the European Economy in the Seventeenth Century, in *PP*, 5 (1954), 33–53.

Hobsbawm, Eric J./Ranger, Terence O. (eds), *The Invention of Tradition*, Cambridge 1983.

Hoppál, Mihály (ed.), *Shamanism in Eurasia*, Göttingen 1984.

Horton, Robin, African Traditional Thought and Western Science, in *Africa*, 37 (1967), 50–71, 155–87.

Hsia, Ronnie Po-Chia/Scribner, Robert W. (eds), *Problems in the Historical Anthropology of Early Modern Europe*, Wiesbaden 1997.

Hufford, David, *The Terror That Comes in the Night: An Experience-centered Study of Supernatural Assault Traditions*, Pennsylvania University Press 1989.

Hughes, M. K./Diaz, H. F. (eds), *The Medieval Warm Period*, Dordrecht 1994 (= *Climatic Change*, 26 (1994), Special Issue).

Hunter, Michael/Wootton, David (eds), *Atheism from the Reformation to the Enlightenment*, Oxford 1992.

Iliffe, John, *Africans. The History of a Continent*, Cambridge 1995.

Jones, Ernest, *On the Nightmare*, London 1949.

Jones, Phil D. /Ogilvie, Astrid E. J./Davies, Trevor D./Briffa, Keith R., *History and Climate. Memories of the Future?*, Dordrecht 2001.

Jordan, William Chester, *The Great Famine. Northern Europe in the Early Fourteenth Century*, Princeton 1996.

Jung, Carl Gustav, *Archetypes and the Collective Unconscious* (= *The Collected Works of C. G. Jung*, vol. 9, part I), London 1968.

Kamen, Henry, *The Iron Century 1550–1650*, London 1971.

Kamen, Henry, *The Phoenix and the Flame. Catalonia and the Counter Reformation*, New Haven 1993.

Kister M. C./Patterson C. J., Children's Conceptions of the Causes of Illness: Understanding of Contagion and Use of Immanent Justice, in *Child Development*, 51 (1980), 839–46.

Klein, Melanie, *The Psychoanalysis of Children*, London 1989.

Kleivan, Inge, West Greenland before 1950, in *HNAI*, vol. 5, Washington 1984, 595–621.

Klibansky, Raymond/Saxl, Fritz/Panofsky, Erwin, *Saturn and Melancholy. Studies in the History of Natural Philosophy, Religion and Art*, New York 1964.

Krige, Eileen Jensen/Krige, Jacob Daniel, *The Realm of the Rain Queen. A Study of the Pattern of Lovedu Society*, London 1943.

Kuhn, Thomas S., *The Structure of Scientific Revolutions*, Chicago 1962.

La Barre, Weston, Materials for a History of Studies of Crisis Cults: A Bibliographical Essay, in *Current Anthropology*, 12 (1971), 3–44.

Lan, David, *Guns and Rain. Guerillas and Spirit Mediums in Zimbabwe*, London 1985.

Lanczkowski, Günter, *Götter und Menschen im alten Mexiko*, Olten 1984.

Lanternari, Vittorio, *The Religions of the Oppressed. A Study of Modern Messianic Cults*, London 1963.

Lecouteux, Claude, *Fantomes et Revenants au Moyen Age*, Paris 1986.

Lederer, David, *A Bavarian Beacon. Spiritual Physic and the Birth of an Asylum, 1495–1803*, Ph.D., New York, MS prepared for print 2003.

Lévi-Strauss, Claude, *The Savage Mind*, Chicago 1968.

Lévy-Bruhl, Lucien, *Primitive Mentality*, London 1923.

Linton, Ralph, Nativistic Movements, in *AA*, 45 (1943), 230–40.

Liu, Kwang-Ching, World-View and Peasant Rebellion. Reflections on Post-Mao Historiography, in *JAS*, 40 (1981), 295–326.

Livi-Bacci, Massimo, *Population and Nutrition*, Cambridge 1991.

Luterbacher, Jürg, The Late Maunder Minimum (1675–1715) – Climax of the 'Little Ice Age' in Europe, in Jones/Ogilvie/Davies/Briffa (2001), 29–54.

Mair, Lucy P., Independent Religious Movements in Three Continents, in *CSSH*, 1 (1958/59), 113–36.

Malinowski, Bronislaw, *Argonauts of the Western Pacific*, London 1922.

Malinowski, Bronislaw, The Pan-African Problem of Culture Contact, in *AJS*, 48 (1943), 649–65.

Mannheim, Karl, Das Problem der Generationen, in *Kölner Viertel-jahreshefte für Soziologie*, 7 (1928), 157–85, 309–30.

Mbiti, John S., *African Religion and Philosophy*, New York 1970.

Merton, Robert K., *Social Theory and Social Structure*, New York 1968.

Midelfort, H. C. Erik, *Mad Princes of Renaissance Germany*, Charlottesville/Va. 1994.

Midelfort, H. C. Erik, *A History of Madness in Sixteenth-Century Germany*, Stanford/Calif. 1999.

Monahan, W. Gregory, *Year of Sorrows. The Great Famine of 1709 in Lyon*, Columbus/Ohio 1993.

Monter, William, *Ritual, Myth and Magic in Early Modern Europe*, Brighton 1983.

Moore, Henrietta L./Sanders, Todd, Magical Interpretations and Material Realities: An Introduction, in Moore/Sanders (2001), 1–27.

Moore, Robert Ian, *The Formation of a Persecuting Society. Power and Deviance in Western Europe, 950–1250*, Oxford 1987.

Mormando, Franco, *The Preacher's Demons. Bernardino of Siena and the Social Underworld of Early Renaissance Italy*, Chicago 1999.

Mühlmann, Wilhelm E. (ed.), *Chiliasmus und Nativismus*, Berlin 1964.

Münzel, Mark, *Schrumpfkopfmacher? Jibaro-Indianer in Südamerika*, Frankfurt 1977.

Nadel, Siegfried Ferdinand, *A Black Byzantium. The Kingdom of the Nupe of Nigeria*, London 1942.

Nadel, Siegfried Ferdinand, *Nupe Religion*, London 1954.

Naphy, William G., *Plagues, Poisons and Potions. Plague-Spreading Conspir-acies in the Western Alps, c.1530–1640*, Manchester 2002.

Naphy, William G./Roberts, Penny (eds), *Fear in Early Modern Society*, Manchester 1997.

Nash, June, Death as a Way of Life, in *AA*, 69 (1967), 455–70.

Nash, Manning, Witchcraft as Social Process in a Tzeltal Community, in *America Indígena*, 20 (1961), 121–6.

Nirenberg, David, *Communities of Violence. Persecution of Minorities in the Middle Ages*, Princeton 1996.

Parker, Geoffrey/Smith L. M. (eds), *The General Crisis of the Seventeenth Century*, London 1978.

Parkin, David (ed.), *The Anthropology of Evil*, Oxford 1985.

Peters, Edward, *Torture*, Philadelphia 1985.

Pfister, Christian, *Klimageschichte der Schweiz 1525–1860*, Bern 1988.

Pfister, Christian/et al. (eds), Climatic Variability in Sixteenth Century Europe and its Social Dimension (= *Climatic Change*, 43, Special Issue), Dordrecht 1999.

Pfister, Christian/Brazdil, Rudolf, Climatic Variability in Sixteenth Century Europe and its Social Dimensions: A Synthesis, in *Climatic Change*, 43 (1999), 5–53.

Pfister, Oskar, *Das Christentum und die Angst. Eine religionspsychologische, historische und religionshygienische Untersuchung*, Zurich 1944.

Phelps-Brown, Henry/Hopkins, Sheila, Seven Centuries of the Prices of Consumables Compared with Builders' Wage Rates, in *Economica*, 23 (1956), 296–314.

Piaget, Jean, *The Child's Conception of Physical Causality*, London 1930.

Piaget, Jean/Inhelder B., *On the Origin of the Idea of Chance in Children*, London 1975.

Popkin, Richard H., *The History of Scepticism from Erasmus to Descartes*, Assen 1960.

Porter, Roy, *Mind Forg'd Manacles. A History of Madness in England from the Restoration to the Regency*, London 1987.

Propp, Vladimir, *Morphology of the Folk Tale* (1st edn Leningrad 1946), New York 1968.

Rabb, Theodore K., *The Struggle for Stability in Early Modern Europe*, Princeton 1975.

Ranger, Terence O., Religious Movements and Politics in Sub-Saharan Africa, in *African Studies Review*, 29 (1986), 1–69.

Ranger, Terence O./Kimambo, Isaria N. (eds), *The Historical Study of African Religion*, London 1972.

Redfield, Robert, *The Folk Culture of Yucatan*, Chicago 1941.

Repgen, Konrad (ed.), *Krieg und Politik, 1618–1848*, Munich 1988.

Richards S., *Luck, Chance, and Coincidence*, Wellingborough 1985.

Rokeach, Milton, *The Open and the Closed Mind. Investigations into the Nature of Belief Systems and Personality Systems*, New York 1960.

Rosen, George, Emotion and Sensibility in Ages of Anxiety. A Comparative Historical Review, in *American Journal of Psychiatry*, 124 (1967), 771–84.

Rossi, Paolo, *Francis Bacon. From Magic to Science*, trans. S. Rabinovitch, London 1968.

Rubin, Miri, *Corpus Christi*, Cambridge 1991.

Ryan, Barbara, Ideological Purity and Feminism. The US Women's Movement from 1966 to 1975, in *Gender and Society*, 3 (1989), 239–57.

Saladin d'Anglure, Bernard, Inuit of Quebec, in *HNAI*, vol. 5, Washington 1984, 476–507.

Salmon, John H. M., *Society in Crisis. France in the Sixteenth Century*, London 1975.

Schneider, Gerhard, *Der Libertin*, Stuttgart 1970.

Schoeffelers, J. Matthew, *Guardians of the Land. Essays on Central African Territorial Cults*, Gwelo 1979.

Seaver, Kirsten A., *The Frozen Echo. Greenland and the Exploration of North America, ca. A.D. 1000–1500*, Stanford/Ca. 1996.

Selby, Henry A., *Zapotec Deviance. The Convergence of Folk and Modern Sociology*, foreword by Howard S. Becker, Austin/Texas 1974.

Shirokogoroff, Sergej M., *Psychomental Complex of the Tungus*, Shanghai/London 1935.

de Silva, Shanaka L./Zielinski, Gregory A., Global Influence of the A.D. 1600 eruption of Huanyaputina, Peru, in *Nature*, 393 (1998), 455–8.

Simmel, Georg, The Sociology of Secrecy and of Secret Societies, in *AJS*, 11 (1905), 441–98.

Simmons, Marc, History of the Pueblo-Spanish Relations to 1821, in *HNAI*, vol. 9 (1979), 178–93.

Skaria, Ajay, Shades of Wilderness. Tribe, Caste, and Gender in Western India, in *JAS*, 56 (1997), 726–45.

Smelser, Neil J., Toward a Theory of Modernization, in Etzioni-Halevy/Etzioni (1973), 268–84.

Smith M., Changing Sociological Perspectives on Chance, in *Sociology* (1993), 513–31.

Sundkler, Bengt, *Bantu Prophets in South Africa*, London/New York 1961.

Swann, Julian/Coward, Barry (eds), *Conspiracies and Conspiracy Theory in Early Modern Europe*, Aldershot 2003.

Taussig, Michael, *Shamanism, Colonialism and the Wild Man*, Chicago 1987.

Thomas, Keith, History and Anthropology, in *PP*, 24 (1963), 3–24.

Thompson, Edward P., Anthropology and the Discipline of Historical Context, in *Midland History*, 3 (1971/1972), 41–55.

Thrupp, Sylvia (ed.), *Millennial Dreams in Action*, The Hague 1962.

Tilly, Charles (ed.), *The Formation of National States in Western Europe*, Princeton 1975.

Trevor-Roper, Hugh Redwald, *Princes and Artists. Patronage and Ideology at Four Habsburg Courts, 1517–1633*, London 1976.

Tuck, Richard, *Philosophy and Government, 1572–1651*, Cambridge 1993.

Turner, Victor, *The Ritual Process*, New York 1966.

Tylor, Edward B., *Primitive Culture*, London 1871.

Utterström, Gustav, Climatic Fluctuations and Population Problems in Early Modern History, in *Scandinavian Economic History Review*, 3 (1955), 1–47.

Vansina, Jan, *Oral Tradition. A Study in Historical Method*, London 1965.

Vansina, Jan, The Bushong Poison Ordeal, in Douglas/Kaberry (1969), 245–60.

van Valkenburgh, Richard, *A Short History of the Navaho People*, Window Rock 1938.

Wallace, Anthony F., Revitalization Movements, in *AA*, 58 (1956), 264–81.

Wallace, Anthony F., Origins of the Longhouse Religion, in *HNAI*, vol. 15 (1978), 442–8.

Wallerstein, Immanuel, *The Modern World System*, 4 vols, New York 1974.

Weber, Max, Objectivity in Social Science and Social Policy (1904), in *The Methodology of the Social Sciences*, eds Edward Shils/H. Finch, New York 1949, 50–112.

Weber, Max, *The Protestant Ethic and the Spirit of Capitalism* (1904/1905), trans. Talcott Parsons, New York 1930, with an introduction by Anthony Giddens, London 1985.

Weber, Max, *Economy and Society. An Outline of Interpretive Sociology*, trans. G. Roth and C. Wittich, 2 vols, Berkeley/Calif. 1978.

Webster, Charles, *From Paracelsus to Newton. Magic and the Modern Science*, Cambridge 1982.

Westerkamp, Marilyn J., *Women and Religion in Early America, 1600–1850. The Puritan and Evangelical Traditions*, London 1999.

Whyte, Susan Reynolds, *Questioning Misfortune. The Pragmatics of Uncertainty in Eastern Uganda*, Cambridge 1997.

Wiesner, Merry E., *Women and Gender in Early Modern Europe*, Cambridge 1993.

Wilson, Bryan R., Millennialism in Comparative Perspective, in *CSSH*, 6 (1963), 93–114.

Wilson, Bryan R., *Magic and the Millennium. A Sociological Study of Religious Movements of Protest among Tribal and Third-World Peoples*, London 1973.

Wilson, Monica Hunter, *Good Company. A Study of Nyakyusa Age-Villages*, London 1951.

Wilson, Stephen, *The Magical Universe. Everyday Ritual and Magic in Pre-Modern Europe*, London 2000.

Wolf, Eric, *Europe and the People without History*, Berkeley/Calif. 1982.

Worsley, Peter, *The Trumpet Shall Sound: A Study of 'Cargo' Cults in Melanesia*, London 1957.

Yates, Frances Amelia, *The Rosicrucian Enlightenment*, London 1972.

Yates, Frances Amelia, *The Occult Philosophy in the Elizabethan Age*, London 1979.

Zagorin, Perez, *Ways of Lying. Dissimulation, Persecution, and Conformity in Early Modern Europe*, Cambridge/Mass. 1990.

Zaleski, Carol, *Otherworld Journeys. Accounts of Near-Death Experience in Medieval and Modern Times*, New York/Oxford 1987.

Index

Aborigines 17, 32, 237
abundance 131, 204, 232
acculturation 8, 26, 87
adoration 35, 57, 59–60, 62, 64,
  68–9, 73, 93, 115, 131, 133, 144,
  147, 233
African churches 225–6, 230, 239
African people 4, 39; Agni 42;
  Azande 23–4, 40; Bakweri
  199; Bechuana 199; bushong
  209; Cewa 14; Dinka 80;
  Giriami 204–5, 208; Kerebe
  51; Lala 204; Lele 206; Maka
  224; Matumbi 202; Mijkenda
  216; Ndebele 199–200;
  Ndongo 51; Ngindo 202;
  Nupe 203; Nyoro 199;
  Oromo-Galla 205; Pondo
  200; Songe 203; Sukuma 208,
  212–13, 217; Temne 51; Tiv
  206; Tuareg 14; Yoruba 43,
  208–9, 237; Zulu 15, 39, 51,
  200
Africanization 11, 211, 223–5
Afro-Americans 141, 146–7,
  202
age groups 4, 120, 211–12, 215
agency 2, 4, 9, 15, 45, 50, 245

aggression 6, 27, 38–40, 42–3, 54,
  69, 89, 185, 195, 211
Agobard of Lyon see Lyon
agriculture 65, 104, 134, 160, 161,
  205
Agrippa von Nettesheim 38, 98,
  139, 163, 167–8, 171
AIDS 15–16, 212, 214, 217, 247
Aix-en-Provence 141, 156
Albania 144, 153
Alciati, Andrea 140, 167, 171,
  181, 243
Alps 32, 57, 60–2, 65–7, 69, 74,
  78, 88, 92, 108, 128, 140, 154–5,
  158, 167
Alsace 54, 71–2, 76–7, 90–1, 97,
  122, 156, 161
alter ego 19, 218, see also nagual
American Indians: Apache 19;
  Delaware 201; Hurons 27;
  Iroquois 200–1; Jivaro
  218–19; Maya 4, 39, 218;
  Nambikwara 4; Native
  Americans 8, 13, 18–19, 27–9,
  144, 146, 200–2, 219, 221, 237;
  Navaho 18, 27, 220–1; Nez-
  Percé 33; Ottawa 201;
  Pueblo 19, 144–5, 220; Seneca

200–1; Shawnee 201–2; Tzeltal 39, 218; Zuni 220–1

Amsterdam 80, 128, 183

amulet 4, 22–3, 35, 244

Anabaptism 81, 121, 183, 204

ANC Youth League 1, 215, 226–7

ancestor 1, 16, 71, 196, 214; cults 165, 213; spirits 7, 14, 44

ancient civilizations 3, 5, 12–13, 18, 22, 31, 33, 47–50, 89, 92, 131–2, 144, 151, 165, 243

angels 137, 141, 184, 201

Anglicanism 122, 133, 146, 185

Angola 51, 209, 227; Jonas Savimbi 209–10, 226–7

animals 2–3, 12–13, 18–19, 29, 35, 69, 76, 132, 134, 147, 193, 198, 211, 218, 223; alligator 23, 147; ants 66; bull 19; calves 91; cats 69, 91, 147; chicken 147; cobra 80; cows 28; crab 15; dog 147; eagle 19; frog 15; goats 147, 231; leopard 211; lion 19; lizard 15; mice 140; owl 12, 19, 30; parrot 147; peacock 53; rabbit 140; rooster 231; snake 93, 204–5; wolf 30, 64, 81, 88, 221

animism 17–18, 217

anthropology 2–3, 6–8, 13, 17–18, 23–6, 29, 39–40, 44, 114, 145, 198–9, 201, 206, 208, 212, 216, 218–19, 226, 228, 238, 242, 247; Ray Abrahams 17, 223; Andrew Apter 39, 208–9; Adam Ashforth 1, 15–16, 242; Joanna Ball 213; Paul Baxter 160; Helen Berger 238; Willem de Blécourt 23; Francis Boas 18, 29; George C. Bond 11, 229; James Brain 40, 191; Cynthia Brantley 205; Diane M. Ciekawy 11, 229; Jean and John Comaroff 29, 196; Mary Douglas 7, 17; Adolphus P. Elkin 17; Edgar E. Evans-Pritchard 2–3, 7, 14,

16, 23–5, 45; Reo F. Fortune 17; George M. Foster 25; James G. Frazer 237; Peter Geschiere 7, 216, 224, 226, 247; Max H. Gluckman 14, 39, 45; Esther Goody 39; Linda Heywood 210; Sohaila Kapur 18; Clyde Kluckhohn 18, 27, 221; Adam Kuper 28; Nancy Levine 18; Claude Lévi-Strauss 4, 40; Lucien Lévy-Bruhl 23; Shirley Lindenbaum 17; Lucy Mair 7, 199, 202; Bronislaw Malinowski 6–7, 13, 17, 24, 196, 198, 206, 228; Max Marwick 14, 17, 28, 200, 207; Marcel Mauss 36; Philip Mayer 29; Simeon Mesaki 212–13; Siegfried F. Nadel 39; Isak Niehaus 7, 28, 214, 216; Stephen Nissenbaum 146; Geoffrey Parrinder 13; Victor Ralushai 2, 16–17, 44–5, 214, 216, 225; Terence O. Ranger 6; Audrey Richards 198; Isaac Schapera 16; Henry A. Selby 25, 44; Sergej M. Shirokogoroff 29; David Silverman 27; Louise Spindler 29; Nathan Wachtel 19, 219; Deward E. Walker 19, 33; Anthony Wallace 200; Bryan Wilson 200; Monica Wilson 244; Eric Wolf 198; Mary Zelienitz 17

anti-Semitism 60, 62, 71, 232, 235

anti-witchcraft: campaigns 11–12, 69, 73, 95, 124, 205–6, 208, 211, 227; cults 17, 21, 199, 202; movements 6–7, 17, 24, 27, 168, 198, 202, 204–9, 211–12, 222, 225; pogroms 45, 50, 84, 128, 144, 163, 222; shrines 17, 38, 202, 206

Antwerp 101, 128

anxiety 6–7, 26–8, 38, 42–3, 48, 50, 54, 56, 61, 77, 124, 198, 201, 209, 215, 219, 229, 239, 244, 247–8; *see also* fears

Aosta Valley   63, 65
apostasy   38, 52, 57, 59–60, 73,
   172–3
Arabia   22, 51, 56, 218
Aragon   35, 53, 148; King
   Ramiro I   53
Ardennes   100, 156, 163
Arles   32; Bishop Caesarius of
   Arles   32
artists: Albrecht Altdorfer   76,
   231; Giuseppe Arcimboldo
   129; Hans Baldung Grien   76,
   231; Pieter Brueghel   131, 231;
   Lukas Cranach   80, 231;
   Niklaus Manuel Deutsch   76;
   Albrecht Dürer   76, 231; Urs
   Graf   76; David Teniers   231
Asia   8, 12–3, 17–8, 24, 28–9, 48,
   50, 143, 169, 196, 217, 227, 243
Assyrian Empire   47; King
   Esarhaddon   47
atheism   133, 167, 185
attribution   2, 11, 14–15, 19, 23,
   25, 28, 39–40, 45, 49, 87, 99, 103,
   108, 123, 145, 158, 165, 201, 206,
   209, 211, 219
Augsburg   52, 71, 83, 85, 98, 108,
   110, 117, 120, 162, 169, 176, 188
Augustine (St)   4, 6, 33, 35, 52,
   73
Australia   8, 12–13, 17, 32, 44,
   194, 196, 237
Austria   8, 72, 79, 83, 101, 120,
   122, 127, 139, 150, 153, 166, 168,
   176, 190–3, 239; Archduke
   Ferdinand I   79; Giulio Cesare
   127; Maria Theresia   191; *see
   also* Emperors, Habsburg
authoritarianism   43, 57, 163,
   226
Avignon   57, 62, 66, 91, 156
Aztec empire   18, 39, 50, 243;
   Emperor Motecuhzoma II   50

baby   13, 67, 189, 193
Babylonia   47, 132
Bacon, Francis   11, 22, 83, 95,
   184, 245

Baltics   92, 135, 138–9, 152
Bamberg   98, 109–15, 117, 120,
   130, 149, 154, 176, 229; Prince-
   Bishop Johann Georg II Fuchs
   von Dornheim   109, 112, 120;
   Johann Philipp von Gebsattel
   111
banishment   45, 80, 155–6, 205
Basel   62, 66, 68–9, 79–80, 168,
   171–2
Basque territories   107, 182–3
Basse, Nikolaus   98, 230
Bavaria   98, 100, 113, 116, 120–2,
   125, 139, 174–80, 184, 188–9,
   192–3; Duke Albrecht V   120;
   Duke/Prince-Elector
   Maximilian I   121, 180; Prince-
   Elector Max III Joseph   192;
   Duke Wilhelm V, 'the Pious'
   121–2
beating   189, 220–3
beggars   139–40, 188–9
behaviour   2, 13, 22, 45, 81, 148,
   189, 245
Bekker, Balthasar   139, 186
Belgium   8, 104, 106, 130, 149–50,
   182, 207
benediction   22, 37
Benin/Dahomey   11–12 , 28,
   207–8, 216, 226–8; President
   Mathieu Kérékou   11, 227
Bernard of Como   62, 102
Berne   66, 80, 84, 92, 123
Binsfeld, Peter   93, 95–7, 100–2,
   104, 106–7, 111, 117, 142, 173–4,
   176
birth   18, 40–1, 43
Black Death *see* epidemic
   diseases/plague
blaming   24, 39, 60, 64, 144, 172,
   189, 248
blasphemy   57, 173, 189, 194
Blocksberg   80, 240
blood   9, 15, 19, 41, 60, 80, 97,
   147, 167–8, 180, 196, 209, 219,
   223, 235
Bodin, Jean   6, 91, 96, 102, 107,
   171–3, 182, 229

body parts 13, 127, 214, 219
Boguet, Henry 102, 105–7
Bohemia 71, 77, 126–7, 192
Bolivia 19, 208, 219, 244
Bologna 79, 155, 177
Bombay/Mumbai 18, 217, 241
bones 147, 205, 241
book 5, 31–2, 56–7, 66, 68, 70–1,
 73–4, 77, 79, 98, 100–1, 104–6,
 138, 142, 167–8, 171, 179–80,
 185, 191, 230, 234, 236–7, 240
Bordeaux 106, 108, 156, 182, 188
Bosnia 153, 221
Botswana 6, 200
Brabant 101, 128
Brandenburg 54, 125, 157, 187
Brazil 4, 13, 21, 144, 148, 182,
 202
breast 15, 38, 40, 222
Breisgau 91, 122
Brescia 78, 168; Bishop Paolo
 Zane 78
Breslau/Wroclaw 117, 154;
 Prince-Bishop Carl Ferdinand
 of Poland 154
Brixen/Bressanone 32, 72, 118,
 154, 166; Prince-Bishop Georg
 II Golser 72–3; Prince-Bishop
 Cardinal Nicolaus of Cusa 32,
 72, 166
Brussels 54, 73, 129
Buddhism 17–18
Bulgaria 144, 153
Bullinger, Heinrich 90, 98, 102
Burchard of Worms *see* Worms
bureaucracy 26, 138
Burgundy 77, 104–5, 107, 120,
 131, 156, 169, 181
Burma 17, 217

Cahors 57; Bishop Hugues
 Géraud 57
California 238
Calvin, Jean 80, 90, 163, 170, 182
Calvinism 24–5, 80, 82, 84, 92,
 122–3, 125–6, 130, 132, 139, 170,
 172–4, 183, 186, 190, 229
Cambodia 243

Cambridge 132, 185, 222
Cameroon 200, 216, 224–5;
 President Ahmadou Ahidjo
 224
Canada 19, 107, 144, 160, 201,
 221
Canary Islands 148, 182
Canisius SJ, Peter 83, 122, 133
cannibalism 2, 12–13, 15, 30–1,
 42, 240
Canon Episcopi 30–2, 69, 165–6
canon law 4, 31–2, 166, 171
capitalism 25, 87, 169, 194, 209,
 232, 247–8
Cardano, Girolamo 35, 98
Carmichael, James 124, 133
Carolina 86–7, 99, 169–70, 177
Caribbean 21, 141, 202
Cartagena de Indias 144
Cassinis, Samuel de 102, 166
Catalonia 67, 81, 131, 148
Cathars 57, 59, 62
Catholic League 92, 100–1,
 120–1, 174, 181
Catholicism 9, 12, 19, 21–2, 24–5,
 37, 74, 80–1, 83–4, 86, 90, 92–3,
 96, 99–100, 103–4, 108–12, 116,
 119–23, 126, 128, 130, 133, 139,
 143, 148, 150, 157, 169–70,
 173–4, 176, 178–81, 190–2, 220,
 232, 234, 239–40
Cautio Criminalis 102, 117,
 180–1
ceremonies 4, 17–18, 37
Champagne 92, 100, 131
changeability 37–8, 40–1
charisma 39, 45, 202, 205, 207,
 225, 230
childhood 13, 24, 42, 71, 142, 240
children 9, 13, 22, 38–42, 57, 71,
 85, 111, 114, 119, 138, 142, 199,
 212, 222, 240; abuse 143, 241;
 as accusers 145, 189; as
 beggars 140; as members of
 street gangs 140, 189–90; as
 members of new witchcraft
 238; as victims of ritual murder
 28, 50, 147, 241; as victims of

children (cont'd)
  witches   12, 30, 35, 44, 64, 91,
    114, 220, 240; as witches   138,
    140–3, 146; as witnesses in
    court   142–3, 146; fantasies
    143; morbidity   41, 65, 216,
    223; mortality   12, 40, 65, 202,
    216, 221
China   18, 29, 51, 131, 196, 243–4;
  Emperor Chuang-Lieh Ti   131
Cicero   90, 122, 170, 179
classification   9–10, 32, 40–1,
  45–6, 49, 69, 96, 145, 178, 198
climate   51, 56, 61, 65, 68, 72,
  87–8, 93, 104, 113–14, 119, 124,
  127, 137, 158–62; Tambora
  Freeze   51, 162–3
Colmar   54, 91
Cologne *see* Köln
Colombia   144, 239
colonialism   11, 13, 16–17, 19, 51,
  137, 143–7, 160–1, 169, 194,
  196–202, 204–12, 217, 223–4, 226
communism   18, 26, 222, 232
Como   62, 78, 102
compassion   163, 173–4, 222
comrades   1, 95, 210, 212, 214
concubines   110–11, 119
confessionalization   84, 109,
  173–4
conflict   8, 16, 19, 23–4, 26–8, 34,
  39, 41, 51, 109, 111, 128, 131,
  134, 157, 161, 166, 168, 212, 228,
  232
Congo   204, 206–9, 211–12, 227;
  Mobutu Sese Seko   211, 227
Connecticut   145–6
conspiracy   2, 5, 9, 13, 48, 55–6,
  60, 64–5, 67, 71, 80–1, 97, 100,
  103, 123–4, 146, 163, 171, 204–5,
  208, 232, 235–6, 244
Constance   65, 76, 80, 108, 119
Constantinople   50, 60
contingency   2, 23–4, 26, 43, 134;
  lacking concept of   7, 23–4
Contzen SJ, Adam   176
Copenhagen   81, 123–4, 126
Council: of Ancyra   31; of Basel

62, 66, 68–9; of Constance   65;
  of Ferrara   68; First Vatican
  232; 4th Lateran   59; of Pisa
  63; of Trent   110, 119, 121
counter-magic   16, 23–4, 36–7,
  230
Counter-Reformation   83,
  99–100, 106, 108–12, 116,
  119–21, 128, 154–5, 174–6, 178,
  194, 229
covenant: with demons   35, 52,
  93; with the devil   3, 52, 59, 98,
  115, 132–3, 141, 170, 188, 190,
  229; with God   133, 170, 229
crimen exceptum   5, 108, 120,
  122, 159, 173, 176
Croatia   150, 153, 189, 191
crop failure   13, 37, 48, 51, 53–6,
  65, 88, 91, 93, 97, 99, 104,
  113–14, 116, 124, 131, 144, 148,
  160–2, 200, 212, 221, 228
Crowley, Aleister   233, 237
culture   3, 5, 7, 18, 23, 27, 29–30,
  40, 45, 49, 65, 107, 117, 140–1,
  145, 161, 201–2, 235, 240, 242,
  245, 247; change   8, 27–8, 51,
  198, 200, 206, 208
cursing   1, 35, 64–5, 147, 189
Czech Republic   150; *see also*
  Bohemia

Dahomey *see* Benin
Dalarna   138–9, 146, 188
Daly, Mary   235–6
dancing   9, 42, 59–60, 77, 80, 84,
  107, 115–16, 124, 131, 133–4,
  138, 141, 147, 211, 220, 234,
  239–41
Daneau, Lambert   91, 98, 102,
  170
danger   4, 7–8, 16, 18, 23, 25,
  31–2, 36, 40–1, 46, 52, 59–60, 79,
  84, 86, 88–9, 97, 117, 121, 133–4,
  138, 140, 144, 150, 160–1, 172,
  174, 178–9, 196, 222, 228, 231,
  240, 247
darkness   2, 19, 22, 76, 114, 120,
  185, 192, 235

Dauphiné   63, 66–8, 102, 105, 130, 156
death   1, 7, 13, 15–19, 21, 28, 34, 44–5, 57, 77, 85, 111, 128, 145, 201–2, 206, 218, 224; mysterious 103; sudden   40, 49, 53, 193
death penalty   31, 33–4, 45, 47–8, 50–5, 61, 85, 89, 92, 95, 106, 145–8, 151, 153–5, 156, 159, 169, 173, 178, 182–3, 185, 187–90, 195, 199, 205, 217, 223, 235, 240; by beating   221, 223; by burning   1–2, 9, 30–3, 37, 46–8, 50, 52–8, 61–64, 67–8, 76–81, 83–4, 87, 89–93, 96, 99–100, 103–4, 108, 111–12, 114–15, 117, 122–6, 128–9, 131, 139, 143–4, 147–9, 152–9, 168, 170, 174, 177–80, 183–4, 187–9, 191, 199, 202, 205, 209, 213–14, 219–20, 223–4, 235, 240; by decapitation   50, 103–4; by drowning   53, 81; by necklacing   213–14, 225; by stoning   22, 48, 53, 153, 164, 215, 218, 221
Dee, John   98, 129
Della Porta, Gianbattista   35, 98
Delrio SJ, Martin   101–7, 122, 173–4, 177
demonology   3–4, 9, 33, 43, 67, 73, 82, 86, 91, 93, 98, 101, 103–6, 126, 141, 146, 173, 177, 185, 192, 229, 231, 244
Denich: Joachim   177–8; Kaspar SJ   178
Denmark   8, 55, 61, 80–1, 99, 102, 105, 123, 126, 130, 135, 139, 149–52, 223; Princess Anne 123; King Christian III   80; Christian IV   152; Frederick II 126; Harald   55; Queen Margarethe   61
denunciation   48, 87, 113, 115, 138, 159, 170, 173, 177, 181, 210
Descartes, René   5, 184
desire   6, 37–9, 41, 71, 87, 196, 237, 241

deviance   2, 6, 19, 43–4, 146
devil   3–5, 21–2, 31, 33, 35–7, 42, 52, 57, 59, 67–70, 73, 79, 81, 91, 93, 98, 114, 132, 142, 146, 157, 166, 183–90, 231, 233; baptism by   138; book of   138; intercourse with   76, 143, 188; mark by   132, 168, 242; pact with   98, 115, 132–3, 141, 170, 188, 190, 219; possessed by 141; worship of   35, 57, 59–60, 62, 64, 68, 69, 115, 124, 133, 144
Dijon   156, 188
Dillingen   120, 140
disenchantment   6, 165
dissidence   6, 60, 236
divination   3, 24, 29–30, 33, 35–6, 44, 48, 50, 52, 54, 63, 78, 90, 93, 148, 182, 202, 211, 224–5, 230, 244, 248
division of labour   26, 39–40, 161, 194
Dole   106, 120
domination   3, 26, 28, 61, 109; female   209; male   43, 209; Mongol   152
dreams   15, 31–2, 44, 46, 192, 235, 242–3, 246
dress   97, 107, 201, 241
drought   51, 56, 65, 160, 189, 200, 212, 219, 221–2
drugs   141, 212
dualism   45, 59, 62
ducking   86, 132, 146, 164, 186, 222, 230

ecology   51, 65, 134, 159, 211–13, 235, 237
economy   6, 8, 11, 14–15, 17, 26–9, 40, 51, 57, 61, 96, 104, 119, 124, 128, 134, 148, 162, 194, 200, 206, 208–9, 211–12, 215–16, 219, 224, 228–9, 244
ecstasies   6, 29–30, 168, 201, 242
Ecuador   218–9
education   12, 14, 21, 26, 40, 95, 108, 110, 120, 137, 143, 169, 172, 176, 191, 194, 205, 212, 226, 248

Egypt   23, 50
Eichstätt   98, 108–9, 112–14, 117,
    164, 176, 178; Prince-Bishop
    Johann Christoph I von
    Westerstetten   109, 112–13,
    176, 178
Ellwangen   105, 109, 112–14, 117,
    119, 130
emotions   2, 20, 25–6, 42, 96–7,
    103, 127, 129, 131, 161, 166, 180,
    236, 243, 244, 247–8; *see also*
    envy, greed, guilt, hatred,
    laughter, love, jealousy
Emperor: Arnulf   53;
    Charlemagne   30, 33, 52, 54;
    Charles V   169; Ferdinand I
    79; Joseph II   192–3; Leopold I
    129; Louis of Bavaria   57;
    Maximilian I   73, 98, 169, 170,
    177; Maximilian II   85, 89;
    Rudolf II   127, 129, 131, 176
England   24, 53, 54, 56–7, 84, 91,
    101–2, 123, 127, 131–5, 148–9,
    160, 172, 176, 185–7, 223, 230,
    233, 244; King Alfred of Wessex
    34; Edgar   53; Edward III   57;
    Edward IV   57; Queen
    Elizabeth I   91, 98, 129; King
    Henry IV   57; Henry VIII
    151; James I   6–7, 99, 102, 123,
    126, 152
Enlightenment   5, 21, 36–7, 104,
    139, 143, 158, 162, 186–9, 192,
    221, 248
envy   2, 11, 20, 22, 25–6, 40–2, 87,
    92, 161, 194, 244
epidemic disease   12, 16, 28, 48,
    51, 56, 60–1, 114, 140, 142, 153,
    160, 162, 189, 198, 200–1, 205,
    219, 221, 245; AIDS   15–16,
    212, 214, 217, 247; cholera   200;
    influenza   194; malaria   212;
    meningitis   200, 216; plague
    28, 57, 60–2, 162, 200; sleeping
    sickness   200, 212; smallpox
    28, 61, 200, 212; tetanus   12,
    216; tuberculosis   212; yellow
    fever   200, 212

eradication   5, 18, 37, 50–1, 55,
    73, 93, 112, 115, 128, 163, 175,
    202, 204, 206–8, 210–11, 228,
    230, 234–5, 243
Erasmus of Rotterdam   79, 163,
    167
Erfurt   108–9
Essex   91, 127, 132
Estonia   39, 126, 139, 150–1, 158
evil   2–5, 7, 10, 12–13, 15, 17–20,
    22–3, 29, 33, 35, 37, 41–2, 44–6,
    48, 50, 53, 55, 64, 82, 89, 114,
    128, 141, 147, 163, 170, 198, 202,
    210–11, 214–15, 226, 240, 243–5
executioner   86–7, 93, 199, 218,
    220
exorcism   83, 106, 141, 192, 221,
    225
experiment   6, 8, 89, 98, 122,
    183–4, 231, 238
eye   18–19, 22–3, 53, 86, 95, 107,
    164, 168, 173, 225
Eymeric, Nicolas   35, 74

Faenza   181; Bishop Giulio
    Monterenzi   181
fairies   2, 31, 35, 54, 78, 240; fairy
    queen   31
fairy tales   9, 30, 32, 192, 231,
    237
familiar spirits   132, 134, 223
family   15–16, 19, 24, 53, 111–12,
    115, 120, 177–8, 219, 221, 243
famine   50–1, 56, 61, 113–14, 152,
    160, 162, 189, 200, 205, 212, 217,
    219, 245
fanatism   72, 74, 77, 119–20, 134,
    165, 228
fantasy   2–3, 5–6, 9, 13, 26, 28, 31,
    35, 41–2, 60–1, 69–71, 76, 89, 93,
    103, 132–3, 140–3, 168, 172, 175,
    225, 230–1, 233, 235–6, 240, 242,
    244, 248
fascination   2, 9–10, 25, 98, 107,
    140, 143, 183, 211, 233, 236,
    239–40
fat: of babies   13, 67; of children
    114; of humans   19, 28, 219

fears   3–4, 23, 26, 144, 162, 185;
  apocalyptic   67, 72, 132;
  collective   3, 60; common   95;
  constant   4, 16; millennial   77,
  132; of authority   57; of
  bewitchment   6–7, 18, 21–2, 24,
  27, 39, 57, 146, 152, 201, 205,
  212, 217, 222, 230, 240, 244; of
  conspiracy   56, 123; of
  conspiracy of witches   204; of
  death   77; of the devil   146; of
  devilish conspiracy   67; of envy
  25; of the evil eye   22, 53; of
  krsniki   30; of mystical powers
  146; of poisoners   80; of
  shamans   146; of sorcery   57;
  of spiritual powers   145; of
  streghe   60; of sudden illness
  77; of witch-hunts   217;
  popular   77; strange   80
feasting   16, 42, 116, 133, 138
female sphere   40–3, 209
feminism   6, 9, 40–1, 157–8,
  232–3, 235–7, 239–40
Ferrara   68, 78
fetish   38, 144, 202
Feugeyron, Ponce   63, 66
Finland   39, 126, 138–40, 150, 158
fire   30, 46, 79, 86, 153, 158, 180,
  186–7, 201, 223–4, 239; bonfire
  37, 92
Flade, Dietrich   96–7, 100, 103
flooding   51, 65, 85, 88, 104, 189
Florence   154, 167, 183
flying   2, 4, 13, 17, 29, 30–1, 42,
  50, 59–61, 64, 91, 93, 166, 168,
  196, 230
folklorists: Anti Aarne   32; Maja
  Boskovic-Stulli   30; Mircea
  Eliade   29; Jeanne Favret-
  Saada   23; Jacob Grimm   5–6,
  231–2, 234, 240; Kirsten
  Hastrup   39; Gustav
  Henningsen   107; Ake
  Hultcrantz   29; Sabina
  Magliocco   238; Ernesto de
  Martino   23, 36; Vladimir
  Propp   13, 32; Shelley

Rabinovitch   237; Rosemary
  Ruether   236; Inge Schöck
  23; Stith Thompson   32
football   14–15, 241
foreigners   54–5, 110, 145, 148–9,
  196, 198, 219, 235, 242
Förner, Friedrich   111–12, 176
France   53, 57, 61, 66–8, 72, 74,
  77–8, 83, 91–3, 106–7, 122, 131,
  135, 150, 155–6, 160, 164, 168,
  176, 181–2, 192–3, 223, 226, 241;
  Charlemagne   30, 33, 52, 54;
  King Charles II   34; Francis I
  151; Queen Fredegunde   54;
  King Henry III   92; Henry IV
  100, 107, 182; Louis XIV   135;
  Philip IV   57
Franche-Comté   105–6, 130
Franconia   102, 108, 110, 113–14,
  125, 137, 151, 161, 170, 175,
  178
Frankfurt/Main   108, 125, 128
fraud   18, 58, 186
Freiburg: Breisgau   120, 168, 177;
  Fribourg/Üchtland   63, 68
Freising   55, 103, 116, 139–40,
  188
Friuli   30, 90
frost   65, 88, 97, 104, 113–14, 131,
  160
Fründ, Hans   63–6
Fulda   110–11, 113, 117, 119,
  177–8; Prince-Abbot Balthasar
  von Dernbach   110–11
fundamentalism   10, 103, 112,
  120, 163, 212, 232

Galileo, Galilei   95, 184
Gardner, Gerald B.   233, 237
Gassendi, Pierre   183, 185
Gelderland   80, 171
gender   4, 10, 37–43, 56, 69, 158,
  235, 247; conflict   39, 41;
  distribution   56, 69, 158;
  relations   247; struggle   39
Geneva   80, 90, 126, 163, 171
Genoa   154–5
Georgia   222

Germanic peoples   30, 51;
   Alemanns   30; Anglo-Saxons
   51, 53; Danes   55; Franks   30,
   51–2, 54; Lombards/Longobards
   30, 67; Ostrogoths   51–2;
   Saxons   30–1, 33, 52; Visigoths
   51–2
Germany   8, 21, 23, 56, 71–2, 74,
   77, 79–81, 83, 91, 93, 98, 100,
   102, 106, 199–200, 125, 130–1,
   135, 139–40, 149–51, 154, 157,
   166, 168, 174–5, 178, 180–1, 184,
   187, 191–3, 223, 233, 235, 241,
   244
Ghana   14, 199, 207–8, 216–17,
   225, 227; Jerry Rawlings   216,
   227
ghost   9, 192, 220
Glanvill, Joseph   133, 139, 185
Glarus   139, 190
globalization   25, 29, 104, 160,
   238, 242, 247
God's: covenant   133, 170, 229;
   honour   9, 163, 175, 194; law
   47; permission   5, 9;
   punishment   55; revenge   163,
   175; wrath   55, 67, 89
Goddesses   30–1, 69; Diana
   30–1, 69; Fortuna   31; Good
   Lady   32; Holda   31–1;
   Richella   32; Venus   30, 78
Goedelmann, Johann Georg
   173, 176
Goya, Francisco   231, 246
grain   11, 64–5, 88, 91, 97, 104,
   113, 131, 161
Grandier, Urban   142, 184
grapevines   56, 88, 91, 113–14,
   131, 161
Gratian of Bologna   31, 166
Graubünden/Grison   128, 139,
   155, 190
Graz   55, 101, 176
Great Britain   36, 150, 169, 188,
   193
Greece   30, 48, 134, 141, 144, 153,
   165, 241
greed   2, 42, 180

Greenland   21, 56, 61, 88
Gregory of Tours *see* Tours
Gregory of Valencia   121–2, 176
Greifswald   99, 125
Gretser SJ, Jacob   122, 176–7
Guatemala   218
Guazzo, Francesco   106, 231
Guernsey   85, 127
guerrillas   211, 209–10, 219
Gui, Bernardo   32, 35
guilt   25, 33, 41, 45, 47–8, 53–4,
   56, 89, 127, 145, 169, 171, 179,
   188, 199–200, 205, 220, 224–5,
   232, 244

Haan: Catharina   112; Georg
   Adam   112; Georg   111–12,
   179; Magdalena   112; Maria
   Ursula   112; Ursula, née
   Neudecker   112
hailstorm   37, 40, 54–5, 65, 88–91,
   97, 113, 131
hair   107, 147
hatred   2, 14, 25–6, 38, 92–3, 127,
   161
healer   6, 15–16, 30, 33, 39, 44, 54,
   78, 106, 146, 198, 202, 210, 214,
   218, 224, 230
heart   38, 44, 61, 115, 159–60,
   214, 224
Hell: Kaspar   177; Kaspar SJ
   177–8
Hemmingsen, Nils   102, 126
hereditability   3, 142, 209, 219
heresy   4, 33–5, 54, 56–7, 59–63,
   66–9, 73, 81–2, 93, 96, 99, 116,
   119, 170, 173, 175, 182
Herodotus   48, 53
Hessen   5, 91, 123
Hildesheim   103, 108, 116, 121,
   180
Hinduism   18, 39, 240
historians: Wilhelm Abel   160;
   Chantal Ammann-Doubliez
   64; Julio Caro Baroja   103;
   Thomas Becker   116; Robert
   Bireley SJ   120, 174; Andreas
   Blauert   67; Monica Blöcker

40; Paul Boyer 146; Robin Briggs 99; George L. Burr 159, 232; Fritz Byloff 68, 161; Stuart Clark 9, 172, 202; Norman Cohn 2, 56, 58; Denis Crouzet 100; Jane Davidson 76; Owen Davies 194; Jane Davidson 76; Jean Delumeau 60; Bernhard Duhr SJ 142; Richard van Dülmen 239; Jonathan Durrant 42, 112; Marc Forster 119; Carlo Ginzburg 29–30; Frantisek Graus 60; Rune Hagen 151; Joseph Hansen 5–6, 51, 58, 64, 159, 232; Jörg Haustein 34; Christopher Hill 233; Eric J. Hobsbawm 6; Jens Johansen 69; Peter Kamber 92; Henry Kamen 129, 148; Carol F. Karlsen 146; Richard Kieckhefer 58; Gábor Klaniczay 30; Philip Kuhn 18; Eva Labouvie 239; Karen Lambrecht 153; Christina Larner 40–1, 49, 123–4, 170; Henry Charles Lea 232; Hartmut Lehmann 129; Brian Levack 156–7; Alan Macfarlane 25–6; Laura de Mello e Souza 13; Jules Michelet 5–6, 232, 234, 240; H. C. Erik Midelfort 8, 49, 127; Katrin Moeller 125; Bill Monter 49, 100, 105–6, 108, 156–7; Robert Muchembled 40, 155; Hans Eyvind Naess 151; Martine Ostorero 63; Jonathan Pearl 160; Richard Popkins 184; Diane Purkiss 236; Theodore K. Rabb 129, 134; Sigmund Riezler 7; Brigitte Rochelandet 106; Lyndal Roper 41–2, 159; Stephen Runciman 233; Gustav Roskoff 157; William Ryan 152; August Ludwig Schlözer 5, 190; Gerhard

Schormann 115–16, 123; James Sharpe 101, 132–3; Wilhelm Gottlieb Soldan 5, 159; Alfred Soman 155; Janusz Tazbir 153; Keith Thomas 24–6, 36; Hugh R. Trevor-Roper 129; Helfried Valentinitsch 161; Rita Voltmer 95; Hans de Waardt 183; Gary K. Waite 81; Rainer Walz 25–6; Marilyn Westerkamp 145; Merry Wiesner 235; Heide Wunder 40; Charles Zika 76

Hobbes, Thomas 185, 187
Hohenems 129; Count Ferdinand Carl Franz 129
holocaust 7, 62, 157, 167, 236, 243
Holstein 125–6, 130, 135, 157
Holy Roman Empire 72, 76, 85, 98, 100, 106, 108–10, 115, 117–18, 120–2, 127, 135, 151, 154, 156, 166, 169, 176, 180, 187–8, 231; *see also* Emperor
Hopkins, Matthew 102, 116, 132–3
Horace 33, 165
house search 53, 244
Hungary 8, 32, 92, 105, 130, 140, 150–1, 154, 189–90; King Coloman 32
Hutchinson, Francis 133, 185
hygiene 134, 194; *see also* pollution, purity

Iceland 53, 61, 81, 126, 135, 140, 150, 158, 161
Illereichen 85, 87; Lord Hans von Rechberg 85–7
illness 13, 19, 21, 34, 48, 77, 206, 218, 228, 240, 247; mental 5, 106, 141, 171; psychosomatic causes of 44
illusion 4, 31, 67, 81, 134, 177, 191, 248
Imperial Chamber Court 85, 111, 128, 135, 137, 156, 176
impotence 64, 134

Inca Empire   19, 28, 50, 218–19,
243; Garcilaso de la Vega Inca
19; Titu Cusi Yupanqui Inca
28
India   18–19, 107, 217, 226–7,
243; Indira Ghandi   227;
Jawaharlal Nehru   227
Indonesia   17–18, 163, 196, 217,
226–7, 240; President Suharto
227
industrialization   5, 11, 19, 21,
161, 194, 219, 232
infanticide   2, 193
infertility   35, 40–2, 44, 64–5, 88,
93, 131, 198, 202
Ingolstadt   120–1, 177–8
Innsbruck   72–4, 76, 122, 128, 154
Inquisition   32, 35, 65–6, 74, 90,
103, 167, 169, 184; in Africa
143, 148, 169; in Asia   169; in
the Atlantic Isles   148; in
Brazil   144, 148, 169, 182; on
the Canary Islands   182;
Episcopal   32, 54, 62–3, 168; in
Latin America   143–4, 154,
169, 182; on the Mediterranean
islands   143; in Mexico   143;
in Naples   90, 154–5; papal
32, 35, 58–9, 63, 65, 72–3, 76,
78, 166, 168, 170; in Peru   143;
on the Philippines   143;
Portuguese   90, 148, 169;
Roman   81, 91, 128, 154–5, 164,
168, 181–2, 184; in Sicily   99,
154; Spanish   34, 81, 92, 107,
143–4, 148, 154–5, 168–9, 182–3,
193
insecurity   15, 119, 212
instability   51, 124, 129, 134–5
Institoris *see* Kramer
institutions   7, 10, 25–6, 39, 52,
81, 119–21, 123–5, 138, 163, 166,
168–9, 194, 202, 209–10, 228,
237, 243–4
Inuit   19, 29, 45, 221
inversion: of Christian ritual   65;
of the covenant with God
133; of moral norms   2, 33,

198; of positive values   45, 198,
244; of the witch stereotype
140
invisibility   2, 15, 50, 64, 102, 146
Ireland   22, 31, 57, 122, 144, 148,
150, 193
isidliso   15–16, 247
Islam   17–18, 39, 60, 198, 205,
217–18, 244
Italy   32, 36, 48–9, 52, 57, 61, 63,
65–8, 71–2, 77–9, 81, 102, 106,
130, 139, 150, 154–5, 160, 164,
166–8, 170, 176, 181–2, 187,
191–2, 241, 244
Ivory Coast   14, 42, 202, 207

Jamaica   147
Japan   29, 51, 107, 244
jealousy   2, 20, 26–7, 161
Jersey   85, 127
Jews   34, 47, 60–1, 63, 67, 71, 76,
115, 183, 234–6
Joan of Arc   68
Jülich-Kleve   5, 106; Duke
Johann Wilhelm   106; Duke
Wilhelm V   171
Junius: Johannes   114–15; Maria
Anna   115
Jutland   81, 223

Kant, Immanuel   192, 248
Kempten   85, 117, 119, 129, 190;
Prince-Abbot Rupert von
Bodman   129; Honorius Roth
von Schreckenstein   190
Kent   102, 127, 133
Kenya   205–6, 208, 216–17, 227;
President Yomo Kenyatta
206, 227; Daniel Arap Moi
227
Kepler: Johannes   176, 184;
Katharina   184
kinship   4, 14, 27, 37, 57, 114, 142,
194, 208–9
Knox, John   170, 229
Köln/Cologne   73, 77, 109–10,
113, 115–18, 121, 130, 135, 171,
174; Prince-Archbishop/Prince-

Elector Ernst of Bavaria 103,
115–16; Ferdinand of Bavaria
109, 115–16, 119, 180; Gebhardt
II Truchsess von Waldburg
110
Korea 29
Kotkel 53; Grima 53; Hallbjorn
Kotkelsson 53; Stigandi 53
Kramer, Heinrich 4, 6, 38, 71–8,
86, 101–2, 104, 142, 170, 236

labelling 5–6, 18, 25, 31, 33, 37,
43–4, 60, 62, 68, 70, 82, 87–8,
111, 115, 121, 135, 168, 171,
173–5, 177, 179, 184, 187–8, 192,
204, 212, 220, 245
Labourd 102, 107, 182
Lancashire 133–4
Lancre, Pierre de 106–8, 156,
182
Landshut 188–9
Languedoc 131, 156
Lausanne 63; Bishop George de
Saluces 63
law 3–7, 87, 89, 95, 101, 111–12,
126, 140, 167, 169–74, 186,
193, 195–6, 216–17, 223, 225,
243–4; African 45; Alemannic
30, 52; Ancient
Mesopotamian/Babylonian
47, 132; Anglo-Saxon 34;
Assyrian 47; Austria 193;
Bavarian 126, 193;
biblical/Jewish/Mosaic 4, 34,
47–8, 52; British 185–6, 224;
British colonial 147, 196, 205;
canon/Church/ecclesiastical 4,
31, 36, 92, 95, 132, 164, 166;
Cameroon 224; Carolingian
55; Chinese 18; colonial
197–8, 205, 224; customary
153; Danish 81, 125; divine
47; Ecuadorian 219; English
84–5, 164, 185–6, 224; European
45, 50, 52, 198; Frankish 30–1,
34, 52; French 34, 66, 193;
German 52; Germanic 51;
Imperial 86–7, 89, 95, 109, 122,

125, 143, 169–70, 173, 177;
Inquisitorial 84; Irish 193;
Kenyan 223–4; Lombard 30;
Malawi 224; Ostrogothic 52;
Polish 190, 193; procedural
169; Roman 30, 33, 36, 48–9,
51–2, 59, 67, 73, 84, 86–7, 92,
128; Salic 30, 52; Savoyan 61;
Saxon 31; Scottish 85, 186;
secular 5, 35, 59, 67, 73, 92,
164; Serbian 153; South
African 44–5, 216, 225;
Spanish 85; Swedish 193;
Ugandan 223; US/American
220; Venetian 52; Visigothic
52
laws of nature 5, 7, 172, 184,
245
Lebowa 213–14
legislation 18, 21, 30–1, 33, 52,
85, 100, 115, 125, 153, 169–70,
186, 193, 196, 223, 226
Leibniz, Gottfried W. 181, 184
Leipzig 99, 128
leniency 5, 31, 34, 51, 104, 119,
125, 148, 156
leprosy 60, 134
liberation 209–11; forces 225;
movements 17, 208, 219, 226;
war 210, 213, 220, 227, 230;
women's 245
libertines 167, 183
Liège 101, 103, 116, 121, 180;
prince-bishops: *see*
Köln/Cologne
Lima 107, 143
Lippe 25, 123
Lisbon 81, 144, 148
Lithuania 150, 152–3, 190;
Grand-Duke Jagiello 34
Little Ice Age 87–8, 104, 114,
159, 160
livestock 13, 37, 44, 54, 80, 85,
88, 99, 114, 168, 200, 223
Livonia 139, 151
Livy 48–9
Lombardy 30, 67, 69; King
Rothari 30

London   53, 78, 128, 183, 232, 241
Loos, Cornelius   96–7, 173
Lorraine   49, 54, 68, 80, 93,
    99–102, 106, 108, 112, 121–3,
    130, 135, 149, 156, 161, 177, 208;
    Princess Antoinette   106;
    Duke Charles III   99, 106, 121;
    Elisabeth of Lorraine-
    Vaudémont   121; Duke
    Henry II   99; Renata   121
love   5, 26, 31, 41, 53, 61, 90, 134,
    147, 170, 172, 221, 228
Lucerne   64, 80, 164, 190
Lucian of Samosata   33, 165
Lucius Cornelius Sulla   49
Ludendorff, Mathilde   234, 236
Luther, Martin   24, 79–81, 108,
    167, 170, 182
Lutheranism   5, 80, 83, 85, 89, 98,
    121, 124–6, 130, 170, 180
Luxembourg   8, 85, 93, 99–100,
    105–6, 130, 149–50, 182
Lyon   66, 68, 74, 106, 128, 188;
    Archbishop Agobard of Lyon
    54–5

Macedonia   153
Machiavelli, Niccolo   166–7, 185,
    248
Madagascar   198, 244; King
    Andrianampoinimerina   198;
    King Radama I   199; Queen
    Ranavalona I   199
Madrid   92, 128, 144, 183
magic   3–4, 6–7, 9–11, 13, 19, 23,
    29–30, 33–9, 42, 50, 52–3, 57, 60,
    86, 90, 93, 97–8, 101–2, 112,
    127–8, 140, 143, 145, 148, 158,
    167, 170, 182–91, 193, 214, 230,
    236, 239, 244–5, 247–8;
    beneficial   3, 33; black   3–4,
    25, 33, 36, 62, 66, 114, 241; evil
    4; harmful/maleficient   19, 24,
    37, 44–5, 48, 52, 54, 59–62,
    89–90, 133–4, 169, 186, 188–90,
    198, 219, 230, 240; love   53, 90,
    134, 221, 228; Native American
    146; natural   9, 35, 98, 129, 131;

popular   66, 115; posthumous
    154; sympathetic   13; weather
    52, 55, 76, 89, 93, 99; witch-
    finding   36; white   3–4, 33, 36,
    169; *see also* counter-magic,
    frost, hailstorms, *maleficium*,
    sorcery, witchcraft
Mainz/Mayence   34, 95, 98, 101,
    108–9, 113, 117, 127, 130, 135,
    177, 181; Prince-
    Archbishop/Prince-Elector
    Johann Adam von Bicken
    108–9; Johann Schweikhard von
    Cronberg   108–9; Georg
    Friedrich von Greiffenklau
    108–9; Archbishop Hrabanus
    Maurus   34; Johann Philipp
    von Schönborn   181
Malawi/Nyasaland   204, 206–8,
    211, 224, 227; President
    Hastings Banda   207, 211,
    227–8
Malaysia   17, 217
maleficium   19, 24, 33, 35–7, 44,
    48, 50, 52, 54, 56–7, 59–61,
    89–90, 133–4, 169, 188–90, 198,
    219, 223, 230
Malleus Maleficarum   4–5, 37–8,
    42–3, 66, 71–4, 76–9, 83–4, 90,
    93, 99, 101–2, 122, 142, 166,
    168–70, 173–4, 225, 229–30, 236,
    239
Mantua   154–5
Marxism   11, 28, 196, 203, 209,
    228, 234
masks   43, 144, 202, 204, 211
Massachusetts   145–6, 238
Mather, Cotton   102, 139, 146
Mecklenburg   124, 126, 130, 135,
    139, 149, 157, 208
medical care   5, 15, 33, 119, 133,
    194, 196
medicine   3, 15, 134, 167, 171,
    196, 212; folk   5, 239, 241;
    humoral   171; Western   16
melancholy   5, 127, 141, 171–2
Melanesia   17–18
Memmingen   77, 98

Mergentheim 111, 130
Mesopotamia 22, 47; King Hammurapi 47
Metz 54, 76, 100, 168
Mexico City 19, 144, 241
Mexico 18–19, 39, 50, 143–4, 218, 226–7, 243–4
midwives 87, 143
Milan 32, 54, 67–8, 78, 98, 102, 106, 130, 154–5; Archbishop Carlo Borromeo, St 115, 155, 229
milk 11, 15, 25, 28, 41, 64, 71, 194, 221
millennarism 77, 120, 129, 132, 200, 202, 204, 208, 221, 230
miracle 82, 149, 170, 202
Mirandola, Pico della 78–9
misery 12, 104, 114, 119, 164, 200, 214, 247
misfortune 2–3, 7, 11, 14–15, 17, 21, 23–4, 39, 45, 56, 67, 85, 89, 165, 202, 204–5, 218, 228, 230, 240–1, 244, 245, 247–8
misogyny 3, 9, 37–8, 43, 87
modernization 26, 29, 87, 194, 196, 199–200, 211
Molitor, Ulrich 74, 76, 98, 166, 231
monks *see* religious Orders
Montaigne, Michel de 172–3
Montbeliard 91, 126, 156
Montenegro 153, 221
moral entrepreneur 67, 133, 163, 228–9, 243
moral 2–3, 24, 44–5, 48, 67, 163, 190, 195, 201, 228, 247
Moravia 189, 191
Moscow 56, 60, 152, 160
motherhood 41–2, 193
movement: anti-colonial 202; anti-witchcraft 6–7, 17, 24, 26–7, 55, 116, 144, 168, 198, 202–212, 222, 225–6; dualistic 59; feminist 158, 232, 234, 236; heretical 4; liberation 17, 208, 211, 219, 226, 230; millenarian 200, 208, 230;

nativistic 28, 145, 200, 220, 230; neo-Christian 208; neo-pagan 6, 157, 233–4; New Age 236; 'new witches' 6, 10, 233–8; Observant reform 66; occultist 232–3; pogrom 163; prophetic 201–2, 207; purification 206; revitalization 200; revivalist 186, 225; Religious reform 194; Waldensian 59; Watchtower 204; Wicca 233, 236–7; witch-cleansing 204–5, 208, 243; witchcraft eradication 18, 51, 202, 206–8, 228; youth 226
Mozambique 207, 217
Müller-Reimerdes, Friederike 235
Munich 121, 176–9
Münster 81, 103, 116, 118, 121, 180, 230; Prince-Bishops *see* Köln
murder 19, 44, 52–4, 56, 71, 73, 89, 153, 173, 190, 198, 198, 210, 215–18, 220–1, 223, 241; judicial 5, 89, 168, 179, 193; magical 48, 214; *muti* 214–15, 241; ritual 2, 28, 60, 211, 214, 241; *see also* lynching
Murray, Margaret 233, 237
music 9, 107, 111, 116, 134, 209, 239
Muslim 12, 22, 34, 144, 153, 205
muti 15, 210, 214–15, 241
mutilation 215, 222

nagual 18–19, 218
Naples 90, 98, 128, 131, 154–5
Nassau 105, 123, 130; Maurice of Nassau-Orange 123
nativism 27–8, 145, 200, 220, 230
neighbours 4, 8, 11, 13–14, 16–17, 23, 25, 28, 36, 41, 43, 49, 57, 64, 86, 88, 138, 143, 149, 153, 159, 161, 172, 195, 219, 222–3, 228, 242–3, 247
neo-paganism 6, 157–8, 233–8
Nepal 18

Netherlands 8, 23, 53, 77, 80, 83, 101–2, 123, 127, 131, 135, 144, 148–50, 160, 169, 183, 186–7, 193, 196, 213, 230
Neuchatel 63, 68, 123
Neudecker: Anna 112; Georg 112; Anna Barbara 112; Magdalena 112
New England 102, 144, 146, 166
New France 144, 160
New Mexico 27, 220
New York City 235–6, 241
New Zealand 217
nganga 198, 205, 210, 224
Nicolaus of Cusa *see* Brixen
Nider, Johannes 62, 66–7, 102
Nigeria 28, 39, 199, 204, 206–8, 225, 241
nomadism 14, 19–20, 27, 48, 160, 213
Normandy 39, 91, 97, 156
norms 2, 6, 16, 198
Norway 8, 56, 61, 81, 83, 123, 125, 135, 150–2
nudity 2, 82, 231
Nuremberg 76, 98, 128, 164, 172, 231
Nuss, Balthasar 111, 113, 178
nutrition 134, 161, 212

occultism 9–10, 42–3, 129, 224, 229, 232–3, 238, 245, 248
old age 1, 4, 9, 12, 21, 25, 40–2, 50, 55–6, 85, 88, 97, 120, 139, 146–7, 158, 168, 171, 217, 221–4, 233
omnipotence 6, 13, 235, 240
oracles 23–5, 32, 36, 54, 63, 198
ordeals 47, 52–6, 59–60, 186, 199, 205; by baptism 204; by cold water 47, 55–6, 59, 86, 93, 132, 146, 153, 186, 222, 230; by hot iron 54, 59; by poison 198–9, 209; by torture 59–60; *see also* swimming test, ducking
Osnabrück 90, 97, 117
Ossory 57; Bishop Richard Ledrede 57

Ottoman Empire 60, 92, 144, 150, 153, 189, 221
Oudewater 230, 240
outsider 65, 87, 144, 174, 195, 242, 245; external 14; internal 39, 144

Paderborn 108, 116–17, 121, 180
paganism 4, 31, 34–5, 53, 69, 163, 233
Palatinate 116, 123, 126–7; Prince-Elector Friedrich V 126
Papua New Guinea 4, 17, 45, 217, 226–7
Paracelsus 35, 86
paradigm 5, 25, 45, 72, 167, 171, 191, 231–2, 237, 244, 247; Alciati 167; charity-refused 25; medical 171; Rational 184, 232; Romantic 5, 231; Soldan 5; Weyer 171; witchcraft 7, 17, 45, 191, 244, 247
paradigm shift 8, 33, 69, 83, 90, 128, 167, 184
paradox 7, 10, 39
Paris 52, 54, 78, 91–2, 100–1, 106, 128, 135, 155, 158, 163, 171, 181, 183, 228, 232
Passau 98, 118, 139–40
patriarchy 39, 41–3, 235, 245
peasant 6, 36, 48, 54, 60, 65–6, 79–80, 85–8, 92, 109, 119, 123–4, 128–9, 161, 212, 221; society 87; uprisings 18, 51, 131; war 81, 86; women 28
periphery 53, 137–9, 146–8; internal 191
Perkins, William 9, 101, 133
Peru 18, 28, 50, 143–4, 208, 219, 243; *see also* Inca empire
Phasha: Abraham Madibeng 215; Michael Morudi 215; Moses 215
Philippines 33–4, 143
Piedmont 61–3, 67
piety 77, 170
plague 28, 65, 77, 80, 134, 154

poison 15, 30, 48, 52, 55, 60, 80,
87, 103, 114, 124, 154, 173, 188,
198–9, 209, 218
Poland 125, 130, 149–54, 164,
181, 187, 189–91, 193; Wladislaw
II Jagiello 34
politicians 7, 22, 99, 198, 112–13,
121–2, 135, 167–8, 174–8, 181,
186–8, 201, 226, 231, 234
pollution 2, 14, 46, 48
Pomerania 125–6, 130, 139, 153,
187
Pope: Alexander VI 63;
Eugenius IV 61–3, 68; Felix V
62; Gregory VII 55; Hadrian I
52; Innocence VIII 72; John
XXII 57; John Paul II/Karol
Woityla 21, 218, 240; Leo X
168; Martin V 63, 67; Pius IX
232; Urban VIII 120, 175
Portugal 13, 81, 122, 144, 148,
150, 160, 169, 182
postmodernism 6, 8, 29, 237–8,
245, 247
poverty 9, 25, 88, 92–3, 97, 121,
124, 160, 171, 194, 247
power 247–8; devilish 79, 183,
186, 245; divine 18, 22;
divinatory 30, 78, 248;
economic 97, 128, 209, 211;
female 9, 209, 235–6, 245;
healing 30, 78; legal 25;
limited 39; magical 23, 236;
military 27, 79, 135, 201, 221;
mystical 2, 33, 146, 198, 202,
218; occult 9; political 28, 48,
62, 72, 95, 108, 110, 127–8, 135,
160, 169, 183, 206, 210, 228–9;
prophetic 30; protective 37;
sacramental 60; satanic 9;
spiritual 79, 145, 210–11, 236;
supernatural 2, 13, 31, 36–7,
45, 147, 206, 218; of witches
76, 93, 209–11, 218, 223, 225,
236
Prague 108, 127, 129, 176
Prätorius, Anton 170, 172–3,
185

Prättigau 128–9
preaching 37, 63, 57, 77, 83, 89,
95, 152, 166, 172, 174, 176, 204,
228
pregnancy 15, 40, 193, 221
pricking test 43, 86, 95, 182
primitivism 6–7, 144, 242
prison 42, 50, 107, 111, 126, 129,
133–4, 141, 147, 151, 155, 157,
159, 169, 177, 178, 180, 182, 188,
190, 206, 215, 220, 222–4
prophets 28, 30, 48, 50, 77, 131,
152, 200–2, 207, 211, 221, 225;
Bwanali 207; Lighton Chunda,
alias Chikanga 207–8;
Chiwere 211; Handsome Lake
200–1; Kajiwe 205–6;
Kinjikitile Ngwale 202; Marie
Lalou 202; Alice Lenshina
225, 230; Moses 47;
Mpulumutsi 207; Thomas
Müntzer 82; Neolin 201;
Tomo Nyirenda 204; Taqui
Ongo 28; Tenskwatawa
201–2
protection 22, 25, 37–40, 86, 140,
159, 173, 202, 217; cults 38, 212
Protestantism 22, 24–5, 38, 80–1,
89–92, 98–9, 101, 104, 109–10,
119–21, 126, 135, 138–9, 148,
157, 169–70, 172–3, 175–6, 180,
183, 187–8, 190–2, 194, 229;
Anglicanism 122, 133, 146,
185; Methodism 186; Pietism
180, 187; Presbyterianism 124,
133, 185; Quakerism 201;
Zwinglianism 122; *see also*
African Churches, Anabaptism,
Calvininism, Lutheranism,
Spiritualism
Prüm 31; Prince-Abbot Regino
of Prüm 31
Prussia 125, 151, 157, 187, 190,
193; King Friedrich Wilhelm I
187
psychology 3, 6, 9, 13, 24, 40–3,
103, 119–20, 133, 146, 163, 237,
242–5; Wilhelm Fliess 42;

psychology (cont'd)
  Sigmund Freud   6, 13, 18, 41–3,
  163; Melanie Klein   41; Fritz
  Morgenthaler   42; Paul Parin
  and Goldy Parin-Mathey   42;
  Oskar Pfister   163; Jean Piaget
  24
psychosomatic reactions   7, 15,
  44, 243
Puritanism   9, 91, 101, 133, 146
purity   46, 48, 67, 175, 199, 202,
  204–5, 208, 227–8 , 233, 235, 243
Pyrenees   83, 131, 134

queens   31, 39, 54, 61, 98, 123,
  125, 129, 199

Rarogne   64ff.; Hildebrand de
  64; Peterman de   64
rationalism   2–3, 5–7, 36, 135,
  193, 232, 247
reality   4–7, 9–10, 16, 24–5,
  28–32, 34, 38, 44, 60, 69, 73, 97,
  109, 123, 128, 142, 144, 149, 156,
  166, 169, 176, 242, 244–5, 247
reason of state   127, 167
rebellion   51, 123, 131, 144, 147,
  201–2, 217, 230, 240
Reformation   24, 37, 68, 71, 74,
  76, 79–81, 84, 87, 99, 124, 130,
  151, 157, 170, 194
Regensburg   118, 140, 174
religious Orders: Ambrosians
  106; Augustinian hermits   191;
  Benedictines   55, 103;
  Capuchins   127, 131;
  Dominicans   4, 32, 38, 54, 63–7,
  69, 71, 74, 77–9, 81, 89, 93, 115,
  142, 166–8, 181, 236; Franciscans
  52, 57, 63, 144, 166, 189, 191;
  Jesuits   27, 83, 95–7, 101, 107,
  110, 117, 121–2, 127, 142,
  174–80, 188, 190–2, 244;
  Theatines   192
Rémy: Claude   99; Nicolas
  99–102, 105–7, 177
Renaissance   76, 78, 111, 165–6,
  248

Rentzin, Anna   85–7
resurrection   207, 225
revenant   53, 154, 213–14
revenge   38, 53, 87, 92, 97, 111,
  158, 175, 218–19
revivalism   152, 186, 201–2, 212,
  225, 238
revolution   19, 79–80, 131, 134,
  193, 212, 225; Bolshevik   222;
  English   131, 134; French   5,
  159, 193, 231–2; Glorious   185;
  Industrial   194; political   80,
  193, 212; Printing   73, 166;
  religious   79–80, 82; Scientific
  184–5; Shaka's military   51;
  social   193, 212
Rhineland   108, 110, 135, 151,
  161, 230
Rhodesia *see* Zimbabwe
Richel: Bartholomäus   178;
  Maria   178
ritual   9, 15, 22, 35–7, 46, 59, 65,
  82, 121, 144, 177, 198–9, 202,
  205, 207, 209, 211, 233, 237–8,
  240–2; murder   2, 28, 60, 71,
  198, 211, 214, 225, 241
Roberts, Alexander   38, 133
Roman Empire   48–50;
  Constantius II   33, 50;
  Diocletian   33; Justinian I   33;
  Valens   50; Valentinian I
  50
Romania   144, 151, 153, 189
Romanticism   5, 231, 235–6, 240,
  245
Rome   62, 67, 72, 78–9, 83, 128,
  154, 183, 243; *see also* Pope
Rostock   99, 124
Rouen   106, 156
rumour   87, 95–6, 131, 182, 210,
  212, 226
Russia   13, 29, 56–7, 61, 141, 146,
  150, 152, 157, 193, 196, 221–2,
  243; Boris Godunov   152;
  Catherine the Great   221;
  Dmitri   152; Ivan IV the
  Terrible   152; Peter I   221
Rwanda   212, 243

Saarland 135, 239
saints 3, 19, 34, 37, 39, 67, 82,
121, 170; St Bernardino da
Siena 67; St Boniface 30; St
Carlo Borromeo 115, 155, 229;
St Simon Unferdorben 71; St
Vincent Ferrer 67; *see also*
(St) Augustine; (St) Petrus
Canisius; (St) Thomas Aquinas
Salazar Frias, Alonso de 107,
138, 182
Salem Village 49, 117, 145–6,
239–40
Salzburg 139–40, 188
Sampson, Agnes 123–4
Santa Fe 145, 221
Santori, Giulio A. 155, 181
Savoy 32, 60–8, 80, 91, 97, 102,
105, 130, 154, 244; Duke
Amadeus VIII 61, 68
Saxony 90, 125, 157
Scandinavia 137, 160–1, 187
scapegoats 42–3, 46, 65, 68, 77,
87–8, 248
scepticism 31, 33–4, 43, 52, 54,
57, 106, 133, 165–7, 169, 171–2,
181, 183
Schleswig 69, 125–6, 130, 151
Schlettstadt/Séléstat 71, 76–7
Schultheis, Heinrich von 102,
117, 180
Scot, Reginald 102, 140, 170, 172
Scotland 8, 49, 85, 92, 99, 102,
123–4, 126–7, 130, 133, 139, 160,
186, 188, 230, 241, 244; James VI
6–7, 99, 102, 123, 126, 152
secrecy 2–3, 9, 35, 43–4, 48, 54,
60, 114, 129, 147, 154, 170, 203,
205, 209, 211, 218, 221, 224, 235,
242
secret societies 43, 203, 205, 209,
211, 221, 224
secularization 26–7, 119, 134,
140
seduction 42, 61, 143, 189
semen 15, 41
Serbia 144, 153, 189; King
Stephan Dusan 153

sexuality 2, 9, 15–16, 21, 41–2,
57, 59, 67–8, 76, 82, 93, 115,
132–3, 138, 142–3, 182, 193, 214,
231, 242
shamanism 3, 7, 13, 18, 21,
29–30, 33, 48, 50, 140–1, 144–6,
158, 196, 198, 202, 218–20, 239,
242, 244
shape-shifting 2, 12–13, 15,
18–19, 29–30, 67, 74, 76, 115,
132–4, 210–11
Sicily 52, 83, 99, 154
sickness 18, 26, 44, 53, 96, 200,
212, 241
Siena 90, 128, 155
Sierra Leone 51
Silesia 151, 153–4, 190
Sion/Sitten 62–5; Prince-Bishop
William V of Rarogne 64ff.;
André di Benzi de Gualdo 64
slavery 13, 45, 51, 144–7, 155,
198–9, 220
sleep 15, 140, 231, 246;
deprivation 133
Slovakia 150, 189, 191
Slovenia 68–9, 150, 189
smallpox 27–8, 61, 200, 212
snow 88, 104, 131
sociology 3, 6, 29, 43–4, 107, 146,
236, 245; Theodor W. Adorno
43, 229; Howard S. Becker
163; Nachman Ben-Yehuda
238; Émile Durkheim 6, 26,
36, 45, 167; Kai Erikson 145;
Erving Goffman 43; Thomas
S. Kuhn 167; Karl Mannheim
120; Robert K. Merton 43;
Milton Rokeach 163; Neil
Smelser 26; Marcello Truzzi
240; Max Weber 6, 9, 21, 165,
194
sodomy 56, 73, 193, 214
Solomon Islands 217
sorcery 4, 14, 17–19, 21, 23, 31,
33–6, 40, 44, 47–54, 57, 60–3,
66–9, 73–4, 79–80, 85, 93,
114–15, 117, 128, 139, 141, 143,
145, 147–8, 152–3, 156, 158, 165,

sorcery (cont'd)
170, 183, 188–9, 191, 193, 196,
198–9, 202, 204–5, 207, 215,
219–21, 223–4, 244
South Africa   1–2, 4, 15–17, 39,
44, 51, 146, 200, 213–17, 225–7,
241; President Nelson Mandela
2, 214, 227, 241; Winnie
Mandela   213; President Thabo
Mbeki   215, 247; *see also* Zulu
empire
Soviet Union   196, 222, 234; *see
also* Russia
Spain   28, 34, 53, 77, 101, 106–7,
122, 143–6, 148, 150–1, 154, 164,
168–70, 181–3, 208; Charles I
151, 169–70; Charles IV   231;
Philip II   99, 101
Spanish Netherlands   85, 90,
93, 99–101, 104, 122, 130, 135,
157, 182; Albrecht VII   129;
Isabella of Spain   129;
see also Belgium
Spee, Friedrich   102, 117, 120,
140, 151, 159, 163, 174–5,
178–81, 244
spells   35–7, 44–5, 131, 189, 204,
240, 244
Speyer   73, 85, 118–19, 128, 135
Spina, Bartolomeo   78, 102
spirit   2, 9, 35, 48, 64, 98, 141, 170,
184, 192, 196, 202, 210, 226;
helper   29, 33, 132, 145;
medium   44–5, 95, 141, 202,
210; possession   18, 28, 106,
127, 131, 141–2, 145–6, 189, 191,
205, 221–2, 225, 228
Spiritualism   5, 82, 167, 170
Sprenger, Jacob   76–7
Sri Lanka/Ceylon   18
stages: of economic development
8, 26–7, 148, 194, 211, 215; of
infant development   9, 13; of
life   18, 101; in technology
138, 194, 215
state: contraction   212;
disintegration   131, 212, 216,
248; formation   7, 17, 26, 51,

61, 81, 84, 87, 108, 110, 116, 119,
123, 126–7, 135, 138, 166, 194,
199, 212, 215–16, 248;
fragmentation   125, 135, 154,
159, 228
Stavelot   103, 116–17, 121, 177;
Prior Gilles de Harzé   103;
Antonius von Salm   103;
prince-abbot, *see* Köln/
Ferdinand of Bavaria
Stearne, John   102, 132–3
stereotyping   9, 21, 38–9, 41, 43,
60, 63, 97, 101, 114, 127, 139–40,
148, 158–9, 245, 247
stigma   16, 43, 132, 168, 236,
242
Stirnerin, Anna   85–7
Stockholm   128, 138, 183
storms   37–8, 53–5, 65, 88, 91, 97,
99, 104, 123–4
Strasbourg   71, 91, 108, 117
striga   30–2, 52, 54, 62–3, 102,
166–7
Stuttgart   89, 113
Styria   55, 79, 161, 239
subconscious   6, 13, 32, 42, 45,
242
Sudan   23, 80, 203
suddenness: change of mind   84;
child death   40, 193; death
49, 53, 77; disease   23, 40, 53,
77; price rise   162
suicide   1, 141, 189, 198
superstition   4, 18, 32–3, 43, 63,
71, 83–4, 93, 135, 138, 143, 148,
167, 170, 172, 182, 185, 238, 242,
244
Swabia   110, 120, 122, 151, 161
Sweden   61, 81, 126, 138–9,
149–50, 188, 193; King Charles
XI   138; Queen Christina
125; King Gustav II Adolph
180; Queen Margarethe   61
swimming test   47, 56, 59, 93, 132,
186, 222, 230
Switzerland   8, 32, 61–3, 65–8, 72,
77–8, 80, 82, 84, 90–2, 97, 102,
106, 108, 123, 128, 130, 149–51,

155, 160, 163, 181, 188, 190, 192–3
symbolism 4, 13, 19, 25, 34, 41–2, 45, 98, 110, 121, 131, 178, 211, 233, 235–6, 240, 245
Synagogue 60, 62, 64, 67–8
Syria 49–50, 218, 234

Tanner, Adam 117, 174–5, 177–9, 244
Tanzania 17, 207–8, 211–13, 217, 226–7; Julius Nyerere 213, 227
Texas 219
Thailand 17
theft 11, 28, 48, 53, 73, 107, 189
Third World 23, 26–8, 77, 140, 239, 241
Tholosan, Claude 66–8, 102
Thomas Aquinas (St) 34, 73
Thomasius, Christian 140, 187
threat 14, 25, 28, 37, 41, 43, 48, 50, 60, 64, 72, 111, 117, 119, 126, 147, 172, 180, 186, 189, 194, 201, 205–6, 211, 214, 219, 222–3, 226, 228, 243
thunderstorm 55, 65, 88–9
Thuringia 108, 125, 180
Tibet 18
Tinctoris, Jean 69–70
Torrenté; Uldry de 63, 65–6
torture 3, 16, 24, 27, 42–3, 48–50, 52–3, 55, 59–60, 62, 64, 72, 84, 87–8, 95–6, 112–15, 117, 122, 126, 129, 141, 152, 159, 169–70, 173–5, 177, 179–81, 188, 195, 220, 223, 225
Toul 100; Prince-Bishop Charles of Lorraine-Vaudémont 106
Toulouse 54, 83, 156, 181
Tours 54; Bishop Gregory of Tours 54
Transylvania 151, 154, 189
trauma 27, 40, 110, 183
treason 19, 50, 57, 59, 152, 177, 210, 214
Trent/Trient/Trento 71, 110, 118–19, 121, 154; Prince-Bishop

Johannes IV von Hinderbach 71
tribal chiefs 16, 27, 29, 44, 50, 198, 201, 204, 208, 211, 213–14, 220; Chichimecatecuhtli 144; Cornplanter 201; Olaf Hoskuldsson 53; Manuelito 220; Mihigo 51; Mukama Kabarega 199; Pontiac 201; Sechele 200; Shaiwila 204; Tecumseh 201
Trier/Treves 76, 95–8, 100–3, 107, 109, 117, 123, 130, 135, 142, 173, 176–7; Prince-Archbishop/Prince-Elector Johann VII von Schönenberg 93, 95–7, 109
Turkey 50, 150, 189, 221, 243; *see also* Ottoman Empire
Tyrol 32, 54, 68, 72, 122, 128, 139, 154, 174; Archduke Sigmund 72, 74

Uganda 199, 223, 227; President Milton Obote 223, 227
Ukraine 48, 56, 152, 153, 190, 222
uncertainty 7, 14–15, 28, 38, 62–3, 65, 74, 113, 131, 135, 152, 168, 194, 205, 209, 212, 226, 228, 245
unguent 13, 67, 113, 205
United Kingdom 12, 130, 193, 226, 230
urbanization 6, 22, 26, 28, 53, 56, 128, 152, 176, 183, 212
USA 12, 195, 219–20, 226, 233, 236, 240–1; Thomas Jefferson 201; George Washington 201

Vagh, Cosmas 175, 177
vaginal fluid 15
Valais/Wallis 61, 63–6, 68, 105, 108, 130, 161, 208
Valcamonica 78, 168
values 21, 24, 27, 29, 45–6, 89, 159, 181, 198, 216, 226, 244
vampires 19, 154

Vasoldt Ernst   111; Karl   111
Vaud/Waadtland   61, 92, 105, 123, 130, 149
Vauderie   68–70
Vaulx, Jean de   103
Venda   2, 214, 216, 225
Venice   52, 74, 78, 90, 128, 153–4, 168, 183; Vice-Doge Luca Tron 168
Verdun   100, 106; Prince-Bishop/Cardinal Charles of Lorraine-Vaudémont   106; Eric de Lorraine   106
Vienna   108, 128, 141, 231–2
Vikings   53, 56, 61, 88
violence   2, 21, 27–8, 39–40, 44, 119–20, 144, 169, 172, 183, 209, 211–12, 214, 223, 244
Visconti, Girolamo   69, 102
visions   6, 169, 201–2, 225
Vladimir   56; Bishop Serapion 56
Voltaire   33, 188
voodoo   21, 35; dolls   35, 53
Vorderösterreich   105, 122, 130

Wagnereckh, Johann Simon   175, 177
Wagstaffe, John   185, 187
Waldensians   57, 59, 61–2, 66–71
wealth   11–12, 25, 28, 39, 57, 87, 96–7, 112, 114, 123, 138, 158, 160, 194, 211, 219, 224, 248
weather magic   19, 21, 37, 52, 54, 56, 65, 68, 76, 80, 88–9, 91, 93, 99, 131, 133, 189
Webster, John   185, 187
Wecker, Johann J.   9, 98
werewolves   30, 63–4, 81, 88
Westphalia   53, 115–16, 134, 180, 230
Weyer, Johann   5–6, 9, 79, 88–90, 96–8, 102, 140, 142, 158–9, 163, 165, 170–2, 181, 243
Wicca   233, 236–7, 240
widows   40, 53, 158, 220, 222, 240

Wiesensteig   83, 85, 87, 89; Count Ulrich XVII von Helfenstein 83
witch villages: sanctuaries/protected settlements   146, 216–17
witchcraft paradigm   7, 17, 45, 191, 244, 247
witchcraft: definition   3–7, 29, 35, 45, 48; terminology   12–14, 16–17, 19, 21–2, 29–32, 54–5, 61–4, 68–9, 76, 48, 219
witch-doctor   3, 14, 23–4, 36, 39, 44–5, 78, 86, 93, 144, 168–9, 198, 200, 205, 208, 215, 220–1, 224–5, 230
witches': activities   96; assemblies 57, 133; conspiracy   100, 103, 124, 171; dance   59–60, 84, 115, 124, 234, 239; dreams   242; flight   13, 67, 69–70, 74, 76, 93, 134, 166, 176, 189; mark   95, 242; mountains   240; patrons 173, 216; power   4–5, 74, 76, 99, 236; Sabbat   60, 63, 65, 67, 69, 74, 84, 93, 95–7, 103, 107, 115, 133, 138, 142–3, 166, 169, 176–7, 188–9; sect   69, 77, 103; sexual intercourse   57, 59, 68, 76, 93; shot   71, 76; synagogues   60, 62, 64, 67–8; *see also* covenant, dancing, dreams, flying, sexuality, shape-shifting
Witches' Hammer, see Malleus
witch-finder   21, 23, 25, 30, 36, 86, 116, 131–2, 148, 164, 198, 204, 226, 240
witch-hunt: definition   49; large-scale witch-hunt   49, 50, 57, 63–4, 66–7, 79–80, 104, 111–15, 122–3, 133, 145, 148–9, 153–6, 158–9, 161, 168, 180, 190, 209; major persecution   49, 57, 200; massive witch-hunt/persecution 34, 48–9, 51, 59, 66–7, 78, 88, 91, 100–1, 105, 107–8, 115, 125, 128–9, 137, 142, 166, 171, 191, 243; panic trial   1, 48–9, 51,

53–4, 56, 66–7, 77, 79–81, 85, 90, 92, 98, 101, 107, 115, 125, 131, 134–5, 144–5, 148, 153, 155, 161, 178, 181, 188, 190, 204, 217, 219, 224, 244; permanent persecution 49, 66, 100, 112

Witekind, Herman 98, 172–4, 184

Wolff, Christian 187, 192

women 15, 21–3, 28, 30–5, 37–43, 48, 50, 54–6, 61, 63–4, 68–9, 71–2, 74, 76, 81, 87, 89, 91, 93, 96, 107, 111, 116, 119, 123, 127–8, 132, 134, 140, 145–6, 153, 157, 159, 161, 164, 166, 171, 188, 190, 193, 202, 208–9, 213–14, 217, 221–2, 230–1, 233–7, 243–5; old 12, 25, 40, 55–6, 171; wise 5, 35, 231–2, 236

woodcut 28, 70–1, 76, 79–80, 93, 97, 106, 230

words 22–3, 38, 40, 199

Worms 108, 118, 181; Bishop Burchard of Worms 4, 31

Württemberg 85, 89, 98, 116, 125–6, 184

Würzburg 98, 109–11, 113–15, 117, 120, 130, 154, 181, 191; Johann Gottfried von Aschhausen 111; Julius Echter von Mespelbrunn 109, 115, 120; Philipp Adolf von Ehrenberg 109, 115; Johann Philipp von Schönborn 181

Yucatan 107; Bishop Diego de Landa 107

Zambia 14–15, 39, 204, 207–8, 211, 225, 230; President Kenneth Kaunda 211

zeal 72, 84, 92, 100, 108, 110–11, 116, 119–20, 125, 133, 163, 167, 174–7; zealots 119–20, 133, 167, 174–8

Zimbabwe 44, 204, 207, 210, 225, 227; King Lobengula 200; Robert Mugabe 210–11, 227–8

Zulu empire 15, 39, 51, 200; king Cetshwayo Ka Mpande 200; King Shaka 51, 200

Zurich 80, 90

Zwingli, Huldrich 90, 122, 170